Criminal Justice

02/03

Twenty-Sixth Edition

EDITORS

Joseph L. Victor
Mercy College, Dobbs Ferry

Joseph L. Victor is professor and chairman of the Department of Law, Criminal Justice, and Safety Administration at Mercy College. Professor Victor has extensive field experience in criminal justice agencies, counseling, and administering human service programs. He earned his B.A. and M.A. at Seton Hall University, and his Doctorate of Education at Fairleigh Dickinson University.

Joanne Naughton
Mercy College, Dobbs Ferry

Joanne Naughton is assistant professor of Criminal Justice at Mercy College. Professor Naughton is a former member of the New York City Police Department, where she encountered most aspects of police work as a police officer, detective, sergeant, and lieutenant. She is also a former staff attorney with The Legal Aid Society. She received her B.A. and J.D. at Fordham University.

McGraw-Hill/Dushkin
530 Old Whitfield Street, Guilford, Connecticut 06437

Visit us on the Internet
http://www.dushkin.com

Credits

1. **Crime and Justice in America**
   Unit photo—© 2002 by PhotoDisc, Inc.
2. **Victimology**
   Unit photo—© 2002 by Cleo Freelance Photography.
3. **The Police**
   Unit photo—© 2002 by PhotoDisc, Inc.
4. **The Judicial System**
   Unit photo—© 2002 by PhotoDisc, Inc.
5. **Juvenile Justice**
   Unit photo—© 2002 by Cleo Freelance Photography.
6. **Punishment and Corrections**
   Unit photo—Criminal Justice Publications, NY—photo by Alex Von Kleydorff.

Copyright

Cataloging in Publication Data
Main entry under title: Annual Editions: Criminal Justice. 2002/2003.
1. Criminal justice—Periodicals. I. Victor, Joseph L., *comp.* II. Title: Criminal justice.
ISBN 0–07–250709–8   658'.05   ISSN 0272–3816

Twenty-Sixth Edition

Cover image © 2002 PhotoDisc, Inc.
Printed in the United States of America   1234567890BAHBAH5432   Printed on Recycled Paper

Editors/Advisory Board

Members of the Advisory Board are instrumental in the final selection of articles for each edition of ANNUAL EDITIONS. Their review of articles for content, level, currentness, and appropriateness provides critical direction to the editor and staff. We think that you will find their careful consideration well reflected in this volume.

To the Reader

In publishing ANNUAL EDITIONS we recognize the enormous role played by the magazines, newspapers, and journals of the public press in providing current, first-rate educational information in a broad spectrum of interest areas. Many of these articles are appropriate for students, researchers, and professionals seeking accurate, current material to help bridge the gap between principles and theories and the real world. These articles, however, become more useful for study when those of lasting value are carefully collected, organized, indexed, and reproduced in a low-cost format, which provides easy and permanent access when the material is needed. That is the role played by ANNUAL EDITIONS.

During the 1970's, criminal justice emerged as an appealing, vital, and unique academic discipline. It emphasizes the professional development of students who plan careers in the field, and attracts those who want to know more about a complex social problem and how this country deals with it. Criminal justice incorporates a vast range of knowledge from a number of specialties, including law, history, and the behavioral and social sciences. Each specialty contributes to our fuller understanding of criminal behavior and of society's attitudes toward deviance.

In view of the fact that the criminal justice system is in a constant state of flux, and because the study of criminal justice covers such a broad spectrum, today's students must be aware of a variety of subjects and topics. Standard textbooks and traditional anthologies cannot keep pace with the changes as quickly as they occur. In fact, many such sources are already out-of-date the day they are published. *Annual Editions: Criminal Justice 02/03* strives to maintain currency in matters of concern by providing up-to-date commentaries, articles, reports, and statistics from the most recent literature in the criminal justice field.

This volume contains units concerning crime and justice in America, victimology, the police, the judicial system, juvenile justice, and punishment and corrections. The articles in these units were selected because they are informative as well as provocative. The selections are timely and useful in their treatment of ethics, punishment, juveniles, courts, and other related topics.

Included in this volume are a number of features designed to be useful to students, researchers, and professionals in the criminal justice field. These include the *table of contents*, which summarizes each article, and feature key concepts in bold italics; a *topic guide* for locating articles on specific subjects; a list of relevant *World Wide Web* sites; a comprehensive section on crime statistics, a *glossary*, and an *index*. In addition, each unit is preceded by an *overview* that provides a background for informed reading of the articles, emphasizes critical issues, and presents key points to consider.

We would like to know what you think of the selections contained in this edition of *Annual Editions: Criminal Justice*. Please fill out the postage-paid *article rating form* on the last page and let us know your opinions. We change or retain many of the articles, based on the comments we receive from you, the reader. Help us to improve this anthology—annually.

Joseph L. Victor
Editor

Joanne Naughton
Editor

Contents

UNIT 1
Crime and Justice in America

Eight selections focus on the overall structure of the criminal justice system in the United States. The current scope of crime in America is reviewed, and topics such as criminal behavior, organized crime, and terrorism are discussed.

The concepts in bold italics are developed in the article. For further expansion, please refer to the Topic Guide and the Index.

UNIT 2
Victimology

Five articles discuss the impact of crime on the victim. Topics include the rights of crime victims and the consequences of family violence.

UNIT 3
The Police

Six selections examine the role of the police officer. Some of the topics include the stress of police work, multicultural changes, and ethical policing.

The concepts in bold italics are developed in the article. For further expansion, please refer to the Topic Guide and the Index.

UNIT 4
The Judicial System

Five selections discuss the process by which the accused are moved through the judicial system. The courts, the jury process, and judicial ethics are reviewed.

The concepts in bold italics are developed in the article. For further expansion, please refer to the Topic Guide and the Index.

UNIT 5
Juvenile Justice

Four selections review the juvenile justice system. The topics include effective ways to respond to violent juvenile crime and juvenile detention.

UNIT 6
Punishment and Corrections

Five selections focus on the current state of America's penal system and the effects of sentencing, probation, and capital punishment on criminals.

The concepts in bold italics are developed in the article. For further expansion, please refer to the Topic Guide and the Index.

The concepts in bold italics are developed in the article. For further expansion, please refer to the Topic Guide and the Index.

Topic Guide

This topic guide suggests how the selections in this book relate to the subjects covered in your course. You may want to use the topics listed on these pages to search the Web more easily.

On the following pages a number of Web sites have been gathered specifically for this book. They are arranged to reflect the units of this *Annual Edition*. You can link to these sites by going to the DUSHKIN ONLINE support site at *http://www.dushkin.com/online/*.

ALL THE ARTICLES THAT RELATE TO EACH TOPIC ARE LISTED BELOW THE BOLD-FACED TERM.

<table>
<tr><td valign="top">

Adolescence

  25. Why the Young Kill

Aggression

  25. Why the Young Kill

Bias

  21. Q: Should Juries Nullify Laws They Consider Unjust or Excessively Punitive?

Candidate selection

  18. Police Officer Candidate Assessment and Selection
  19. Improving the Recruitment of Women in Policing

Capital punishment

  33. The Death Penalty on Trial

Corrections system

  29. The Past and Future of U.S. Prison Policy: Twenty-Five Years After the Stanford Prison Experiment
  30. Bringing College Back to Bedford Hills
  31. Crime and Punishment
  32. Ex-Cons on the Street
  33. The Death Penalty on Trial

Court system

  16. Crime Story: The Digital Age
  20. How to Improve the Jury System
  21. Q: Should Juries Nullify Laws They Consider Unjust or Excessively Punitive?
  22. Looking Askance at Eyewitness Testimony
  23. The Creeping Expansion of DNA Data Banking
  24. Community Prosecution

Crime

  1. What Is the Sequence of Events in the Criminal Justice System?
  2. The Road to September 11
  3. America Is Getting Even Safer
  4. Toward the Ideal of Community Justice
  5. Making Computer Crime Count
  6. When It's No Longer a Game: Pathological Gambling in the United States
  7. Land of the Stupid: When You Need a Used Russian Submarine, Call Tarzan
  8. The Well-Marked Roads to Homicidal Rage
  22. Looking Askance at Eyewitness Testimony
  25. Why the Young Kill
  31. Crime and Punishment

Crime statistics

  3. America Is Getting Even Safer
  11. Telling the Truth About Damned Lies and Statistics

Criminal justice system

  1. What Is the Sequence of Events in the Criminal Justice System?
  2. The Road to September 11
  3. America Is Getting Even Safer

</td><td valign="top">

  4. Toward the Ideal of Community Justice
  5. Making Computer Crime Count
  6. When It's No Longer a Game: Pathological Gambling in the United States
  7. Land of the Stupid: When You Need a Used Russian Submarine, Call Tarzan
  8. The Well-Marked Roads to Homicidal Rage
  13. A LEN Interview With Susan Herman, Director of the National Center for Victims of Crime
  14. Ethics and Criminal Justice: Some Observations on Police Misconduct
  20. How to Improve the Jury System
  21. Q: Should Juries Nullify Laws They Consider Unjust or Excessively Punitive?
  23. The Creeping Expansion of DNA Data Banking
  25. Why the Young Kill
  29. The Past and Future of U.S. Prison Policy: Twenty-Five Years After the Stanford Prison Experiment
  33. The Death Penalty on Trial

Death penalty

  33. The Death Penalty on Trial

Discretion

  1. What Is the Sequence of Events in the Criminal Justice System?
  21. Q: Should Juries Nullify Laws They Consider Unjust or Excessively Punitive?
  24. Community Prosecution

DNA

  23. The Creeping Expansion of DNA Data Banking

Education

  30. Bringing College Back to Bedford Hills

Ethics

  14. Ethics and Criminal Justice: Some Observations on Police Misconduct
  17. Policing the Police
  25. Why the Young Kill

Evidence

  22. Looking Askance at Eyewitness Testimony
  23. The Creeping Expansion of DNA Data Banking

Eyewitnesses

  22. Looking Askance at Eyewitness Testimony

Genetics

  25. Why the Young Kill

Gun control

  8. The Well-Marked Roads to Homicidal Rage

Jury system

  20. How to Improve the Jury System

</td></tr>
</table>

World Wide Web Sites

The following World Wide Web sites have been carefully researched and selected to support the articles found in this reader. The easiest way to access these selected sites is to go to our DUSHKIN ONLINE support site at *http://www.dushkin.com/online/*.

AE: Criminal Justice 02/03

The following sites were available at the time of publication. Visit our Web site—we update DUSHKIN ONLINE regularly to reflect any changes.

General Sources

American Society of Criminology
http://www.bsos.umd.edu/asc/four.html

This is an excellent starting place for study of all aspects of criminology and criminal justice, with links to international criminal justice, juvenile justice, court information, police, governments, and so on.

Federal Bureau of Investigation
http://www.fbi.gov

The main page of the FBI Web site leads to lists of the most wanted criminals, uniform crime reports, FBI case reports, major investigations, and more.

National Archive of Criminal Justice Data
http://www.icpsr.umich.edu/NACJD/index.html

NACJD holds more than 500 data collections relating to criminal justice; this site provides browsing and downloading access to most of these data and documentation. NACJD's central mission is to facilitate and encourage research in the field of criminal justice.

Social Science Information Gateway
http://sosig.esrc.bris.ac.uk

This is an online catalog of thousands of Internet resources relevant to social science education and research. Every resource is selected and described by a librarian or subject specialist. Enter "criminal justice" under Search for an excellent annotated list of sources.

University of Pennsylvania Library: Criminology
http://www.library.upenn.edu/resources/subject/social/criminology/ criminology.html

An excellent list of criminology and criminal justice resources is provided here.

UNIT 1: Crime and Justice in America

Campaign for Equity-Restorative Justice
http://www.cerj.org

This is the home page of CERJ, which sees monumental problems in justice systems and the need for reform. Examine this site and its links for information about the restorative justice movement.

Crime Times
http://www.crime-times.org/titles.htm

This interesting site, listing research reviews and other information regarding biological causes of criminal, violent, and psychopathic behavior, consists of many articles that are listed by title. It is provided by the Wacker Foundation, publisher of *Crime Times*.

Ray Jones
http://blue.temple.edu/~eastern/jones.html

In this article, subtitled "A Review of Empirical Research in Corporate Crime," Ray Jones explores what happens when business violates the law. An extensive interpretive section and a bibliography are provided.

Sourcebook of Criminal Justice Statistics Online
http://www.albany.edu/sourcebook/

Data about all aspects of criminal justice in the United States are available at this site, which includes more than 600 tables from dozens of sources. A search mechanism is available.

UNIT 2: Victimology

Connecticut Sexual Assault Crisis Services, Inc.
http://www.connsacs.org

This site has links that provide information about women's responses to sexual assault and related issues. It includes extensive links to sexual violence–related Web pages.

National Crime Victim's Research and Treatment Center (NCVC)
http://www.musc.edu/cvc/

At this site, find out about the work of NCVC at the Medical University of South Carolina, and click on Related Resources for an excellent listing of additional Web sources.

Office for Victims of Crime (OVC)
http://www.ojp.usdoj.gov/ovc

Established by the 1984 Victims of Crime Act, the OVC oversees diverse programs that benefit the victims of crime. From this site you can download a great deal of pertinent information.

UNIT 3: The Police

ACLU Criminal Justice Home Page
http://aclu.org/issues/criminal/hmcj.html

This "Criminal Justice" page of the American Civil Liberties Union Web site highlights recent events in criminal justice, addresses police issues, lists important resources, and contains a search mechanism.

Introduction to American Justice
http://www.uaa.alaska.edu/just/just110/home.html

Prepared by Darryl Wood of the Justice Center at the University of Alaska at Anchorage, this site provides an excellent outline of the causes of crime, including major theories. An introduction to crime, law, and the criminal justice system as well as data on police and policing, the court system, corrections, and more are available here.

Law Enforcement Guide to the World Wide Web
http://leolinks.com/

This page is dedicated to excellence in law enforcement. It contains links to every possible related category: community policing, computer crime, forensics, gangs, and wanted persons are just a few.

www.dushkin.com/online/

National Institute of Justice (NIJ)
http://www.ojp.usdoj.gov/nij/lawedocs.htm

The NIJ sponsors projects and conveys research findings to practitioners in the field of criminal justice. Through this site, you can access the initiatives of the 1994 Violent Crime Control and Law Enforcement Act, apply for grants, monitor international criminal activity, learn the latest about policing techniques and issues, and more.

Violent Criminal Apprehension Program (VICAP)
http://www.state.ma.us/msp/unitpage/vicap.htm

VICAP's mission is to facilitate cooperation, communication, and coordination among law enforcement agencies and provide support in their efforts to investigate, identify, track, apprehend, and prosecute violent serial offenders. Access VICAP's data information center resources here.

UNIT 4: The Judicial System

Center for Rational Correctional Policy
http://www.correctionalpolicy.com

This is an excellent site on courts and sentencing, with many additional links to a variety of criminal justice sources.

Justice Information Center (JIC)
http://www.ncjrs.org

Provided by the National Criminal Justice Reference Service, this JIC site connects to information about corrections, courts, crime prevention, criminal justice, statistics, drugs and crime, law enforcement, and victims.

National Center for Policy Analysis (NCPA)
http://www.public-policy.org/~ncpa/pd/law/index3.html

Through the NCPA's "Idea House," you can click onto links to an array of topics that are of major interest in the study of the American judicial system.

U.S. Department of Justice (DOJ)
http://www.usdoj.gov

The DOJ represents the American people in enforcing the law in the public interest. Open its main page to find information about the U.S. judicial system. This site provides links to federal government Web servers, topics of interest related to the justice system, documents and resources, and a topical index.

UNIT 5: Juvenile Justice

Gang Land: The Jerry Capeci Page
http://www.ganglandnews.com

Although this site particularly addresses organized-crime gangs, its insights into gang lifestyle—including gang families and their influence—are useful for those interested in exploring issues related to juvenile justice.

Institute for Intergovernmental Research (IIR)
http://www.iir.com

The IIR is a research organization that specializes in law enforcement, juvenile justice, and criminal justice issues. Explore the projects, links, and search engines from this home page. Topics addressed include youth gangs and white collar crime.

National Criminal Justice Reference Service (NCJRS)
http://virlib.ncjrs.org/JuvenileJustice.asp

NCJRS, a federally sponsored information clearinghouse for people involved with research, policy, and practice related to criminal and juvenile justice and drug control, provides this site of links to full-text juvenile justice publications.

National Network for Family Resiliency
http://www.nnfr.org

This organization's CYFERNET (Children, Youth, and Families Education and Research Network) page will lead to a number of resource areas of interest in learning about resiliency, including Program and Curriculum for Family Resiliency .

Partnership Against Violence Network
http://www.pavnet.org

The Partnership Against Violence Network is a virtual library of information about violence and youths at risk, representing data from seven different federal agencies—a one-stop searchable information resource.

UNIT 6: Punishment and Corrections

American Probation and Parole Association (APPA)
http://www.appa-net.org

Open this APPA site to find information and resources related to probation and parole issues, position papers, the APPA code of ethics, and research and training programs and opportunities.

The Corrections Connection
http://www.corrections.com

This site is an online network for corrections professionals.

Critical Criminology Division of the ASC
http://www.critcrim.org/

Here you will find basic criminology resources and related government resources, provided by the American Society of Criminology, as well as other useful links. The death penalty is also discussed.

David Willshire's Forensic Psychology & Psychiatry Links
http://members.optushome.com.au/dwillsh/index.html

This site offers an enormous number of links to professional journals and associations. It is a valuable resource for study into possible connections between violence and mental disorders. Topics include serial killers, sex offenders, and trauma.

Oregon Department of Corrections
http://www.doc.state.or.us/links/welcome.htm

Open this site for resources in such areas as crime and law enforcement and for links to U.S. state corrections departments.

Prison Law Page
http://www.prisonwall.org

This page, edited by Arnold Erickson, contains articles and resources on prisons, death row, and the death penalty debate, prison news, and other criminal justice information.

We highly recommend that you review our Web site for expanded information and our other product lines. We are continually updating and adding links to our Web site in order to offer you the most usable and useful information that will support and expand the value of your Annual Editions. You can reach us at: *http://www.dushkin.com/annualeditions/.*

UNIT 1

Crime and Justice in America

Unit Selections

Key Points to Consider

- In your view, what is behind the dramatic drop in crime?

- What steps do you believe could be taken to prevent gun-related crimes?

- Are alcohol and drug arrests on your campus on the rise? Are you familiar with treatment modalities that have proven effective in helping chronic drug users to break away from addiction? Explain.

 **Links: www.dushkin.com/online/**
These sites are annotated in the World Wide Web pages.

Campaign for Equity-Restorative Justice
  http://www.cerj.org
Crime Times
  http://www.crime-times.org/titles.htm
Ray Jones
  http://blue.temple.edu/~eastern/jones.html
Sourcebook of Criminal Justice Statistics Online
  http://www.albany.edu/sourcebook/

Crime continues to be a major problem in the United States. Court dockets are full, our prisons are overcrowded, probation and parole caseloads are overwhelming, and our police are being urged to do more. The bulging prison population places a heavy strain on the economy of the country. Clearly crime is a complex problem that defies simple explanations or solutions. While the more familiar crimes of murder, rape, and assault are still with us, drugs are an ever-increasing scourge. The debate continues about how best to handle juvenile offenders, sex offenders, and those who commit acts of domestic violence. Crime committed using computers and the Internet is already an issue to be dealt with.

Annual Editions: Criminal Justice 02/03 focuses directly upon crime in America and the three traditional components of the criminal justice system: police, the courts, and corrections. It also gives special attention to crime victims in the victimology unit and to juveniles in the juvenile justice unit. The articles presented in this section are intended to serve as a foundation for the materials presented in subsequent sections.

The unit begins with "What Is the Sequence of Events in the Criminal Justice System?" which reveals that the response to crime is a complex process, involving citizens as well as many agencies, levels, and branches of government. Then, in "The Road to September 11," Evan Thomas' *Newsweek* article chronicles the missed clues and missteps in a manhunt that is far from over. In "America is Getting Even Safer," the unprecedented drop in violent crime is discussed. "Toward the Ideal of Community Justice" looks at the concept of community justice. Computer crime is the subject of the next article, "Making Computer Crime Count" by Marc Goodman. The problem of addictive gambling is examined in Charles Wellford's "When It's No Longer a Game: Pathological Gambling in the United States." In "Land of the Stupid: When You Need a Used Russian Submarine, Call Tarzan," Robert Friedman traces a Russian organized crime figure from his birthplace in Odessa to Miami, providing insight into this version of the now-familiar phenomenon of organized crime in America. The last article in this unit, "The Well-Marked Roads to Homicidal Rage," is part of a *New York Times* series on rampage killers. It discusses how relatives, colleagues, and officials overlook the warning signs projected by the killers.

What is the sequence of events in the criminal justice system?

The private sector initiates the response to crime

This first response may come from individuals, families, neighborhood associations, business, industry, agriculture, educational institutions, the news media, or any other private service to the public.

It involves crime prevention as well as participation in the criminal justice process once a crime has been committed. Private crime prevention is more than providing private security or burglar alarms or participating in neighborhood watch. It also includes a commitment to stop criminal behavior by not engaging in it or condoning it when it is committed by others.

Citizens take part directly in the criminal justice process by reporting crime to the police, by being a reliable participant (for example, a witness or a juror) in a criminal proceeding and by accepting the disposition of the system as just or reasonable. As voters and taxpayers, citizens also participate in criminal justice through the policymaking process that affects how the criminal justice process operates, the resources available to it, and its goals and objectives. At every stage of the process from the original formulation of objectives to the decision about where to locate jails and prisons to the reintegration of inmates into society, the private sector has a role to play. Without such involvement, the crim-

inal justice process cannot serve the citizens it is intended to protect.

The response to crime and public safety involves many agencies and services

Many of the services needed to prevent crime and make neighborhoods safe are supplied by noncriminal justice agencies, including agencies with primary concern for public health, education, welfare, public works, and housing. Individual citizens as well as public and private sector organizations have joined with criminal justice agencies to prevent crime and make neighborhoods safe.

Criminal cases are brought by the government through the criminal justice system

We apprehend, try, and punish offenders by means of a loose confederation of agencies at all levels of government. Our American system of justice has evolved from the English common law into a complex series of procedures and decisions. Founded on the concept that crimes against an individual are crimes against the State, our justice system prosecutes individuals as though they victimized all of society. However, crime victims are involved throughout the process and many justice

agencies have programs which focus on helping victims.

There is no single criminal justice system in this country. We have many similar systems that are individually unique. Criminal cases may be handled differently in different jurisdictions, but court decisions based on the due process guarantees of the U.S. Constitution require that specific steps be taken in the administration of criminal justice so that the individual will be protected from undue intervention from the State.

The description of the criminal and juvenile justice systems that follows portrays the most common sequence of events in response to serious criminal behavior.

Entry into the system

The justice system does not respond to most crime because so much crime is not discovered or reported to the police. Law enforcement agencies learn about crime from the reports of victims or other citizens, from discovery by a police officer in the field, from informants, or from investigative and intelligence work.

Once a law enforcement agency has established that a crime has been committed, a suspect must be identified and apprehended for the case to proceed through the system. Sometimes, a suspect is apprehended at the scene; however, identification of a suspect sometimes requires an extensive investigation. Often, no one is identified or apprehended. In some instances, a suspect is arrested and later the police determine that no crime was committed and the suspect is released.

Prosecution and pretrial services

After an arrest, law enforcement agencies present information about the case and about the accused to the prosecutor, who will decide if formal charges will be filed with the court. If no charges are filed, the accused must be released. The prosecutor can also drop charges after making efforts to prosecute (*nolle prosequi*).

A suspect charged with a crime must be taken before a judge or magistrate without unnecessary delay. At the initial appearance, the judge or magistrate informs the accused of the charges and decides whether there is probable cause to detain the accused person. If the offense is not very serious, the determination of guilt and assessment of a penalty may also occur at this stage.

Often, the defense counsel is also assigned at the initial appearance. All suspects prosecuted for serious crimes have a right to be represented by an attorney. If the court determines the suspect is indigent and cannot afford such representation, the court will assign counsel at the public's expense.

A pretrial-release decision may be made at the initial appearance, but may occur at other hearings or may be changed at another time during the process. Pretrial release and bail were traditionally intended to ensure appearance at trial. However, many jurisdictions permit pretrial detention of defendants accused of serious offenses and deemed to be dangerous to prevent them from committing crimes prior to trial.

The court often bases its pretrial decision on information about the defendant's drug use, as well as residence, employment, and family ties. The court may decide to release the accused on his/her own recognizance or into the custody of a third party after the posting of a financial bond or on the promise of satisfying certain conditions such as taking periodic drug tests to ensure drug abstinence.

In many jurisdictions, the initial appearance may be followed by a preliminary hearing. The main function of this hearing is to discover if there is probable cause to believe that the accused committed a known crime within the jurisdiction of the court. If the judge does not find probable cause, the case is dismissed; however, if the judge or magistrate finds probable cause for such a belief, or the accused waives his or her right to a preliminary hearing, the case may be bound over to a grand jury.

A grand jury hears evidence against the accused presented by the prosecutor and decides if there is sufficient evidence to cause the accused to be brought to trial. If the grand jury finds sufficient evidence, it submits to the court an indictment, a written statement of the essential facts of the offense charged against the accused.

Where the grand jury system is used, the grand jury may also investigate criminal activity generally and issue indictments called grand jury originals that initiate criminal cases. These investigations and indictments are often used in drug and conspiracy cases that involve complex organizations. After such an indictment, law enforcement tries to apprehend and arrest the suspects named in the indictment.

Misdemeanor cases and some felony cases proceed by the issuance of an information, a formal, written accusation submitted to the court by a prosecutor. In some jurisdictions, indictments may be required in felony cases. However, the accused may choose to waive a grand jury indictment and, instead, accept service of an information for the crime.

In some jurisdictions, defendants, often those without prior criminal records, may be eligible for diversion from prosecution subject to the completion of specific conditions such as drug treatment. Successful completion of the conditions may result in the dropping of charges or the expunging of the criminal record where the defendant is required to plead guilty prior to the diversion.

Adjudication

Once an indictment or information has been filed with the trial court, the accused is scheduled for arraignment. At the arraignment, the accused is informed of the charges, advised of the rights of criminal defendants, and asked to enter a plea to the charges. Sometimes, a plea of guilty is the result of negotiations between the prosecutor and the defendant.

If the accused pleads guilty or pleads *nolo contendere* (accepts penalty without admitting guilt), the judge may accept or reject the plea. If the plea is accepted, no trial is held and the offender is sentenced at this proceeding or at a later date. The plea may be rejected and proceed to trial if, for example, the judge believes that the accused may have been coerced.

If the accused pleads not guilty or not guilty by reason of insanity, a date is set for the trial. A person accused of a serious crime is guaranteed a trial by jury. However, the accused may ask for a bench trial where the judge, rather than a jury, serves as the finder of fact. In both instances the prosecution and defense present evidence by questioning witnesses while the judge decides on issues of law. The trial results in acquittal or conviction on the original charges or on lesser included offenses.

After the trial a defendant may request appellate review of the conviction or sentence. In some cases, appeals of convictions are a matter of right; all States with the death penalty provide for automatic appeal of cases involving a death sentence. Appeals may be subject to the discretion of the appellate court and may be granted only on acceptance of a defendant's petition for a *writ of certiorari*. Prisoners may also appeal their sentences through civil rights petitions and *writs of habeas corpus* where they claim unlawful detention.

Sentencing and sanctions

After a conviction, sentence is imposed. In most cases the judge decides on the sentence, but in some jurisdictions the sentence is decided by the jury, particularly for capital offenses.

In arriving at an appropriate sentence, a sentencing hearing may be held at which evidence of aggravating or mitigating circumstances is considered. In assessing the circumstances surrounding a convicted person's criminal behavior, courts often rely on presentence investigations by probation agencies or other designated authorities. Courts may also consider victim impact statements.

The sentencing choices that may be available to judges and juries include one or more of the following:

- the death penalty
- incarceration in a prison, jail, or other confinement facility
- probation—allowing the convicted person to remain at liberty but subject

Entry into the system

Prosecution and pretrial services

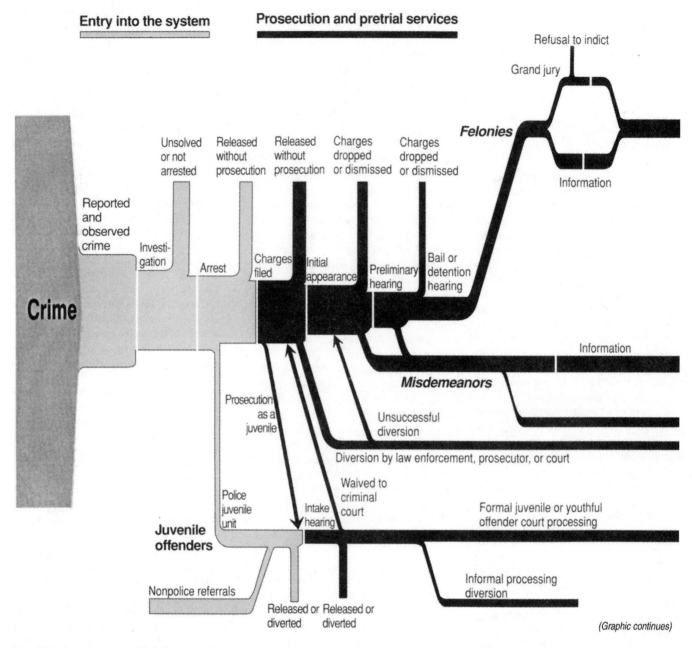

Note: This chart gives a simplified view of caseflow through the criminal justice system. Procedures vary among jurisdictions. The weights of the lines are not intended to show the actual size of caseloads.

to certain conditions and restrictions such as drug testing or drug restrictions such as drug testing or drug treatment

• fines—primarily applied as penalties in minor offenses

• restitution—requiring the offender to pay compensation to the victim. In some jurisdictions, offenders may be sentenced to alternatives to incarceration that are considered more severe than straight probation but less severe

than a prison term. Examples of such sanctions include boot camps, intense supervision often with drug treatment and testing, house arrest and electronic monitoring, denial of Federal benefits, and community service.

In many jurisdictions, the law mandates that persons convicted of certain types of offenses serve a prison term. Most jurisdictions permit the judge to set the sentence length within certain limits, but some have determinate sentencing laws that stipulate

a specific sentence length that must be served and cannot be altered by a parole board.

Corrections

Offenders sentenced to incarceration usually serve time in a local jail or a State prison. Offenders sentenced to less than 1 year generally go to jail; those sentenced to more than 1 year go to prison. Persons admitted to the Federal system or a State prison system may be held in prison with

Article 1. What is the sequence of events in the criminal justice system?

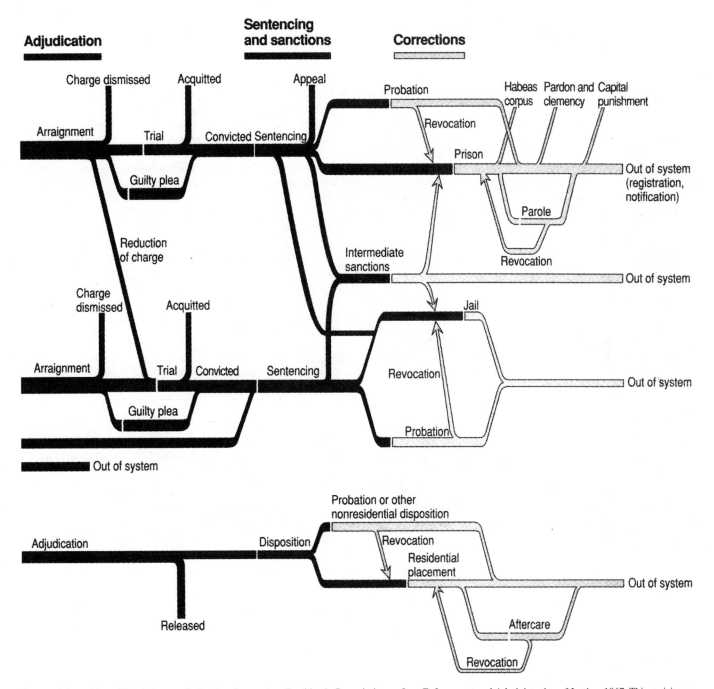

Source: Adapted from *The challenge of crime in a free society*. President's Commission on Law Enforcement and Administration of Justice, 1967. This revision, a result of the Symposium on the 30th Anniversary of the President's Commission, was prerpared by the Bureau of Justice Statistics in 1997.

varying levels of custody or in a community correctional facility.

A prisoner may become eligible for parole after serving a specific part of his or her sentence. Parole is the conditional release of a prisoner before the prisoner's full sentence has been served. The decision to grant parole is made by an authority such as a parole board, which has power to grant or revoke parole or to discharge a parolee altogether. The way parole decisions are made varies widely among jurisdictions.

Offenders may also be required to serve out their full sentences prior to release (expiration of term). Those sentenced under determinate sentencing laws can be released only after they have served their full sentence (mandatory release) less any "goodtime" received while in prison. Inmates get goodtime credits against their sentences automatically or by earning them through participation in programs.

If released by a parole board decision or by mandatory release, the releasee will be under the supervision of a parole officer in the community for the balance of his or her unexpired sentence. This supervision is governed by specific conditions of release, and the releasee may be returned to prison for violations of such conditions.

Discretion is exercised throughout the criminal justice system

Discretion is "an authority conferred by law to act in certain conditions or situations in accordance with an official's or an official agency's own considered judgment and conscience."[1] Discretion is exercised throughout the government. It is a part of decisionmaking in all government systems from mental health to education, as well as criminal justice. The limits of discretion vary from jurisdiction to jurisdiction.

Concerning crime and justice, legislative bodies have recognized that they cannot anticipate the range of circumstances surrounding each crime, anticipate local mores, and enact laws that clearly encompass all conduct that is criminal and all that is not.[2]

Therefore, persons charged with the day-to-day response to crime are expected to exercise their own judgment within limits set by law. Basically, they must decide—
- whether to take action
- where the situation fits in the scheme of law, rules, and precedent
- which official response is appropriate.[3]

To ensure that discretion is exercised responsibly, government authority is often delegated to professionals. Professionalism requires a minimum

level of training and orientation, which guide officials in making decisions. The professionalism of policing is due largely to the desire to ensure the proper exercise of police discretion.

The limits of discretion vary from State to State and locality to locality. For example, some State judges have wide discretion in the type of sentence they may impose. In recent years, other states have sought to limit the judge's discretion in sentencing by passing mandatory sentencing laws that require prison sentences for certain offenses.

Notes

1. Roscoe Pound, "Discretion, dispensation and mitigation: The problem of the individual special case," *New York University Law Review* (1960) 35:925, 926.
2. Wayne R. LaFave, *Arrest: The decision to take a suspect into custody* (Boston: Little, Brown & Co., 1964), p. 63–184.
3. Memorandum of June 21, 1977, from Mark Moore to James Vorenberg, "Some abstract notes on the issue of discretion."

Bureau of Justice Statistics (*www.ojp.usdoj.gov/bjs/*). January 1998. NCJ 167894. To order: 1-800-732-3277.

Who exercises discretion?

These criminal justice officials...	must often decide whether or not or how to—
Police	Enforce specific laws Investigate specific crimes; Search people
Prosecutors	File charges or petitions for adjudication Seek indictments Drop cases Reduce charges
Judges or magistrates	Set bail or conditions for release Accept pleas Determine delinquency Dismiss charges Impose sentence Revoke probation
Correctional officials	Assign to type of correctional facility Award privileges Punish for disciplinary infractions
Paroling authorities	Determine date and conditions of parole Revoke parole

Recidivism

Once the suspects, defendants, or offenders are released from the jurisdiction of a criminal justice agency, they may be processed through the criminal justice system again for a new crime. Long term studies show that many suspects who are arrested have prior criminal histories and

those with a greater number of prior arrests were more likely to be arrested again. As the courts take prior criminal history into account at sentencing, most prison inmates have a prior criminal history and many have been incarcerated before. Nationally, about half the inmates released from State prison will return to prison.

The juvenile justice system

Juvenile courts usually have jurisdiction over matters concerning children, including delinquency, neglect, and adoption. They also handle "status offenses" such as truancy and running away, which are not applicable to adults. State statutes define which persons are under the original jurisdiction of the juvenile court. The upper age of juvenile court jurisdiction in delinquency matters is 17 in most States.

The processing of juvenile offenders is not entirely dissimilar to adult criminal processing, but there are crucial differences. Many juveniles are referred to juvenile courts by law enforcement officers, but many others are referred by school officials, social services agencies, neighbors, and even parents, for behavior or conditions that are determined to require intervention by the formal system for social control.

At arrest, a decision is made either to send the matter further into the justice system or to divert the case out of the system, often to alternative programs. Examples of alternative programs include drug treatment, individual or group counseling, or referral to educational and recreational programs.

When juveniles are referred to the juvenile courts, the court's intake department or the prosecuting attorney determines whether sufficient grounds exist to warrant filing a petition that requests an adjudictory hearing or a request to transfer jurisdiction to criminal court. At this point, many juveniles are released or diverted to alternative programs.

All States allow juveniles to be tried as adults in criminal court under certain circumstances. In many States, the legislature *statutorily excludes* certain (usually serious) offenses from the jurisdiction of the juvenile court regardless of the age of the accused. In some States and at the Federal level under certain circumstances, prosecutors have the *discretion* to either file criminal charges against juveniles directly in criminal courts or proceed through the juvenile justice process. The juvenile court's intake department or the prosecutor may petition the juvenile court to *waive* jurisdiction to criminal court. The juvenile court also may order *referral* to criminal court for trial as adults. In some jurisdic-

tions, juveniles processed as adults may upon conviction be sentenced to either an adult or a juvenile facility.

In those cases where the juvenile court retains jurisdiction, the case may be handled formally by filing a delinquency petition or informally by diverting the juvenile to other agencies or programs in lieu of further court processing.

If a petition for an adjudicatory hearing is accepted, the juvenile may be brought before a court quite unlike the court with jurisdiction over adult offenders. Despite the considerable discretion associated with juvenile court proceedings, juveniles are afforded many of the due-process safeguards associated with adult criminal trials. Several States permit the use of juries in juvenile courts; however, in light of the U.S. Supreme Court holding that juries are not essential to juvenile hearings, most States do not make provisions for juries in juvenile courts.

In disposing of cases, juvenile courts usually have far more discretion that adult courts. In addition to such options as probation, commitment to a residential facility, restitution, or fines, State laws grant juvenile courts the power to order removal of children from their homes to foster homes or treatment facilities. Juvenile courts also may order participation in special programs aimed at shoplifting prevention, drug counseling, or driver education.

Once a juvenile is under juvenile court disposition, the court may retain jurisdiction until the juvenile legally becomes an adult (at age 21 in most States). In some jurisdictions, juvenile offenders may be classified as youthful offenders which can lead to extended sentences.

Following release from an institution, juveniles are often ordered to a period of aftercare which is similar to parole supervision for adult offenders. Juvenile offenders who violate the conditions of aftercare may have their aftercare revoked, resulting

in being recommitted to a facility. Juveniles who are classified as youthful offenders and violate the conditions of aftercare may be subject to adult sanctions.

The governmental response to crime is founded in the intergovernmental structure of the United States

Under our form of government, each State and the Federal Government has its own criminal justice system. All systems must respect the rights of individuals set forth in court interpretation of the U.S. Constitution and defined in case law.

State constitutions and laws define the criminal justice system within each State and delegate the authority and responsibility for criminal justice to various jurisdictions, officials, and institutions. State laws also define criminal behavior and groups of children or acts under jurisdiction of the juvenile courts.

Municipalities and counties further define their criminal justice systems through local ordinances that proscribe the local agencies responsible for criminal justice processing that were not established by the State.

Congress has also established a criminal justice system at the Federal level to respond to Federal crimes such as bank robbery, kidnaping, and transporting stolen goods across State lines.

The response to crime is mainly a State and local function

Very few crimes are under exclusive Federal jurisdiction. The responsibility to respond to most crime rests with State and local governments. Police protection is primarily a function of cities and towns. Corrections is primarily a function of State governments. Most justice personnel are employed at the local level.

From the *Report to the Nation on Crime and Justice,* January 1998. © 1998 by the U.S. Department of Justice, Office of Justice Programs, Bureau of Justice Statistics. Reprinted by permission.

The Road to September 11

It was a long time coming. For a decade, America's been fighting a losing secret war against terror. A NEWSWEEK investigation into the missed clues and missteps in a manhunt that is far from over.

He was more than a little suspicious. At the Airman Flight School in Norman, Okla., the stocky aspiring pilot with the heavy French accent acted oddly. He was abrupt and argumentative, refusing to pay the whole $4,995 fee upfront (he shelled out $2,500 in cash instead). He had been dodgy in his e-mails. "E is not secure," explained Zacarias Moussaoui, 33, who preferred to use his Internet alias, "zuluman tangotango." A poor flier, he suddenly quit in mid-May, before showing up at another flight school in Eagan, Minn. At Pan Am Flying Academy, he acknowledged that the biggest plane he'd ever flown was a single-engine Cessna. But he asked to be trained on a 747 flight simulator. He wanted to concentrate only on the midair turns, not the takeoffs and landings. It was all too fishy to one of the instructors, who tipped off the Feds. Incarcerated because his visa had expired, Moussaoui was sitting in the Sherburne County Jail when some other pilot trainees drove their hijacked airliners into the World Trade Center and the Pentagon.

It's not that the U.S. government was asleep. America's open borders make tracking terrorists a daunting exercise. NEWSWEEK has learned that the FBI has privately estimated that more than 1,000 individuals—most of them foreign nationals—with suspected terrorist ties are currently living in the United States. "The American people would be surprised to learn how many of these people there are," says a top U.S. official. Moussaoui almost exactly fits the profile of the suicide hijackers, but he may or may not have been part of the plot. After Moussaoui's arrest on Aug. 17, U.S. immigration authorities dutifully notified the French (he was a passport holder), who responded 10 days later that Moussaoui was a suspected terrorist who had allegedly traveled to Osama bin Laden's training camps in Afghanistan. Ten days may seem like a leisurely pace for investigators racing against time to foil terrorist plots, but in the real world of international cooperation, 10 days, "c'est rapide," a French official told NEWSWEEK. Fast but, in the new age of terror, not fast enough.

As officials at the CIA and FBI sift through intelligence reports, they are berating themselves for missing warning signs on the road to Sept. 11. Those reports include intercepted messages with phrases like "There is a big thing coming," "They're going to pay the price" and "We're ready to go." Unfortunately, many of those messages, intercepted before the attack, did not reach the desks of intelligence analysts until afterward. In the bureaucracy of spying, 24-hour or 48-hour time lags are not unusual. None of the intercepted traffic mentioned the Pentagon or the World Trade Center. Some hinted at a target somewhere on the Pacific Rim. Nonetheless, an intelligence official told NEWSWEEK: "A lot of people feel guilty and think of what they could have done."

ALL ACROSS THE WORLD LAST WEEK, intelligence services were scrambling to catch the terrorists before they struck again. The scale of the roundup was breathtaking: in Yemen, a viper's nest of terror, authorities hauled in "dozens" of suspected bin Laden followers. In Germany, police were searching for a pair of men believed to be directly involved in the hijacking plot. In France, more than half a dozen were being held for questioning, while in Britain, Belgium and the Netherlands—and Peru and Paraguay—police raided suspected terror hideouts. In the United States, where the FBI has launched the greatest manhunt in history, authorities detained about 90 people. Most of them were being held for minor immigration charges, but investigators were looking for mass murderers. The gumshoes swept up pieces of chilling evidence, like two box cutters stuffed into the seat of a Sept. 11 flight out of Boston—another hijacking target? Boston was jittery over threats of an attack last Saturday. An Arab in a bar was overheard to say that blood would flow in Boston on Sept. 22, and U.S. intelligence intercepted a conversation between Algerian diplomats talking about "the upcoming Boston tea party on Sept. 22." It turned out that some women really were holding a tea party that day. Some federal officials were spooked when manuals describing crop-duster equipment—to spray deadly germs?—were found among Moussaoui's possessions. But a top U.S. official told NEWSWEEK, "I'm not getting into the bunker and putting on a gas mask. We're used to seeing these threats." (Nonetheless, crop-dusters were barred from flying near cities.)

The vast dragnet was heartening, unless one considers that after two American embassies were bombed in 1998, a similar crackdown swept up a hundred potential suspects from Europe to the Middle East to Latin America—and bin Laden's men were still able to regroup to launch far more devastating attacks. Catching foot soldiers and lieutenants will not be enough to stop even greater cataclysms. Last week the authorities were searching for a single man who might have triggered the assault on Washington and New York. In past attacks by bin Laden's Qaeda organization, "sleeper" agents have burrowed into the target country to await their orders. FBI officials now believe that the mastermind was Mohamed Atta, the intense Egyptian who apparently piloted the first plane, American Airlines Flight 11, into the North Tower of the World Trade Center. ("Did he ever learn to fly?" Atta's father, Mohamed al-Amir Atta, said to NEWSWEEK. "Never. He never even had a kite. My daughter, who is a doctor, used to get

him medicine before every journey, to make him combat the cramps and vomiting he feels every time he gets on a plane.") Though intelligence officials believe they have spotted the operation's paymaster, identified to NEWSWEEK as Mustafa Ahmed, in the United Arab Emirates, Atta was the one hijacker who appeared to have the most contacts with conspirators on other aircraft prior to the attacks, and he was the one who left a last testament. According to a top government source, it included this prayer: "Be prepared to meet your God. Be ready for this moment." Atta's role "doesn't fit the usual pattern," said one official. "It looks like the ringleader went down with the plane."

You could rate the arrival of the international jihad in America on the rainy night of Nov. 5, 1990, when a terrorist walked into a Marriott and killed Meir Kahane. The cops bungled the case.

The ultimate ringleader may be somewhere in the mountains of Afghanistan, hiding from U.S. bombs and commandos—but also no doubt plotting his next atrocity. In history's long list of villains, bin Laden will find a special place. He has no throne, no armies, not even any real territory, aside from the rocky wastes of Afghanistan. But he has the power to make men willingly go to their deaths for the sole purpose of indiscriminately killing Americans—men, women and children. He is an unusual combination in the annals of hate, at once mystical and fanatical—and deliberate and efficient. Now he has stirred America's wrath and may soon see America's vengeance. But the slow business of mopping up the poison spread by bin Laden through the Islamic world was almost pitifully underscored after the attack by a plea from FBI Director Robert Mueller. The nation's top G-man said the FBI was looking for more Arabic speakers. A reasonable request, but perhaps a

little late in the game. It's hard to know your enemy when you can't even speak his language.

For most Americans, life was instantly and forever changed on Sept. 11, 2001. But the terror war that led up to the attack had been simmering, and sometimes boiling over, for more than 10 years. It can be recalled as a tedious bureaucratic struggle—all those reports on "Homeland Defense" piling up unread on the shelves of congressmen, droning government officials trying to fatten their budgets with scare stories relegated to the back pages of the newspaper. Or it can be relived—as it truly was—as a race to the Gates of Hell. Before the world finds out what horrors lie beyond, it's worthwhile retracing a decade-long trail of terror to see how America stumbled. The enemy has clearly learned from experience. In December 1994, the Armed Islamic Group (GIA), an Algerian-based terrorist band that would go on to play a prominent role in bin Laden's global army, hijacked an Air France Airbus with 171 passengers aboard. The plan: to plunge into the Eiffel Tower. The problem: none of the hijackers could fly. The Air France pilot landed instead in Marseilles, where French police stormed the plane. It was not too long afterward that the first terrorists began quietly enrolling in flight schools in Florida.

THE UNITED STATES HAS BEEN A LITTLE slower on the uptake. Money has not really been the obstacle. The counterterrorism budget jumped from $2 billion to $12 billion over a decade. The United States spends $30 billion a year gathering intelligence. Nor has bin Laden been in any way ignored. For the past five years, analysts have been working through the night in a chamber, deep in the bowels of CIA headquarters, known as the Bin Laden Room. Some experts argued that the CIA was too focused on bin Laden—that, in an effort to put a face on faceless terror, the gaunt guerrilla fighter had been elevated to the role of international bogeyman, to the neglect of shadowy others who did the real killing. Now, as the Washington blame game escalates—along with the cries for revenge—intelligence officials are cautioning that terror cells, clannish and secretive, are extremely difficult to penetrate; that for every snake beheaded two more will crawl out of the swamp; that swamps can never be drained in land that drips with the blood of martyrs; that even the most persuasive interrogations may not crack a suspect who is willing to die.

All true. But the inability of the government to even guess that 19 suicidal terrorists might turn four jetliners into guided missiles aimed at national icons was more than a failure of intelligence. It was a failure of imagination. The United States is so strong, the American people seemed so secure, that the concept of Homeland Defense seemed abstract, almost foreign, the sort of thing tiny island nations worried about. Terrorists were regarded by most people as criminals, wicked and frightening, but not as mortal enemies of the state. There was a kind of collective denial, an unwillingness to see how monstrous the threat of Islamic extremism could be.

In part, that may be because the government of the United States helped create it. In the 1980s, the CIA secretly backed the mujahedin, the Islamic freedom fighters rebelling against the Soviet occupation of Afghanistan. Arming and training the "Mooj" was one of the most successful covert actions ever mounted by the CIA. It turned the tide against the Soviet invaders. But there is a word used by old CIA hands to describe covert actions that backfire: "blowback." In the coming weeks, if and when American Special Forces helicopters try to land in the mountains of Afghanistan to flush out bin Laden, they risk being shot down by Stinger surface-to-air missiles provided to the Afghan rebels by the CIA. Such an awful case of blowback would be a mere coda to a long and twisted tragedy of unanticipated consequences. The tale begins more than 10 years ago, when the veterans of the Mooj's holy war against the Soviets began arriving in the United States—many with passports arranged by the CIA.

Bonded by combat, full of religious zeal, the diaspora of young Arab men willing to die for Allah congregated at the Al-Kifah Refugee Center in Brooklyn, N.Y., a dreary inner-city building that doubled as a recruiting post for the CIA seeking to steer fresh troops to the mujahedin. The dominant figures at the center in the late '80s were a gloomy New York City engineer named El Sayyid Nosair, who took Prozac for his blues, and his sidekick, Mahmud Abouhalima, who had been a human minesweeper in the Afghan war (his only tool was a thin reed, which he used as a crude probe). The new immigrants were filled not with gratitude toward their new nation, but by implacable hatred toward America, symbol of West-

ern modernity that threatened to engulf Muslim fundamentalism in a tide of blue jeans and Hollywood videos. Half a world away, people who understood the ferocity of Islamic extremism could see the coming storm. In the late '80s, Pakistan's then head of state, Benazir Bhutto, told the first President George Bush, "You are creating a Frankenstein." But the warnings never quite filtered down to the cops and G-men on the streets of New York.

The international jihad arrived in America on the rainy night of Nov. 5, 1990, when Nosair walked into a crowded ballroom at the New York Marriott on 49th Street and shot and killed Rabbi Meir Kahane, a mindless hater who wanted to rid Israel of "Arab dogs" ("Every Jew a .22" was a Kahane slogan). The escape plan was amateur hour: Nosair's buddy Abouhalima was supposed to drive the getaway car, a taxicab, but the overexcited Nosair jumped in the wrong cab and was apprehended.

> **In the mid-'90s Ramzi Yousef took flying lessons and talked of crashing a plane into the CIA or a nuclear facility. At the time the FBI thought the plans grandiose. Now they look like blueprints.**

With a room full of witnesses and a smoking gun, the case against Nosair should have been a lay-down. But the New York police bungled the evidence, and Nosair got off with a gun rap. At that moment, Nosair and Abouhalima may have had an epiphany: back home in Egypt, suspected terrorists are dragged in and tortured. In America, they can hire a good lawyer and beat the system. The New York City police hardly noticed any grander scheme. A search of Nosair's apartment turned up instructions for building bombs and photos of targets—including the Empire State Building and the World Trade Center. The police never bothered to inventory most of the evidence, nor were the documents translated—that is, until a van with a 1,500-

pound bomb blew up in the underground garage of the World Trade Center on Feb. 26, 1993. The (first) World Trade Center bombing, which killed six people and injured more than 1,000, might have been a powerful warning, especially when investigators discovered that the plotters had meant to topple the towers and packed the truck bomb with cyanide (in an effort to create a crude chemical weapon). But the cyanide was harmlessly burned up in the blast, the buildings didn't fall and the bombers seemed to be hapless. One of them went back to get his security deposit from the truck rental.

The plotters were quickly exposed as disciples of Sheik Omar Abdel-Rahman, the "Blind Sheik" who ranted against the infidels from a run-down mosque in Jersey City. The Blind Sheik's shady past should have been of great interest to the Feds—he had been linked to the plot to assassinate Egyptian President Anwar Sadat in 1981. But the sheik had slipped into the United States with the protection of the CIA, which saw the revered cleric as a valuable recruiting agent for the Mooj. Investigators trying to track down the Blind Sheik "had zero cooperation from the intelligence community, zero," recalled a federal investigator in New York.

ONE WORLD TRADE CENTER PLOTTER who did attract attention from the Feds was Ramzi Yousef. Operating under a dozen aliases, Yousef was a frightening new figure, seemingly stateless and sinister, a global avenging angel. Though he talked to Iraqi intelligence and stayed in a safe house that was later linked to bin Laden, Yousef at the time appeared to be a kind of terror freelancer. Yousef's luck ran out when the apartment of an old childhood friend, Abdul Hakim Murad, burst into flames. Plotting with Yousef, Murad had been at work making bombs to assassinate the pope and blow up no fewer than 11 U.S. airliners. Murad's arrest in January 1995 led investigators to capture Yousef in Pakistan, where he was hiding out. Murad and Yousef were a duo sent by the Devil: Murad had taken pilot lessons, and the two talked about flying a plane filled with explosives into the CIA headquarters or a nuclear facility. At the time, FBI officials thought the plans were grandiose and far-fetched. Now they look like blueprints.

The capture of Yousef was regarded as a stirring victory in the war against terrorism, which was just then gearing up in Washington. But Yousef's arrest illustrates the difficulties of cracking terrorism even when a prize suspect is caught. At his sentencing, Yousef declared, "Yes, I am a terrorist, and I am proud of it." He has never cooperated with authorities. Instead, he spent his days chatting about movies with his fellow inmates in a federal maximum-security prison, Unabomber Ted Kaczynski and, until he was executed, the Oklahoma City bomber Timothy McVeigh.

By the mid-'90s, counterterror experts at the FBI and CIA had begun to focus on Osama bin Laden, the son of a Saudi billionaire who had joined the Mooj in Afghanistan and become a hero as a battlefield commander. Bin Laden was said to be bitter because the Saudi royal family had rebuffed his offer to rally freedom fighters to protect the kingdom against the threat of Saddam Hussein after the Iraqi strongman invaded Kuwait in 1990. Instead, the Saudi rulers chose to be defended by the armed forces of the United States. To bin Laden, corrupt princes were welcoming infidels to desecrate holy ground. Bin Laden devoted himself to expelling America, not just from Saudi Arabia, but—as his messianic madness grew—from Islam, indeed all the world.

Tony Lake, President Bill Clinton's national-security adviser, does not recall one single defining moment when bin Laden became Public Enemy No. 1. It was increasingly clear to intelligence analysts that extremists all over the Middle East viewed bin Laden as a modern-day Saladin, the Islamic warrior who drove out the Crusaders a millennium ago. Setting up a sort of Terror Central of spiritual, financial and logistical support—Al Qaeda (the Base)—bin Laden went public, in 1996 telling every Muslim that their duty was to kill Americans (at first the *fatwa* was limited to U.S. soldiers, then broadened in 1998 to all Americans). From his home in Sudan, bin Laden seemed to be inspiring and helping to fund a broad if shadowy network of terrorist cells. On the rationale that no nation should be allowed to harbor terrorists, the State Department in the mid-'90s pressured the government of Sudan to kick out bin Laden. In retrospect, that may have been a mistake. At least in Sudan, it was easier to keep an eye on bin Laden's activities. Instead, he vanished into the mountains of Afghanistan, where he would be welcomed by extremist Taliban rulers and enabled to set up training bases for terrorists. These camps—crude collections of mud huts—appear to have provided a sort of Iron John bonding experience for thou-

sands of aspiring martyrs who came for a course of brainwashing and bombmaking.

With the cold war over, the Mafia in retreat and the drug war unwinnable, the CIA and FBI were eager to have a new foe to fight. The two agencies established a Counter Terrorism Center in a bland, windowless warren of offices on the ground floor of CIA headquarters at Langley, Va. Historical rivals, the spies and G-men were finally learning to work together. But they didn't necessarily share secrets with the alphabet soup of other enforcement and intelligence agencies, like Customs and the Immigration and Naturalization Service, and they remained aloof from the Pentagon. And no amount of good will or money could bridge a fundamental divide between intelligence and law enforcement. Spies prefer to watch and wait; cops want to get their man. At the White House, a bright national-security staffer, Richard Clarke, tried to play counterterror coordinator, but he was given about as much real clout as the toothless "czars" sent out to fight the war on drugs. There was no central figure high in the administration to knock heads, demand performance and make sure everyone was on the same page. Lake now regrets that he did not try harder to create one. At the time, Clinton's national-security adviser was too preoccupied with U.S. involvement in Bosnia to do battle with fiefdoms in the intelligence community. "Bosnia was easier than changing the bureaucracy," Lake told NEWSWEEK.

Bitter after the Saudis allied themselves with the American infidels against Saddam, bin Laden, his messianic madness growing, devoted himself to destroying the United States.

AN EMPIRE BUILDER WITH A MESSIANIC streak OF his own, FBI Director Louis Freeh was eager to throw G-men at the terrorist threat all over the world. When a truck bomb blew up the Khobar Towers, a U.S. military barracks in Saudi Arabia,

Freeh made a personal quest of bringing the bombers to justice. As Freeh left office last summer, a grand jury in New York was about to indict several conspirators behind the bombing. But, safely secluded in Iran, the suspects will probably never stand trial. The Khobar Towers investigation shows the limits of treating terrorism as a crime. It also reveals some of the difficulties of working with foreign intelligence services that don't share the same values (or rules) as Americans. Freeh's gumshoes got a feel for Saudi justice when they asked to interview some suspects seized in an earlier bombing attack against a U.S.-run military compound in Riyadh. Before the FBI could ask any questions, the suspects were beheaded. An attempt by the FBI to play the role of Good Cop to the Saudis' Bad Cop was thwarted by American sensitivities. After the bombing, FBI agents managed to corner Hani al-Sayegh, a key suspect in Canada. Cooperate with us, the gumshoes threatened, or we'll send you back to Saudi Arabia, where a sword awaits. No fool, the suspect hired an American lawyer. The State Department was convinced that sending the man back to Saudi Arabia would violate international laws banning torture. Their leverage gone, the Feds were unable to make the suspect talk.

The CIA did have some luck in working with foreign security services to roll up terror networks. In 1997 and 1998, the agency collaborated with the Egyptians—whose security service is particularly ruthless—to root out cells of bin Laden's men from their hiding places in Albania. But just as the spooks were congratulating themselves, another bin Laden cell struck in a carefully coordinated, long-planned attack. Within minutes of each other, truck bombs blew up the U.S. embassies in Tanzania and Kenya, killing more than 220. The failure of intelligence in the August 1998 embassy bombings is a case study in the difficulty of penetrating bin Laden's network.

For some of the time that bin Laden's men were plotting to blow up the two embassies, U.S. intelligence was tapping their phones. According to Justice Department documents, the spooks tapped five telephone numbers used by bin Laden's men living in Kenya in 1996 and '97. But the plotters did not give themselves away. Bin Laden uses couriers to communicate with his agents face to face. His Qaeda organization is also technologically sophisticated, sometimes embedding coded messages in innocuous-seeming Web sites. Intelligence experts have worried for some time that the supersecret-code breakers at the National Security Agency are going deaf, overwhelmed by the sheer volume of telecommunications and encryption software that any consumer can buy at a computer store.

If high-tech espionage won't do the job, say the experts, then the CIA needs more human spies. It has become rote to say that in order to crack secretive terrorist cells the CIA needs to hire more Arabic-speaking case officers who can in turn recruit deep-penetration agents—HUMINT (human intelligence) in spy jargon. Actually, the CIA had a sometime informer among the embassy bombers. Ali Mohamed was a former Egyptian Army officer who enlisted in the U.S. Army and was sent to Fort Bragg, N.C., in the early 1980s to lecture U.S. Special Forces on Islamic terrorism. In his free time, he was a double agent. On the weekends he visited the Al-Kifah Refugee Center in Brooklyn, where he stayed with none other than El Sayyid Nosair, the man who struck the first blow in the holy war by murdering Rabbi Kahane. Ali Mohamed went to Afghanistan to fight with the Mooj, but after the 1993 World Trade Center bombing, he flipped back, telling the Feds about bin Laden's connection to some of the bombers. He described how the Islamic terrorist used "sleepers" who live normal lives for years and then are activated for operations. What he did not tell the spooks was that he was helping plan to bomb the U.S. embassies in Africa. Only after he had pleaded guilty to conspiracy in 1999 did he disclose that he had personally met with bin Laden about the plot. He described how bin Laden, looking at a photo of the U.S. Embassy in Nairobi, "pointed to where the truck could go as a suicide bomber."

The story of Ali Mohamed suggests that the calls by some politicians for more and better informants may be easier to preach than practice. The CIA's skills in the dark arts of running agents have atrophied over the years. The agency was purged of some of its best spy handlers after the 1975 Church Committee investigation exposed some harebrained agency plots, like hiring the Mafia to poison Fidel Castro. During the Reagan years, the agency was beefed up, but a series of scandals in the late '80s and the '90s once more sapped its esprit. America's spies were once proud to engage in "morally hazardous duty," said Carleton Swift, the CIA's Baghdad station chief in the late 1950s. "Now the CIA has become a standard government bureaucracy instead of a bunch of special guys."

A number of lawmakers are calling to, in effect, unleash the CIA. They want to do away with rules that restrict the agency from hiring agents and informers with a record of crimes or abusing human rights. Actually, case officers in the field can still hire sleazy or dangerous characters by asking permission from their bosses in Langley. "We almost never turn them down," said one high-ranking official. But that answer may gloss over a more significant point—that case officers, made cautious by scandal, no longer dare to launch operations that could get them hauled before a congressional inquisition.

THE WEAKNESSES OF THE CIA'S DIRECTorate of Operations, once called "the Department of Dirty Tricks," can be overstated. When the CIA suspected that the Sudanese government was helping bin Laden obtain chemical weapons, a CIA agent was able to obtain soil samples outside the Al Shifa pharmaceutical plant that showed traces of EMPTA—a precursor chemical used in deadly VX gas. The evidence was used to justify a cruise-missile attack on the factory in retaliation for the embassy bombings. At the same time, 70 cruise missiles rained down on a bin Laden training camp in Afghanistan.

The Clinton administration was later mocked for this showy but meaningless response. Clinton's credibility was not high: he was accused of trying to divert attention from the Monica Lewinsky scandal. In classic American fashion, the owner of the pharmaceutical plant in Sudan hired a top Washington lobbying firm to heap scorn on the notion that his plant was being used for chemical weapons. But Clinton's national-security adviser at the time, Sandy Berger, still "swears by" the evidence, and insists that the cruise missiles aimed at bin Laden's training camps missed bin Laden and his top advisers by only a few hours.

The Clinton administration never stopped trying to kill bin Laden. Although a 1976 executive order bans assassinations of foreign leaders, there is no prohibition on killing terrorists—or, for that matter, from killing a head of state in time of war. In 1998, President Clinton signed a "lethal finding," in effect holding the CIA harmless if bin Laden was killed in a covert operation. The agency tried for at least two years to hunt down bin Laden, working with Afghan rebels opposed to the Taliban regime. These rebels once fired a bazooka at bin Laden's convoy but hit the wrong

vehicle. "There were a few points when the pulse quickened, when we thought we were close," recalled Berger.

By the final year of the Clinton administration, top officials were very worried about the terrorist threat. Berger says he lay awake at night, wondering if his phone would ring with news of another attack. Administration officials were routinely trooping up to Capitol Hill to sound warnings. CIA Director George Tenet raised the specter of bin Laden so many times that some lawmakers suspected he was just trying to scare them into coughing up more money for intelligence. The Clinton Cassandras emphasized the growing risk that terrorists would obtain weapons of mass destruction—chemical, biological or nuclear. But the threat was not deemed to be imminent. Bin Laden was generally believed to be aiming at "soft" targets in the Middle East and Europe, like another embassy. The experts said that a few bin Laden lieutenants were probably operating in the United States, but no one seriously expected a major attack, at least right away.

The millennium plots should have been a wakeup call. Shortly before the 2000 New Year, an obscure Algerian refugee named Ahmed Ressam was caught by a wary U.S. Customs inspector trying to slip into the United States from Canada with the makings of a bomb. Ressam was a storm trooper in what may have been a much bigger plot to attack the Los Angeles airport and possibly other targets with a high symbolic value. A petty criminal who lived by credit-card fraud and stealing laptop computers, Ressam was part of a dangerous terrorist organization—GIA, the same group that hijacked the Air France jet in 1994 and tried, but failed, to plunge it into the Eiffel Tower. A particularly vicious group that staged a series of rush-hour subway bombings in Paris in the mid-'90s, GIA is a planet in Al Qaeda's solar system. Ressam later told investigators that he had just returned from one of bin Laden's Afghan training camps, where he learned such skills as feeding poison gas through the air vents of office buildings. Some of Ressam's confederates in the millennium plots were never picked up and are still at large. The Canadian Security Intelligence Service is believed to have fat files on the GIA, but like many secret services, the CSIS does not share its secrets readily with other services, at home or abroad. Some U.S. investigators believe that bin Laden was using Canada as a safe base for assaults on the United States. U.S.

border authorities now believe that several of the suicide hijackers came across the border via a ferry from Nova Scotia in the days before the attack on the World Trade Center.

In hindsight, the Ressam case offered clues to another bin Laden trademark: the ability of Al Qaeda-trained operatives to hide their tracks. While renting buildings in Vancouver, Ressam and his confederates frequently changed the names on the leases, apparently to lay a confusing paper trail. A kind of terrorist's how-to manual ("Military Studies in the Jihad Against the Tyrants") found at the home of a bin Laden associate in England last year instructs operatives to deflect suspicion by shaving beards, avoiding mosques and refraining from traditional Islamic greetings. Intelligence officials now suspect that bin Laden used all manner of feints and bluffs to throw investigators off the trail of the suicide hijackers. Decoy terrorist teams and disinformation kept the CIA frantically guessing about an attack somewhere in the Middle East, Asia or Europe all last summer. Embassies were shuttered, warships were sent to sea, troops were put on the highest state of alert in the Persian Gulf. The Threat Committee of national-security specialists that meets twice a week in the White House complex to monitor alerts sent out so many warnings that they began to blur together. One plot seemed particularly concrete and menacing. At the end of July, authorities picked up an alleged bin Laden lieutenant named Djamel Begal in Dubai. He began singing—a little too fast, perhaps—about a plan to bomb the American Embassy in Paris. Was the threat real—or a diversion?

The United States is heavily dependent on foreign intelligence services to roll up terror networks in their own countries. But typically, intelligence services prefer to keep an eye on suspected terrorists rather than prosecute them.

To persuade a foreign government to turn over information on a terrorist suspect, much less arrest him, requires heavy doses of diplomacy. The task is not made easier if different branches of the American government squabble with each other. Last October, the USS Cole, a destroyer making a refueling stop in the Yemeni port of Aden, was nearly sunk by suicide bombers in a small boat. (An earlier attempt, against a different American warship docking in Yemen, fizzled when the suicide boat, overloaded with explosives, sank as it was leaving the dock. Bin Laden,

nothing if not persistent, apparently ordered his hit men to try again.) FBI investigators immediately rushed to the scene, where they were coolly received by the Yemeni government. The G-men became apprehensive about their own security and demanded that they be allowed to carry assault rifles. The U.S. ambassador, Barbara Bodine, who regarded the FBI men as heavy-handed and undiplomatic, refused. After an awkward standoff between the G-men and embassy security officials in the embassy compound, the entire FBI team left the country—for three months. They did not return until just recently.

It now appears that the same men who masterminded the Cole bombing may be tied to the devastating Sept. 11 assault on the United States. Since January 2000 the CIA has been aware of a man named Tawfiq bin Atash, better known in terrorist circles by his nom de guerre "Khallad." A Yemeni-born former freedom fighter in Afghanistan, Khallad assumed control of bin Laden's bodyguards and became a kind of capo in Al Qaeda. According to intelligence sources, Khallad helped coordinate the attack on the Cole. These same sources tell NEWSWEEK that in December 1999, Khallad was photographed by the Malaysian security service (which was working with the CIA to track terrorists) at a hotel in Kuala Lumpur. There, Khallad met with several bin Laden operatives. One was Fahad al-Quso, who, it later turned out, was assigned to videotape the suicide attack on the Cole (not all of Al Qaeda's men are James Bond: al-Quso botched the job when he overslept). Another was Khalid al-Midhar, who was traveling with an associate, Nawaf al-Hazmi, on a trip arranged by an organization known to U.S. intelligence as a "logistical center" and "base of support" for Al Qaeda.

> **American intelligence agencies intercepted a number of messages pointing to an imminent terrorist assault. But none was analyzed until after the deadly September 11 attacks.**

Those two names—al-Midhar and al-Hazmi—would resonate with intelligence officials on Sept. 11. Both men were listed among the hijackers of American Airlines Flight 77, the airliner that dive-bombed the Pentagon. Indeed, when one intelligence official saw the names on the list of suspects, he uttered an expletive. Just three weeks earlier, on Aug. 21, the CIA asked the INS to keep a watch out for al-Midhar. The INS reported that the man was already in the country; his only declared address was "Marriott Hotel" in New York. The CIA sent the FBI to find al-Midhar and his associate. The gumshoes were still looking on Sept. 11.

AT LEAST ONE OTHER NAME FROM THE list of hijackers had shown up in the files of Western intelligence services: Mohamed Atta. He is an intriguing figure, both because of his role as the apparent senior man among the suicide hijackers, and because his background offers some disturbing clues about the high quality of bin Laden's recruits. The stereotype of an Islamic suicide bomber is that of a young man or teenage boy who has no job, no education, no prospects and no hope. He has been gulled into believing that if he straps a few sticks of dynamite around his waist and presses a button, he will stroll through the Gates of Paradise, where he will be bedded by virgins. Atta in no way matches that pathetic creature. He did not come from a poor or desperate fundamentalist family. His father, Mohamed, described himself to NEWSWEEK as "one of the most important lawyers in Cairo." The Atta family has a vacation home on the Mediterranean coast. Their Cairo apartment, with a sweeping view of downtown, is filled with ornate furniture and decorated with paintings of flamingos and women in head scarves.

If anything, Atta seemed like a prodigy of Western modernism. His two sisters are university professors with Ph.D.s. Atta won a bachelor's degree in Cairo in 1990 and went to Germany for graduate work in urban studies.

His thesis adviser in Hamburg, where he studied at the Technical University, called Atta "a dear human being." Only in retrospect does it appear ominous that in his thesis dedication he wrote "my life and my death belong to Allah, master of all worlds." Atta went to bars and rented videos ("Ace Ventura," "Storm of the Century"), but he also grew a beard and began to dress more in Islamic style. He spoke often of Egypt's "humiliation" by the West.

While polite, he also could be haughty. He scorned women, refusing to shake their hands.

That was the only worry of Atta's proud father. "I started reminding him to get married," Atta senior recounted to NEWSWEEK, as he chain-smoked cigarettes ("American blend"). "Many times I asked him to marry a woman of any nationality—Turkish, German, Syrian—because he did not have a girlfriend like his colleagues. But he insisted he would marry an Egyptian. He was never touching woman, so how can he live?" In October 1999, "we found him a bride who was nice and delicate, the daughter of a former ambassador," said Atta senior. But Atta junior said he had to go back to Germany to finish his Ph.D. Actually, he was going to Florida to enroll in flight school.

During his years as a student in Hamburg, Atta would disappear for long periods of time—possibly, to meet with his handlers. U.S. intelligence believes that Atta met in Europe this year with a midlevel Iraqi intelligence official. The report immediately raised the question of Saddam Hussein's possible role in the Sept. 11 atrocity, but intelligence officials cautioned against reading too much into the link. Atta was in close communication with his superiors. On Sept. 4, one week before the bombing, he sent a package from a Kinko's in Hollywood, Fla., to a man named Mustafa Ahmed in the United Arab Emirates. "We don't know for sure what was in the package," said a senior U.S. official. "But Mustafa could be the key to bin Laden's finances. We're taking a hard look at him." (Several of the hijackers also wired money to Ahmed.) There are indications that Atta prepared very carefully for the attack, casing the airport in Boston and flying coast to coast on airliners. He may have had a backup plan: NEWSWEEK has learned that Atta had round-trip reservations between Baltimore and San Francisco in mid-October.

Atta's father refuses to accept his son's role as a suicide bomber. "It's impossible my son would participate in this attack," he said, claiming that he was a victim of a plot by Israeli intelligence to provoke the United States against Islam. "The Mossad kidnapped my son," said Atta. "He is the easiest person to kidnap, very surrendering, no physical power, no money for bodyguards. They used his name and identity… Then they killed him. This was done by the Mossad, using American pilots." Atta's rant was wild and sad—yet it was matched by the vituperations of the virulently anti-American Egyptian press, which spun fantastic plots featuring Mossad agents as the villains.

Atta appears to have been inseparable from another hijacker, Marwan al-Shehhi, up to the moment they parted ways at Logan airport on the morning of Sept. 11. The FBI believes that al-Shehhi piloted the second jetliner, United Airlines Flight 173, into the South Tower of the World Trade Center. Al-Shehhi and Atta roomed together in Florida and were tossed out of Jones Flying Service School for unprofessional behavior. (Instructors complained about their "attitude.") They signed up together for a one-month membership at a gym, the Delray Beach Health Club. They went to Las Vegas, where the FBI believes that several hijackers kept girlfriends. They ate American, but told the employees at Hungry Howie's to hold the ham when they ordered their favorite pizza, a pie with all the toppings called "The Works."

As investigators piece together the lives of the hijackers, details that once seemed innocuous now loom large. Ziad Samir Jarrahi, a Lebanese man, took martial-arts lessons at a Dania, Fla., gym. "What he wanted to study was street-fighting tactics—how to gain control over somebody with your hands, how to incapacitate someone with your hands," gym owner Bert Rodriguez told NEWSWEEK. Did Jarrahi use those tactics in the last, desperate struggle in the cockpit of Flight 93, which crashed in a field outside Pittsburgh? Top law-enforcement officials reported that the voice recorder from Flight 93 picked up sounds of Arab and American voices shouting as the plane went down. Some very brave passengers stormed the cockpit in a last-ditch effort to seize control of the plane. Did they encounter Jarrahi and his newly honed fighting skills?

THE AVAILABLE EVIDENCE SUGGESTS A death match. When the hijackers struck, at about 9:35 a.m., air-traffic controllers listening in on the frequency between the cockpit and the control center in Cleveland could hear screams, then a gap of 40 seconds with no sound, then more screams. Then, sources say, a nearly unintelligible voice said something like "Bomb onboard." The controllers tried to raise the captain but received no response. Then radar showed the plane turning sharply—toward Washington, D.C. A voice in thickly accented English said, "This is your captain. There is a bomb onboard. We are returning to the airport."

In the passenger cabin, there was bloodshed and fear. At least one passenger was dead, probably with his throat slashed. In the back of the plane, however, five men, all burly athletes, were plotting a rush at the hijackers. "We're going to do something," Todd Beamer told a GTE operator over the air phone. "I know I'm not going to get out of this." He asked the operator to say the Lord's Prayer with him. "Are you ready, guys?" he asked. "Let's roll." The cockpit voice recorder picked up someone, apparently a hijacker, screaming "Get out of here! Get out of here!" Then grunting, screaming and scuffling. Then silence.

Such stories of heroic struggle will be—and should be—told and retold in the years to come. But now investigators are groping with uncertainty, asking: Who else is still out there? And will they strike again? A congressional delegation to CIA headquarters last week reported that mattresses were strewn on the floors. The race is still on, round the clock. Some investigators were trying to follow the money. They learned that in the week before the Sept. 11 attack, the hijackers began sending small amounts of money back to their paymasters in the Middle East. "They were sending in their change," an intelligence source told NEWSWEEK. "They were going to a place where they wouldn't need money." The hijackers apparently didn't need all that much to begin with: law enforcement estimates that the entire plot, flight lessons and all, cost as little as $200,000. That is 10 times more than was spent on the first World Trade Center bombing, but still a low-enough sum so the money could be moved in small denominations among trusted agents. Still, Al Qaeda is reputed to be expert at money laundering. Last week the pressure was on banks all over the world to open up their books (and on the banking lobby in the United States to drop its opposition to new laws that would make it easier for investigators to follow the money). The trail is likely to lead in some diplomatically awkward directions. Moderate Arab regimes are said to try to buy off terrorists. Much of bin Laden's money has come from wealthy Saudis who ostensibly give to Islamic charities. Some of those charities resemble the "widows and orphans" funds the Irish Republican Army uses to finance its bombmaking.

The money trail led investigators last week to a suspect whose background and motives could be the stuff of nightmares. Nabil al-Marabh, a former Boston taxi driver of Kuwaiti descent, is suspected of funneling thousands of dollars in wire transfer through Fleet Bank to the Middle East. The money was allegedly sent to a former Boston cabby implicated in a terrorist plot in Jordan that was foiled at the time of the millennium celebrations. At the same time, investigators say, al-Marabh may have exchanged phone calls with at least two of the Sept. 11 hijackers. Al-Marabh, who like a number of terrorists seems to have used Canada as a sometime sanctuary, was hard to track down. Canadian authorities first informed U.S. Customs about al-Marabh in July, and investigators opened a money-laundering probe. Last week the FBI raided an apartment in Detroit, where al-Marabh had been living. They found instead three men who had once worked as caterers at the Detroit airport (and kept their airport ID badges). In the apartment was a diagram of an airport runway and a day planner filled with notations in Arabic about "the American base in Turkey," the "American foreign minister" and the name of an airport in Jordan. The FBI arrested the men, but al-Marabh was at the time getting a duplicate driver's license at the state department of motor vehicles.

Not just any license. Al-Marabh's license would permit him to drive an 18-wheel truck containing hazardous materials. As it turned out, two of his housemates had also been going to school to learn how to drive large trucks. Carrying what, exactly? And heading where?

This story was written by EVAN THOMAS *with reporting from* MARK HOSENBALL, MICHAEL ISIKOFF, ELEANOR CLIFT *and* DANIEL KLAIDMAN *in Washington*, PEG TYRE *in New York*, CHRISTOPHER DICKEY *in Paris*, ANDREW MURR, JOSEPH CONTRERAS *and* JOHN LANTINGUA *in Florida*, KAREN BRESLAU *in San Francisco*, SARAH DOWNEY *in Minneapolis*, STEFAN THEIL *in Hamburg*, TOM MASLAND *in Dubai and* ALAN ZARENBO *in Cairo*

America is getting even safer

In 2000, violent crime dropped 15 percent—the largest decline ever recorded.

By Alexandra Marks
Staff writer of The Christian Science Monitor

NEW YORK—America just keeps getting safer and safer.

Violent crime plummeted a surprising 15 percent last year, the biggest decline ever recorded by the Justice Department's National Crime Victimization Survey. The drop, across almost all categories from simple assault to rape, also affected all demographic groups—women, men, blacks, Hispanics, and whites.

In all, there were 1 million fewer crimes in 2000 than in 1999.

The drop, as well as its size, surprised many criminologists—in part, because a recently released FBI crime report found a leveling off of the crime rate after eight straight years of declines. The difference in the findings can be attributed to the different types of crime the two reports measure.

But it appears the factors that led to the almost decade-long drop in crime—the increased police presence on the streets, declining drug use, the aging population, and increased incarceration rates—are still working to make Americans safer in their daily lives.

"That's surprising. We've had a lot of good news," says Carolyn Rebecca Block, senior research analyst for the Illinois Criminal Justice Information Authority in Chicago. "But everybody's holding their breath, aren't they?"

That's at least partly because many criminologists expected that the crime rate would soon begin inching up again as the economy softens and a large number of young people start to come into their peak crime-committing years. The FBI's report this year appeared to reinforce that expectation.

It is drawn from police statistics from around the country, but doesn't include simple assaults—the largest type of crime in the US. The Victimization Survey is derived from the nation's second-largest household survey, which is done by the Census Bureau and includes unreported, as well as reported, crime. While it includes simple assault, it excludes homicide rates, which the FBI report includes.

As a result, the survey tends to be weighted more toward less serious crime than the FBI report.

Criminologist James Fox compared the two to weather measures—the FBI's statistics are like temperature, while the Victimization Survey is more like the wind chill factor. "The thing about wind chill factor—it's not just temperature, its how hard the wind is blowing," he says. "That's why temperature sometimes can give you a poor indication of how cold it feels. And for many people, it's the less serious things that make life unpleasant."

Able to walk in the park

For Maria Then, it wasn't just the little things. She felt imprisoned by the crime in her neighborhood. The Dominican pharmacist moved to New York's Washington Heights 13 years ago at the height of the crack epidemic. The streets were full of drug dealers, gangs of armed kids, and gunshots. The dark-eyed mother wouldn't even let her three children walk to the local bodega for a carton of milk in the middle of the day.

That has all changed now. She even takes her children to play into the park across the street, an unthinkable notion just a few years ago. "You can live more freely now," she says.

As in Washington Heights, declining drug use and the violence associated with it—along with a more community-oriented police practices—helped bring down the crime rate across the US.

16

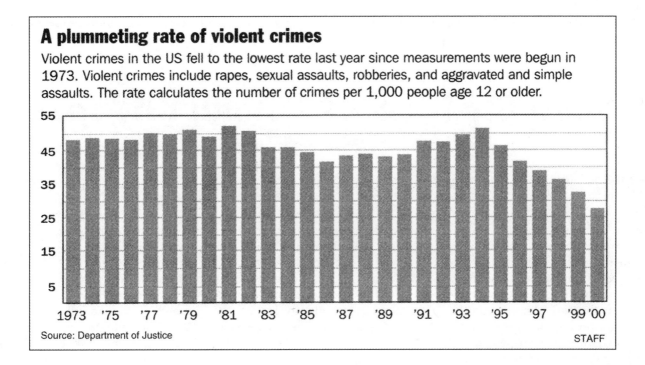

A plummeting rate of violent crimes

Violent crimes in the US fell to the lowest rate last year since measurements were begun in 1973. Violent crimes include rapes, sexual assaults, robberies, and aggravated and simple assaults. The rate calculates the number of crimes per 1,000 people age 12 or older.

Source: Department of Justice

STAFF

But those are just two of the myriad reasons criminologists point to to explain the continuing drop. "The factors involved also include the good economy, high incarceration rates, and ... an older population," says Margaret Zahn, a criminologist at North Carolina State University. "People have also learned more about how to protect their property."

Many more people are also working together to reclaim their neighborhoods, like Jose Fernandez, a New York bodega owner. A few months ago, two armed men walked into one of his stores in the Bronx, stole $10,000, and threatened to kill the employees.

It made him so angry, he decided to take safety prevention into his own hands.

"We're reaching out to community leaders to try to get everyone involved," says Mr. Fernandez, who is also president of the New York State Bodega Owners Association. "It's a question of education and learning the impact that small things, like not reporting trouble, can have on everyone in the neighborhood."

Still 6.3 million crimes

Still, some criminologists worry that reports of the continuing crime rate drop could lead to complacency. And

Calli Rennison, who wrote the Crime Victimization Survey, agrees. "We can't forget that there are still 6.3 million violent crimes that we're measuring in one year.... There's still a lot of work left to be done."

That's the general attitude in the financially ailing city of East St. Louis, Ill., where abandoned storefronts outnumber businesses, which seem split between check-cashing operations and used-clothing stores.

Inside Fashion Guys, manager Brian Jackson laughs when told about the new crime statistics. "Are you kidding?" he asks.

Things are certainly better than when he started at the store 10 years ago, when the city was dubbed the US "murder capital." But it's become only marginally less dangerous, and at night, "all bets are off." The only statistic that matters to him, he says, is that he doesn't become one.

Craig Savoye in St. Louis and Sara Miller in New York contributed to this report.

Toward the Ideal of Community Justice

by Todd R. Clear and David R. Karp

In recent years, there has been a rapid growth in approaches to criminal justice that center on "community." Most familiar is community policing, now almost universally accepted as the new orthodoxy in the field, but the community paradigm has been adopted in virtually every component of the criminal justice system, from prosecution through corrections. Neighborhood-based prosecution centers in jurisdictions such as Portland, Oregon, and New York City; community courts in Manhattan and elsewhere; reparative probation statewide in Vermont; and community justice councils in Travis County, Texas, are among the manifestations. The trend, however, is not confined to the United States. Indeed, some initiatives underway in this country were originated abroad. Family group conferencing for juvenile offenses, now being adopted here, began in New Zealand and is widespread in Australia. Sentencing circles are rooted in the traditional peacemaking rituals of both Native Canadians and Native Americans.

Community Justice Defined

Two central elements grafted from policing—problem solving and community orientation—animate community justice. The approach, which is proactive rather than focused on criminal events, is handled on a case-by-case basis. Community justice taps into the problem-solving skills of citizens instead of relying solely on the expertise of professionals. It is localized and flexible rather than centralized and standardized. And whereas in traditional criminal justice the outcome of a case generally involves restricting the offender's freedom, in community justice, restoring what the victim and the community have lost as a result of the crime is at the forefront. In this respect, it closely resembles restorative justice.[1]

Community justice might be best described as an ethic that transforms the aim of the justice system into enhancing community life or sustaining community. To achieve that aim, the community partners with the justice system to share responsibility for social control.

Community justice might be best described as an ethic that transforms the aim of the justice system into enhancing community life or sustaining community. To achieve that aim, the community partners with the justice system to share responsibility for social control. This means some control devolves from the justice system, a powerful mechanism of formal social control, to the community, which through churches, schools, civic organizations, families, and similar institutions, exercises the informal social control that fosters civil behavior and public safety.

Still in an embryonic stage, community justice is not yet a fully identifiable practice, nor is it based on a systematically derived theory or grounded in a body of empirical research. Without a full articulation of the philosophy underlying community justice, it might be dismissed as a fad or as a term applied to programs that consist of little substantive change. The ideal of community justice is presented here to begin elaboration of the concept and to guide practitioners who may be interested in adopting the approach.

Crime, Communities, and Criminal Justice

As currently configured, the justice system responds to crime in ways that may actually diminish the quality of life of a community. Strong mechanisms of informal social control in a community not only help reduce crime, but by augmenting the work of the agents of formal control, make that work easier.[2] By contrast, when informal social controls are weak, formal social control fills the void, and as it becomes the main regulating force, citizens may begin to view it as the appropriate agent to deal with all conflict, not just crime.[3] Incarcerating large segments of a neighborhood's population is evidence of strong formal social control, but it signals the breakdown of informal control mechanisms and can further weaken an already fragile social order.[4] Community justice, by contrast, is based on the notion that formal social control is neither the only response to crime nor the one best suited to improve the quality of community life.

Under community justice, offender accountability for crime remains a vital element, but it is set in the context of repairing the damage to both victims and the community. Embracing the idea of community is a profound shift because it changes the focus of justice from what is to be done about people (offenders) to what is to be done about the places in which people live and work.

"Supportive" Justice. In exercising conventional formal control, the justice system functions as a force acting upon the community, whereas in a community justice model it is a resource to strengthen and support the community in dealing with crime and disorder. Drawing on the community's capacity for self-regulation, the justice system helps build up the forces of social control that occur naturally in a community.

Under community justice, offender accountability for crime remains a vital element, but it is set in the context of repairing the damage to both victims and the community. Embracing the idea of community is a profound shift because it changes the focus of justice from what is to be done about people (offenders) to what is to be done about the places in which people live and work. And while in the community justice paradigm incarceration remains a means to ensure public safety, what to do about released offenders also becomes a concern.

Underlying Community Ideals. Community justice is guided by certain fundamental moral and social ideals of effectively functioning communities. As ideals, they are never fully realized, but they can serve as benchmarks against which public policy and programs based on community justice are measured. They extend beyond the protection of rights that is a hallmark of traditional liberalism and embrace contemporary concern for cultivating meaningful social relationships, responsible citizenship, and democratic participation.[5]

Strengthening social ties refers to the role of community in imparting wisdom; inspiring a sense of belonging; responding collectively to individuals' needs; promoting relations based on reciprocal interests, commitment, and cooperation; and fostering self-definition and realization. By promoting intimate, supportive relationships in this way, communities serve as a countervailing force to the tendency of complex societies to base human relations on marketplace considerations.

Communities promote the common good while protecting the rights of individuals, an ideal expressed as *reconciling order and autonomy*. Far from being incompatible, order and autonomy are interdependent. Indeed, autonomy depends on a foundation of order. When conflict arises, the community justice ideal would be neither to balance the two nor to choose one over the other, but rather to recognize collective needs while acknowledging each individual's full autonomy as a shared interest.

Ideally, obedience to the law derives from motives other than self-interest or fear of sanctions. People obey the law because they believe it is morally valid and thus they see enforcement as legitimate. This ideal, *voluntary cooperation*, refers to the cultivation of socially astute, emotionally intelligent citizens who are as concerned with and engaged in the life of the community as they are with their own lives. Concern for the collective good becomes the motivating force in obeying the law.

Beyond the Adversarial Model. These community ideals are "operationalized" or fulfilled through such institutions as schools, churches, and civic associations; through the multiple informal mechanisms that socialize community members by transmitting behavioral norms and standards; and through civic activism, which enables people to assess their own views and demonstrate common purpose. The current adversarial configuration of the justice system militates against the full realization of these ideals. Thus, for example, when criminal justice is reduced to fighting and controlling crime, aggressive and even brutal police tactics can shatter a normative order based on institutional legitimacy and individual autonomy. If cooperation is a product of coercion, the spirit of voluntarism vital to a community declines, and narrow self-interest replaces it. Crime increases fear, and because the justice system does not address that fear, the response to crime can be withdrawal from civic participation.

By offering a model in which crime is understood as something that happens to a community, community justice builds and sustains communities. It does so by applying democratic principles that increase the roles and responsibilities of offenders, victims, and other members of the community affected by a crime, thereby engaging them more fully in community life. In the same sense, the egalitarian principles on which community justice is based help ensure commitment to crime prevention by cultivating concern, particularly for societal inequities.

Principles of Democratic Community Justice

In community justice, criminal events are considered and dealt with as social acts that shatter community life. They are not simply violations of the law but renunciation by offenders of their moral and social obligations to the community as a whole as well as to the victim. When crime is viewed this way, it shows the State's role as sole arbiter of the offender-victim conflict to be flawed, because com-

Figure 1: Core Responsibilities of All Parties in Community Justice

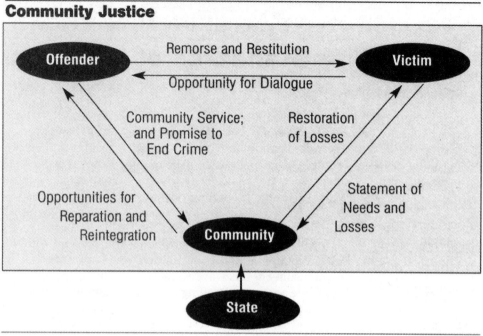

munity members are isolated from the conflict.

At the heart of community justice is civic participation. Through the problem-solving process, all parties carry out tasks derived from their relationship to the criminal event. These tasks are based on principles that define an essentially democratic vision of justice. Citizens participate in processes that affirm community standards of conduct, restore the quality of community life, and reduce the likelihood of further crime. The tasks of each party are reciprocal, linking them in a network of mutual obligation. (See figure 1.)

The Roles of Victim, Offender, and Community. The offender must strive for readmission to the community. This involves admitting the wrong, working to undo the effects of the offense, and taking steps to convince the community that the crime will not occur again. Victims, too, have responsibilities. In community justice their goal is to recover their capacity to fully function in the community. Recovery begins when the victim articulates the losses, intangible as well as tangible, and esti-

mates the resources, financial and otherwise, needed to restore the losses.

Because community laws have been violated and community life disrupted, it is incumbent on community institutions to play a role in recovery. That may involve clarifying norms and standards of conduct, expressing to the offender in particular what is and is not acceptable. (For an example of how this operates in practice, see "Vermont's Reparative Probation; Upholding Standards of Community Behavior)". The community provides opportunities for making restitution and offers the support and supervision needed for the offender to live in the community crime-free. To the victim, the community provides support in achieving recovery.

The Role of the Justice System. For the justice system, the role shifts from that of defender of law and order to that of resource to the community, bearing ultimate responsibility for the justice process. In the community justice model, the justice system helps the victim, community, and offender to carry out their tasks

by designing and managing a process that facilitates participation. In the ideal conception, community justice workers assume that role.

Community justice workers might, for example, organize and convene victim-offender mediation sessions, family group conferences, reparative citizen boards, sentencing circles, or similar practices based on restorative justice.[6] The justice system also would design and oversee a risk management plan that differs from the conventional approach in allowing the community to accept or reject it.

Principles of Egalitarian Community Justice

Community justice works not just through the personal response of each individual stakeholder—victim, offender, and community—after a crime is committed. It works by cultivating the community's social obligation to prevent crime. In this more broad conception, the ideal of justice is fundamentally egalitarian. Egalitarianism in this context means applying principles relevant to key indicators of the quality of commu-

Vermont's Reparative Probation: Upholding Standards of Community Behavior

Vermont's Reparative Probation Program exemplifies how democratic community justice seeks to reaffirm norms and standards of acceptable conduct. Offenders and their victims come together in a forum in which the offender acknowledges his or her wrongdoing and has the opportunity to express remorse and make amends. Community Reparative Boards, consisting of citizens who have a stake in the outcome, represent the community as the custodian of behavioral norms.[1]

In what is essentially a community-based restorative justice program, more than 60 boards operating throughout the State handle the cases of people whom the courts have sentenced to reparative probation for non-violent offenses, including some property felonies. The sentence is conditioned on the offender's meeting with the board, which negotiates an agreement or contract specifying how the offender will repair the harm inflicted on the victim and the community. Victims meet with the board if they wish to do so, and all participants, including the victims, must agree to the terms of the contract.

The board works with the offender in three ways. First, it seeks to demonstrate to him or her the effects of the crime on the victim and the community; second, it identifies ways the offender can repair the damage; and third, it works with the offender to devise a strategy to reduce the likelihood of reoffending. With the victim, the board works to acknowledge the harm done, to listen to the victim's concerns, and to demonstrate the community cares and will act on the victim's behalf.

The Community Reparative Boards of Vermont create a vital opportunity for citizen participation in the justice system. The boards do not establish guilt or innocence, but rather clarify, communicate, and enforce standards of acceptable behavior following the court's decision. By removing sanctioning from the courtroom to the informal problem-solving setting of the community, the process forces offenders to face their peers directly.[2]

Notes

1. See Perry, John G., and John F. Gorczyk, "Restructuring Connections: Using Market Research in Vermont," *Corrections Management Quarterly* 1 (1997): 26–35.
2. The success of Vermont's program led to its designation in 1998 as a winner in the prestigious Innovations in American Government competition.

---

nity life: Community members treat each other fairly (equality), tolerate the attitudes and behaviors of others (inclusion), balance self-interest with concern for the collective good (mutuality), and are willing to put the common good above their own wants and needs (stewardship).[7] Community justice is responsive not only to crime, but also to the conditions such as economic deprivation that may foster it.

From Crime Control to Crime Prevention

The principle of equality refers to fair treatment of all community members, grounded in repudiation of social subordination.[8] Because neighborhood disadvantage correlated strongly with criminality,[9] it suggests community justice must respond to social inequity if the quality of community life is to improve.

Whether that can be done is open to question, however, given the demise of the manufacturing sector that once meant full employment in the cities and the persistent spatial isolation of an economic underclass (consisting disproportionately of African Americans) in many urban cores.

Reducing the marginalization of those who challenge the accepted code of behavior and fail to conform is an ongoing pursuit in community justice. The tension between tolerating nonconformity and promoting predictability of social interaction is resolved with "pre-emptive strikes" of socialization and informal social control. Shaming is one such means.[10] It works because people want to avoid disapproval. The risk is that shaming may stigmatize the deviant and lead to ostracism, which in turn may impel the deviating person to seek the company of other outcasts. The challenge is to build the norm violator's stake in the com-

munity by cultivating a sense of inclusion.

Rational choice theorists have long pondered whether or not cooperation is possible among "egoists"[11]—that is, whether there can be common purpose among people who are less concerned about the general welfare than about their own lives. The issue has been explored in the experimental gaming literature,[12] where at least one theorist has concluded that while self-interest yields short-term benefits, cooperation achieves the greatest long-term gains.[13] That highlights the imperative of building long-term relationships based on mutual interest, which offer the greatest incentive to cooperate. In the context of community justice, the issue translates as how to mobilize support for crime prevention and develop strategies that reduce incentives to commit crime. The principle of mutuality assumes mobilization is feasible because people have a stake in community life, but there need to be strategies that make this stake manifest.

Stewardship is the principle that may place the greatest demand on community members because it requires that they empathize with people whom they may not know personally. In the words of criminologist James Q. Wilson, stewardship involves the creation of a "moral sense" based on sympathy, fairness, self-control, and duty.[14] Stewards of the community not only demonstrate concern for the welfare of the whole, but they are willing even to sacrifice their own desires and needs. Like equality, stewardship may require tackling structural societal problems. As a principle of justice, it requires examining local standards of behavior and adjudicating the conflict between them and acts that may not reflect those standards. In such examination, a chief concern is the effect of individual acts on the good of the whole. (For an example of how this operates in practice, see "Austin's Community Justice Councils: Promoting Stewardship of the Community.")

Can It Work?

Particularly for practitioners who wish to develop community justice initiatives, it is important to note that there is no standard formula for adopting the principles. The design will depend on the nature of community organizations, justice system practices, and crime problems in the targeted neighborhood. Myriad models are plausible, and a community might adopt and reject several options before finding a good fit.

Community justice is not problem-free. Citizens are not likely to be eager to participate; justice system officials also may be resistant. The history of community organization and community development offers ample proof of the difficulty of mobilizing and engaging people, particularly on a sustained basis.

Operational difficulties will abound. Offenders will fail—sometimes dramatically so. Yet there are reasons to believe community justice is a good idea.

Any call for change that does not recognize the loss of credibility in the justice system is bound to fail. Because it is the community that has lost faith, faith can be restored to the extent the community is involved. The ideal of community has an almost inherent appeal, as it holds out the prospect for inclusion—providing incentives for victims and offenders to participate—and offers opportunities to improve the quality of community life. Finally, community justice is already happening, as criminal justice agencies throughout the country reach out to the communities they serve, bring them more actively into the justice process, and form partnerships with organizations representing local interests. What remains is for those interested in advancing the aims of community justice to harvest the results achieved thus far and use them to further develop the concept.

Notes

1. Community justice is more broadly conceived than restorative justice. Like restorative justice, it attends to the sanctioning of offenders, but community justice also addresses crime prevention. Community justice focuses explicitly on the location of justice activities at the local level and concentrates on community outcomes. For a more extensive description of restorative justice and community justice, see *Incorporating Restorative and Community Justice into American Sentencing and Corrections,* by Leena Kurki, Research in Brief—Sentencing & Corrections: Issues for the 21st Century, Washington, DC: U.S. Department of Justice, National Institute of Justice/Corrections Program Office, September 1999 (NCJ 175723).

2. Bursik, Robert J., and Harold G. Grasmick, *Neighborhoods and Crime: The Dimensions of Effective Community Control.* New York: Lexington Books, 1993.

3. Black, Donald, *The Behavior of Law,* New York: Academic Press, 1976.

4. Clear, Todd R., and Dina R. Rose, *When Neighbors Go to Jail: Impact on Attitudes About Formal and Informal Social Control,* Research Preview, Washington, DC: U.S. Department of Justice, National Institute of Justice, July 1999 (FS 000243).

5. Selznick, Philip, *Moral Commonwealth: Social Theory and the Promise of Community,* Berkeley, CA: University of California Press, 1992.

6. Bazemore, Gordon, "The 'Community' in Community Justice: Issues, Themes, and Questions for the New Neighborhood Sanctioning Models," in *Community Justice: An Emerging Field,* ed. David R. Karp, Lanham, MD: Rowman and Littlefield, 1998: 327–371.

7. This conceptualization was borrowed from Philip Selznick. See his "Social Justice: A Communitarian Perspective," in *The Responsive Community* 6 (1996): 13–25.

8. Rawls, John, *A Theory of Justice,* Cambridge, MA: Belknap, 1971; and Selznick, "Social Justice."

9. Braithwaite, John, *Inequality, Crime, and Public Policy,* London: Routledge and Kegan Paul, 1979; and Sampson, Robert J., "The Community," in *Crime,* ed. James Q. Wilson and Joan Petersilia, San Francisco: Institute for Contemporary Studies, 1995: 193–216.

10. Braithwaite, John, *Crime, Shame, and Reintegration,* Cambridge, England: Cambridge University Press, 1989; and Karp, David R., "Judicial and Judicious Use of Shame Penalties," *Crime and Delinquency* 44 (1998): 277–294.

11. Yamagishi, Toshio, "Social Dilemmas," in *Sociological Perspectives on Social Psychology,* ed. Karen S. Cook, Gary A. Fine, and James House, Boston: Allyn and Bacon, 1994: 317.

12. Pruitt, Dean G., and Melvin J. Kimmell, "Twenty Years of Experimental Gaming: Critique, Synthesis, and Suggestions for the Future," *Annual Review of Psychology* 28 (1977): 363–392.

13. Axelrod, Robert, *The Evolution of Cooperation,* New York: Basic Books, 1984.

14. Wilson, James Q., *The Moral Sense,* New York: Free Press, 1993.

For More Information

The ideal of community justice presented here is one of a number of conceptions of how to build greater community participation in the justice system. Others can be found in the following sampling of resources.

• *Balanced and Restorative Justice: Program Summary,* Washington, DC: U.S. Department of Justice: Office of Juvenile Justice and Delinquency Prevention, 1994 (NCJ 149727).

• "Beyond Community Policing: Community Justice," by Thomas J. Quinn, *Police Chief* 64 (10) (October 1997): 107–108.

• *Change Lenses: A New Focus for Crime and Justice,* by Howard Zehr, Scottsdale, PA: Herald Press, 1990.

• "The Community," by Robert J. Sampson, in *Crime,* ed. J. Q. Wilson and J. Petersilia, San Francisco: Institute for Contemporary Studies, 1995: 193–216.

• "Community Courts: Prospects and Limits," by David B. Rottman, *National Institute of Justice Journal* 231, August 1996: 46–51.

• *Community Prosecution Profiles,* by Victor Wolf and Robert V. Wolf, New York: Center for Court Innovation, 2000.

• "Conferences, Circles, Boards, and Mediation: The 'New Wave' of Community Justice Decisionmaking," by Gordon Bazemore and Curt Taylor Griffiths. *Federal Probation* 61 (2) (June 1997): 25–37.

• *Crime, Shame, and Reintegration,* by John Braithwaite, Cambridge, England: Cambridge University Press, 1989.

• *Engaging the Community: A Guide for Community Justice Planners,* by Greg Berman and David Anderson, New York: Center for Court Innovation, 1999.

• *Incorporating Restorative and Community Justice into American Sentencing and Corrections,* by Leena Kurki, Research in Brief—Sentencing & Corrections: Issues for the 21st Century, Washington, DC: U.S. Department of Justice, National Institute of Justice/Corrections Program Office, September 1999. NCJ 175723.

• *Juvenile and Family Drug Courts: An Overview,* rev. ed., Washington, DC: U.S. Department of Justice: Office of Justice Programs, Drug Courts Program Office, 1999.

• *Model Courts Serve Abused and Neglected Children,* by Mary Mentaberry, Washington, DC: U.S. Department of Justice, Office of Juvenile Justice and Delinquency Prevention, OJJDP Fact Sheet #90, January 1999 (FS 9990).

• *Neighborhoods and Crime: The Dimensions of Effective Community Control,* by Robert J. Bursik and Harold G. Grasmick, New York: Lexington Books, 1993.

• *Responding to the Community: Principles for Planning and Creating a Community Court,* by John Feinblatt and Greg Berman, Washington, DC: U.S. Department of Justice, Bureau of Justice Assistance, November 1997 (NCJ 166821).

• *Restorative Community Justice: Background, Program Examples, and Research Findings,* by Thomas J. Quinn, Technical Assistance Report, Washington, DC: U.S. Department of Justice, National Institute of Justice, 1996.

• "Restorative Justice," by John Braithwaite, in *Handbook of Crime and Punishment,* ed. M. Tonry, New York: Oxford University Press, 1998: 323–344.

• "Restorative Justice and Earned Redemption," by Gordon Bazemore, *American Behavioral Scientist* 41 (1998): 768–813.

• *Restorative Juvenile Justice: Repairing the Harm of Youth Crime,* ed. Gordon Bazemore and Lode Walgrave, Monsey, NY: Criminal Justice Press, 1999.

• *Restoring Justice,* by Daniel Van Ness and Karen Heetderks Strong, Cincinnati, OH: Anderson Publishing Company, 1997.

• "Therapeutic Jurisprudence and the Emergence of Problem-Solving Courts," by David Rottman and Pamela Casey, *National Institute of Justice Journal,* July 1999, 12–19 (JR 000240).

• *Victim Meets Offender: The Impact of Restorative Justice and Mediation,* by Mark S. Umbreit, Monsey, NY: Criminal Justice Press, 1994.

• **The authors' own perspective on community justice is more fully elaborated in:**

• *The Community Justice Ideal: Preventing Crime and Achieving Justice,* by Todd R. Clear and David R. Karp, Boulder, CO: Westview Press, 1999 (supported by NIJ grant number 1997–IJ–CX–0032).

• "Community Justice: A Conceptual Framework," by David R. Karp and Todd R. Clear, in *Boundary Changes in Criminal Justice Organizations: Criminal Justice 2000, Volume 2,* ed. Charles M. Friel, Washington, DC: U.S. Department of Justice, National Institute of Justice, July 2000: 323–368 (NCJ 182409).

• *Community Justice: An Emerging Field,* ed. David R. Karp, Lanham, MD: Rowman and Littlefield, 1998.

• **Related to community justice are the following sampling of problem-solving policing and community-oriented policing:**

• *Community Policing, Chicago Style,* by Wesley G. Skogan, New York: Oxford University Press, 1997.

• *Problem-Oriented Policing,* by Herman Goldstein, New York: McGraw-Hill Publishing Company, 1990.

• *Problem-Oriented Policing (POP): Crime-Specific Problems, Critical Issues, and Making POP Work, volume 1,* ed. T. O. Shelly and A. C. Grant, Washington, DC: Police Executive Research Forum, 1998.

• *Problem-Oriented Policing (POP): Crime-Specific Problems, Critical Issues, and Making POP Work, volume 2,* ed., Corina Sole Brito and Tracy Allan, Washington, DC: Police Executive Research Forum, 1999.

• *Tackling Crime and Other Public Safety Problems: Case Studies in Problem Solving,* by Rana Sampson and Michael S. Scott, Washington, DC: U.S. Department of Justice, Office of Community Oriented Policing Services, 1999.

about the authors

Todd R. Clear, Ph.D., is Distinguished Professor in the John Jay College of Criminal Justice, City University of New York; David R. Karp, Ph.D., is a Professor in the Department of Sociology at Skidmore College.

Making Computer Crime Count

By MARC GOODMAN

Does computer crime pose a serious threat to America's national security? Recent highly publicized computer virus attacks have shown that computer crime has become an increasing problem. Unfortunately, the absence of a standard definition for computer crime, a lack of reliable criminal statistics on the problem, and significant underreporting of the threat pose vexing challenges for police agencies.

Sensational headlines, such as "Nation Faces Grave Danger of Electronic Pearl Harbor,"[1] "Internet Paralyzed by Hackers,"[2] "Computer Crime Costs Billions,"[3] have become common. Law enforcement organizations cannot determine exactly how many computer crimes occur each year. No agreed-upon national or international definition of terms, such as computer crime, high-tech crime, or information technology crime, exists. Thus, as a class of criminal activities, computer crime is unique in its position as a crime without a definition, which prevents police organizations from accurately assessing the nature and scope of the problem.

Internationally, legislative bodies define criminal offenses in penal codes. Crimes, such as murder, rape, and aggravated assault, all suggest similar meanings to law enforcement professionals around the world. But what constitutes a computer crime? The term covers a wide range of offenses. For example, if a commercial burglary occurs and a thief steals a computer, does this indicate a computer crime or merely another burglary? Does copying a friend's program disks constitute a computer crime? The answer to each of these questions may depend on various jurisdictions.[4]

The United States Department of Justice (DOJ) has defined computer crime as "any violation of criminal law that involved the knowledge of computer technology for its perpetration, investigation, or prosecution."[5] Some experts have suggested that DOJ's definition could encompass a series of crimes that have nothing to do with computers. For example, if an auto theft investigation required a detective to use "knowledge of computer technology" to investigate a vehicle's identification number (VIN) in a state's department of motor vehicle database, under DOJ guidelines, auto theft could be classified as a computer crime. While the example may stretch the boundaries of logic, it demonstrates the difficulties inherent in attempting to describe and classify computer criminality.

Over the past 15 years, several international organizations, such as the United Nations, the Organization of Economic Cooperation and Development (OECD), the Council of Europe, the G-8,[6] and Interpol, all have worked to combat the problem of computer crime.[7] These organizations have provided guidance in understanding this problem. Yet, despite their efforts, no single definition of computer crime has emerged that the majority of criminal justice professionals use. Although many state and federal laws define terms, such as "unauthorized access to a computer system" and "computer sabotage," neither Title 18 nor any of the state penal codes provide a definition for the term computer crime.

Defining criminal phenomena is important because it allows police officers, detectives, prosecutors, and judges to speak intelligently about a given criminal offense. Furthermore, generally accepted definitions facilitate the aggregation of statistics, which law enforcement can analyze to reveal previously undiscovered criminal threats and patterns.

Benefits of Reporting Computer Crime Statistics

Crime statistics serve an important role in law enforcement. First, they allow for the appropriate allocation of very limited resources. For example, if a community suffered a 73 percent increase in the number of sexual assaults, police administrators immediately would take steps to address the problem by adding more rape investigators, extra patrol in the specific area, and increased community awareness projects. The aggregation of crime data allows police to formulate a response to a problem. Anecdotal evidence suggests that computer crime presents a growing problem for the public, police, and governments, all who rely on crime statistics for the development of their criminal justice policies and the allocation of extremely limited resources. For police to respond successfully to these crimes in the future, they

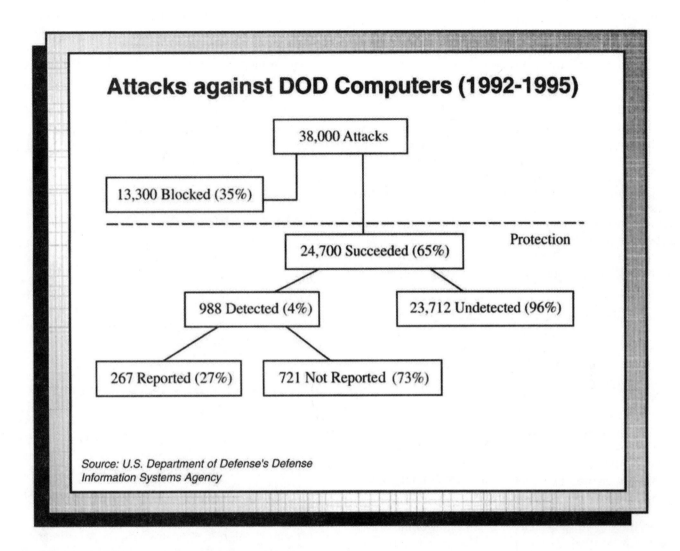

Attacks against DOD Computers (1992-1995)

38,000 Attacks

13,300 Blocked (35%)

Protection

24,700 Succeeded (65%)

988 Detected (4%)

23,712 Undetected (96%)

267 Reported (27%)

721 Not Reported (73%)

Source: U.S. Department of Defense's Defense Information Systems Agency

must increase the resources their departments currently dedicate to the problem—a difficult task.

Agencies must justify training, equipment, and personnel costs necessary to create a computer-competent police force. How can law enforcement managers justify these costs to community leaders without appropriate data to substantiate their claims? Police must document the problem with factual data not information based on media sensationalism or a few notorious attacks.

Second, accurate statistics on computer crime are important for public safety reasons. Computer crimes not only affect corporations but hospitals, airports, and emergency dispatch systems as well. Furthermore, surveys have indicated that many individuals fear for their safety in the on-line world and worry about criminal victimization.[8]

Businesses and individuals rely on law enforcement crime statistics when making important decisions about their safety. Many citizens contact a local police station prior to the purchase of a home in a particular neighborhood to inquire about the number of burglaries and violent crimes in the area. Just as these data provide important information for communities in the "real world," the same is true in cyberspace. For individuals and organizations to intelligently assess their level of risk, agencies must provide accurate data about criminal threats. Access to reliable and timely computer crime statistics allows individuals to determine their own probability of victimization and the threat level they face and helps them begin to estimate probable recovery costs.[9] Law enforcement organizations traditionally have taken a leading role in providing crime data and crime prevention education to the public, which now should be updated to include duties in cyberspace.

Crime statistics facilitate benchmarking and analysis of crime trends. Crime analysts use criminal statistics to spot emerging trends and unique modi operandi. Patrol officers and detectives use this data to prevent future crimes and to apprehend offenders. Therefore, to count computer crime, a general agreement on what constitutes a computer crime must exist.

In many police departments, detectives often compile and report crime data. Thus, homicide detectives count the number of murders, sexual assault investigators examine the number of rapes, and auto detectives count car thefts. Computer crime, on the other hand, comprises such an ill-defined list of offenses that various units within a police department usually keep the related data separately, if they keep them at all. For example, the child abuse unit likely would maintain child pornography arrest data and identify the crime as the sexual exploitation of a minor. A police department's economic crimes unit might recap an Internet fraud scam as a simple fraud, and an agency's assault unit might count an on-line stalking case as a criminal threat. Because most police organizations do not have a cohesive entity that measures offenses where criminals either criminally target a computer or use one to perpetrate a crime, accurate statistics remain difficult to obtain.

The Underreporting Problem

Generally, crime statistics can provide approximations for criminal activity. Usually, people accurately report serious crimes, such as homicide, armed robbery, vehicle theft, and major assaults. Many other criminal offenses, however, remain significantly underreported.

Police always have dealt with some underreporting of crime. But, new evidence suggests that computer crime may be the most underreported form of criminal behavior because the victim of a computer crime often remains unaware that an offense has even taken place. Sophisticated technologies, the immense size and storage capacities of computer networks, and the often global distribution of an organization's information assets increase the difficulty of detecting computer crime. Thus, the vast majority of individuals and organizations do not realize when they have suffered a computer intrusion or related loss at the hands of a criminal hacker.

The U.S. Department of Defense's (DoD) Defense Information Systems Agency (DISA) has completed in-depth research on computer crime. From 1992 to 1995, DISA attacked their own DoD computer systems using software available on the Internet. System administrators did not detect the majority of attacks against DoD computers. Of the 38,000 attacks perpetrated, 96 percent of the successful attacks went undetected. Furthermore, of the detected attacks, only 27 percent were reported. Thus, approximately 1 in 140 attacks were both detected and reported, representing only 0.7 percent of the total. If the detection and reporting of computer crime is less than 1 percent in the nation's military systems, how often might these crimes go unreported when the intended victim is an individual or a small business owner?

Convincing victims who have suffered a loss to report the crime to police constitutes another hurdle facing law enforcement agencies. Surprisingly, many individuals, network administrators, and corporate managers do not realize that attacks against their networks constitute a crime. Worse, many victims who understand that a crime

has taken place may deliberately keep these facts from the police. Victims may have serious doubts about the capacity of the police to handle computer crime incidents in an efficient, timely, and confidential manner.[10] These concerns are true particularly among large corporations who fear damage to their reputation or, worse, their bottom line. In banking and financial sectors, reputation is everything. Information that a criminal has infiltrated a bank's computers and accounts potentially could drive thousands of customers to its competitors.

" . . . accurate statistics on computer crime are important for public safety reasons."

Businesses suffer a variety of losses, both tangible and intangible when hackers attack them. They can lose hundreds of millions of dollars of value, brand equity, and corporate reputation when a business falls prey to a hacker.[11] Most of the companies that suffer Web attacks see their stock prices fall.[12] Furthermore, in recent denial of service attacks, for example, the Yankee Research Group estimated that direct revenue losses due to blocked online transactions and the need for security infrastructure upgrades exceed $1 billion.[13] Because of the high price of victimization, most companies would not want to involve law enforcement and risk a very public arrest or trial attesting to the organization's security and business failings.

The difficulties in computer crime detection and the challenges posed by the reluctance of businesses to admit victimization might demonstrate the underestimation of all statistics related to cybercrimes. However, some less reputable computer security consulting companies may overestimate computer crime and security problems to scare business leaders who, they hope, will turn to these organizations for consulting services and support.

An annual report compiled by the Computer Security Institute in San Francisco, California, and the FBI provides a variety of statistics on computer crime by surveying computer security practitioners in both the private and public sectors.[14] The anonymity offered to survey respondents may contribute to the accuracy of their data. However, the report does not directly poll law enforcement organizations about the number of computer crimes reported to police. Many experts believe that such a task should be carried out by the government, but to date, no single governmental body maintains responsibility for asking police forces about the prevalence of computer crimes reported and investigated.

The Development of a Definition

The development of a simple, widely agreed-upon definition of computer crime among law enforcement may form the first step in counting computer crimes. This definition would help police to communicate more effectively about these offenses and begin to accurately assess the prevalence of criminal victimization.

The earliest work in computer security provides a good foundation upon which police can build such a definition. Traditionally, all computer security efforts have sought to protect the confidentiality, integrity, and availability of information systems.[15]

Confidentiality in computer systems prevents the disclosure of information to unauthorized persons. Individuals who trespass into another person's computer system or exceed their own authority in accessing certain information, violate the legitimate owner's right to keep private information secret. Crimes that violate the confidentiality of computer systems include "unauthorized access crimes" as defined by Title 18, U.S.C. Section 1030(a)(2). Because breaking into a computer begins with unauthorized access to an information system, many believe this represents the foundational computer crime offense.

Integrity of electronically stored information ensures that no one has tampered with it or modified it without authorization. Thus, any nonsanctioned corruption, impairment, or modification of computer information or equipment constitutes an attack against the integrity of that information. Many of the malicious hacking activities, such as computer viruses, worms, and Trojan horses, fall within this category. The same is true for individuals who purposefully change or manipulate data either for profit or some other motivation, such as revenge, politics, terrorism, or merely for the challenge.

" . . . computer crime has become an increasing problem."

Availability of computer data indicates the accessibility of the information and that its associated programs remain functional when needed by the intended user community. A variety of attacks, such as the often-cited denial of service incidents, constitute a set of criminal activities that interferes with the availability of computer information.

Together, computer crime incidents that attack the confidentiality, integrity, or availability of digital information or services constitute an extremely precise and easily understood foundational definition of computer crime. In effect, these offenses might represent "pure-play" computer crimes because they involve a computer system as the direct target of the attack.

These three types of crimes should form the basis for an internationally agreed-upon definition of computer crime. In reality, they already are becoming the definition of computer crime because each state has some law that prohibits these offenses. Furthermore, an analysis of penal legislation in nearly 50 nations suggests that at least one-half of those countries surveyed—including most industrialized nations—had laws in place or legislation pending that prohibited crimes affecting the confidentiality, integrity, and availability of a computer.[16] A variety of international organizations also support legislative efforts prohibiting pure-play computer crimes. Groups, such as the United Nations, the G8, the Council of Europe, the OECD, and Interpol, each have delineated confidentiality, integrity, and availability offenses as forming the minimum basis of proscribed computer criminal behavior. The Council of Europe, the 41-nation body of which the United States is an observer, has been working on a draft treaty on cybercrime for several years. If adopted as currently drafted, the treaty would ensure that confidentiality, integrity, and availability offenses were outlawed in all signatory nations to the treaty, an extremely significant step forward in policing these crimes.[17]

Computer-Mediated Offenses

Defined broadly, the term computer crime or even the more common "computer-related crime" has described a wide variety of offenses. Traditional crimes, such as fraud, counterfeiting, embezzlement, telecommunications theft, prostitution, gambling, money laundering, child pornography, fencing operations, narcotics sales, and even stalking, all could be computer related. Computer technology could facilitate or perpetrate each of these offenses.

These crimes, which represent traditional offenses perpetrated in new and, perhaps, more effective ways, differ from pure-play computer crimes, which involve a computer system as the direct target of attack. Additionally, these crimes, as a group, demonstrate that offenders can use a computer as a tool to commit the crime. The fact that a computer is not necessary to commit the crime sets these offenses apart from the pure-play computer crimes. Prostitution, counterfeiting, and frauds have taken place for hundreds of years without any computer connection. The computer-mediated forms of these crimes pose problems for law enforcement as well.

A traditional crime perpetrated with a new, high-tech twist raises the same investigative and legal challenges for police as pure-play computer offenses. The unique nature of information technology and computer networks moving at Internet speed often are highly incompatible with traditional legal models of policing. Crimes involving high technology cross multiple jurisdictions, are not covered by a single cohesive international law, become harder to track because of anonymity, result in expensive investigations, complicate efforts in obtaining forensic evidence, and require police to have specialized knowledge for a successful investigation. Because computer-related crimes pose many of the same investigative difficulties as pure-play computer crimes, documenting these criminal offenses proves useful. Once captured, these data can help police to further refine their allocation of resources and determine relevant crime trends for computer-mediated illegal activities.

Offenses where a computer is completely incidental to the crime represents the third type of criminal activity with possible computer involvement. In these cases, although a criminal might have used a computer before, during, or after the crime, it was not related directly to the offending criminal activity. For example, a man who murders his wife and confesses 3 weeks later in an electronic document has not committed a computer crime—he has committed a homicide. Leaving behind computer-related evidence that will require specialized forensic methods does not turn murder into "cyber-homicide." For this reason, police should not count offenses that generate computer-related evidence incidental to the perpetration of the offense as either a computer crime or as a computer-related crime.

Law Enforcement's Response

How can agencies capture, analyze, and report data on these offenses in an efficient manner? In 1930, the U.S. Congress required the Attorney General to produce data on the incidence of crime in America. In turn, the Attorney General designated the FBI to serve as the national clearinghouse for the statistics collected. Since that time, the FBI has administered the Uniform Crime Reporting (UCR) Program, which obtains data based on uniform classifications and procedures for reporting from the nation's law enforcement agencies and presents this information in the annual *Crime in the United States* publication.[18] While the traditional UCR Summary Reporting System[19] tracks only eight criminal offenses (murder and nonnegligent manslaughter, forcible rape, robbery, aggravated assault, burglary, larceny-theft, motor vehicle theft, and arson), the new UCR National Incident Based Reporting System[20] (NIBRS) tracks 46 criminal offenses in 22 categories, including crimes perpetrated using computers.[21] However, because the transition from the traditional system to NIBRS will take considerable time, law enforcement executives proactively should review their internal procedures to ensure that they have appropriate policies in place to track and recap pure-play computer crimes.

Agencies should consider adding the following question to crime and arrest reports: "Was a computer used in the perpetration of this offense?" Many agencies already include similar questions about the use of firearms or the occurrence of hate crimes on their internal reports. In fact, hate crimes may provide a useful lens through which to examine computer-related crime. Hate crimes often involve other crimes, such as assault, vandalism, and even murder. But, knowing what percentage hate actually

motivates vandalism becomes a useful tool for police administrators attempting to understand and address community disorder problems.

Several efforts have begun to promote law enforcement's understanding of the prevalence and effects of computer crime. The FBI and the National White Collar Crime Center recently took a big step forward in counting computer-related fraud. In 2000, these organizations established the Internet Fraud Complaint Center (IFCC)[22] to create a national reporting mechanism for tracking fraud on the Internet. The center will track statistics on the number and type of complaints and forward reported incidents to the appropriate law enforcement agency. While IFCC will prove helpful in tracking Internet fraud data, it does not deal directly with pure-play computer crimes that violate the confidentiality, integrity, and availability of data. Therefore, federal, state, and local criminal justice agencies must take a more comprehensive approach.

Conclusion

To combat computer crime, law enforcement must build an internal capacity to define, track, and analyze these criminal offenses. Even if law enforcement has a highly sophisticated and well-developed system to count computer crime, agencies still must overcome the public's underreporting problem. Underreporting these crimes results from a failure on the part of the victim to realize a crime has taken place and an unwillingness to report discovered incidents to police.

To decrease the incidence of computer crime, law enforcement agencies must work with private organizations to ensure that businesses become aware of potential threats they face from computer crime. These partnerships could include working with technical experts from within and outside the government to develop solutions that improve the prevention and detection of computer crimes. Of course, even after detecting these crimes, police still must convince victims to report them.

Police agencies must work with the business community to gain trust. Many community and problem-oriented policing techniques can help law enforcement as they deal increasingly with computer crime investigations. Government and industry partnerships, and police sensitivity about businesses concerns, will help increase the number of these offenses brought to the attention of the police.

Most police agencies do not have the staff or funding to deal adequately with computer crime. Though the recent series of virus and denial of service attacks have increased public awareness of the problem, law enforcement organizations must prepare for offenses by developing a strategic and preventative approach to deal with this problem.

"*Several efforts have begun to promote law enforcement's understanding of the prevalence and effects of computer crime.*"

Law enforcement managers must ensure that they remain capable of responding to the changing faces of criminal activity in the 21st century. When compared to murder, rape, or violent assaults, computer crime may seem trivial. But, a person who asks an executive who loses his life savings due to the theft of intellectual property from his computer hard drive will get a different answer. The teacher who receives daily calls from credit agencies because she was the victim of on-line identity theft understands the importance of policing computer related crime as well. Similarly, so does the AIDS researcher who has 5 years of work destroyed by a computer virus. The mother of the 13-year-old girl who was lured across state lines by a pedophile will certainly demand a computer-competent police force capable of helping her. Each of these computer or computer-related crimes and their victims are real. Law enforcement agencies have a responsibility to protect and serve the public, regardless of advances in technology—a role that cannot be abdicated.

Defining the problem, gathering crime data, and analyzing the nature and scope of the threat represent natural steps in any problem-oriented policing approach. New forms of criminality do not differ—a lesson law enforcement agencies must learn to make computer crime count.

Endnotes

1. Andrew Glass, "Warding Off Cyber Threat: "Electronic Pearl Harbor Feared," *The Atlanta Journal and Constitution*, June 25, 1998.
2. Anick Jesdanun, "Internet Attacks Raise Concerns About Risks of Growth," *San Francisco Examiner*, February 14, 2000.
3. Michael Zuckerman, "Love Bug Stole Computer Passwords," *USA Today*, May 10, 2000.
4. Jodi Mardesich, "Laws Across the Country Become Relevant in Connected World: Jurisdiction at Issue in Net Legal Cases," *San Jose Mercury News*, October 8, 1996, 1E.
5. Catherine H. Conly, *Organizing for Computer Crime Investigation and Prosecution*, National Institute of Justice, July 1989, 6.
6. These countries, several major industrial nations in the world, include the United States, the United Kingdom, France, Germany, Japan, Canada, Italy, and Russia.
7. "International Review of Criminal Policy: United Nations Manual on the Prevention and Control of Computer-Related Crime," United Nations Crime and Justice Information Network Vienna: United Nations, 1994.
8. Tina Kelley, "Security Fears Still Plague Cybershopping," *The New York Times*, July 30, 1998, G5; Michael Stroh, "On-line Dangers, Offspring Protection; Security: Parents Can Find Allies on the Family Computer to Protect their Children from Harm on the Internet," *The Baltimore Sun*, May 10, 1999, 1C.
9. M.E. Kabay, "ISCA White Paper on Computer Crime Statistics," International Computer Security Association (1998), *http://www.icsa.net/html/library/whitepapers/index.shtml*; accessed November 8, 2000.
10. P.A. Collier and B.J. Spaul, "Problems in Policing Computer Crime," *Policing and Society* 307, no. 2 (1992).
11. Larry Kamer, "Crisis Mode: It s About Values," *The San Francisco Examiner*, February 23, 2000, A15.
12. Carri Kirbie, "Hunting for the Hackers: Reno Opens Probe Into Attacks That Disabled Top Web Sites," *The San Francisco Chronicle*, February 10, 2000, A1.
13. "7 Days: Web Attacks Raise Security Awareness," *Computing*, February 17, 2000, 17.
14. R. Power, "2000 CSI/FBI Computer Crime and Security Survey," *Computer Security Issues and Trends* 6, No. 1, Spring 2000.
15. These three themes provide the basis for the Organization for Economic Cooperation and Development's (OECD) *Guidelines for the Security of Information Systems* and are included in most textbooks, legislative acts, and media articles on computer crime. The OECD document is available at *http://www.oecd.org/dsti/sti/it/secur/prod/reg97-2.htm*; accessed November 8, 2000.
16. Based upon research conducted by the author.
17. For further information, see *http://conventions.coe.int/treaty/EN/cadreprojets.htm*.
18. U.S. Department of Justice, Federal Bureau of Investigation, *Crime in the United States* (Washington, DC, 1999).
19. In the summary program, law enforcement agencies tally the number of occurrences of the offenses, as well as arrest data, and submit aggregate counts of the collected data in monthly summary reports either directly to the FBI or indirectly through state UCR programs.
20. In NIBRS, law enforcement agencies collect detailed data regarding individual crime incidents and arrests and submit them in separate reports using prescribed data elements and data values to describe each incident and arrest.
21. NIBRS provides the capability to indicate whether a computer was the object of the crime and to indicate whether the offenders used computer equipment to perpetrate a crime. This ensures the continuance of the traditional crime statistics and, at the same time, "flags" incidents involving computer crime. For additional information on NIBRS, contact the NIBRS Program Coordinator, Criminal Justice Information Services, 1-888-827-6427.
22. Jerry Seper, "Justice Sets Up Web Site to Combat Internet Crimes," *The Washington Times*, May 9, 2000, A6, *www.ifccfbi.gov*; November 8, 2000.

For further information regarding computer crime, contact the author at digitalpolice@yahoo.com.

When It's No Longer A Game: *Pathological Gambling in the United States*

by Charles Wellford

This article summarzies a book-length report, *Pathological Gambling: A Critical Review*, by the Committee on the Social and Economic Impact of Pathological Gambling, National Research Council (Washington, D.C.: National Academy Press, 1999), National Academy of Sciences (NAS). The summary is published with permission of NAS. The full report is available from the National Academy Press and is online at its Web site: http://www.nap.edu. Readers who wish to consult the author's citations to the research literature will find them in the full report.

Even the most determined opponents of gambling cannot dispute its popularity. Anyone who succumbs to the temptation to play the lottery when the jackpot rises into the millions can attest to it. Anyone who resists the temptation to join a long ticket queue that promises fabulous, instant wealth can attest to it. Hard facts confirm gambling's pervasiveness as well as its broad appeal. It is now legal in all but 3 States, and 37 States have lotteries. More than 8 in 10 adults say they have played casino games, bet on the races on and off the track, bought lottery tickets, or in some other way engaged in recreational gambling. In a single recent year, Americans collectively wagered more than half a trillion dollars.

The wider availability of gambling in the past two decades, the introduction of new forms of gambling, the rise in the number of people who play games of chance, and the increasing amount of money they are wagering have raised concerns about gambling's social and economic effects. One focus of concern is "pathological" gambling —the inability to resist the impulse to gamble. Identified as a psychiatric disorder, pathological gambling can have a number of harmful consequences for the compulsive gambler and his or her family. The justice system enters the picture when destructive behavior becomes criminal behavior.

Concern about the effects of gambling has been voiced at the highest levels of government, prompting the U.S. Congress to order a comprehensive study. Included in the study was an assessment of pathological gambling. (For details of the mandate, see "Why Study Pathological Gambling?") The assessment covered the nature and extent of the problem; its effects on individuals, families, and communities; treatment approaches and their effectiveness; and ways to improve the understanding of pathological gambling. The study found considerable gaps in what is known, concluding that pathological gambling requires further study.

Rapid Expansion of Legalized Gambling

When Americans gamble, they are observing a time-honored tradition. In this country, gambling predates the republic. Opponents have at times succeeded in banning or otherwise stigmatizing it, but even after protracted periods of interdiction, recreational or social gambling always revived, most notably with relegalization in Nevada in the 1930's.

The current era of legalized, socially acceptable gambling (or "gaming," as the industry terms it) dates from the 1960's, when the first State lottery was established. The advent of State lotteries marked a major pol-

Why Study Pathological Gambling?

The study of pathological gambling was conducted in response to a congressional mandate. Rapid expansion of gambling and new forms of gambling prompted Congress in 1996 to order a comprehensive study of its social and economic effects. Congress recognized that State, local, and Native American tribal governments were instituting gambling as a way to create jobs and generate revenue and that new forms such as Internet gambling could affect interstate and international matters that come under Federal jurisdiction. The most recent Federal Government study of gambling was conducted almost 25 years ago, so the jurisdictions that established gambling had no recent information about the impact of these new developments.

One of the missions of the National Gambling Impact Study Commission (NGISC), the body established to conduct the study, was to assess the effects of pathological or problem gambling.[1] Congress stipulated that NGISC contract with the National Research Council for assistance in studying pathological gambling. In response, the Council established the Committee on the Social and Economic Impact of Pathological Gambling, whose mission was to identify and analyze the full range of research on the nature of pathological and problem gambling, highlighting key issues and data sources that might provide evidence of prevalence and effects.

The Commission reports, including the report on pathological gambling, are available on the Web site at http://www.ngisc.gov.

1. In addition to pathological gambling, the Commission examined Federal, State, local, and tribal government policies on gambling; the relationship between gambling and crime; the impact of gambling on individuals, families, businesses, and the economy; the extent to which gambling generates government revenues; and interstate and international effects of electronic gambling.

---

icy shift—away from mere tolerance on the part of government and toward active sponsorship and aggressive marketing.

One focus of concern is "pathological" gambling— the inability to resist the impulse to gamble. Identified as a psychiatric disorder, pathological gambling can have a number of harmful consequences for the compulsive gambler and his or her family.

State sponsorship reflected a lifting of social and moral barriers and initiated an expansion of gambling that continues today. No doubt it lent added legitimacy to gambling. It did not mean that all opposition ceased. Many State legislatures, for example, oppose casinos and State-sanctioned sports betting. Still, the growth of legalized gambling continues apace. The Indian Gaming Regulatory Act, passed in 1988, allows Indian tribes to operate any form of gambling that is legal in the State where the tribe lives. New forms of gambling are emerging, most notably those based on advanced electronic technologies (Internet-based gambling, for example).

Benefits of Gambling

If the opponents of gambling cannot dispute its popularity, they would also be hard-pressed to dispute its benefits. The States earn revenue from taxes on commercial gambling enterprises and from the proceeds of government-sponsored gambling. In fact, State budgets have become increasingly dependent on these revenues. Economically depressed communities in which gambling is offered appear to have benefitted from it.

If a gambling enterprise is operating in a community, that can mean more jobs and higher incomes, enhanced opportunities for tourism- and recreation-based business, and higher property values. Indian communities in particular have benefit-

ted socially and economically from gambling enterprises. Unquestionably, gambling produces numerous economic benefits, although there is not enough information available to calculate the amount or to determine with any accuracy whether they exceed the costs of gambling, including those associated with problem and pathological gambling.

When Does Gambling Become Pathological?

If gambling has benefits, it also has costs. Pathological gambling, with its adverse effects for individuals, families, and communities, is one of them. Most adults who gamble view it solely as entertainment, and they wager only small amounts of money. Pathological gambling is different. Someone with this problem is unable to control the urge to gamble, and that inability may grow progressively worse. The condition has been defined by the psychiatric profession as a mental health disorder. (More details of the definition are in "A Mental Health Problem.")

About 1.5 percent of adults in this country have been pathological gamblers at some point in their lives. In a given year, 0.9 percent of adults in this country (1.8 million) are

A Mental Health Problem

Pathological gambling is a mental health disorder. The condition is difficult to define, but the American Psychiatric Association (APA), an authority on mental problems, developed criteria that can be used to diagnose it. APA first classified pathological gambling as a definitive diagnosis in 1980, including it among impulse-control disorders.[1]

The condition can be described as a disorder characterized by continuous or periodic loss of control of one's gambling behavior, a preoccupation with gambling and obtaining money with which to gamble, irrational thinking, and a continuation of this behavior despite adverse consequences. The inability to resist the compulsion to gamble can produce undesirable outcomes ranging from borrowing excessive amounts of money from family or friends, to losing time from work, to being arrested for offenses committed to support the gambling habit.

The APA criteria appear to have worked well for clinicians who treat the disorder, but because they are based only on populations who seek treatment, they cannot be used to define the nature and causes of pathological gambling or to estimate prevalence.

1. See the APA's *Diagnostic and Statistical Manual of Mental Disorders* (DSM). Pathological gambling also was included in the 1994 edition, DSM-IV.

pathological gamblers. There are differences by gender and age, with men more likely than women to be pathological gamblers, and adolescents more likely than adults.

In the currently expanding gambling environment, it might seem likely that the number or proportion of pathological gamblers would increase. Although public health and policy officials are concerned about that possibility, studies thus far offer no certain answers.

Links to Crime

Pathological gamblers engage in various forms of destructive behavior. They may amass large debts, damage their relationships with family members and friends, and even kill themselves. They also may commit crimes, including theft, embezzlement, domestic violence, and child abuse and neglect. Precise tallies of these social costs of pathological gambling are needed, but again, the current state of knowledge makes it impossible to identify the extent to which legalized gambling affects crime rates. (For an examination of crime in several communities where this form of gambling has been introduced, see "Casino Gambling: Burden or Boon?")

Pathological gambling can co-occur with such problems as substance abuse. Substance abusers admitted to treatment programs are three to six times more likely than the general population to be problem gamblers. A study of people seeking treatment for cocaine abuse revealed that those who had gambling problems were more likely than those who did not to have additional drug problems, such as overdosing or using opiates.

Heavy use of alcohol is linked to multiple gambling problems and increased spending on gambling, and pathological gambling increases with the number of illicit substances used.

The link to crime is often a byproduct of the financial losses incurred. Pathological gamblers may spend inordinate amounts of money on their addiction, tapping into family savings or borrowing money. As these sources are depleted and debts pile up, they may resort to crime to obtain money.

Attempts have been made to estimate the proportion of pathological gamblers who commit crimes such as fraud, theft, embezzlement, forgery, and blackmail, but the results vary widely. As many as one-half to two-thirds of pathological gamblers may have committed a crime to obtain gambling money. Evidence also suggests that a sizable proportion of pathological gamblers have criminal charges pending as a result of illegal activity to fund their habit.

More Questions Than Answers

Much of what is known about pathological gambling is limited in scientific value. The extent and causes of pathological gambling are not well understood. Neither is it possible to determine whether the number of pathological gamblers is rising. Nor is there enough information to state with certainty whether particularly vulnerable populations—the elderly and people who are economically disadvantaged—tend disproportionately to be pathological gamblers. Although there is no doubt that gambling creates certain economic benefits for communities, these too are difficult to measure precisely, as are the social costs of gambling. Problem gambling is linked to crime, but exactly how legalized gambling affects local and national crime rates is unknown.

This information deficit means that the assessment of pathological gambling is greatly influenced by a relatively small number of newer, better studies. Notably, information about the onset and progression of the disorder is beginning to come to light. It reveals, for example, that the earlier someone starts to gamble, the more likely he or she is to become a pathological gambler and the pathological gamblers are more likely than other gamblers to have parents who were pathological gamblers.

The origins and nature of pathological gambling and the changes taking place in it over time could be better understood through long-term studies and cross-sectional studies (which examine a population at a specific point in time). One way

Casino Gambling: Burden or Boon?

The research described below was conducted independently of the study of pathological gambling. It is based on *Effects of Casino Gambling on Crime and Quality of Life in New Casino Jurisdictions*, by B. Grant Stitt, Mark Nichols, and David Giacopassi, November 29, 2000, draft report of grant 98-IJ-CX-0037, submitted to NIJ.

Proposals to establish casino gambling often have generated rancorous debate among community residents, with proponents touting the anticipated economic benefits and opponents predicting inevitable social problems. Residents' perceptions are important, because the establishment or continued existence of a gambling enterprise can depend on them. Nevertheless, though these opinions are forcefully expressed, they have not been based on hard data, because studies of many key questions about the effects of gambling have been incomplete or nonexistent. A recent NIJ-sponsored study, which examined crime data as well as residents' opinions, showed that perceptions of gambling's effects on crime can be at odds with more objective measures.

The study covered seven communities where casino gambling (on riverboats or barges) had been introduced in the past 10 years: Alton and Peoria/East Peoria, Illinois; Sioux City, Iowa; St. Joseph, St. Louis, and St. Louis County, Missouri; and Biloxi, Mississippi. Community leaders and residents were asked their views of the impact on crime, and more objective sources of information in the form of crime data also were examined.

Community residents and community leaders were divided in their views, with residents believing casinos increased crime and community leaders seeing little effect and

creased crime and community leaders seeing little effect and believing casinos enhanced the quality of life and benefitted the economy. Perhaps not surprisingly, communities most heavily dependent economically on gambling were the ones that embraced it most warmly.

Perceptions did not reflect reality. There is no single "casino effect" on crime. The impact of the casinos varied from community to community. Three communities experienced a significant increase in several types of crime, while the opposite was true in three others.

One other saw no change in the vast majority of crimes. The mixed results suggest that certain factors may be operating in some communities and not others. One factor might be tourism. Biloxi, with its nine casinos drawing tens of thousands of visitors annually, saw the largest increase in crime of all the communities studied.

Interviews with the police chiefs of these communities revealed that law enforcement agencies need to prepare to make changes in their operations when a casino comes to town, because crime patterns may change and crimes once unknown to the community may appear. Several chiefs stressed that preparedness is the key to avoiding problems. For example, the department might want to develop communications with other casino communities and cultivate a good working relationship with casino security staff. Where citizens' perceptions of increased crime do not square with reality, the police will want to make doubly sure that accurate information about crime rates is widely reported so as to alleviate unfounded fears. Where crime has increased, the police will want to find additional resources.

to obtain this kind of information would be to include measures of pathological gambling in the annual surveys conducted by the Centers for Disease Control and Prevention and the National Institutes of Health.

The effects of pathological gambling (debt, for example) could be added to other long-term studies of health or mental health. Prevention and treatment of pathological gam-

bling need to be aggressively pursued. For that to happen, a great deal more light needs to be shed on the subject by filling in the many information gaps identified in the assessment. In short, pathological gambling is a problem significant enough to warrant more sustained, comprehensive, and scientific research than now exists.

NCJ 187712

ABOUT THE AUTHOR

Charles Wellford, professor of criminology and criminal justice at the University of Maryland, is director of its Maryland Justice Analysis Center. He chairs the National Research Council's (NRC's) Committee on Law and Justice and has served as chair of the NRC's Committee on the Social and Economic Impact of Pathological Gambling, which produced the report on which this article is based. He can be reached at 301-405-4701 or cwellford@crim.umd.edu.

ANNALS OF CRIME

LAND OF THE STUPID

When you need a used Russian submarine, call Tarzan.

BY ROBERT I. FRIEDMAN

On a September day last year, at the tail end of Hurricane Floyd, I took a taxi ride to the Federal Detention Center in downtown Miami to interview a man known as Tarzan. His real name is Ludwig Fainberg, and until recently he was the ringleader of the Russian mob in South Florida. When I got to the prison, the guards took my passport, my keys, and a pack of chewing gum I had in my pocket. ("It'll cost us two thousand dollars to unjam a lock from that gum if an inmate gets hold of it," one of the guards said.) I was led to a large rectangular room where prisoners in gray jumpsuits silently waited for their lawyers and guests.

In a glass-walled cubicle at the back I spotted Tarzan, a pallid man in his early forties, glaring grimly as he slumped over a brown Formica table. He used to have wild, acid-rock hair, but now it had been shorn; he once took pride in a steroid-enhanced physique, but today he looked like a deflated tire. Tarzan slammed a thick document down on the table. It was his indictment, and it consisted of thirty counts, among them conspiring to distribute cocaine and heroin, buying stolen property, counterfeiting, and money laundering. "'United States versus Tarzan,'" he said, paraphrasing a bit. "I already spent a million dollars on

lawyers. Who can fight the U.S. government?"

Since the collapse of Communism, the Mafiya, as it is known to outsiders (Russian gangsters affect disdain for the term), has become bigger, more brutal, and better armed; it is widely believed to be richer than any other criminal cartel—richer, even, than its counterpart in Colombia. The Russian mob buys and swaps drugs, money, handguns, assault carbines, submachine guns, anti-aircraft missiles, helicopters, plutonium, enriched uranium, and submarines. In 1996, James Moody, who was then the F.B.I.'s deputy assistant director in charge of organized crime, warned Congress that the Russian mob, which has thirty crime syndicates operating in more than seventeen North American cities, has "a very real chance" of becoming "the No.1 crime group in the United States." And, until recently, the No. 1 Russian crime figure in Miami was Ludwig Fainberg.

I began investigating the world of Russian organized crime in the late nineteen-eighties, venturing into strip clubs in New York and Miami, suburban homes in cities like Denver, and prison cells across the United States. Of all the mobsters I came into contact with, Tarzan was

certainly the most garrulous. He first became conspicuous in Miami in the early nineties. A strip club he owned in a warehouse district near Hialeah Race Track—Porky's, inspired by the film of that name—attracted so many Russian mobsters, from Tashkent to Brighton Beach, that local policemen referred to it as Redfellas South. It was the place to go for recreational drugs, bootleg cigarettes, and stolen bottles of Stolichnaya—or, for bigger spenders, thousand-dollar-a-night Eurasian prostitutes and Colombian cocaine. At various times, Fainberg also owned not only a residence in Miami but a restaurant, several luxury cars, and a pleasure boat.

As we chatted in the prison cubicle, Tarzan spoke expansively about his disreputable past, but he also took pains to mention his eleemosynary activities, and described numerous fund-raisers that he had held for Jewish charities at a restaurant and night club he owned called Babushka. Fainberg, who is Jewish, insists that he never stole from Jewish organizations. "You've got to be kidding!" But, according to statements that he made to undercover agents for the Drug Enforcement Agency, the operating costs for these events tended to run high—eighty-five cents of every dollar. He certainly had the qualities of a mobster: he was greedy (he allegedly stole tip money from the strippers at his club); he was ruthless (he once forced a woman to eat gravel); and he was ambitious (he brokered a complicated negotiation involving the transfer of a Russian military submarine to Colombian narcotraffickers). In Russia, Fainberg told me, dishonesty is a trait that is bred in the bone. Deprivation has taught Russians to be cunning predators—it's the only way to survive, he said. "We lived by the eleventh commandment—don't get caught." Americans, by contrast, were trusting souls, he thought. Their rules were made to be broken. "America is the land of the stupid" he said. "The land of make-believe. If you ask me to describe America in one word, I would tell you this is Disneyland. And I'm surprised that Mickey Mouse is not yet the President."

Fainberg was born in 1958 in Odessa, a Black Sea port that was once the Marseilles of the Soviet Union. His parents soon divorced, and when he was three he moved with his mother, who had remarried, and his stepfather to Czernowitz, a small city in Ukraine. He sang in a boys' choir and participated in a boxing program set up by the Soviet military. More to the point, his stepfather, who worked for a Soviet factory that made rugs and fur hats, was a prosperous dealer on the burgeoning black market. He'd trade merchandise for choice cuts of meat, theatre tickets, and fresh vegetables. " My mother had nice clothes and jewelry," Fainberg said. "We took a vacation once a year to Odessa, a stunning city with a boardwalk and gorgeous beaches." It was a city, he said, "filled with mobsters and entertainers."

One day in 1972, when Fainberg was fourteen, his mother and stepfather announced that they were moving the family to Israel, where they hoped to increase their already considerable wealth. Ludwig, who had

never known the family to identify with Judaism in any way, was confused. "Jew" was just something stamped on their passports, he thought, signifying their ethnic group. "I knew only that I was circumcised."

Before leaving, the Fainbergs converted their money into gold and diamonds, stashing some in shoes with hollow heels and hiding the rest in secret compartments in specially built tables and a piano, which they shipped to Israel. There they lived on a kibbutz. Fainberg, with his wild mane and his flair for daredevil stunts—he once jumped off a second-story roof—soon acquired his nickname. "One of the kids said, 'You look like Tarzan'—you know, build, hair, muscles."

At eighteen, Fainberg, who was now six feet one, was drafted into the Israeli Navy, and he applied to an élite Navy Commando unit. He washed out during basic training, and served the remaining three years of his service in the weapons-control room of a destroyer. In 1979, Fainberg moved to West Berlin, claiming to be a boxer defecting from the Soviet Union. Like many young Russian émigrés he says, he joined a mob crew. His specialty was credit-card fraud. Then he tried his hand at extortion. Working for a local racket—run, he later learned, by a notorious gangster named Efim (Fima) Laskin, who had sold weapons to the Red Brigades, in Italy—he was ordered to go to a certain restaurant and abduct a Russian named Leonid, who owed the gang money. Fainberg and his accomplices drove Leonid to a bank so that Leonid could get cash for them. But shortly after they arrived the hostage's friends—a group of rival mobsters—showed up and dealt Fainberg's men a severe beating. Fainberg, who happened to be in a store buying cigarettes at that moment, escaped, but the rival mob put out a contract on him. He fled to Cologne and went into hiding. A few years later, he landed in Brooklyn, at Brighton Beach.

From the middle to the late nineteen-seventies, the Soviet government was under intense diplomatic pressure from the West to let Jews emigrate freely. In response, the authorities searched the Gulag for Jewish criminals—some of them quite recent converts to the faith—and shipped them to America. (During the Cold War, criminal-background information was unavailable to United States immigration officials, and their ability to screen criminals was severely limited.) More than forty thousand Russian Jews settled in Brighton Beach. Most were decent, hardworking citizens, but the criminals among them resumed their careers as thieves and swindlers. By the time Fainberg arrived, in 1984, Brighton Beach had already become the seat of the Organizatsiya, as the Russian Jewish mob was called. "It was the Wild West," Fainberg told me. "I took my gun everywhere."

Fainberg quickly discovered that there were two distinct communities in Brighton Beach. Affluent Russians lived in well-kept Art Deco apartment buildings near the ocean; poor Russians lived–sometimes ten to a room—in decaying clapboard houses amid crack dens on the area's many side streets. Even the local McDonald's had folded. Bordered on one side by the shore and on another by an enormous middle-class housing project, referred to by the émigrés as "the great wall of China," the Russians built a closed world. It was modelled on Odessa. On frigid winter mornings, beefy men in fur hats strolled the boardwalk, stopping at vendors to buy piroshki. Movie houses showed first-run Russian-language films; the conversations in the cafés were in Russian and Ukrainian. Tarzan spent much of his time in mob haunts, flirting with the wives of big-time mafiosi and "getting into fistfights," as he recounts it. Soon after he arrived in Brooklyn, he married Maria Raichel, a princess of the Russian Mafiya and a beauty. (Maria's grandfather was said to have stabbed a man to death in Russia. Her first husband and his brother, known as Psyk—Russian for psycho—became high-level extortionists, but, because of their uncontrollable behavior, they eventually fell into violent conflict with other Russian gangsters, who ordered hits on them.)

Fainberg took up with a fellow-émigré named Yossif Roizis, known to his friends as Gregory, or Grisha. Their families had been friends in Ukraine and were neighbors in Israel. Roizis had spent three years in prison in Siberia for hitting a man who was recovering from an appendectomy—hitting him so hard that his fist penetrated the abdominal cavity and killed him. Now Roizis headed one of the most feared Russian gangs in Brighton Beach. He owned a wholesale furniture store with branches in Coney Island, Italy, and Russia, which the D.EA and a knowledgeable figure in the Genovese underworld say fronted for a heroin business involving Italian and Russian mobsters. Fainberg says that he helped Roizis's crew with torch jobs and extortion. He also went into business with the owners of a furniture store in nearby Bensonhurst. Roizis wanted Tarzan's partners, a brother and sister, to stock their store with his store's furniture. "I can't get them to do that," Tarzan said. "Well, then it's time for them to disappear," Roizis replied. They did. ("I asked Roizis what happened to them," Fainberg said, "but he never told me anything.") Tarzan took over the business.

Inevitably, the Russian mobsters crossed paths with their Italian counterparts. One day, according to Fainberg, an old woman walked into the furniture store and asked to buy a twin-size mattress on credit. "You've got to be crazy," a clerk replied. Fainberg overheard the conversation and gave the woman the mattress and box spring as a gift. He even loaded it onto his truck and delivered it to her house. He said he felt sorry for her, and, besides, they had samples to spare. Two years later, a powerfully built Italian sauntered into a video store that Fainberg

owned and asked for him. "I was scared shitless," Fainberg recalled. "He looked like Luca Brasi in 'Godfather.'" Introducing himself as Frank, the man said, "I'm the son of the old woman you gave the mattress to. I owe you. Anything you want is yours."

Fainberg was awestruck. "You could feel his power," he said. "He was the kind of man who wouldn't take no for an answer."

Over the next several months, if the landlord attempted to raise the rent at the video store Tarzan would call Frank. When an Italian extortionist tried to shake Tarzan down, Frank's boys had the thug pistol-whipped. As we spoke, Tarzan repeatedly assured me that he didn't know the identity of his patron until, one day in 1987, he saw him identified in the *Times* as the late Frank Santora, a notable member of the Colombo organized-crime family. Santora had been shot twice at close range outside a dry-cleaning store on a quiet Brooklyn street.

After that, life became more dangerous for Fainberg and his friends. One of those singled out for merciless treatment was Alexander Slepinin, nicknamed the Colonel, a three-hundred-pound, six-foot-five black belt who claimed to have served with the Russian Special Forces in Afghanistan. Slepinin had tattoos of a panther and a dragon on his upper torso—signs that he had spent time in Soviet prisons. He was trained in a variety of martial arts, and kept a large collection of knives and machetes, which he used to dismember extortion victims in his bathtub before disposing of the body parts.

On a June morning in 1992, while Slepinin was sitting in his Cadillac on a residential street in the Sunset Park section of Brooklyn, he was ambushed by a group of Russians. According to eyewitnesses, the big man, wheezing heavily, begged his assailants for mercy. "We are not in the church," one of the hit men replied. Slepinin tried to squeeze out of the car through the passenger door, but he was shot three times in

the back. The bullets were aimed to insure that his death would be agonizing. Thrashing and moaning, Slepinin continued to beg for his life. Two bullets to the back of the head finally finished him off. "He was a big, huge motherfucker—a monster, a cold-blooded killer," one of the alleged assassins, an infamous Russian gangster named Monya Elson, told me during an interview at the Metropolitan Correctional Center in Manhattan. He was being held there on charges of heading a racketeering outfit called Monya's Brigade, which was responsible for three murders, including Slepinin. (The case is still pending.) Although Elson maintained that he was innocent, he also said, "The F.B.I. and everybody have to fucking give me an award."

Fainberg is more sentimental. "My mother loved the Colonel," he recalled gloomily. Even before Slepinin's death, Tarzan had decided that it was time once again to move to a safer neighborhood. He had not been getting along with his wife anyhow, he said, and in 1989 he left her, and Brighton Beach, and headed south.

Long before Fainberg got to Florida, in 1990, the Miami Beach Police Department had noticed that an inordinate number of newly arrived Russian taxi-drivers were involved in many of the same crimes that had made the Italian Mafia so powerful: extortion, narcotics gambling, and prostitution. Diana Fernandez, an assistant United States Attorney, says that, following the collapse of the Soviet Union, in 1991, "Miami was a boomtown for the Russian mob." The mobsters had become rich in the era of privatization, and they bought rows of luxury condominiums in North Miami Beach or spent millions for mansions on Fisher Island, one of the city's most fashionable residential areas. Several of the buyers were former high-ranking Russian military officers and ex-K.G.B. officials. They had found their perfect dacha: a base for money laundering which was also convenient to South American cocaine.

In Miami, Fainberg met William Seidle, a very successful car dealer. A veteran D.E.A. agent told me that Seidle has been under investigation by numerous federal agencies for more than twenty years, although he has never been indicted. Seidle's friends respond to these allegations with bafflement. "Bill Seidle is a great guy," William Lehman, a former Democratic congressman, told me. Lehman, who represented North Dade County for twenty years and has known Seidle for fifty years, says that Seidle enjoyed Fainberg's "outrageousness" but that he himself ran a "kosher" business.

Seidle liked Fainberg from the moment they met. "Tarzan was a boisterous, bigmouthed yiddel," he told me in Miami, speaking with obvious affection. "He's a Jewboy, you know. Just a bigmouth kid, always bragging, boisterous—but very nice, very kind." Seidle saw in Fainberg a younger version of himself: a risk-taker. In Miami, Fainberg ran a furniture and moving company out of a warehouse owned by Seidle. A local charitable foundation gave Fainberg donated clothes, which he sold for profit. Before long, Seidle and Fainberg decided that there was a lot of money to be made in strip clubs. According to government informants, in 1991 Seidle staked Tarzan to the club that became Porky's, in return for a hidden share of the off-the-book profits. Tarzan was proud of his upward mobility in his adopted land: "From schmattes to the big tits!" he told me. "Can you imagine! What a country!" Seidle, for his part, denies receiving club profits, acknowledging only that he collected rent as the club's landlord.

At Porky's, Fainberg held court for visiting dons from the former Soviet Union. One of the most powerful was Anzor Kikalischvili, a Moscow-based businessman who had long been on a C.I.A list of prominent Soviet organized-crime figures and, in a conversation taped by the F.B.I., once boasted that he

had more than six hundred "soldiers" in South Florida. In one conversation, Kikalischvili warned a Russian couple with whom he had a partnership in a Miami deli that if they didn't pay him two hundred and fifty thousand dollars for his share he would skin them like animals. The couple fled the country, and Fainberg, who had introduced them to Kikalischvili, became a partner in the deli.

In addition to extortion, Fainberg had a habit of degrading women. "This is cultural," he explained to me, in an effort to defend himself. "In Russia, it was normal for men to beat women. In the stories Dostoyevsky, Chekhov, and Gorky wrote, to slap a woman is normal, it's part of life. And to do something like that in America, something that you grew up with—you're arrested, for domestic violence!" In an incident observed by the F.B.I. and the D.E.A. from surveillance cars across the street from Porky's, Fainberg chased a girlfriend out of the club and decked her. On another occasion, he allegedly beat a girlfriend's head against the door of his Mercedes until the car was covered with blood; and he regularly abused his common-law wife, a frail young woman named Faina Tannenbaum whom he had brought with him from New York. When the police arrived at their home in response to 911 calls, she would quiver in fear, and was sometimes found huddled inside a locked car with her daughter. Tannenbaum never pressed charges, however. In 1996, as she was driving to pick up her daughter at a day-care center, her car hit a tree and she was killed. Her blood-alcohol level was far over the legal limit, and the car was travelling at more than ninety miles per hour in a thirty m.p.h. zone.

Fainberg's ambitions went beyond strip clubs. According to F.B.I. wiretap affidavits and Fainberg's own admissions to under-

cover agents, he and Seidle had a "grow lab" for hemp in a warehouse near Hialeah, with giant halogen lights. (Seidle denies this.) Fainberg boasted to two government undercover agents that he had a connection for "tons" of marijuana from Jamaica.

For Fainberg, marijuana was just a gateway drug. In the early nineties, the Mafiya had little contact with the Colombian drug cartels, but Fainberg helped forge a connection, brokering cocaine deals between the Colombians and the most powerful mob family in Russia's St. Petersburg. In one instance, according to the D.E.A., he conspired to smuggle more than a hundred kilograms of cocaine a month in crates of frozen shrimp which were flown from Guayaquil, Ecuador, to St. Petersburg. He also ran small amounts of cocaine directly out of Miami. (He denies this.) And wiretap affidavits allege that his couriers "bodied" cocaine by the kilo.

Fainberg's principal link to the Colombians was through two men, Juan Almeida and Fernando Birbragher. Almeida, who is the son of a Cuban-American real estate and construction mogul in Miami, had been a major cocaine dealer since the mid-nineteen-eighties, according to the D.E.A. Birbragher, a Colombian and a friend of Seidle's, had strong ties to the Medellín and the Cali cartels. He was indicted in 1982 on charges of laundering seventy-three million dollars for Colombian drug lords; he pleaded guilty in 1984 to a lesser charge of conspiring to defraud the United States government. One D.E.A. agent told me that Birbragher was a very close friend of the late Pablo Escobar, the notorious leader of the Medellín cartel. "Birbragher used to buy Escobar sports cars and do a lot of favors for him," the agent said. D.E.A. officials also strongly suspect that Birbragher laundered drug money for Manuel Noriega, the former Panamanian President, who was convicted in 1992 of drug trafficking, racketeering, and money laundering.

Fainberg worked closely with Almeida, who told him that they wouldn't have trouble with the law as long as they didn't sell drugs in America. According to F.B.I. sources, Fainberg's cocaine business did so well that he soon found himself fending off hostile takeover attempts from other Russian mobsters eager to do business with the Colombians.

By the mid-nineties, the Colombians had a thriving arrangement with the Russians—the Colombians supplied the cocaine and the Russians laundered the money. Now, according to D.E.A. officials, Fainberg and Almeida saw a way to expand this business. The Mafiya had access to military hardware from the former Soviet Union. Goods stored in deteriorating facilities and guarded by indifferent, bribable soldiers were easily available—everything from aircraft and armored personnel carriers to submarines.

In the fall of 1992, Fainberg travelled to Latvia, where, he told me, he knew people who could help him procure six heavy-lift Russian military helicopters. The choppers were intended for Pablo Escobar, who hoped to use them to transport chemicals to cocaine-refining laboratories in the jungle. (Fainberg told undercover agents that a "rich American Jew"—thought by the D.E.A. to be Seidle—was financing ten per cent of the cost of the trip, a charge Seidle heatedly denies.) Fainberg was accompanied by Almeida, Birbragher, and a group of Colombian and Cuban thugs. The trip was a failure, and Almeida and Birbragher blamed Fainberg. "He is an idiot," Almeida told me with disgust. "He didn't know anybody."

But in mid-1993 Fainberg succeeded. According to the D.E.A., he and Almeida bought as many as six MI-8 Russian military helicopters for something under a million dollars each. Fainberg later boasted to undercover agents that he had bought the helicopters to traffic cocaine for a group of "Colombian drug barons"

headed by Escobar, and, after purchasing the helicopters, he stayed behind in Moscow to oversee the final details. At the request of the Colombians, Fainberg later said, the helicopters' seats were removed and fuel bladders were added to extend their range. With everything set, Fainberg went to a final meeting with the sellers. He was taken into a conference room and left alone with two big Russian guys. "They were like heavy weight lifters," he told me. "They were incredible hulks. I was in deep shit." One of the men opened the window. Parked outside were a Range Rover, a Mitsubishi Montero, a Lexus, and a Mercedes. When the man whistled, the doors opened and out came men armed with automatic weapons. "Well, that's my people," the man said to Fainberg. "I was waiting for your people."

"At that point, I understood I'm not going to leave Russia," Fainberg recalled. "I'm going to be buried in the motherland." The weight lifters informed him that he had neglected to pay the local Mafiya for permission to buy the helicopters. Fortunately for Fainberg, "his people" — the Colombians—held a certain mystique for the Russians, and by alluding to his close connections with them he was able to buy time.

He telephoned Anzor Kikalischvili, the Russian don, who happened to be visiting Miami. Kikalischvili, who wanted Fainberg's help in obtaining a green card, said he'd make some calls and try to smooth things over, but meanwhile Fainberg would have to explain why he hadn't cut "the boys" in for a share. In another series of frantic phone calls, Fainberg described his predicament to Almeida. Almeida advised him to tell the Russians that the helicopters were for Pablo Escobar and that no one had told Escobar he was required to pay a bribe. Fainberg and Almeida hoped that the Russians might make an exception for Escobar, but the Russians were stubborn. If Escobar wanted the choppers, they replied, he would have to come to Moscow himself.

Almeida says he decided that the only way to get the helicopters—and to save Fainberg—was to pose as Escobar. At Sheremetyevo Airport, in Moscow, Almeida, dressed like the Colombian, was welcomed by a motorcade of thick-necked men driving black Mercedeses. (This is Almeida's account. Tarzan never mentioned an Escobar impersonation to me.) Almeida says he was escorted like a head of state to a five-star hotel in the center of the city and led into a dark room, where more thick-necked men sat around a long conference table. Almeida walked past them to the head of the table, where the don presided. There was a nervous silence. Suddenly, the Russian seized him in a bear hug and cried, "Pablo! Pablo Escobar! What took you so long? Let's do some real shit. Cocaine!"

To celebrate their new friendship, the Russians took Almeida and Fainberg out for a night on the town. They went to a dingy boxing ring called the Samurai Club, where chain-smoking mobsters and their girlfriends, wearing Italian designer clothes, had gathered to watch a match. Young men dressed in street clothes were led into the ring. Mafiya rules: only one could walk out alive. Blood spattered the crowd as spectators swilled vodka and placed bets on their favorite combatant. As implausible as this seems, Fainberg and Almeida have separately offered almost identical versions of the incident. The spectacle went on through the night. There was no air-conditioning in the club, and the stench of blood, Tarzan says, nearly made him vomit. The following day, he was permitted to fly out of Moscow. The helicopters, Fainberg told various federal undercover agents, were subsequently delivered to the Colombian drug barons.

Meanwhile, in the United States, the activities of the Russian mob were alarming a great many law-enforcement agencies. In 1994, Louis J. Freeh, the director of the F.B.I. said that the Russian Mafiya posed "a significant direct threat to the United States." In a few years, the Russians had supplanted the Cubans as one of the top crime groups in South Florida. Local, state, and federal officials set up a task force called Operation Odessa, and eventually developed ties with Canadian, Russian, and German police. Richard Gregorie, a bearded, professorial assistant U.S. Attorney who helped launch Operation Odessa, says of the Russians, "Their obvious sophistication far exceeds that of La Cosa Nostra at its infant stage."

Operation Odessa's agents had so far been unable to infiltrate Fainberg's close-knit world. That assignment fell to Fainberg's old Brighton Beach friend Grisha Roizis, who had by this time acquired the nickname the Cannibal. (A booking sergeant in Brooklyn had once called him "a fucking dirty Jew," and Roizis, although handcuffed, managed to bite off the tip of the sergeant's nose.) Roizis was by now indebted to the D.E.A. In 1992, he had been jailed in Romania on a U.S. warrant for heroin trafficking, and he became an informant in return for his release. He had no trouble getting close to Fainberg. "Gregory and I were like brothers," Fainberg told me. "He's the one who helped me when I arrived in Brighton Beach. He *loved* me!"

In October of 1994, Roizis, using seventy-two thousand dollars in cash supplied by the D.E.A., bought a managing partnership in Babushka, Fainberg's restaurant. Many people found the Cannibal's presence in the restaurant disturbing. A Brooklynite named Vladimir Ginzburg, who the F.B.I. believe was a key operative in Fainberg's cigarette-bootlegging operation, had repeatedly told Fainberg that his buddy was working for the federal government. "I warned Tarzan about the rumors," Ginzburg said. "Tarzan didn't listen. So I asked Tarzan why he trusted him. He said they were both from the same town. He knew his father. He had his friends checked out. And Roizis had a cruel criminal past. That counts for a lot. Tarzan didn't have a compara-

ble past—and Tarzan wasn't so smart. He had steroids for brains. He had a big-muscle peanut brain."

With Fainberg's confidence secured, Roizis got to his work. One day, a man named Alexander Yasevich walked into Babushka, posing as an arms-and-heroin dealer, and Roizis embraced him like a long-lost comrade. Fainberg dimly recognized Yasevich from Brooklyn; Yasevich had moved there from Odessa as a teen-ager. But, unbeknownst to Fainberg, Yasevich had joined the Marines, and then become an undercover agent for the D.E.A.

Five days later, they met again, at Porky's. Fainberg was in a mood to boast, and told Yasevich of his criminal exploits. The two men began to hang out together. Yasevich was offered free sex at the hotel next door to Porky's, and ate in expensive Japanese restaurants. They consumed enormous amounts of exotic concoctions, such as raw quail eggs drenched in *sake* and ice-cold vodka. The drinking and kibbitzing paid off for Yasevich. He learned that Fainberg was in the midst of executing his most audacious caper yet: the purchase of a hundred-million-dollar Soviet-era diesel-powered submarine, for "the people associated with the late Pablo Escobar." (Escobar had been hunted down and killed by Colombian authorities in December of 1993.) As a gift, Yasevich gave Fainberg a "safe" cell phone, which, of course, was closely monitored by the D.E.A.

W hen Fainberg was first approached about the submarine, the prospect unnerved him. The Russian helicopters had nearly cost him his life. But this time he made sure to clear the deal through Anzor Kikalischvili, whom he met with in Helsinki and, later, in Moscow. Finally— through the most powerful crime boss in St. Petersburg, a man named Misha Brave—Tarzan, Almeida, and Nelson Yester, a Cuban-American on the lam from a federal cocaine indictment, met two corrupt, high-

ranking Russian military officers. Fainberg and Yester were taken to the front gate of Kronstadt, a sprawling naval base in the Baltic, where numerous abandoned diesel submarines bobbed on their sides, leaking oil, fluid, and battery acid into the harbor. Richard Palmer, who was a C.I.A. station chief in the former Soviet Union, told me that at such bases "anything is available—the Soviet fleet is rotting, and the sailors haven't been paid for months."

Initially, the Miamians wanted to buy a huge attack submarine for Escobar's East Coast drug trade. But a retired Russian submarine captain whom Fainberg nicknamed the Admiral suggested that they operate on the West Coast, where America's anti-submarine net was less active. According to the D.E.A., a Russian active-duty officer suggested that Fainberg and his associates buy a small, diesel-powered Piranha-class submarine. Made of titanium and much quieter than other models, the Piranhas are used to plant saboteurs, troops, and spies behind enemy lines. But the Colombians considered the Piranha too expensive, and they wanted a submarine with greater range.

They finally agreed on a three-hundred-foot-long Foxtrot-class attack submarine, a model manufactured between 1958 and 1984, with a range of several thousand miles. It could disappear for days at a time and resurface, when required, to deliver drugs. Drug lords calculated that it could carry up to forty tons of cocaine. The Admiral told Fainberg that he had slipped a similar submarine past the Americans during the Cuban missile crisis. The Colombians planned to base the sub, which would be demilitarized and retrofitted to resemble an oceanographic-research vessel, in Panama or somewhere else on the Pacific side of Central or South America. From there, it would transport the drugs underwater to a ship outside Santa Barbara's territorial waters. The ship would then deliver the cocaine to ports along the Pacific Coast. A consortium of St. Petersburg mobsters and two active-duty admirals wanted twenty million dollars for the vessel. Fainberg bargained them down to $5.7 million. (A million of that would be his fee.) The money was to be passed through a dummy company in Switzerland in order to give an air of legitimacy to the oceanographic-research front. Fainberg planned to hire the retired captain for five hundred dollars a month and to secure a crew of seventeen to twenty-five men for a two-year contract; he even got permission to take photographs of the vessel to send to the Colombians. Tarzan told undercover agents that, at a party at a dacha, Misha Brave, the St. Petersburg crime boss, made a side deal with him to procure a "test shipment" of ten kilograms of cocaine from Miami for thirty thousand dollars a kilo. (Fainberg's cost per kilo was four thousand dollars.) To Tarzan, everything looked good.

On Tuesday, January 21,1997, Fainberg was pulled over on a Miami street by a marked Metro-Dade Police Department vehicle. He was driving a white 1996 Jaguar convertible. As he spoke with the officers, two agents from the D.E.A., Brent Eaton and Detective Joseph McMahon, who had been trailing him in an unmarked car, approached. Eaton and McMahon introduced themselves and invited him to join them in their car. They told Fainberg that he was in trouble and would be arrested. They asked him to accompany them to a place where they and a few other officers could speak with him confidentially. Fainberg argued that he was a "nicer person" than they thought and said that he hadn't "done anything wrong."

At the interview site, a D.E.A. training room near Miami International Airport, Fainberg was offered a seat and a cup of coffee. McMahon told him that he was giving him a chance to work with the government rather than be arrested. Fainberg replied that he could be very useful to

the government but was not well acquainted with United States laws and preferred to consult with his attorney before making a decision. Eaton told Fainberg that although he certainly had a right to consult with his lawyer, a man named Kieran Fallon, it might not be a wise decision, since Fallon represented other targets of the investigation. "I thought you would tell me what you have and ask me questions," Fainberg said, according to a transcript of the interrogation. "I don't know what to say, because I don't know what you think I have done."

McMahon asked Fainberg if he had ever bought liquor for Porky's or for Babushka from any source other than a legitimate wholesaler or liquor store. "Never!" Fainberg declared.

The detective asked him about his relationship with Anzor Kikalischvili.

"Anzor! I know nothing about what he does in Russia," Fainberg said. "I met him at my club. He is a sex maniac, always looking for girls. I helped him once when he opened a bagel store in Aventura."

"Tell us about Juan Almeida's activities," McMahon said.

"I don't know what he is up to," Fainberg said. "He speaks Spanish most of the time."

"You mean you travel all over the world with Almeida and you don't know what he's up to?"

"Yes."

"You know that those helicopters you get go to Colombian drug traffickers," McMahon said.

"They go to legitimate people," Fainberg replied.

When the officers accused him of lying, Fainberg said, "Maybe I should go to jail, then find out what you have."

The agents had had enough. They placed him under arrest, handcuffed him, and drove him to the D.E.A. processing room, where he was fingerprinted, photographed, and allowed to call his attorney.

Almeida surrendered to the authorities several days later. (His accom-

plice Nelson Yester remains at large.) Not only had Fainberg bragged about their activities to various undercover agents but he had even introduced Almeida to Yasevich, the D.E.A. undercover agent. At the time, Almeida told Yasevich that he represented a client with unlimited funds who was interested in buying a Russian diesel submarine; he added, with a laugh, that the vessel was going to be used to transport stolen gold off the coast of the Philippines.

Almeida, a suave man with a salesman's charm, told me in Miami that the sub was intended for an underwater museum in South Florida. (Fainberg makes a similar claim.) After Almeida was arrested, his lawyer, Roy Black, said that the sub was intended to carry tourists around the Galápagos Islands. As for the Russian helicopters, Almeida claimed that the aircraft were actually contracted by Helitaxi, a Bogotá-based company, to do heavy lifting at oil rigs in South America.

The investigation produced five hundred and thirty wiretapped conversations, in English, Russian, Hebrew, Yiddish, and Spanish. (It took a team of twenty translators a year to transcribe and analyze the tapes.) On the tapes and in conversations with the undercover agents, Fainberg implicated himself and others in numerous crimes. Louis J. Terminello, Fainberg's civil lawyer, says the only thing that his client is guilty of is having a big mouth. "It's the high-school kid who wants the high-school girl to believe that he's got the biggest dick in the world."

After months of sullen denial, Fainberg decided to coöperate. "He's admitted to everything," a D.E.A agent named Pamela Brown told me several months after his arrest. "He keeps saying, 'Well, this would have all been legal in Russia.'" But then, after negotiating at least six proffer agreements, the feds decided to let him stand trial. They could not corroborate much of his information, and he said that he would never testify unless he was released on bail. There was little likelihood of that happening. The feds had a good idea what Fainberg would do if he obtained bail: informants reported that he was working with several powerful Israeli drug dealers in Miami who were going to help him flee to Israel; it is difficult to extradite Israeli nationals.

Finally, Fainberg, who faced a possible life sentence, pleaded guilty to one count of federal racketeering, which included conspiring to sell cocaine, heroin, and the Russian submarine, and sundry other crimes. He testified against Almeida, who was convicted of conspiracy to smuggle and distribute. "Tarzan's big mouth ruined my life," Almeida says. According to well-placed government sources, Almeida, who is awaiting sentencing, made threats against the judge and the prosecution team.

As for the Cannibal, Grisha Roizis—the man who helped the feds the most—in July of 1998 he seemed to be without a care in the world as he stood erect, his Popeye-like arms bulging out of a lime-green polo shirt, calmly awaiting sentencing in Federal District Court. In return for services rendered to the government, the judge sentenced him to time served and waived further jail time.

Less than a year later, Roizis was in trouble again: he was arrested by the Italian police in Rimini for money laundering, extortion, kidnapping, and racketeering. Most of his victims were small-time Russian entrepreneurs in Italy. Some of his illicit gains were allegedly passed through the Bank of New York. Apparently, shortly after working for the D.E.A. Roizis had begun to run a thriving criminal empire on the Adriatic Coast.

The Russian mob in South Florida today is the hub of a sophisticated and ruthless operation. But Ludwig Fainberg is no longer a member. At the conclusion of my conversations with him in prison in September, he said ruefully, "America's built on Mafia! All over the world, when you ask 'What do you know about America?' they say, 'Mafia, "Godfather," Bugsy Siegel, Meyer Lansky!' I swear, I can't believe John Gotti got life in jail. How can you kill your own history?"

Then, in October, after living in America for fifteen years, Fainberg was deported to Israel, with fifteen hundred dollars in his pocket. He had served a mere thirty-three months. His light sentence was in return for his operation which reportedly included providing intelligence on several alleged Russian mob heavyweights. Even as he awaited deportation, Fainberg told me that, given what he knows about the sex industry, he'll soon be rich again. He was already cooking up a new scheme. "I'm going to Cuba. A few of my Russian friends already own resorts there." But his enthusiasm for the land he was leaving was undimmed. "I love this country!" Tarzan said. "It's so easy to steal here!"

From *The New Yorker*, April 10, 2000, pp. 40–49. © 2000 by Robert I. Friedman.

The Well-Marked Roads to Homicidal Rage

By LAURIE GOODSTEIN and WILLIAM GLABERSON

Shots explode at a school in Oregon, a brokerage office in Atlanta, or a church in Fort Worth, and the nation is witness to another sudden, seemingly random violent rampage. Before the ambulances leave, the news crews arrive. The killers' neighbors, friends or families submit to interviews, and inevitably, they say something like this: "He just snapped."

But the killers do not just snap. An examination by The New York Times of 100 rampage murders found that most of the killers spiraled down a long slow slide, mentally and emotionally. Most of them left a road map of red flags, spending months plotting their attacks and accumulating weapons, talking openly of their plans for bloodshed. Many showed signs of serious mental health problems.

But in case after case, the Times review found, the warning signs were missed: by a tattered mental health care system; by families unable to face the evidence of serious mental turmoil in their children or siblings; by employers, teachers and principals who failed to take the threats seriously; by the police who, when alerted to the danger by frightened relatives, neighbors or friends, were incapable of intervening before the violence erupted.

James Davis, whose co-workers had nicknamed him Psycho, warned his colleagues at a tool warehouse in Asheville, N.C., "If they ever decide to fire me, I'll take two or three of them with me." His employers did fire him, and feared he would respond with violence, but despite his threats, they failed to protect his co-workers when Mr. Davis returned to take his revenge.

In 34 of the 100 cases, however, families or friends of the killers desperately did try to find help for a person they feared was a ticking time bomb, but were rebuffed by the police, school administrators or mental health workers.

Sylvia Seegrist caromed in and out of mental institutions 12 times in 10 years, while her parents searched for a residential program where she could stay in treatment. They knew she was dangerous. She had stabbed a psychologist and tried to strangle her mother, and had hidden a gun in her apartment. But each time, she was released from the hospital when she seemed to improve.

"We were always fearful that maybe some tragedy would happen," said Ruth S. Seegrist, Sylvia's mother. "She threatened it: 'Someday before I kill myself, I'll bring some people down with me.'" Sylvia opened fire in a suburban Philadelphia shopping mall in 1985, killing three people and wounding seven.

In response to the recent spate of rampage-style mass shootings in schools, workplaces, stores and other public places, The New York Times re-examined 100 such violent incidents that occurred in the United States over the last 50 years. The Times gathered extensive information on all 100, and looked closely at more than 25 of the cases, a surprising number of which attracted little but local attention. The examination included reviews of court cases, news coverage and mental health records, and interviews with families and friends, psychologists and victims, in an effort to glean what the people closest to each tragedy had learned. In some cases, reporters questioned the killers themselves.

Based on this information, The Times found that in 63 of the 100 cases (which involved 102 killers), the killers made general threats of violence to others in advance. Fifty-five of the 100 cases involved killers who regularly expressed explosive anger or frustration, and 35 killers had a history of violent behavior and assaults. They were so noticeably unstable that even in their very separate circles they had been awarded similar nicknames: "Crazy Pat," "Crazy John," "Crazy Joe."

And in 40 cases, family members and others said they noticed a sudden change in behavior in the period before the rampage.

"The more you find out about each of these cases, the more it makes sense," said Prof. Dewey G. Cornell, a clinical psychologist at the University of Virginia and director of the Virginia Youth Violence Project, which studies school safety and violence prevention. "This notion that someone just snaps is based on ignorance and denial," Professor Cornell said. "People don't just snap. Pressures build up."

Many psychologists caution that it is impossible to predict violent behavior, and that most people who threaten violence never follow through. Often, it is only in retrospect that each killer's life appears to be a coherent chilling narrative foretelling obvious danger. Looking back, it is easy to marvel, how could the people who knew the murderer have failed to see it coming? In particular, how could so many psychiatric workers, and even the police, have missed the warning signs?

In many cases, there was no single person in the potential killer's life to put together the lethal clues. Colleagues, friends, family members, mental health professionals, teachers and the police may have independently sensed something disturbing, but they did not communicate with one another. Frightened neighbors or co-workers decided it was safest to keep their distance. Friends laughed off homicidal talk. Parents did not know where to turn, or just hoped the irrational fury was merely a phase.

"It's like looking at the night sky," said Robert Granacher Jr., a psychiatrist in Lexington, Ky., who has examined the records of several rampage murderers. "If you only see one or two stars, you may not see the whole constellation. It's the same with these fragmentary bits of information; no one has the whole picture."

In the end, the review of these cases suggests that if people understood more about mental illness and connected the clues, many of these types of rampage killings could be prevented.

IN rural Giles County, Tenn., on Nov. 15, 1995—before school shootings regularly made headlines—a slight 17-year-old strode down the hall of Richland School with his black .22 Remington Viper.

His name was Jamie Rouse, and as always, he was dressed in black. He walked up to two female teachers who were chatting in the hall, and without a word shot each of them in the head. One teacher was gravely wounded, the other died. Then Jamie Rouse smiled and aimed for the school's football coach. But a student named Diane Collins happened to cross his path. A bullet tore through her throat. She was 16 when she died that day.

Jamie Rouse had sent distress signals for years to the adults in his life. More startling, the police say he had told as many as five teenage friends exactly how he planned to bring his rifle to school and begin killing. None of them had called anyone for help. In fact, the night before, word of the planned massacre was passed like macabre gossip along a chain of students, from Jamie, to his close friend Stephen Abbott, to a teenager that Mr. Abbott worked with at the gas station, Billy Rogers.

"He told me something was going to happen at school the next day, that I was going to lose a couple of friends," Mr. Rogers later testified. "Steve told me if there was a God he better make it snow tonight so we ain't got school tomorrow."

The rampage killers in the study, young and old, often talked for months in advance about their murderous plans. And in 54 of the 100 cases, killers like Jamie Rouse provided explicit descriptions of who, where or when they intended to kill.

Charles Whitman, the infamous sniper who shot 45 people, killing 14, from atop the tower on the campus of the University

of Texas at Austin in 1966, had told a college psychiatrist four months before the attack that he had been "thinking about going up on the tower with a deer rifle and start shooting people."

Michael Carneal, a high school freshman in Paducah, Ky., told schoolmates that "it would be cool" to shoot into a student prayer group. He did as he had promised, killing three people and injuring five in 1997.

Andrew Wurst, 14, showed a group of friends a gun hidden in his father's dresser drawer and told them he planned to use nine shells to kill nine people he hated, and then kill himself. In 1998, he started shooting at his eighth-grade prom, killing a popular teacher and injuring three other people.

In case after case, friends, family members and others who heard the threats and did not take action later said they did not act because it seemed unfathomable that a human being would carry through with such threats. Others said they had heard the killer boast of violence so often that, like the villagers hardened to the boy who cried wolf, they just did not take it seriously.

In testimony, Stephen Ray, one of Jamie Rouse's closest friends, said that it had sounded ridiculous when Mr. Rouse "might have" said something about shooting someone the day before the killings, when Mr. Rouse was fuming over a fender-bender with a schoolmate's car.

Mr. Ray, now 21 and a college student in Knoxville, trembled in an interview in his dormitory this winter when he said it was hard to tell at the time that Jamie Rouse's blustery threats were real. Even when Mr. Rouse showed up in the morning with a rifle and a box of bullets, Mr. Ray said, he did not believe Jamie would really do it.

"It wasn't a joke," Mr. Ray said in a tone of amazement. "It wasn't a high school prank. It was something real."

Tennessee prosecutors said they were frustrated that legal rules barred them from charging Mr. Ray with a crime because he did nothing active to foster the plan. They did prosecute the teenager who drove Mr. Rouse to school that morning.

Failing to act in the face of warning signs, the prosecutors said, was not a crime. In retrospect, there were many people guilty of that.

In ninth grade, Jamie had scratched an inverted cross on his forehead, a symbol other students had told him was a sign of Satan worship. Many people, including teachers, had noticed the mark, which

lasted a few weeks, and talked about it among themselves.

At home during his junior year, Jamie held his brother Jeremy at gunpoint and threatened to kill him. As punishment, Jamie's parents took away his gun.

As his senior year began, he submitted his entry for the yearbook: "I, Satan, James Rouse, leave my bad memories here to my two brothers." By that time, according to testimony at his trial, Jamie Rouse was working nights, taking Max Alert to stay awake and Sominex to get to sleep, and listening to heavy metal music cranked very loud because it drowned out the voices in his head that he later told psychiatrists he had been hearing at the time.

The spring before the shootings Mr. Rouse got into a violent fight with two other boys at school. But when teachers broke it up, "Jamie just would not calm down," recalled Ronald W. Shirey Jr., the football coach that Jamie had missed shooting, in an interview in his living room a few miles from the school. "He was just totally out of control, and saying, 'I will kill you,'" Mr. Shirey said.

The school called the police after that fight. Mr. Rouse faced juvenile charges and was suspended for three days.

But time passed. His mother later said it had not occurred to her to get counseling for him. And when hunting season started, Jamie's parents gave him his rifle back.

Long after the crime, Mr. Shirey said, when government investigators sought to study ways to prevent school shootings, they asked him to circulate a survey among the teachers at Richland School, which has students from kindergarten through 12th grade, to gather information about Jamie Rouse. No survey came back with more than a paragraph, he said.

"You can't find a teacher up there that was close to Jamie Rouse since elementary school," Mr. Shirey said. "Nobody knew enough about him to say anything."

The adults noticed Jamie Rouse but did not know him, and the teenagers who knew him did not tell.

SHE was dressed in the green Army fatigues and knit cap she wore all four seasons of the year as she drove into the parking lot of the Springfield Mall in suburban Philadelphia. She leaped out of her car firing a Ruger semiautomatic rifle, and continued spraying bullets as she ran through the mall, killing three people and injuring seven, all strangers. Among the dead was a 2-year-old boy whose family had been shopping for a church charity fashion show.

Sylvia Seegrist was 25 the day of her murder spree in 1985. Her crime was the culmination of 10 years of mounting psychosis, crippling delusions and violent assaults on people who tried to help her.

Her mother, in a recent interview in her apartment a few miles from the site of Ms. Seegrist's rampage, remembered the "feelings of hopelessness, helplessness, despair, of incredible sadness" as she and her husband watched their only daughter overtaken by schizophrenia.

They also feared her. "I'll take you out," Mrs. Seegrist recalls her daughter threatening.

The Times' study found that many of the rampage killers, including Sylvia Seegrist, suffered from severe psychosis, were known by people in their circles as being noticeably ill and needing help, and received insufficient or inconsistent treatment from a mental health system that seemed incapable of helping these especially intractable patients.

Only a small percentage of mentally ill people are violent, and many advocates bristle at any link between mental illness and violence out of concern that it will further stigmatize an already mistreated population.

However, the Times investigation of this particular style of violence—public rampage killings—turned up an extremely high association between violence and mental illness. Forty-seven of the killers had a history of mental health problems before they killed; 20 had been hospitalized for psychiatric problems; 42 had been seen by mental health professionals.

Psychiatric drugs had been prescribed at some point before the rampages to 24 of the killers, and 14 of those people were not taking their prescribed drugs when they killed. Diagnoses of mental illness are often difficult to pin down, so The Times tabulated behavior: 23 killers showed signs of serious depression before the killings, and 49 expressed paranoid ideas.

Some of the killers who survived their rampages have made it clear they preferred to be thought of as criminal rather than mentally ill. Back in 1966, Robert Benjamin Smith, an 18-year-old high school senior in Mesa, Ariz., said he believed he was God when he herded five women and two children into the back room of a beauty school, forced them to lie down in a circle and methodically shot each person in the head, killing five of them.

In a letter Mr. Smith sent to a Times reporter from prison in January, he brushed off questions about illness and wrote, "Lessons? The sole thing I have learned worth the telling is the ironclad necessity of retaining control over one's essential bodily fluids." He blamed "sexual self-stimulation" for his crime and noted that he had tried to amputate his penis while in prison using the pull-tab from a can of diet soda.

"The more ill they are, the less sensibility there is" in the violent attack itself, said Anthony G. Hempel, chief forensic psychiatrist at the Vernon campus of North Texas State Hospital. Dr. Hempel, who has studied mass murderers, said that in contrast to the killers who "go postal," gunning for their bosses, "when someone goes and kills strangers or they kill children, the odds of them being mentally ill are higher."

Sylvia Seegrist was first hospitalized at 16, and schizophrenia was diagnosed. Each of the dozen times she was discharged, psychiatrists deemed that she no longer posed a threat to herself or others.

No one said she was getting better, though. At the local health club Ms. Seegrist was seen taking steam baths in her camouflage clothing. At the library, she spouted a tangle of theories about nuclear weapons, energy shortages and famine. Between her daughter's hospitalizations, Mrs. Seegrist found a gun in Sylvia's apartment, she said. Ms. Seegrist told her mother she planned to use it to kill her parents and then herself.

Mrs. Seegrist said the family could not afford private rehabilitation programs, and their insurance covered only short-term hospitalization.

Sylvia Seegrist, now 39, is serving a life sentence at a prison in Pennsylvania. She declined an interview, instead writing two letters to The Times, a weave of lucid fragments and unintelligible passages about benzene and Styrofoam. On the back of an envelope, she writes that her killings were a form of public service.

She also seems to assert that she had to kill to ensure she would be imprisoned instead of being sent yet again to a state mental hospital.

"Sure had all kinds of theories in my head," she wrote, "expressed them at political meetings, just doll, understand, please 10 yrs. of beat-up, orphan in state hospitals that are 300 % worse than even Sing-Sing prison. All the throwaways retarded smearing feces on themselves, when I read research materials at Ivy league colleges,

and watched nothing but CNN and C-Span at home."

She said she had no choice. "It had to be 'a serious crime' or I'd get the state hospital i.e. Nazi camp."

ROXIE M. WALLACE knew something was wrong when her grown son Jeffrey visited her, and padlocked his room. He sometimes slept with a knife by his bed. He was growing increasingly paranoid, she realized. He would talk incessantly about evil forces. Most disturbing, she said in interviews and letters, her son sometimes growled "like a small dog or a wolf."

Mr. Wallace offers a glimpse into how difficult it can be to shake someone out of a delusional universe, even when friends and relatives notice and want to do something about it. Mr. Wallace, like other rampage killers, was convinced he was defending himself against an intricate conspiracy. Of the 100 cases in the study, 49 involved killers who had shown extreme, irrational suspicion and mistrust. In their paranoia, they think they must defend themselves against threats that other people do not see.

Even now, incarcerated in an isolated Florida prison, Mr. Wallace, 38, insists that he had no choice but to open fire in 1997 at a Key West bar where he once worked, killing one person and injuring three others.

In a long prison interview, Mr. Wallace was unable to deviate from his convoluted theory that the bar was the center of an organized-crime drug and prostitution ring with ties—he was sure—to Satanism, President Clinton and Garrison Keillor, host of the public radio program "Prairie Home Companion."

Mr. Wallace's lawyers argued unsuccessfully that he was insane, but Mr. Wallace insists his actions were perfectly rational.

"The best example I can give," Mr. Wallace said, "is you're in your house and somebody breaks in and you have to defend yourself and you end up killing somebody. It's terrible but what else can you do?"

From her home in Tennessee, Mrs. Wallace said she had tried for years to maneuver her son toward help when he did not want it. "I was afraid he was either going to kill himself or he was going to 'fight back' to save himself like a caged animal," she said.

Many rampage killers are extremely difficult to treat, say psychiatrists who have interviewed them. They may deny their illness and resist medication and treatment, and are often shrewd about masking symptoms to avoid being hospitalized involuntarily.

Even those who do receive psychiatric treatment do not always get the help they need.

Joseph Brooks Jr. was a policeman's son from Detroit and one of the few black students to win entrance to both a prestigious local preparatory school and the Massachusetts Institute of Technology. Friends in the fraternity house where Mr. Brooks lived recall no hint of anger or illness, only that Mr. Brooks was absurdly meticulous about his chores, and studied so compulsively that they nicknamed him Books. But in his third year at M.I.T., he tried to commit suicide, was hospitalized for obsessive-compulsive disorder, and later received a diagnosis of paranoid schizophrenia.

Back in Detroit, living alone, Mr. Brooks, 28, sought treatment with Dr. Reuven Bar-Levav, a well-known local psychiatrist who ran group therapy sessions in Southfield attended by a close-knit clientele of upper-middle-class patients coping with depression or anxiety disorders—nothing as severe as paranoid schizophrenia. Mr. Brooks joined the group sessions, but refused to take the medication he had been prescribed, telling friends that the drugs made him tremble, gain weight and lose concentration.

Ronald Rissman, a fellow patient in the therapy group Mr. Brooks joined, said in an interview, "It was obvious he was not in touch with reality. He would laugh inappropriately. Within a matter of two or three group sessions, it became apparent to most of the senior patients that he did not belong there, that he should have been institutionalized."

Mr. Rissman said he and several other patients and therapists in the group practice repeatedly went to Dr. Bar-Levav with their concerns about Mr. Brooks. And in one group session—with Mr. Brooks in the room—a patient named Mary Gregg told the group she was afraid of Mr. Brooks, Mr. Rissman recalled.

After about eight group sessions, Dr. Bar-Levav finally terminated Mr. Brooks's treatment and referred him to other therapists.

Eight months later, on June 11 last year, Mr. Brooks returned to the psychiatrist's office and killed Dr. Bar-Levav. Mr. Brooks then pivoted and fired into the therapy group he had once attended, killing

Mrs. Gregg and wounding four others, including Mr. Rissman, who leapt up to close the door. Mr. Brooks then turned the gun on himself.

Dr. Bar-Levav had been given some warning: while in treatment, Mr. Brooks had handed a gun over to another therapist in the practice and confessed he had come close to killing his girlfriend's mother and committing suicide. And just before the killings, Mr. Brooks sent Dr. Bar-Levav a 52-page manuscript critiquing the therapy he had received from him. The critique contained obsessive, paranoid passages about a "German American woman" humiliating him in his therapy group, and hints of menace. The local police emphasized in interviews with The Times that Dr. Bar-Levav should have alerted them.

"We would have taken that weapon away from him," said Joseph Thomas, the chief of police in Southfield, Mich. But even had the police confiscated the gun, the killing would not have been prevented. Mr. Brooks easily obtained a second permit and a second gun—an expensive limited-edition combat-style handgun, which he used to kill Dr. Bar-Levav.

The psychiatrist's daughter, Dr. Leora Bar-Levav, a therapist herself who worked with her father and is now carrying on his practice, rejected with a pained wince the suggestion of negligence. In a conversation in the practice's new offices in Southfield, she said the problem was instead a permissive society and a narcissistic patient who had rejected treatment.

"You can lead a horse to water, but you can't make him drink it," she said. "Denial is very potent."

A MAN storms a warehouse where he was recently fired, leaving a trail of shell casings, three dead workers and four more wounded. The news story the next day begins, "A disgruntled former employee went on a shooting rampage."

In the turmoil that follows a rampage shooting by a killer like James Davis in Asheville, N.C., there is usually a scramble to pinpoint the cause. And in a world of rapid news cycles, the answers come quickly.

Mr. Davis was the "disgruntled employee." In news coverage last year, Dung Trinh was described as so bereaved at the death of his mother that in September he shot at nurses in a hospital in Anaheim, Calif., where she had once been treated. Sometimes the reason is reported to be a broken marriage, a spurned romance or fi-

nancial misfortune. Mark O. Barton, a rampage killer in Atlanta, was reported to have singled out day traders because he had suffered huge losses in the market.

These are the kinds of events that often result in the observation, "He just snapped."

But the incident that is often simplistically cited as the cause—a firing, a divorce, an eviction—is on closer examination just the final provocation to a troubled, angry person who has already left numerous warning markers, often available for many to see.

When he opened fire in the day-trading office, Mr. Barton already had problems deeper than his recent stock losses. Eight hours earlier, he had killed his second wife and his children, and he was still the prime suspect in the deaths six years earlier of his first wife and her mother.

"You can have it because I probably wouldn't need it much longer."

James Floyd Davis on giving his niece a video game a few days before his workplace rampage

Colin Ferguson, who opened fire on rush-hour commuters on the Long Island Rail Road, had displayed such menacing behavior that he received an eviction notice, which further fueled his fury.

Most of the workplace shooters had been fired or disciplined precisely because they were already threatening violence, behaving bizarrely or getting in fights. Of the 81 adult murderers The Times looked at, 49 were unemployed.

Mr. Davis was no mild-mannered worker who just mysteriously snapped, according to court records and interviews.

He repeatedly picked fights at the tool warehouse where he worked in Asheville, and had often told colleagues that if he were ever fired, he would return to kill his bosses. He had seen combat in Vietnam and been hospitalized with schizophrenia after the war. He lived alone, and co-workers knew he owned a .44 Magnum with a scope and had practiced firing it in his basement.

One Wednesday in May 1995, he got into another fight at work, his last.

That weekend, his family noticed him acting strangely. For example, Mr. Davis, an unemotional recluse, told his sister he loved her. And though James had never given anything to anybody, his brother, William, later said, James had wanted to give his niece a chess set and video game the weekend before. His siblings tried to persuade him to go to a hospital for psychiatric help, but he refused.

That Monday, James Davis was fired. His bosses were so anxious about his reaction that they agreed to break the news in a room where they could use a table to deflect an attack. Some employees planned escape routes when they heard of Mr. Davis's firing.

Just after midnight on Wednesday, William Davis called the police from his house 100 miles away to tell them that James had left home in a nervous frenzy and left all his personal belongings with their mother.

"I don't see why you got to wait till he kills himself or somebody," William Davis told the police, according to a transcript of his telephone call. "If you send a patrol car out to that plant, he's probably sitting there. Or notify them." William Davis told the police, "I don't know for sure, but I know and believe by the warning signs he gave me he's going to die." The Asheville police did drive by James Davis's house, but said that when they saw there was no vehicle in the driveway, there was nothing else they could do.

William Davis testified that he got in his car around 2 a.m. and drove to what he thought was his brother's workplace. But because he had not lived in Asheville for many years, he went to the wrong plant. The gate was shut, so he drove back to his mother's house to sleep.

James Davis never came home. That morning, on Wednesday, May 17, he stormed the Union Butterfield plant. Two of the victims were the bosses who fired him.

"I live for the rest of my life knowing that if someone had listened to me, no one would have died," William Davis said in an interview. "I could have stopped it if someone would have listened."

Last spring, with Mr. Davis already on death row, a jury considered a civil suit claiming that his employers had failed to protect the other employees from a man they knew to be violent. A lawyer for the company argued there was no way anyone could foresee such an attack.

A lawyer for the victims said, "This case is a human tragedy because this could have been prevented."

The jury agreed, awarding the families of two of the victims $7.9 million. An appeal has been filed.

"I am a horrible son. I wish I had been aborted. I destroy everything I touch. I can't eat. I can't sleep. I didn't deserve them. They were wonderful people. It's not their fault or the fault of any person, organization, or television show. My head just doesn't work right. God damn these VOICES inside my head."

From the note Kip Kinkel left on the coffee table in his house after killing his parents

Even the cases that drew wide attention offer fresh insights when re-examined in the context of the Times review.

One spring day, Kipland P. Kinkel, a freckle-faced boy with a history of behavior problems in school, disrupted his ninth-grade literature class by abruptly yelling out loud, "God damn this voice inside my head!"

His teacher took immediate action. He wrote up a disciplinary note. "In the future," it asked, "what could you do differently to prevent this problem?"

Kip dutifully filled out the answer: "Not to say 'Damn.'"

The note was signed by the teacher. Kip took it home to his mother, and she signed it too.

Nobody paid attention to the part about the voice inside Kip's head.

One month later, on May 20, 1998, Kip was suspended from school for buying a stolen gun and stashing it in his locker. That afternoon, back at home in a wooded neighborhood called Shangri La, Kip Kinkel, 15, shot his father and then his mother.

The next morning he drove to his school in Springfield, Ore., and shot 24 people in the cafeteria, killing two students.

Sometimes even concerned parents, like the Kinkels, or other caring adults, find the specter of serious mental or emotional problems in a child so disturbing that they lapse into denial, the study found over and over.

The youngsters themselves often unwittingly assist in the denial by being reluctant to tell someone about hearing voices or having bizarre thoughts, in fear of being labeled mentally ill. Complicating the picture is the fact that in adolescents like Kip, the symptoms are most likely just emerging, psychiatric experts say.

Kip Kinkel's parents, while perhaps unwilling to face the serious implications of his outburst in class, had not been blind to his problems, according to interviews and court records. They were both schoolteachers, and such behavior would have been hard to ignore. Starting at age 6, when Kip hit a boy twice his age with a piece of metal bar, he was susceptible to uncontrollable rages.

As a teenager, like many of the killers in the study, he showed an inordinate fascination with weapons. He collected knives, secretly built explosives and boasted to friends that he wanted to be the next Unabomber. He detonated explosives at a local quarry and was caught by the police throwing rocks at cars off a highway overpass, a prank that some psychologists say is an early indication of a potential for violent tendencies.

His mother took him to a therapist. Kip showed symptoms, the therapist noted, of "major depressive disorder," and was prescribed Prozac.

But William Kinkel, Kip's father, did not approve of therapy, and never attended the sessions, Mark Sabitt, Kip's defense lawyer, said in an interview. Mr. Sabitt said that Mr. Kinkel was "a very proud individual and aware of his image in the community. He was very skeptical of counseling in general and closed to the notion of someone in his family needing treatment, or even worse, being mentally ill. It just didn't fit with the image he had of his kids and what he hoped they would be."

After nine therapy sessions and three months of summer vacation on Prozac, Kip's behavior improved, so his parents discontinued the therapy and the medication. Kip's father bought him the Glock semiautomatic pistol his son had been pestering him for.

At Kip's sentencing hearing, the defense presented a family tree showing severe mental illness, including schizophrenia, affecting three generations on both maternal and paternal sides.

When Kip's victims addressed the judge, some said he was faking insanity. Others said that even if insane, he should be held responsible for ripping apart their lives.

"I don't care if you're sick, if you're insane, if you're crazy," said Jacob Ryker, one

Rampage Killers in 100 Cases

Figures are the number of cases in which the killers had these characteristics.

Mental Health Problems Were Prominent

47 History of mental health problems **42** Previously seen by mental health professional **24** Psychiatric drugs prescribed **14** Off prescribed psychiatric drugs at time of crime

23 Symptoms of depression **20** Previous psychiatric hospitalization **26** Suicide attempt or fixation **49** Paranoid talk

There Were Frequent Warning Signs

63 Made general or specific threat **40** Behavior changed before killing **35** History of violent behavior **25** Displayed weapons in public

But Cultural Influences Seemed Small

 11 Liked violent TV   **6** Played violent video games   **4** Interest in occult or Satanism

NEW YORK TIMES

To compile this data, The New York Times reviewed newspaper reports, court records and psychiatric reports, and interviewed the police, prosecutors, defense attorneys, victims, families, friends, and when possible, the killers themselves.

of the students who finally tackled Kip, despite gunshot wounds in his own chest and arm. "I don't care. I think prison, a lifetime in prison is too good for you. If a dog was to go insane and if a dog got rabid and it bit someone, you destroy it. So I stand here and I ask, why haven't you been destroyed? I question myself for not pulling the trigger."

AN agitated Sgt. William Kreutzer Jr. telephoned a friend in his squad at Fort Bragg, N.C. He said the shooting would begin the next morning at daybreak, just when 1,300 soldiers were on a field stretching before their morning run.

"He said he was going to 'mow them down,'" said his friend, Specialist Burl F. Mays.

True, Sergeant Kreutzer was an odd loner who talked about killing so often that the men in his company had nicknamed him Crazy Kreutzer and Silence of the Lambs. But when Specialist Mays arrived early the next morning and saw Sergeant Kreutzer was not in, he feared that this time it was no idle threat. He told his superiors just before 5 a.m. and was asked to check Sergeant Kreutzer's room.

He found that the bed had not been slept in. On the desk he found a draft of Sergeant Kreutzer's will.

Specialist Mays later testified that when he then tried to alarm superiors, the first sergeant dismissed his concerns, saying something like, "Kreutzer is a pussy, he wouldn't do anything like this."

The case of Sergeant Kreutzer, told in court records and interviews, illustrates an altogether different common case: the depressed and angry misfit provoked by the people around him.

Park Elliott Dietz, a psychiatrist and expert on mass killers, said people who become mass murderers are often "handled in a provocative, ineffective way." Their outrageous fantasies of violence draw public condemnation or ridicule. Humiliation, Dr. Dietz said, often precedes rampage killing.

Sergeant Kreutzer, a gawky perfectionist, had long been the object of ridicule in his squad at Fort Bragg. When his unit was sent to the Sinai, other soldiers tied his shoelaces together while he slept. They filled his boots with sand. Sergeant Kreutzer, 26, had always wanted to be a soldier, but he lagged behind on company runs and sometimes misplaced equipment. He cried when criticized. When he repeatedly threatened to kill other soldiers, they took it as a joke.

Fifteen months before his final ambush, when Sergeant Kreutzer had an outburst in

which he threatened to kill soldiers, and it became common knowledge, his superiors sent him to a military social worker.

"He told me that he had specific plans to kill the people in his squad," the counselor, Darren Fong, told military investigators, the court-martial documents show. But when he was returned to full duty, Sergeant Kreutzer was not referred to Army psychiatrists. He was barred from access to weapons for two weeks.

The morning of Oct. 27, 1995, Sergeant Kreutzer hid in the woods and fired onto a field of American soldiers who thought they were at peace. He wounded 18 of them, and killed Maj. Stephen Mark Badger, an intelligence officer and a father and stepfather of eight children.

Sergeant Kreutzer kept firing until he was tackled from behind by two comrades.

Minutes later, he spoke to a military police officer, Bruce W. Hamrick.

"He said he kept warning people that he was going to kill somebody," Mr. Hamrick testified, "but that nobody would listen."

Reporting for this series was by Fox Butterfield, Ford Fessenden, William Glaberson and Laurie Goodstein, with research assistance from Anthony Zirilli and other members of the news research staff of The New York Times.

UNIT 2
Victimology

Unit Selections

Key Points to Consider

- What is needed in order to switch from calling oneself a victim of crime to a "survivor of crime"?

- Why do we need good statistics to talk sensibly about social problems?

- Why is it difficult to discover the actual number of sexual assaults on college campuses?

 **Links: www.dushkin.com/online/**
These sites are annotated in the World Wide Web pages.

Connecticut Sexual Assault Crisis Services, Inc.
http://www.connsacs.org

National Crime Victim's Research and Treatment Center (NCVC)
http://www.musc.edu/cvc/

Office for Victims of Crime (OVC)
http://www.ojp.usdoj.gov/ovc

For many years, crime victims were not considered an important topic for criminological study. Now, however, criminologists consider that focusing on victims and victimization is essential to understand the phenomenon of crime. The popularity of this area of study can be attributed to the early work of Hans Von Hentig and the later work of Stephen Schafer. These writers were the first to assert that crime victims play an integral role in the criminal event, that their actions may actually precipitate crime, and that unless the victim's role is considered, the study of crime is not complete.

In recent years, a growing number of criminologists have devoted increasing attention to the victim's role in the criminal justice process. Generally, areas of particular interest include establishing probabilities of victimization risks, studying victim precipitation of crime and culpability, and designing services expressly for victims of crime. As more criminologists focus their attention on the victim's role in the criminal process, victimology will take on even greater importance.

This unit provides sharp focus on several key issues. In the lead article, "Coping In Tragedy's Aftermath," a surviving spouse watches accused bombers stand trial, 12 years after PanAm 103 claimed her husband's life. New studies on college victim rates prompt debate in the essay that follows, "In the Campus Shadows, Women Are Stalkers as Well as the Stalked." The need for good statistics to talk sensibly about social problems is the point of the next article, "Telling the Truth About Damned Lies and Statistics." A brief overview of sexual assault issues confronting the nation and current efforts to address these problems is the focus of "Sexual Violence: Current Challenges and Possible Responses." The unit closes with an interview of Susan Herman, Director of the National Center for Victims of Crime.

Coping in Tragedy's Aftermath

Twelve Years After Pan Am 103 Claimed Her Husband's Life, Mary Kay Stratis Watches Accused Bombers Stand Trial

By Angelo Carfagna

The solemn judicial process had concluded and all that was left was the verdict. Warnings had been issued to families and friends to maintain decorum and respect the Scottish High Court and the Dutch hosts. That meant no outbursts, neither from those whose loved ones perished in the sky, nor from those who supported the accused bombers of Pan American Flight 103.

FDU trustee Mary Kay Mastronardy Stratis, BS'69 (R), MAT'71 (T-H), knew she had to be there for this moment; to bear witness to this time in history; to watch the prosecution in action; to see the judges seated under a royal coat of arms, wearing traditional white wigs and white judicial robes; and, perhaps most of all, to look into the eyes of the men believed responsible for the loss of her husband and 269 other people. "It happened so quickly," she recalls. "The judges came in, all rose; they sat, we sat. The question was asked, and the verdict was given."

When the first defendant was pronounced "guilty," she remembers the shoulders of the victims' loved ones collectively falling as if the tension had sprung them to new heights and was suddenly released. "There was a cumulative sigh of relief and some audible gasps, but it was contained," she says, "Justice had been done—halfway [the second defendant was found not guilty]—but it had been done."

For Stratis, this was another round, but a major one, in a long journey of emotional trials that began at 1 a.m. on December 22, 1988, when London authorities called to confirm that her husband of nearly 20 years and her college sweetheart on FDU's Rutherford Campus, Elia Stratis, BS'67

(R), MBA'76 (T-H), was on board the ill-fated Pan Am 103, a flight he was not scheduled to take.

Since that time, Stratis has raised their three children, cared for her handicapped brother and, for a time, her ill mother; and continued an impressive list of voluntary activities, ranging from Sunday school teacher to president of the local high school's parent-faculty association, and now, following in her husband's footsteps, FDU trustee. But through it all, she has never stopped working to preserve her husband's memory, while clinging to the hope that someday those responsible would be brought to justice.

Judgment Day

For Stratis, that day arrived on January 31, 2001, when the Scottish Court, meeting in the Netherlands, sentenced Abdelbaset Ali Mohmed al-Megrahi to life imprisonment, with no possibility of parole for 20 years, for planting the bomb that exploded in the plane, killing all 259 people on board and 11 people in the town below, Lockerbie, Scotland. A second defendant, Al Amin Khalifa Fhimah, was found not guilty.

Scottish law applied to the case because the midair bombing occurred over that country's territory, and the right for the Scottish court to sit in the Netherlands was established by a landmark treaty among the British, Libyan and Dutch governments.

A critical part of the decision by the panel of three judges is the description of Megrahi as a Libyan state intelligence agency official of "fairly high rank." Stratis says, "This was a big step because Megrahi is high in the Libyan intelligence

system and his conviction directly implicates Libya."

Suspicions previously focused on Libya, and United Nations sanctions were imposed on the nation; but up until the time of this writing Libya has denied responsibility, and Megrahi is appealing his conviction. Adding to the legal battles is a civil trial in a U.S. District Court in which more than 200 families, including the Stratis family, are plaintiffs seeking a judgment against the Libyan government and reparations. "To be honest, I'm not even sure where we stand with that case. I've never thought about reparations. I just want the truth about what happened. But I've also come to understand that a message must be sent that engaging in terrorism will be very expensive."

An FDU Romance

The year was 1965. Mary Kay Mastronardy was a bright-eyed college freshman earning tuition credit by working for the University during registration. "I was one of the work-study students lined up at the admissions tables when I saw this big-shot upperclassman walk in. He just approached me and started talking."

The son of a Greek import-export trader, Elia Stratis was born in Sudan and had come to the United States with his family when he was 12. He and Mary Kay hit it off instantly and began dating.

Both were extremely active on the Rutherford Campus. If there were a Mr. and Mrs. FDU, Elia and Mary Kay would have fit the bill. Elia was a leader in student organizations and a member of the soccer and track teams. Mary Kay was a member of the Class Council, Student Education Association and Dean's Advisory Committee and worked on the yearbook. "It was a very friendly atmosphere, and we tried to take advantage of our opportunities."

Elia graduated in 1967 with a BS degree in accounting and began working for the firm of Ernst & Ernst, now Ernst & Young. In 1969, Mary Kay earned her bachelor of arts in secondary education and began graduate courses in the MAT program, and Elia formed his own firm called Campos & Stratis. That same year, the two were married and they later purchased a home in Montvale, N.J.

Elia's partnership grew considerably in the subsequent years. After starting humbly in a rented office, the firm eventually gained an international reputation and opened offices overseas. Elia was a pioneer in the field of forensic accounting. Focusing on serving the insurance industry, the company would investigate claims to sniff out fraudulent cases. The financial detective was in great demand.

In the meantime, Mary Kay became a high school math teacher. Later, she opted to be a full-time mom to Lia, Christopher and Sonia. The young children were enthralled by stories of where daddy had been and the gifts brought home from exotic countries. "Our children always had the best things for show and tell." During the summer, Elia brought Mary Kay and the children wherever he went. "We toured Europe, the Orient, Australia, etc. It was wonderful."

Mary Kay vividly remembers how Elia loved to see the children thrive academically, but how he also relished seeing them develop their physical talents. Elia could constantly be found tumbling with the children, helping with their gymnastics and karate lessons. All three children took quickly to karate, and Elia was their biggest fan.

"I remember in 1988," Mary Kay says, "one young lady in our karate school was selected to represent the United States in an international tournament. My husband told my children that this was a great honor to be proud of. He sent her a telegram and brought flowers to the school. He was so excited."

In a lamentable twist, one year later, just months after Elia's death, both Lia and Christopher were selected to represent the United States in an international competition. In fact, in a span of 10 years, the Stratis children won numerous national championships and represented America in 10 international competitions. "He would have been so proud," Stratis says.

"I clung to the hope that he was on some other plane but it became more and more evident... that he wasn't coming home."

A successful businessman and devoted father, Elia also was a loyal son to the institution he credited with launching his success, Fairleigh Dickinson University. "He was so grateful for the education that was given to him. He wanted to give something back," Mary Kay says. Elia became the first alumnus appointed to the University's Board of Trustees and served as president of the Alumni Association. He also would frequently involve his family with the University, bringing the children to athletic contests and alumni events.

On business trips, Elia helped recruit new students to FDU, and he opened his home to international students. The Stratis family grew to include two students from South Africa, who had been living in undesirable conditions, and another student from Cyprus, whose father was killed in an industrial accident. "He so appreciated his educational experience that he tried to help give others the same opportunity he had."

When Time Stopped

On December 19, 1988, 43-year-old Elia Stratis left the United States for a quick business trip to Germany and the Netherlands. He was scheduled to return December 22, in plenty of time for the Stratis family holiday party. But he wrapped up business quickly and, without having the chance to notify his wife, decided to fly home a day earlier. With him was an insurance executive who grew up in Bergen County and worked for a client's firm. The two checked out of a hotel in Rotterdam, leaving behind a note, which said they were booked on Pan Am Flight 103 departing from London on December 21.

Still believing her husband wasn't due home for another day, Mary Kay Stratis was Christmas shopping with her mother when she heard on the car radio that a plane had gone down. "I remember thinking what a terrible thing but not dwelling on it because my husband was not supposed to be on that flight."

When she got home, news of the crash was on all the networks but she again didn't focus on the incident. A little after 3 p.m., her husband's secretary called and,

not having had access to any news that day, told Mary Kay that Elia was coming home a day early and that he was scheduled to catch a plane out of London.

Stratis was stunned but says she still wanted to believe her husband was not on that flight. "I clung to the hope that he was on some other plane but as the day progressed it became more and more evident that he probably was on the plane and that he wasn't coming home."

Moving On

Heartbroken and faced with raising three children, ages 13, 10 and 7, as well as taking care of her aging mother and brother, Stratis decided that, to the extent possible, life would go on as it had before. "This was such a big change, especially in the children's lives, I was determined to keep everything else the same."

So she continued to help them with their homework, take them to gymnastics and karate classes and volunteer at the schools. "My piece of mind came from knowing that my children were OK. If I saw they were coping, then I was able to cope better."

The children displayed similar concern for their mother. Stratis recalls them huddling together behind closed doors, trying not to worry their mother and discussing issues relating to their father's death. Sometimes, when they urgently needed to raise questions with mom, the older two would send Sonia to get an answer or float a topic. "She was the mouthpiece for the group."

Stratis' main message to her children always has been the same: don't dwell on the tragedy. "Early on, I would tell them, 'Your job is to be the best students you can be.' I've tried to instill in them the importance of cultivating their natural talents and using the gifts they possess."

Through the years, Stratis would try to "explain to them what I think their dad would have done in a certain situation or what he would have said." She adds, "I had known him for almost a quarter century, so I knew him well. I really felt any decisions I made, I made with the two of us in mind."

There were days Stratis felt like "my brain would explode with all that I was trying to process." She says she made it through by taking it not one day at a time, but "one-half day at a time." After school, of course, life was filled taking care of the children. While they were in school, she would tend to her mother and brother and also sort through the legal aspects of the case against Pan Am.

After the explosion, families of the victims filed lawsuits against the airline for its lax security. This suit brought together for the first time Stratis and a fellow Fairleigh Dickinson University graduate Mitch Baumeister, BA'66 (F-M). In 1988, after 16 years of practicing law, Baumeister founded his own law firm, Baumeister & Samuels, P.C., specializing, among other things, in aviation law. In addition to this case, Baumeister has represented plaintiffs and worked with cases relating to the Swissair Flight 111, TWA Flight 800 and Valu-Jet Flight 92 disasters. Another lawyer recommended him to Stratis, who says, "I didn't even know Mitch was an FDU graduate."

Stratis was deeply touched by Baumeister's devotion, which went beyond his routinely intense legal preparations. "When I first retained him, he said he wanted to come to my house to feel my husband's presence and to meet my children in order to get a sense of the loss in their lives. He actually sat in my children's room and talked with them about Elia. That was very special." Baumeister says his role isn't confined to legal issues, but includes "learning about the family and helping them as best I can."

In a three-month trial in 1992, Baumeister, who represented 21 families in the suit against Pan Am, and his fellow attorneys representing other families, successfully showed that Pan Am was "grossly negligent" and "failed to provide adequate security to prevent this disaster." Among other things, Baumeister said Pan Am had ignored bomb warnings and had violated regulations in allowing an unaccompanied bag on board the plane. The total compensation awarded to the families—between $450 and $500 million—was the largest amount of money ever awarded in a commercial aviation disaster.

Stratis remembers Pan Am "putting us through the ringer" with inquiries and questions, including medical statements to prove that Elia wasn't ill (the presumption was that an ill Elia would be worth less). Even the final verdict was not without grief, because on the same day the decision was announced, cancer claimed the life of Mary Kay Stratis' mother.

In the Fields

Lockerbie, a small village community in rural Southern Scotland, was plunged into the global spotlight by the destruction of the Boeing 747 jumbo jet. Over the years, many family members of the victims traveled to this scenic farmland setting where sheep graze and farmhouse lights flicker over endless rolling lands. Mary Kay Stratis was not one of the early visitors.

"As much as I was curious to go there and see what happened, I had three kids in a very vulnerable state. I was not about to tell them mommy was going on a plane." Four years later, Stratis felt the time was right to walk the fields where Pan Am 103 melted into the landscape. Older and more mature, her three children joined her on the journey.

"Like all of the families who went there, we definitely benefited from the experience," she says, "and that's a great tribute to the Scottish people who made sure we had every comfort and access to wherever we wanted to go."

For Stratis, that meant visiting a sheep farm where the aircraft's nose cone, and the portion of the plane where her husband was seated, landed. "The owner of this field took us right to the spot where this happened." Stratis remembers not talking very much with her children, standing amid silence, while trying to process the enormity of what had transpired. "Visiting the location where he was found, the town that was affected, somehow seemed to help. In a way, it made it tangible for me."

In Memory Of

Devoted so heartily to her children, it might have been easy for Mary Kay Stratis to lose herself in her mothering role and leave behind causes she and Elia treasured. She refused to let this happen. A dedicated volunteer, her activities have focused on helping others realize their educational goals. Continuing to reside in Montvale, she has been active with the Parent Faculty Association of Pascack Hills High School in Montvale and has served as its president. To honor Elia's ideals of self-improvement, good sportsmanship and academic excellence, she has established six scholarships (three for males and three for females) at the high school.

Stratis also has been involved in fund raising for the Association of Retarded Citizens, and her service at Westwood (N.J.) United Methodist Church has included positions as a church school teacher and youth group coordinator.

In addition, Stratis has maintained her husband's support for their alma mater and today is a member of the University's Board of Trustees. "Had Elia been here, he would still be playing a big role at the University."

> ## "I know some people are uncomfortable when I mention the bombing, but to forget... would be a show of apathy toward terrorism."

Elia's mark is indelibly stamped on the University he loved. Made possible through the support of Stratis, the University today offers the Elia G. Stratis Memorial Scholarship, which is awarded to an undergraduate accounting major and an incoming freshman on the soccer or track and field team. Thus far, 12 students have earned Stratis Scholarships. FDU also boasts tributes to Elia on both New Jersey campuses: the Elia G. Stratis Lounge in the George and Phyllis Rothman Center on the Teaneck-Hackensack Campus and the Elia G. Stratis Running Track in the Roberta Chiaviello Ferguson and Thomas G. Ferguson Recreation Center on the Florham-Madison Campus. (Stratis also has donated her collection of books about the Pan Am 103 case to the FDU library and another set to the Bergen County library system.)

For Stratis, these efforts are more than just a way to preserve the memory of Elia, they represent a way to keep his ideals alive. "If people see a plaque bearing his name, they might ask who was he and what he stood for."

When asked to speak about her husband, Stratis doesn't shy away from bringing up the cause of Elia's death. In fact, the plaque on the Ferguson Recreation Center track is dedicated to his memory as well as the other victims of Pan Am 103. "I know some people are uncomfortable when I mention the bombing, but to forget about it would be a show of apathy toward terrorism. I decided to put that wording on the plaque so people wouldn't be apathetic toward security or apathetic about punishing terrorism."

Bittersweet Triumphs

As Lia, Christopher and Sonia grew, Stratis says there was no shortage of stories about their father. "Because he was so active at Fairleigh, and because the family attended many University events, the kids heard about the wonderful things he did and the goals he had. That has helped them know what Elia was like and would have been like as they were growing up."

Still, loving words and fond recollections could not fill the void. "I know they've missed him terribly and often wondered how their teen years would have been with him here."

Their dad certainly would have smiled with each triumph. Lia has been married for nearly two years and, like her father, is an accountant. Christopher graduated from Carnegie Mellon University, Pittsburgh, Pa., in May and is working in information systems, and Sonia is studying fashion design at Baylor University, Waco, Texas.

Stratis is obviously proud of her children's achievements, but she says each celebration has been a little "bittersweet. All of the things that the children have accomplished have been fabulous, but the joy is always tempered somewhat because he's not there to see it, and they're missing his pat on the back."

United in Grief

While Stratis' focus was riveted on her family, others who lost loved ones on Pan Am 103 spent time organizing and demanding action. Their outcry was crucial in getting sanctions imposed against Libya, and their continued lobbying in Washington resulted in the Aviation Security Act, which enhanced security standards. As Baumeister says, "Pan Am 103 marked the beginning of family group associations that came together to support each other and lobby for changes."

The voice of the families also was heard when the Anti-Terrorism Bill, which gave Americans the right to sue directly nations that sponsor terrorism, was enacted in 1996. This cleared the way for the civil suit against Libya.

While Stratis has become friends with many of the family members, she hasn't been in the forefront of advocacy efforts. Still, she says, "I think what they have done has been wonderful. I admire and appreciate what they've accomplished."

The close bonds that have developed among family members were never more evident than during the recent trial. Alongside Stratis watching the proceedings in the Netherlands were about 60 members of the victims' families and overall more than 200 relatives attended parts of the trial. "It was good to be among the other family members," Stratis says, "and to discuss what we heard and our feelings. There were so many ups and downs, we were never sure which way the verdict would go."

Stratis especially remembers watching the accused and wondering what they were thinking as the prosecutor described the impact of the bombing and mentioned that more than 400 parents lost a son or a daughter, 46 parents lost their only child, 65 women were widowed, and 11 men lost their wives. "That was overwhelming to hear."

Whether the conviction of Megrahi will withstand appeal is unclear. Baumeister says a decision can be expected by the end of the year. In the meantime, the Bush Administration has promised to keep pressure on the Libyan government to acknowledge its complicity in the bombing. Stratis believes the sanctions need to continue against Libya. "I don't want them to soften on that stand."

Stratis also expects the U.S. government will continue to support the families of the victims, particularly in the civil suit against Libya. Baumeister is representing Stratis and 20 other families in that case before U.S. District Judge Thomas Platt in the Eastern District of New York. According to Baumeister, "The conviction of Megrahi helps the action we have pending since it's a public statement that Libya is responsible. Megrahi was convicted most importantly as an employee/agent of a Libyan government agency."

The question in the civil case, Baumeister says, "is whether the Libyan government will even defend itself. If it doesn't, we could win a default judgment, but it will probably be uncollectible."

Some, though, believe Libya might eventually be willing to pay damages to end the economic sanctions. Baumeister adds that he is confident their side can demonstrate that this was a state-sponsored act of terrorism, and added that many believe other nations also may have been involved, particularly Iran, which could have been looking for retribution following an American attack on an Iranian airliner. One motive commonly attributed to Libya is revenge for U.S. airstrikes in 1986 that killed 37 people. But the final answers to what really happened to Pan Am 103, and why, continue to be elusive.

In His Name

Today, Mary Kay Stratis is a different person from the wife who was waiting for her husband to come home for Christmas in 1988. She has developed a broader outlook

on the world and taken a much deeper interest in international issues. She acknowledges that she is much more cynical about the world, but adds that she has "really tried to curb the anger. I do not want to be an angry person. I just want justice to be done."

She also is quick to admonish those complaining about airport delays due to security measures such as examining passengers' bags. "Don't complain about such things, be glad for them."

On the inside, though, the essence of Mary Kay Stratis, what she shared with her husband, and what has helped her rebuild a life so radically altered, remains the same. "Whatever I have done and whatever I will do, I'm going to give everything I have. That's how Elia lived his life and that has been passed on to my children."

Mitch Baumeister has known Stratis for more than a decade now and continues to marvel at her resiliency. "She's a remarkable person whose warmth, love and courage continue to be an inspiration for all of us."

Stratis had her chance recently to return the tribute when she personally presented Baumeister with the FDU Alumni Association Elia G. Stratis Service Award for outstanding contributions to the University. Fittingly, the presentation took place during the rededication of the Stratis Lounge in the Rothman Center. "That was very special," Stratis says, "and Mitch has since said how much closer he feels to my husband by receiving that award."

Baumeister humbly denies being in "the same league with Elia" when it comes to serving others but says, "I'm truly honored to be mentioned in the same breath. I hope I can carry on his tradition."

Elia's influence has spread so far and wide that Stratis and Baumeister have a lot of company looking to continue his legacy. Last summer, Stratis traveled to South Africa to see two of the students who Elia took into their home. She's happy to report that they are both doing well and are now married. The younger man has a child with an unusual name for a South African. In tribute to the successful businessman who took desperate strangers into his home a continent away, who supported education above all pursuits, whose heart filled with love for his wife and children, whose light was untimely dimmed but whose spirit forever lives on, the child bears the name "Elia."

From the *FDU Magazine*, Summer 2001, pp. 20-25. © 2001 by the Office of Communications and Marketing, Fairleigh Dickinson University, Teaneck, NJ 07666. Reprinted by permission.

In the Campus Shadows, Women Are Stalkers as Well as the Stalked

New studies on college victim rates prompt debate

BY ANDREW BROWNSTEIN

T WICE.

They only kissed twice. To the other freshmen in the Central Michigan University dormitory, the relationship didn't look like much. Nothing that would explain the incessant calls that later came to the room and on the pager. The hang-ups. The watching through the peephole of the dorm-room door.

Police officers would call it a clear-cut case of stalking. What might seem unusual about this story, however, is that the victim was a man.

"I was scared," says Matt Owens, now a senior at Central Michigan majoring in communications. "I kept thinking: This girl is nuts. If that was a guy making countless phone calls and sitting outside the door, he'd be in big trouble."

A new study suggests such experiences are far more prevalent on college campuses than one might expect. The survey of 756 students at Rutgers University and the University of Pennsylvania found that, while women are still more likely to have been stalked, men constitute a surprising 42 percent of victims.

That compares with 22 percent in the most recent survey of the national population. Female stalkers are three times as likely to be found at the two colleges than in the population at large.

UNUSUAL DYNAMICS ON CAMPUSES

The man-bites-dog finding is one of several to emerge from a flurry of studies that point to the unusual dynamics of stalking on college campuses. Later this month, the National Institute of Justice will release results from the largest study of stalking on college campuses thus far. The random survey of more than 4,400 students—all women—found that more than 13 percent said they had been stalked in the past seven months, compared to the national figure of 8 percent.

It should be no surprise that stalking is more common on campuses. It is, in general, a crime against young people, the typical victim being between 18 and 29. If crime is about means, motive, and opportunity, college is the land of opportunity for stalkers.

"Stalking is all about knowing someone's routine," says Bonnie S. Fisher, associate professor of criminal justice at the University of Cincinnati and the principal investigator on the national institute's study. "On college campuses, you know where people live, when their classes are, and you don't have to be a rocket scientist to find their e-mail address. In many ways, they're the perfect targets."

The studies are likely to prompt debate on just what constitutes stalking, how men and women perceive fear, and how campuses should deal with what has become pervasive in dorm rooms and chat rooms alike.

The gender issue is bound to be the most controversial. Stalking is generally thought of as a crime against women. California passed the first anti-stalking law in the nation in 1990 in response to the murder of the actress Rebecca Schaeffer, who was shot to death by an obsessed fan who had stalked her for two years. The original thought was that stalking was a step to more violent crimes, whose perpetrators are overwhelmingly men. The National Institute of Justice found the notion of woman-as-stalking-victim so self-evident that it excluded men from its study.

The authors of the Rutgers survey are bluntly agnostic about what their findings on male victims mean. "We got zilch. We don't have a clue," says Shirley A. Smoyak, professor of planning and public policy at Rutgers and the lead author on that study.

Timothy Baker, adjunct professor of nursing at Penn and a collaborator on the study, has a theory—thus far, unproved—that he predicts will catch him "a lot of flak" within academe: "Women are coming into their own. As women take on the roles traditionally relegated to men, they inevitably take on some of the negative aspects as well." As usual, Mr. Baker suggests, colleges are seeing this trend before the general population.

STALKING IN THE GENERAL POPULATION AND AT 2 COLLEGES

The national information below comes from a 1998 random survey by the National Institute of Justice. Campus data come from a 2000 study of 756 students at the University of Pennsylvania, where participants were surveyed in a victimology class, and Rutgers University at New Brunswick, where they were surveyed randomly. Of those surveyed, 90 students, or 12 percent, said they had been stalked during their lifetimes.

General population	Two colleges
8% of women and 2% of men are stalked.	12% of students were stalked.
78% of stalking victims are women.	58% of victims were female and 42% were male.
87% of stalkers are male.	56% of stalkers were male and 43% were female.
On average, victims are 28 years old when the stalking begins.	On average, victims were 21 years old when the stalking began.
23% of female victims and 36% of males were stalked by strangers.	16% of male victims and 24% of female victims were stalked by strangers.
Half of stalking victims report the situation to the police.	Only 6 stalked students out of 90 reported the stalking to the police.
45% of victims receive overt threats.	Only 18% of victims received overt threats.
75% of victims are spied on or followed.	53% of victims were constantly followed.
The majority of victims are stalked by former intimate partners.	41% of victims were stalked by a classmate, 27% by an acquaintance, 26% by a former intimate partner, 20% by a stranger, 1% by a family member, and 6% reported other.
Stalking episodes average 1.8 years.	Most stalking episodes last less than one year.

The as-yet-unpublished Rutgers study still must be replicated. Some critics argue that two elite universities in the Northeast are not representative of college campuses as a whole. Furthermore, a good portion of the students surveyed came from what researchers call a "convenience sample," a class on victimology at Penn—making the results less than random.

AN EVEN SPLIT

Police officials and victim's advocates are divided in their reactions to the findings, but a surprising number say they're seeing the same, roughly even split between male and female victims in their work.

Judi King, chief of police at California State University at Fullerton, says the breakdown is "pretty much 50-50." Like many researchers, she suspects substantial underreporting by male victims due to sexist stereotypes—this time, against men. "They don't report it because they don't want to be seen as weak," she says. "It's the age-old idea that men are supposed to be able to take care of themselves."

Brian H. Spitzberg, a professor of communication at San Diego State University, finds "no gender differences" among college victims in his research on "obsessive relational intrusion," a term that encompasses stalking and more minor forms of

hounding, such as leaving unwanted gifts or making repeated telephone calls.

But he adds one important caveat: Women are far more likely to be terrorized by such incidents, due to what he calls "the creep factor."

"Our society still constructs a world that's more threatening to women," he says.

Take the story of Amber, a 29-year-old corporate-communications executive who consulted with Mr. Spitzberg in 1996 when she was getting her master's degree at San Diego State.

Amber, who did not want to reveal her last name, initially thought little of the notes she found on the windshield of her car. The words, written in a script too perfect to be a man's, she thought, clearly indicated someone who knew her movements. "I liked your hair today," read one. And another: "Did you enjoy debate class?"

At first, when a lost high-school acquaintance invited her out for coffee, she did not link his out-of-the-blue appearance with the strange notes. The meeting was pleasant, she says, until "he started saying strange things, like he forgave me for going out with my boyfriend."

Then came the obsessive phone calls to her apartment and her parents' house. One day after class, she went to the parking lot to find a funereal display of roses on the hood of her sports-utility vehicle—hun-

dreds of baby roses, red and pink, each intricately ribboned.

One night, after he followed her around the campus parking lot, she called the police. Their subsequent search of his apartment and car yielded enough to give anyone pause: two unlicensed handguns and a shrine of photos that showed he'd been watching her from afar for years.

Last year, Amber's three-year restraining order against her stalker expired. She still lives in fear. "This guy is so mentally unstable," she says. "I have no belief that he will leave me alone in the future."

It is tempting to contrast her situation with that of Mr. Owens, the Central Michigan student who said he was stalked. He had no problem giving his name to a reporter, and even being photographed. Amber, meanwhile, considered her situation so severe that upon graduation, she moved away from San Diego to escape her stalker. Only her family and a few friends have her current address.

It is experiences like Amber's that make Stephen M. Thompson wonder if the authors of the Rutgers study aren't trivializing the experiences of stalking victims. The fact is, men are bigger and stronger, says Mr. Thompson, sexual-assault-services coordinator at Central Michigan and author of *No More Fear*, a study of sexual violence and its victims. Put simply, women have more reason to be afraid.

"In my experience, men report because it's a damn nuisance," he says. "Women report out of a primal fear. I would debate with anybody that it's the same feeling."

He says the study's numbers showing that men make up 42 percent of stalking victims look "damned high"; only 15 percent of the stalking victims who report to his office are men.

DEBATING THE DEFINITIONS

The inevitable problem with any stalking research is the way the act is defined. In the decade since the first statute was passed in California, all of the other states and the federal government enacted their own stalking laws, with their own quirks and nuances. Most statutes use some form of a definition cited in the National Institute of Justice's study: "a repeated behavior that seemed obsessive and made the respondent afraid or concerned for her safety."

But the Rutgers and Penn researchers omitted the definition, instead asking respondents if they had been the object of a set of stalking-related behaviors, from being followed to receiving unwanted e-mail messages.

The results from the national study and the Rutgers research were nonetheless similar in many respects. The telephone topped both lists as the mode of choice for stalkers (it was used in 78 percent of cases, in both studies), with following being a distant second (42 percent in the national study and 53 percent in the Rutgers study). But without additional research to determine how fearful the subjects were, some critics say it is hard to know whether the male and female respondents in the Rutgers study were talking about the same thing.

The Rutgers researchers say they omitted the definition on purpose. The authors believe college students are largely ignorant of what the law says about stalking. To many students, stalkers are like O. J. Stalking victims? That's Letterman and Madonna, not me.

A STALKING POLICY

Such ignorance is one reason that George Mason University enacted a comprehensive stalking policy in 1999. It remains perhaps the only university policy in the country that spells out what stalking is and lists specific punishments for violators.

In a policy that goes further than many laws, George Mason defines activities occurring "on more than one occasion," including "non-consensual touching" and "threatening gestures," to be stalking. It says violators will be subject to disciplinary action and criminal prosecution. And it advises victims to "get caller I.D. if possible," change travel routes frequently, and keep a journal of stalking incidents. (The full policy can be found at the university's Web site (http://www.gmu.edu/facstaff/sexual/ffstalkingcode.html.)

Connie J. Kirkland, the coordinator of sexual-assault services at George Mason, urged the university to enact the policy when she realized that roughly a third of the students who came to her were stalking victims whose problems were unrelated to sexual assault. (Incidentally, she is not seeing higher number of stalking cases against men. She says that 95 percent of the cases she handles are reported by women.)

Another educational effort, the Love Me Not campaign, was unveiled by the Los Angeles district attorney's office last Valentine's Day. Given that the typical stalking victim is college age, the office decided to focus on students by training police officers at five local colleges and flooding campuses with billboards and bookmarks advertising a 24-hour hot line and an advice-filled Web site (http://www.lovemenot.org/). According to Scott Gordon, the deputy district attorney in charge of the city's stalking-and-threat team, more than 300 students have made stalking reports to the hot line since February.

Some colleges find that simply raising awareness goes a long way. "Frequently, stalkers are unaware that they are instilling fear or that they are breaking the law," says Ms. King, of California State at Fullerton. "We usually find that sitting them down in the station and talking to them is all we need to do."

Stalking on college campuses rarely turns violent. Ms. King says she has had only one such case in her year as chief. In the Rutgers study, 12 percent of the female victims and 3 percent of the males said their pursuers had become violent.

In the beginning, the prosecution of stalking was seen primarily as a deterrent to more-destructive actions down the road. Now, the focus is much more on the psychological toll of the act itself. That shift may be the best explanation for the larger number of men appearing as victims, Ms. King says.

"If you know someone is always watching you and won't stop, no matter how many times they are told, that causes fear," she says. "There doesn't have to be any touching. It's mostly a mental issue, and it's been my experience that men are affected much the same as women are."

College Women: How They Were Stalked

The figures are from a random phone survey of 4,446 female students at 223 colleges and universities in the United States. Of those called, 696, or 13 percent, said they had been stalked during a seven-month period in 1997.

Type of behavior	Percentage
Telephoned	78%
Waited outside or inside places	48
Watched from afar	44
Followed	42
Sent letters	31
E-mailed	25
Showed up uninvited	5
Sent gifts	3
Other	11

Note: The totals do not add to 100 percent because some stalking patterns involved more than one type of behavior.

SOURCE: NATIONAL INSTITUTE FOR JUSTICE, UNIVERSITY OF CINCINNATI

In Ms. King's view, it is the psychological instability of the stalker, more so than his or her size or power, that strikes fear in the victim.

In one recent case she handled, a lesbian student obsessed with a female faculty member followed the professor everywhere. She called her incessantly and waited at her apartment door in the morning. She made statements like: "If I can't have you, no one will."

The student is now finishing a two-year jail sentence for violating five restraining orders filed by the faculty member. "That professor is scared to death," Ms. King says. "She wonders all the time: What happens when she gets out?"

Stalking that involves a professor is actually quite rare, representing less than 1 percent of the cases in the national institute's study. The likeliest stalker is a boyfriend or ex-boyfriend (42 percent), followed by a classmate (25 percent) and an acquaintance (10.3 percent).

WHAT MAKES STALKERS TICK

From these studies and others, scholars are trying to determine what makes stalkers tick. A good deal of research shows that stalkers generally had trouble forming nurturing relationships early in childhood, particularly with their parents. Or as Ms. Smoyak of Rutgers likes to put it, "Some-

thing went wrong in attachment-land." That may be one reason stalkers feel rejection so intensely, why they create elaborate fantasies of their relationships to their victims, a neverworld that is often nourished in the anonymity of the Internet.

Ms. Smoyak is hoping to kindle the debate with future research—she is coordinating a national study to further examine the gender issue—and by holding the first conference on collegiate stalking at Rutgers in May. Among the topics: cyberstalking, the administrative response to the crime, and the effect of stalking on victims.

'SHE LOST A SEMESTER'

This last topic is a salient one for George Mason's Ms. Kirkland, who says she has helped several students withdraw from classes because of the disastrous effects of stalking in their lives. Just this fall, she says, she helped a female engineering student with a 4.0 grade-point average drop out for a semester after she faced relentless harassment from an ex-boyfriend.

"She lost her tuition," Ms. Kirkland says. "She lost a semester. And she has to explain it all to parents and her friends. In these cases, it is always the victim who loses."

Telling the Truth About Damned Lies and Statistics

By JOEL BEST

The dissertation prospectus began by quoting a statistic—a "grabber" meant to capture the reader's attention. The graduate student who wrote this prospectus undoubtedly wanted to seem scholarly to the professors who would read it; they would be supervising the proposed research. And what could be more scholarly than a nice, authoritative statistic, quoted from a professional journal in the student's field?

So the prospectus began with this (carefully footnoted) quotation: "Every year since 1950, the number of American children gunned down has doubled." I had been invited to serve on the student's dissertation committee. When I read the quotation, I assumed the student had made an error in copying it. I went to the library and looked up the article the student had cited. There, in the journal's 1995 volume, was exactly the same sentence: "Every year since 1950, the number of American children gunned down has doubled."

This quotation is my nomination for a dubious distinction: I think it may be the worst—that is, the most inaccurate—social statistic ever.

What makes this statistic so bad? Just for the sake of argument, let's assume that "the number of American children gunned down" in 1950 was one. If the number doubled each year, there must have been two children gunned down in 1951, four in 1952, eight in 1953, and so on. By 1960, the number would have been 1,024. By 1965, it would have been 32,768 (in 1965, the F.B.I. identified only 9,960 criminal homicides in the entire country, including adult as well as child victims). By 1970, the number would have passed one million; by 1980, one billion (more than four

times the total U.S. population in that year). Only three years later, in 1983, the number of American children gunned down would have been 8.6 billion (nearly twice the earth's population at the time). Another milestone would have been passed in 1987, when the number of gunned-down American children (137 billion) would have surpassed the best estimates for the total human population throughout history (110 billion). By 1995, when the article was published, the annual number of victims would have been over 35 trillion—a really big number, of a magnitude you rarely encounter outside economics or astronomy.

Thus my nomination: estimating the number of American child gunshot victims in 1995 at 35 trillion must be as far off—as hilariously, wildly wrong—as a social statistic can be. (If anyone spots a more inaccurate social statistic, I'd love to hear about it.)

Where did the article's author get this statistic? I wrote the author, who responded that the statistic came from the Children's Defense Fund, a well-known advocacy group for children. The C.D.F.'s *The State of America's Children Yearbook 1994* does state: "The number of American children killed each year by guns has doubled since 1950." Note the difference in the wording—the C.D.F. claimed there were twice as many deaths in 1994 as in 1950; the article's author reworded that claim and created a very different meaning.

It is worth examining the history of this statistic. It began with the C.D.F. noting that child gunshot deaths had doubled from 1950 to 1994. This is not quite as dramatic an increase as it might seem. Remember that the U.S. population also rose through-

out this period; in fact, it grew about 73 percent—or nearly double. Therefore, we might expect all sorts of things—including the number of child gunshot deaths—to increase, to nearly double, just because the population grew. Before we can decide whether twice as many deaths indicates that things are getting worse, we'd have to know more. The C.D.F. statistic raises other issues as well: Where did the statistic come from? Who counts child gunshot deaths, and how? What is meant by a "child" (some C.D.F. statistics about violence include everyone under age 25)? What is meant by "killed by guns" (gunshot-death statistics often include suicides and accidents, as well as homicides)? But people rarely ask questions of this sort when they encounter statistics. Most of the time, most people simply accept statistics without question.

Certainly, the article's author didn't ask many probing, critical questions about the C.D.F.'s claim. Impressed by the statistic, the author repeated it—well, meant to repeat it. Instead, by rewording the C.D.F.'s claim, the author created a mutant statistic, one garbled almost beyond recognition.

But people treat mutant statistics just as they do other statistics—that is, they usually accept even the most implausible claims without question. For example, the journal editor who accepted the author's article for publication did not bother to consider the implications of child victims doubling each year. And people repeat bad statistics: The graduate student copied the garbled statistic and inserted it into the dissertation prospectus. Who knows whether still other readers were impressed by the author's statistic and remembered it or repeated it? The article remains on the shelf in hundreds of libraries, available to anyone who needs a dramatic quote. The lesson should be clear: Bad statistics live on; they take on lives of their own.

Some statistics are born bad—they aren't much good from the start, because they are based on nothing more than guesses or dubious data. Other statistics mutate; they become bad after being mangled (as in the case of the author's creative rewording). Either way, bad statistics are potentially important: They can be used to stir up public outrage or fear; they can distort our understanding of our world; and they can lead us to make poor policy choices.

T HE NOTION that we need to watch out for bad statistics isn't new. We've all heard people say, "You can prove anything with statistics." The title of my book, *Damned Lies and Statistics*, comes from a famous aphorism (usually attributed to Mark Twain or Benjamin Disraeli): "There are three kinds of lies: lies, damned lies, and statistics." There is even a useful little book, still in print after more than 40 years, called *How to Lie With Statistics*.

We shouldn't ignore all statistics, or assume that every number is false. Some statistics are bad, but others are pretty good. And we need good statistics to talk sensibly about social problems.

Statistics, then, have a bad reputation. We suspect that statistics may be wrong, that people who use statistics may be "lying"—trying to manipulate us by using numbers to somehow distort the truth. Yet, at the same time, we need statistics; we depend upon them to summarize and clarify the nature of our complex society. This is particularly true when we talk about social problems. Debates about social problems routinely raise questions that demand statistical answers: Is the problem widespread? How many people—and which people—does it affect? Is it getting worse? What does it cost society? What will it cost to deal with it? Convincing answers to

such questions demand evidence, and that usually means numbers, measurements, statistics.

But can't you prove anything with statistics? It depends on what "prove" means. If we want to know, say, how many children are "gunned down" each year, we can't simply guess—pluck a number from thin air: 100, 1,000, 10,000, 35 trillion, whatever. Obviously, there's no reason to consider an arbitrary guess "proof" of anything. However, it might be possible for someone—using records kept by police departments or hospital emergency rooms or coroners—to keep track of children who have been shot; compiling careful, complete records might give us a fairly accurate idea of the number of gunned-down children. If that number seems accurate enough, we might consider it very strong evidence—or proof.

The solution to the problem of bad statistics is not to ignore all statistics, or to assume that every number is false. Some statistics are bad, but others are pretty good, and we need statistics—good statistics—to talk sensibly about social problems. The solution, then, is not to give up on statistics, but to become better judges of the numbers we encounter. We need to think critically about statistics—at least critically enough to suspect that the number of children gunned down hasn't been doubling each year since 1950.

A few years ago, the mathematician John Allen Paulos wrote *Innumeracy*, a short, readable book about "mathematical illiteracy." Too few people, he argued, are comfortable with basic mathematical principles, and this makes them poor judges of the numbers they encounter. No doubt this is one reason we have so many bad statistics. But there are other reasons, as well.

Social statistics describe society, but they are also products of our social arrangements. The people who bring social statistics to our attention have reasons for doing so; they inevitably want something, just as reporters and the other media figures who repeat and publicize statistics have their own goals. Statistics are tools, used for particular purposes. Thinking critically about statistics requires understanding their place in society.

While we may be more suspicious of statistics presented by people with whom we disagree—people who favor different political parties or have different beliefs—bad statistics are used to promote all sorts of causes. Bad statistics come from conservatives on the political right and liberals on the left, from wealthy corporations and

powerful government agencies, and from advocates of the poor and the powerless.

In order to interpret statistics, we need more than a checklist of common errors. We need a general approach, an orientation, a mind-set that we can use to think about new statistics that we encounter. We ought to approach statistics thoughtfully. This can be hard to do, precisely because so many people in our society treat statistics as fetishes. We might call this the mind-set of the Awestruck—the people who don't think critically, who act as though statistics have magical powers. The awestruck know they don't always understand the statistics they hear, but this doesn't bother them. After all, who can expect to understand magical numbers? The reverential fatalism of the awestruck is not thoughtful—it is a way of avoiding thought. We need a different approach.

One choice is to approach statistics critically. Being critical does not mean being negative or hostile—it is not cynicism. The critical approach statistics thoughtfully; they avoid the extremes of both naive acceptance and cynical rejection of the numbers they encounter. Instead, the critical attempt to evaluate numbers, to distinguish between good statistics and bad statistics.

The critical understand that, while some social statistics may be pretty good, they are never perfect. Every statistic is a way of summarizing complex information into relatively simple numbers. Inevitably, some information, some of the complexity, is lost whenever we use statistics. The critical recognize that this is an inevitable limitation of statistics. Moreover, they realize that every statistic is the product of choices—the choice between defining a category broadly or narrowly, the choice of one measurement over another, the choice of a sample. People choose definitions, measurements, and samples for all sorts of reasons: Perhaps they want to emphasize some aspect of a problem; perhaps it is easier or cheaper to gather data in a particular way—many considerations can come into play. Every statistic is a compromise among choices. This means that every definition—and every measurement and every sample—probably has limitations and can be criticized.

Being critical means more than simply pointing to the flaws in a statistic. Again, every statistic has flaws. The issue is whether a particular statistic's flaws are severe enough to damage its usefulness. Is the definition so broad that it encompasses too many false positives (or so narrow that it excludes too many false negatives)?

How would changing the definition alter the statistic? Similarly, how do the choices of measurements and samples affect the statistic? What would happen if different measures or samples were chosen? And how is the statistic used? Is it being interpreted appropriately, or has its meaning been mangled to create a mutant statistic? Are the comparisons that are being made appropriate, or are apples being confused with oranges? How do different choices produce the conflicting numbers found in stat wars? These are the sorts of questions the critical ask.

As a practical matter, it is virtually impossible for citizens in contemporary society to avoid statistics about social problems. Statistics arise in all sorts of ways, and in almost every case the people promoting statistics want to persuade us. Activists use statistics to convince us that social problems are serious and deserve our attention and concern. Charities use statistics to encourage donations. Politicians use statistics to persuade us that they understand society's problems and that they deserve our support. The media use statistics to make their reporting more dramatic, more convincing, more compelling. Corporations use statistics to promote and improve their products. Researchers use statistics to document their findings and support their conclusions. Those with whom we agree use statistics to reassure us that we're on the right side, while our opponents use statistics to try and convince us that we are wrong. Statistics are one of the standard types of evidence used by people in our society.

It is not possible simply to ignore statistics, to pretend they don't exist. That sort of head-in-the-sand approach would be too costly. Without statistics, we limit our ability to think thoughtfully about our society; without statistics, we have no accurate ways of judging how big a problem may be, whether it is getting worse, or how well the policies designed to address that problem actually work. And awestruck or naive attitudes toward statistics are no better than ignoring statistics; statistics have no magical properties, and it is foolish to assume that all statistics are equally valid. Nor is a cynical approach the answer; statistics are too widespread and too useful to be automatically discounted.

It would be nice to have a checklist, a set of items we could consider in evaluating any statistic. The list might detail potential problems with definitions, measurements, sampling, mutation, and so on. These are, in fact, common sorts of flaws found in many statistics, but they should not be considered a formal, complete checklist. It is probably impossible to produce a complete list of statistical flaws—no matter how long the list, there will be other possible problems that could affect statistics.

The goal is not to memorize a list, but to develop a thoughtful approach. Becoming critical about statistics requires being prepared to ask questions about numbers. When encountering a new statistic in, say, a news report, the critical try to assess it. What might be the sources for this number? How could one go about producing the figure? Who produced the number, and what interests might they have? What are the different ways key terms might have been defined, and which definitions have been chosen? How might the phenomena be measured, and which measurement choices have been made? What sort of sample was gathered, and how might that sample affect the result? Is the statistic being properly interpreted? Are comparisons being made, and if so, are the comparisons appropriate? Are there competing statistics? If so, what stakes do the opponents have in the issue, and how are those stakes likely to affect their use of statistics? And is it possible to figure out why the statistics seem to disagree, what the differences are in the ways the competing sides are using figures?

At first, this list of questions may seem overwhelming. How can an ordinary person—someone who reads a statistic in a magazine article or hears it on a news broadcast—determine the answers to such questions? Certainly news reports rarely give detailed information on the processes by which statistics are created. And few of us have time to drop everything and investigate the background of some new number we encounter. Being critical, it seems, involves an impossible amount of work.

In practice, however, the critical need not investigate the origin of every statistic. Rather, being critical means appreciating the inevitable limitations that affect all statistics, rather than being awestruck in the presence of numbers. It means not being too credulous, not accepting every statistic at face value. But it also means appreciating that statistics, while always imperfect, can be useful. Instead of automatically discounting every statistic, the critical reserve judgment. When confronted with an interesting number, they may try to learn more, to evaluate, to weigh the figure's strengths and weaknesses.

Of course, this critical approach need not—and should not—be limited to statistics. It ought to apply to all the evidence we encounter when we scan a news report, or listen to a speech—whenever we learn about social problems. Claims about social problems often feature dramatic, compelling examples; the critical might ask whether an example is likely to be a typical case or an extreme, exceptional instance. Claims about social problems often include quotations from different sources, and the critical might wonder why those sources have spoken and why they have been quoted: Do they have particular expertise? Do they stand to benefit if they influence others? Claims about social problems usually involve arguments about the problem's causes and potential solutions. The critical might ask whether these arguments are convincing. Are they logical? Does the proposed solution seem feasible and appropriate? And so on. Being critical—adopting a skeptical, analytical stance when confronted with claims—is an approach that goes far beyond simply dealing with statistics.

Statistics are not magical. Nor are they always true—or always false. Nor need they be incomprehensible. Adopting a critical approach offers an effective way of responding to the numbers we are sure to encounter. Being critical requires more thought, but failing to adopt a critical mind-set makes us powerless to evaluate what others tell us. When we fail to think critically, the statistics we hear might just as well be magical.

Joel Best is a professor of sociology and criminal justice at the University of Delaware. This essay is excerpted from Damned Lies and Statistics: Untangling Numbers From the Media, Politicians, and Activists, *just published by the University of California Press and reprinted by permission. Copyright © 2001 by the Regents of the University of California.*

Sexual Violence:
Current Challenges and Possible Responses

The following is a brief overview of sexual assault issues confronting the nation—drug-facilitated rape, campus sexual assault, male sexual assault, and police responses to victims—and current efforts to address these problems.

Drug-Facilitated Rape

Sexual assaults that are facilitated by the use of incapacitating drugs present a plethora of obstacles to investigators and many barriers to justice for victims. These drugs move quickly through the body and are not easily detectable. A victim must present at a facility shortly after being administered a drug (usually between four and seventy-two hours, depending on the substance) for testing to detect its presence. Because these drugs cause a victim to suffer a mild case of amnesia and to be drowsy for long periods of time, it is often too late to go to the hospital for effective testing once victims regain consciousness and their presence of mind.

Disseminating vital information to the public on the prevalence of drug-facilitated sexual assault and how to protect oneself is crucial to preventing victimization. Informing the public about what to do in the event that they or someone they know may have been drugged and raped will help victims find justice by preserving crucial evidence. For example, victims can save vomit or urine for drug testing. Unexplained bruises on hands and knees after a period of amnesia are indicative of falling down and may signal that a person was drugged. Youth, elderly, and underserved populations need to be included in the development of any successful awareness campaign.

In addition, many states have classified these drugs as dangerous and having no lawful purpose for possession. Lawmakers in many states have also successfully passed legislation to hold offenders accountable by increasing

penalties in rape cases in which drugs have been used to incapacitate a victim.

Campus Sexual Assault

Sexual assaults on college campuses are of increasing concern to the entire campus community, victim advocates and service providers, legislators, and the general public. Campuses are microcosms of the larger community, and many of the same issues and barriers to victim services and justice in society at large also exist in a campus setting. However, campuses also face distinct issues that call for specialized attention.

Sexual assault victims on campuses face several obstacles to having a forensic exam performed. One of those barriers is simply the location of the service provider. Many campus health centers do not perform forensic exams, forcing students to go to a facility off-campus where they may be required by state law to use their insurance. In most cases, students are still covered under their parents' insurance plans, so if a student does not wish to tell her parents about an assault, she may end up paying for the exam herself or not having one at all. Bringing Sexual Assault Nurse Examiners (SANE) programs to college campuses could improve students' access to these exams. With on-campus SANEs available, exams would be provided for under the college health plan and students could stay on campus to receive this important care. Bringing these services to campus communities will help reduce unnecessary stress associated with the justice process.

Campuses should evaluate their judicial procedures, clearly delineate the code of conduct and policies for handling infractions, and ensure that campus-wide awareness campaigns inform the campus community of their responsibilities under the code. Campaigns should also include prevention information, in particular for incoming freshmen. Because one in three females and one in five males has been sexually assaulted by their 18th birthday, campuses should be prepared to discuss repeat victimization with incoming students.

Bringing the community, including rape crisis centers, police, and prosecutors, to the table will help determine the most appropriate response to sexual assault allegations on campus and how to support victims. Institutions may want to consider applying for Violence Against Women Act STOP grants or Grants to Reduce Violent Crimes Against Women on Campus in order to form multidisciplinary teams to create a campus and community-wide response to victimization. Colleges and universities should consider creating statewide intercollegiate coalitions or consortia to facilitate information-sharing on sexual assault issues particular to the campus community.

Lastly, the incidence of sexual violence on campus remains unknown because the majority of numbers are coming from public safety offices and campus police reports, not counseling centers and victim services. We must find a way to discover the actual number of sexual assaults on campuses without jeopardizing confidentiality in order to truly address the issue and support victims.

Male Sexual Assault

Traditionally, sexual violence has existed in the public mind as a crime committed by a man against a woman. In fact, some state laws support that notion by the statutory definition of rape.

This idea permeates our society and serves to alienate, isolate, shame, and humiliate male survivors of sexual violence. Studies have shown that male victims experience many of the same lasting emotional consequences after sexual assault that women do. Male victims may have intense feelings of inadequacy and self-blame because they were not able to protect themselves from the attacker. Men raped by men may find their sexuality questioned, by themselves and by society. Male-on-male rapes are often gang-related; these attacks may result in severe injury to the victim. Male sexual assault victims may be humiliated and ignored by police and the justice system, and may not get the services they need.

Efforts to respond to male sexual assault victims must be fundamentally supported by a concerted public awareness campaign to reduce the stigma surrounding the crime, akin to those that have raised awareness of domestic violence. Society, and in turn, male victims, must be shown that rape is a crime of power and control, not sex, whether the victim is female or male. Public awareness campaigns should include information on resources and services for male victims. Victim service agencies should include information about male victims in all of their outreach events, materials, and literature. Even though sexual assault crisis centers offer services to men, this is not widely known, and male victims are less likely to search out these services than women.

Law enforcement officers need training on responding to male victims, in particular on how to recognize the reactions that are especial to them, so that victims are not alienated by officers' disbelief and insensitivity. Protocols for law enforcement and medical personnel are crucial to assure that male rape victims receive the medical care and legal attention they deserve. In addition, state laws that are not gender neutral should be amended to give all victims an equal opportunity at justice.

Police Response to Victims

A supportive and validating response from law enforcement can have a very positive impact on victims' short- and long-term emotional state, and can bolster a sense of fairness and justice in the system. Victims who experience a positive police response may be less likely to blame themselves, forego medical treatment, and drop charges, and more likely to cooperate with the investigation and prosecution of the case.

Reports from the field convey that in some jurisdictions, law enforcement responses to rape victims range from insensitive to disdainful. Insensitivity to victims from law enforcement is one issue that needs to be addressed. In some jurisdictions, it has been noted that police routinely dismiss sexual assault cases as unfounded—even without investigation. Victims report that they have been forced to take polygraph tests, and in some cases, have been charged with false reporting if police feel they are lying.

States should consider instituting mandatory training for law enforcement on the proper response to victims. Training should cover not only sensitive treatment of victims but also how to recognize the signs of Post-Traumatic Stress Disorder (PTSD) and the varying reactions victims' will present (*e.g.*, not making eye contact, forgetting details) and where to refer victims for counseling, support, and medical treatment. Victims should be made aware of their rights as crime victims, including how to receive information about their case and how to apply for compensation. Law enforcement should be informed of the variations in the dynamics among acquaintance rape, stranger rape, gang rape, same-sex rape, and incest.

Statistics show that the rate of false reporting for sexual assault is no higher than that of other crimes. Therefore, policies and protocols must prohibit polygraphing sexual assault victims. In addition, police department administrations must continuously review the handling of sexual assault cases to ensure that they are being treated as serious crimes, instead of being labeled as unfounded and not worthy of investigation. Polygraphing victims, charging them with false reporting, and shelving or dismissing cases all inhibit victims from coming forward and lead to a lack of trust in the justice system, not only by victims, but by the community as a whole. Sexual assault victims deserve to be believed and trusted just as other victims of crime are.

Communities have been successfully addressing many of the aforementioned issues by creating Sexual Assault Response Teams (SARTs)—a collaboration between sexual assault nurse examiners, law enforcement, and patient/victim advocates to improve the response to sexual assault victims. Where SARTs have been developed, response time by police, nurses, and advocates have been reduced, as well as victims' length of stay in the hospital. SARTs have improved evidence collection and documentation. This coordination of interagency services should be replicated across the country. Advocates may want to consider applying for federal grants, such as Grants to Reduce Violent Crimes Against Women (STOP grants) to support the formation of SARTS in their communities.

Statute of Limitations

Recently, lawmakers have expanded the list of crimes for which DNA samples are collected from convicts. These criminals' DNA profiles are entered into many state databanks and the national electronic database known as CODIS. Investigators can use these databases to search the pool of suspects for a match to forensic crime scene evidence. Recent improvements in the collection and evaluation of DNA evidence, including the speed at which results are available, are encouraging investigators to revisit criminal cases that previously had no potential suspects. As state labs work on reducing the backlog of forensic evidence they hold, new leads for cold cases may surface.

However, in many states, the prosecution of these cases may be inhibited by the running of the statute of limitations. Regrettably, in some cases, even though a perpetrator may be identified through CODIS, charges may not be brought because the statute of limitations has expired.

One creative way that prosecutors have circumvented the statute of limitations issue is by using the specific DNA makeup of an unknown perpetrator to file a "John Doe" indictment. This indictment allows the case to remain active because a specific perpetrator has been identified, just as is done with a perpetrator's name or fingerprints. Granting prosecutors the ability to issue these warrants, in particular in states in which a DNA evidence backlog exists, would give hope to victims whose offenders have been identified only by DNA profile. States should also consider eliminating the statute of limitations for sexual assault. Doing so would remove one barrier that sexual assault victims face in their quest for justice.

While our country currently faces many challenges and obstacles to eradicating sexual assault and securing justice and services for victims, there are many positive advancements to report. States' movement to eliminate the statute of limitations for sexual assault, improvements in DNA-evidence analysis, and the increase in public awareness campaigns have bolstered the anti-sexual assault movement. Thanks in part to the federal funding provided by the Violence Against Women Act of 1994, model programs and unprecedented multidisciplinary teams have been created. The duplication of these efforts across the country will continue to improve the treatment of rape victims and, in turn, will have a significant impact on the elimination of sexual assault.

If you would like more information on any of the topics covered here, or are interested in pursuing legislation, call the National Center's public policy department at 703-276-2880 or e-mail ncvc_public_policy_dept.@ncvc.org.

From the *Victim Policy Pipeline,* Spring 2001, pp. 16-19. © 2001 by the National Center for Victims of Crime. Reprinted by permission of the author, Susan Smith Howley.

A LEN interview with
Susan Herman, Director of the National Center for Victims of Crime

"Over the last few years, we've seen a lot of creative problem-solving [by police]. I don't think, though, that we're seeing a lot of real, genuine partnering, particularly where victims are concerned."

LAW ENFORCEMENT NEWS: Since the late 1970s, the crime victims movement has been steadily picking up steam, with victims seeking financial and legal assistance, restitution, consultation with prosecutors regarding plea bargains, input in parole hearings and notification when offenders were released. Generally speaking, have their needs been met?

HERMAN: Over the last 30 years we've seen an enormous amount to progress in both the legal rights strand and the social services strand of the victims movement. Your question really seems to go to the legal rights stand. We now have legal rights in the form of statutes of constitutional amendments in all 50 states. We have state constitutional amendments guaranteeing victims various rights in 32 states, but every state in the union has a variety of statutes. Many of the things that you listed—the right to be informed of critical proceedings, the right to be present, the right to be heard at critical stages of the criminal justice process—these are all laws that are on the books. And from a recent study that we conducted, we know that in some states where there are stronger protections for victims, victims are more satisfied. They do feel more a part of the process, they do feel more respected and they do feel that they've been included.

We also know, though, that even in states that have stronger protections, these rights are frequently not enforced. Victims don't know they have the rights; they're not given notice about them; and when they try to take advantage of these rights, they're often not permitted to by various criminal justice officials. In many states they have no enforcement mechanisms, so for some, these are hollow rights.

LEN: Why do you think this is the case? One would like to think it's not the victim's fault....

HERMAN: I think in many cases this is just something that people are not focusing on. I don't think in large part this is a malicious or conscious effort to exclude victims;

it's something that falls through the cracks, and there isn't enough monitoring or enforcement to make sure that it's happening. For instance, police departments are supposed to be handing out cards or pamphlets that inform victims of their rights, and we know that in many cases this just isn't happening.

There's very little recourse for a victim if, for instance, they were not consulted prior to a plea agreement; there's not much that victim can do. We don't have an enforcement mechanism that says that the victim's right was violated, so turn back the clock and have another sentencing hearing. Now that's partly because of where victims' rights are. In some places it's just executive law, in some cases it's by state statute, in still others it's a state constitutional amendment. But there's nothing in the U.S. Constitution. So there's a sense that while these rights have proliferated—we now afford victims much more opportunity to participate in the process—there's also a sense that we're saying they don't really rise to the level where it's a fundamental right. And that's critical.

LEN: Apparently you believe strongly that something should be done at the Federal level.

HERMAN: We do, but we think it must include an ability to enforce the rights. It's not enough to say that it's critical that victims have notice or are present or can be heard; they also have to have an opportunity to enforce those rights.

Double indemnity

LEN: Victims often complain that they feel doubly victimized: by the criminal and by the criminal justice system. For example, in giving a statement to police they are sometimes made to feel like they're being interrogated....

HERMAN: I think victims often feel that they are treated as a piece of evidence, helpful only when they help prove the prosecution's case and when they help a police officer find the bad guy. But they often feel disrespected and ignored and that their interests and concerns are irrelevant. I should say that in the survey we did, part of what we asked victims was how satisfied they were with various parts of the criminal justice system. And the part they are the most satisfied with is law enforcement. So while they may feel that the system as a whole is disrespectful and treats them poorly, it's very significant that the performance of the law enforcement officer, who is often the first contact with the victim, was rated highly. I think a lot of time has been spent over the last 10 years providing officers with sensitivity training, helping officers understand that it's better for everyone if they treat victims with respect. We asked victims, for instance, whether they felt that officers tried to be polite, whether they seemed to care about what happened, whether they showed interest in victims feelings, whether they gave them a chance to talk about what happened, whether they seemed interested in catching the offender, and whether they tried to gather all of the evidence necessary. We asked similar questions about other parts of the system. Law enforcement came out very well.

LEN: If the police fared well in this survey, what about the other components of the system? For example, how did prosecutors do?

HERMAN: Prosecutors didn't do quite as well, although the prosecutors in states that had stronger protections for victims did better.

LEN: And what about corrections?

HERMAN: Corrections keeps going down. It's only relatively recently that corrections departments have understood that crime victims are as much clients of theirs as the people in the prisons. They now are starting to realize that it's important, and in some states mandated, that victims be told when an offender is going to be released or transferred to another institution or have a parole hearing. Those are all things the victims care an awful lot about and want timely notice of. And when they don't get it, yes, they feel that they have been poorly treated by the system.

LEN: A growing number of states are now using automated victim-notification systems. How reliable are these systems?

HERMAN: I think that like many automated systems, they function as well as they're programmed. If they have accurate information, they can do a thorough job, and I think they hold enormous potential for victims having access to the kind of information they need. I think every state and every jurisdiction, even the smaller jurisdictions, should look at automated notification systems, and they should look at ones where the information that goes into it is driven by the victims, where they give their own

information to the system. Then if they move they're more likely to update it and it's much more likely to be accurate. They're more likely to seek out information and how it works and understand it before they need to rely on it heavily. If you rely on others giving information about the victim, it's less likely that the directions for how to use the system will be really understood.

Parallel lines

LEN: In a recent speech you talked about dealing with victims' rights in a way that roots them in a new vision of justice. Could you describe that vision?

HERMAN: I believe that we have understandably and appropriately focused an enormous amount of attention trying to have the victim's role in the criminal justice system be as useful and as valuable as possible. But at the most basic, we are tinkering with a system that is about offenders. It's the state first trying to decide whether this accused actually committed the crime, and then it's about the state saying, "You violated our laws, and this is what's going to happen to you." It's not about victims trying to rebuild their lives. I do think they need to participate and can play a critical role in the criminal justice system, but I also think it's time for society to make a similar statement to crime victims, which is, "What happened to you was wrong, and we as a society are going to help you rebuild your life."

I'm talking about a communal response to victims just as we have a communal response to offenders. It's saying that we will marshal all of our resources, all of the government agencies that we have, to help individual victims in the ways they need to be helped to get back on track and rebuild their lives. That means counseling, that means medical care, that sometimes means child care or employment training and counseling, because crime victims often need to find other vocations because they can't go back to the job they had. Sometimes it means being able to say that if you need to move because you can't go back to your old house or neighborhood, we will give you priority help find you another place to live.

We call this the search for parallel justice because we think it's trying to find a path for justice for victims, not just finding justice for offenders. This doesn't in any way say that we can't continue with the criminal justice system, with community justice and restorative justice efforts. Those are good as far as they go, but they don't go far enough in addressing the needs of victims.

LEN: I'd like to explore the idea of "parallel justice" a little further....

HERMAN: I think it's always important to remember that only one out of three victims ever report crimes, and only 20 percent of those cases result in arrest. So if you think about what opportunities the crime system has to provide any relief or justice for victims, you're talking about a very small percentage of crime victims in this country. That's why we need to think about a system that helps all crime victims who are suffering trauma, suffering losses of money, property, jobs, mental health, academic achievement, all of that. We need to find a way to help them, and not rely on a criminal justice system that's not designed for them anyway.

LEN: Are you getting support for your idea?

HERMAN: I am excited that whenever I speak about parallel justice, I see real, instant acceptance of the idea, and a lot of curiosity about where do we go from here. My hope is that as we gather people who are interested in this concept, we'll be able to think through what it would mean to operationalize it.

LEN: Do you have a model in mind?

HERMAN: Well, at the outset, we're thinking about a system where a victim of crime could come to a government agency, say what happened and what losses were sustained and what their needs are, and then that entity could pull together all of the resources that currently exist, like victim's compensation, victim's services, medical care and so forth, and figure out where the gaps are. Over time you'd soon see that you need to be helping victims with housing and relocation. You need to be helping victims with drug treatment because a battered woman who is also a drug abuser has a hard time getting into a battered women's shelter. You need to advocate for women to INS if their status is in jeopardy because their batterer is their husband. It's a combination of advocacy and marshaling existing resources and then filling in the gaps. It means saying; "This is one-stop shopping; we're going to make it convenient for you. We're going to bend over backwards to do what you need."

'Police officers are still so used to not seeing violence between inmates as criminal behavior, so we must take more steps to affirmatively seek arrests.'

Typically, victim services in this country are either system-based—they're housed within a criminal justice agency like the police department or the prosecutor's office or the courts—or they're entirely community-based and have no government authority. I think that the parallel justice system that we need to create needs to have government authority, so I see it as a municipal function. There's a terrific victims' service center in Jacksonville, Fla., that is a municipal agency that tries to coordinate various government functions; it's actually a building that's entirely devoted to crime victims and their issues. But in most areas in the country, you either have a sys-

tem-based advocacy or community-based services, and not much else. There is no total case management, and there is also no sense that this is part of what justice means for victims.

Medical attention

LEN: How cooperative is the medical community when it comes to victims—not only treating them, but also in reporting cases of abuse and so forth? In New York, for example, it's pretty well known that if you go to the hospital with a gunshot wound, it's going to be reported to the police, but what about other kinds of assaults?

HERMAN: You know that because that's the law. They're mandated to report a gunshot wound, and they're not mandated to report domestic violence. Then again, they're also mandated to report child abuse. Over the years we've created laws that mandate reporting for different kinds of abuse or crime by different people, and each one of these has been hotly debated and enacted one at a time. For example, there's great debate about whether elder abuse should be something that is mandated to be reported, the same as child abuse is. There's a great debate about whether domestic violence should be mandated. Right now neither is.

LEN: Should they, in your opinion?

HERMAN: In my opinion, someone who, at minimum, does not have the capacity to report to the system, in that instance there should be mandatory reporting. Or in the case of something that is so vile and is so criminal as a gunshot wound is, yes, there should be mandatory reporting. With domestic violence, at this point, I would say no. We're at a point where we have developed enough cooperation between medical agencies, victim service agencies, domestic violence shelters, social service systems and enough public consciousness, particularly over the last five years, about the availability of services that it would be hard right now to say that there should be mandatory reporting.

LEN: How about problems regarding the treatment of victims, where medical exigencies can sometimes get in the way of the investigative needs of police?

HERMAN: The doctors and nurses in the emergency room only see a suicide attempt, or only see a broken arm, or only see lots of black and blue marks, and don't recognize it as domestic violence—particularly if they don't track people who come to a emergency room frequently, and realize that you've seen this same woman over and over in the last few months. Then you have an identification problem, and I think you're not practicing medicine well because you're not fully understanding the problem. It's the same in other areas. You see a gunshot wound, and you know it's a gunshot wound, but are you also aware that perhaps it involves a gang? Perhaps it involves enough intimidation so that the teenager is too scared to leave the house, or too scared to go to school, or is risking further violence. I think that's part of how people in an emergency room need to look at the cases in front of them.

LEN: Their counter-argument might be: "We don't have time for this, people are coming in with real serious problems, and you want us to sit here and do all this analysis?"

HERMAN: Yes, we know. But research tells us that a gunshot victim who is released from the hospital has a far greater chance of being shot again than anyone else, and probably has a greater chance than being killed. We have wonderful programs developed in the Washington state where doctors are counseling patients about what they need to do or what they need to think about in their life so they don't show up in the emergency room again with a gunshot wound.

To arrest, or not to arrest

LEN: With respect to domestic violence, one aspect of the problem that remains an ongoing topic for debate is the question of mandatory arrest, with some new research suggesting that, for example, if you arrest an abuser who is unemployed, it could result in more, not less, recidivism. With that in mind, how do you think police departments should proceed when it comes to arresting domestic violence offenders?

HERMAN: I think police departments now are looking very hard now at primary aggressor policies, and they're trying to come up with very hard-to-design but critical training as to how to recognize the primary aggressor. Keeping in mind, then, the problem of knowing who that person is, I think mandatory and pro-arrest policies are still appropriate.

I think of mandatory and pro-arrest policies almost as an affirmative action policy; police officers are still so used to not seeing violence between intimates as criminal behavior, so we must take more steps to affirmatively seek arrests. I'm not sure we will always need that, but we do now because the tendency is still not to take it seriously. I think stalking is now where domestic violence was 10 years ago. There are still many law-enforcement agencies around the country that don't know their state has created an anti-stalking law, that stalking has been criminalized. They don't know what behaviors constitute stalking. They don't understand how lethal stalking can be, so it's not taken seriously. Every day there are police officers who will say, "Well, there's nothing I can do about it until he actually lays a hand on you, or until he actually does something harmful to hurt you. Someone just following you or making a lot of phone calls, or send-

ing you threatening e-mail actually hasn't done anything." Well, this is stalking behavior that's criminal, and there's plenty that can be done. It's where I think we were with domestic violence 10 years ago, where people felt it's a private matter between intimates and there's nothing we can do about it anyway; so it doesn't belong in the criminal justice system. Well, the state has said otherwise; it does belong in the criminal justice system. The same holds true for stalking. It's the new arena in which we need to help victims understand how dangerous it can be, how critical early reporting is, how to recognize stalking behavior, and why it's important to act on it. And we need to help criminal justice officials understand what role they can play.

LEN: Reading between the lines of the follow-up study that suggested that arresting the offender has a different impact depending on the offender's employment status, one gets the sense that researchers are really saying that police should try to make an effort to find out if the offender is employed or unemployed, and then exercise discretion accordingly. Doesn't that fly in the face of the notion of equal protection under the law?

HERMAN: I would think it would. I think, though, that it also flies in the face of either pro-arrest or mandatory arrest policies, which is what the country has been moving toward. Mandatory arrest is if you have probable cause, you have to; you shall arrest. Pro-arrest policies are saying, ought to, except, for instance, in New York if the woman says don't. Not every state is like that. It's mandatory if it's a violation of an order of protection, mandatory if it's a felony, mandatory if it's a misdemeanor unless the woman says no, don't.

In some pro-arrest policies, it's basically saying you shall make an arrest unless you have a good reason not too, and you feel that there would be increased danger if you did make an arrest. There's a discretion that's there, but it's encouraging an officer to make an arrest. There's a range of options for departments. But all departments, whatever their arrangements are, are struggling with trying to identify the primary aggressor and add that to the policy so that you're not making joint arrests all the time; you're not arresting both parties.

LEN: Under a recent Federal law, the Lautenberg Amendment, anyone who has ever had a misdemeanor arrest for domestic violence is prohibited from carrying a firearm—including police officers. How do you feel about that particular clause of the gun bill?

HERMAN: I think it sent a very important message to batterers, whether they're uniformed or non-uniformed. It sent a very important message that domestic violence is taken seriously, and that you shouldn't have that kind of professional responsibility if this arrest is in your life.

What's in a name?

LEN: You've mentioned previously that New York is the only state that doesn't specifically define a crime called "stalking"?

HERMAN: That's true. New York criminalizes stalking *behavior*. There's harassment and there's aggravated harassment, so the behavior is criminal, but New York is the only state that doesn't actually use the term "stalking." So it becomes very difficult to educate people about what we're talking about and what they can do about it. Sometimes the naming of it is critical. [*Editor's Note: On Nov. 22, after this interview had been conducted, New York Gov. George Pataki signed legislation creating the new offense of stalking. The offense can be a felony or a misdemeanor, depending on severity.*]

I think there's a lack of understanding about what stalking is and how dangerous it can be. You hear stories about the terror that people feel when they're afraid for their lives, afraid to leave their homes, afraid to walk down the street because they're being followed, because somebody's left a dead animal in their driveway, because somebody's left them disgusting and scary e-mails over and over again. Then after all that, after someone has maybe moved away and tried to hide her location, the stalker might send them flowers to show them they know where they live. Well, if you call the police and say, "I want you to arrest this guy because he sent me flowers," they don't understand unless they really "get" stalking, how it's just part of a pattern of behavior of terrorizing this person. We have a situation now in America where one out of every 12 women has experienced stalking at some time in their lives.

LEN: And who are these stalkers?

HERMAN: In about 60 percent of the cases, it's domestic-violence related. Most domestic violence cases that we see have some elements of stalking in them, but only 60 percent of all stalking cases are domestic-violence related.

LEN: Even if a state has a stalking law on the books, and police and communities have been very well trained to identify the seriousness of it and the patterns of behavior that come with this, what can be done to change the behavior of offenders, if anything?

HERMAN: Well, there's everything from batterers' groups that can be adapted to deal with stalkers to electronic monitoring of stalkers, which in many cases should go on for years and years so that a victim can always have the ability to know when someone is close. There are all kinds of programs that victims are taking advantage of, but these are extremely scary and extremely dangerous situations. It really comes down to education and talking about violence. People need to really understand what af-fection and love and relationships are all about, and we don't do a very good job in our society helping people understand how to have healthy relationships.

> **'30 to 35 million Americans become victims of crime every year, and they rarely emerge unscathed by the experience. We don't have enough empathy or compassion yet to reach out and help these people rebuild their lives.'**

Keeping it to themselves

LEN: You mentioned so many crimes going unreported. Why do you think that is?

HERMAN: A combination of people having had a bad personal experience, so they're afraid to go into the criminal justice system because no one will care about it, or they've already been discouraged: they reported something in the past and nothing happened; nobody was found. Only 20 percent of the cases that are reported result in arrest, so that certainly discourages reporting. With certain kinds of crimes, people are told by police officers, "Don't bother reporting, nothing's going to happen." On a more profound level, in many cases people don't see how putting their case and their situation through the criminal justice system is going to help them. Because, in fact, the system is about what happened to the offender; it's not about what happen to the victim. Even if victims have maximal opportunities to participate in the criminal justice system, if they have all the rights we'd like them to have, and they're implemented and they're enforced, I believe that on some level they will still be disappointed that the system is not about them.

LEN: One often gets the feeling that society blames the victim, and sometimes the victims blame themselves—for instance, when you hear people say, "Well, why was she jogging at that end of the park?" or, "Why did he flash around a wad of bills?" How does that kind of perspective affect policies concerning victims rights?

HERMAN: We run up against this frequently. I think the word 'victim' has become trivialized, and has almost become negative word in our language. People don't like the word victim and don't like victims. It ranges from, "It's their fault," to "Why can't they get over it," to "They're exaggerating." I think this is due to several reasons. I think we as a country, through our media and through our schools and various other institutions, have not helped people understand the impact of crime on individuals, on families, on neighborhoods and on our country as a whole. We focus on the offender and the incident. We also tend to put up shields and pretend that it's somebody's fault when crime happens, so that we can pretend that it will never happen to us. If it's completely your responsibility, you can pretend that you can control it and it will never happen to you. Well, we have 30 to 35 million Americans who become victims of crime every year, and they rarely emerge unscathed by the experience. We don't have enough empathy or compassion yet to reach out and help those people rebuild their lives.

Turning pain into activism

LEN: That many millions represents a very large constituency—one that, if mobilized, could probably accomplish some very big things. Is it difficult to get crime victims to mobilize for action?

HERMAN: There are many people who have come up with incredibly constructive ways to help the system—notification systems, publications that educate victims, advocating for laws that provide more opportunity to participate in the criminal justice system. There are all kinds of victim advocates who have turned their pain into activism and tried to promote a more compassionate societal response. I think victims deal with the process of coping with their trauma and their victimization differently. Some turn to activism, some turn to helping other victims, some take whatever steps they need to take to put their lives back together.

LEN: Does your agency provide a kind of switching post for these organizations? What sort of coordinating role do you play?

HERMAN: One of the services that we offer is an 800-line, 1-800-FYI-CALL, which any individual can call from around the country to find out the location of the nearest most appropriate service. We have a data base of victim services around the country, so that if you need a battered woman's shelter, or you need a victim advocate to talk to a police department, or if you want to hook up with an advocacy organization that's trying to accomplish what you'd like to accomplish as a result of your victimization, we can give you the names of places around the country to talk to. If there is no local victim advocate, or there is no local victim counselor, we step in and do what we can through telephone and e-mail and provide supportive counseling and advocacy to crime victims.

LEN: Do you also do your own lobbying or advocacy, basically trying to get legislators to pay attention?

HERMAN: We have worked on drafting model legislation, we comment on legislation, we provide testimony on the Hill, we devote a lot of time to developing public policies that will help bring resources to victims and secure and protect their rights. We recently launched something called the National Crime Victim Bar Association,

which is an organization that helps promote civil litigation on behalf of crime victims, so that attorneys who would like to help crime victims can receive our publications and help them direct this area of specialization. We have a data base of civil litigation involving crime victims so we can readily jump-start research for attorneys around the country, and we also refer victims to attorneys in their area who will represent them. And that's one we're excited about.

> 'We need to understand how to reach out and serve people from different cultures as well as different neighborhoods, not try and write them off and say that there is no trauma, there is no way to help them.'

LEN: Do you have any projects or anything going on with various crime prevention organizations? After all, one could readily see a connection—to reduce the number of victims, one should prevent crime in the first place....

HERMAN: We work with various crime prevention organizations, but the focus of our work is to forge a national commitment to help victims rebuild their lives, and we focus on individual families and communities. To the extent that people are working with crime victims and their core issues, we often find ways to collaborate, and we enjoy doing that.

Payback time

LEN: How does the compensation of victims typically work? With all 50 states having some type of compensation agency, what are their commonalities and their differences?

HERMAN: One thing they have in common is that they all deal with violent crime. Nonviolent crime or economic crime is excluded in terms of financial compensation. So if you suffered a devastating loss of your life savings, you can't go to victims' comp to help you. But if you had your pocketbook stolen and you were knocked down to the ground, you can go to victims' comp to get some of that money returned. Victims' comp is thought of as the place to go as a last resort, the agency of last resort. So if you have health insurance or other resources that can help you, you have to go there first. States vary as to how much money they give out. The average across the country is about $2,500. There are some states that give out all of the money they have and need more, and many other states that don't give out the amount that they have.

LEN: We've reported on some of these states that have a kind of victims' comp jackpot sitting there, and you have to wonder why.

HERMAN: I think part of the reason why is that victims don't know it's there and haven't been helped to go through all the bureaucratic hurdles you have to go through to get that money. Every victim ought to have a counselor and a victim advocate who can help them with the process and can help them get on with their life. We know that in most of the country that's not the case. And in most of the country it's a system-based person that you're going to see, which means probably there's already been an arrest.

Our goal would be that everyone should know that this help is available—we don't think that most crime victims even know that this is available—and that the payment should be as speedy as possible, between 10 and 90 days. In many cases this can take six months to a year.

LEN: Can you point to any model systems in this area?

HERMAN: When I was in Australia recently, I was fascinated to see an issue that was being hotly debated in the press, as well as at the Restoration of Victims Conference I attended. The issue in the State of Victoria, in Australia, was whether they should return to the system that they had two years ago where every crime victim, regardless of whether the perpetrator was arrested or convicted, every victim appeared before a tribunal and described the crime that they had experienced. If the tribunal believed that the person was in fact a victim of a crime, the victim received a flat payment from the state, essentially as compensation for pain and suffering. So if you were an assault victim, you got, say, $5,000; if you were a survivor of a homicide victim, you might get $20,000, and a burglary victim perhaps $2,500. The proponents of this system say that this was a way for all victims to feel that the state was saying, "What happened to you was wrong, and we're going to do what we can to help you, and here's some money." In addition to that flat payment, they also received specific payment for specific losses that they suffered. So if their property was damaged in some way, or they lost work, they were compensated for that.

What they had moved to was a system where they reimbursed you for the losses that you suffered, and instead of the flat payment that you got because of the crime, they said, "Tell us what you need to rebuild your life and to recover, and we will give you the specific amount of money for that." So if you need to move to get away from the neighborhood where the crime occurred, or if you need to get job training because you lost your job and you're disabled, or if you need to have a family member move in with you because you're too afraid to live in your home alone, you'd be paid for those expenses.

I found this a fascinating debate because, of course, we do neither of these things. We only compensate people for the specific losses— property damage, lost work, medical expenses if they can't be covered elsewhere. We don't help people rebuild their lives, and we don't say the state owes you a certain amount of money because there's been a violation of our criminal law. So we don't do either of those things. It was an eye-opening experience.

LEN: Is the victim expected to know that he or she has this entitlement?

HERMAN: The state there also provides victim advocates through a state system of information and referral. Every crime victim is also entitled to 10 free therapy sessions with a licensed psychologist, and they have victim advocates all over, who'll help you do this sort of planning.

I think we have a lot to learn looking at these two Australian models. Both of them are examples of a more compassionate societal response, of society reaching out and helping victims far more than we are here. I think it's an invitation for us to think through which way do we want to go and why.

Can we talk?

LEN: The notion of "restorative" justice often goes hand in hand with what you're describing as parallel justice. Do you think that such a process affords victims more satisfaction than the regular criminal justice system would?

HERMAN: Restorative justice to me involves trying to restore the relationship and address the harms that have been created by the criminal act. Typically, it involves an offender and a victim in dialogue, sometimes with a community representative on hand in a sort of triangular conversation. This dialogue can be post-sentencing, to try and create more understanding. Perhaps, there's an apology; perhaps there's restitution, or some kind of relationship building. Or it can be post-corrections. It really depends on what kind of program you're talking about.

For many victims this can be a terrific healing experience. It has to be voluntary. Victims have to know what the process is and what it isn't. Again, typically, it's about what that offender can do to help that victim as opposed to all of what that victim may need and what can be done to help the victim. It starts from a dialogue or relationship that exists or should exist or could exist between the offender and the victim. Some victims have no desire to see their offender or have anything to do with them, but I've had long conversations with victims who went through restorative justice processes—not just in shoplifting or car-theft cases, but in murder, too—where they felt it provided a way for them to move on in their lives. It's not for everyone, but I don't see why it can't be an option as long as people do it voluntarily and really understand what it is.

LEN: Couldn't offenders fake their remorse in such a situation—you know, a few tears or something to earn them a few perks in prison or get a few days knocked off their sentences?

HERMAN: Sure, sure. I think you've touched on a very important part of restorative justice, of what the offender gets out of it. If the offender has those kinds of incentives, I think it skews the process. This is for victims and offenders who want to participate in it, and it's typically for offenders who've already admitted guilt.

LEN: The experience of crime victims certainly can differ depending on the offense. What about other factors, such as geography, socioeconomics, etc.?

HERMAN: This is something that we have to try and struggle with a little bit, that the experience of crime is very different for different people—where they're located, the neighborhood that they live in, the kind of day-to-day life they experience. For example, the experience of crime is very different for residents of urban areas, suburban areas and rural areas—very different, whether it's an everyday part of your reality or a once-in-a-lifetime situation for you.

LEN: Even different from one culture to another, one would assume....

HERMAN: Yes. We need to understand how to reach out and serve people from different cultures as well as different neighborhoods, not try and write them off and say that there is no trauma, there is no way to help them. We need greater representation of people of all cultures in the victim-assistance world, and we need to talk to each other more.

Limited partners

LEN: Has the recent evolution to a community-oriented model of policing affected the dynamic between police and crime victims?

HERMAN: Well, I think a lot of the changes in the last few years may influence how people view police. It seems to me there are really two components to community policing that we emphasize. One is partnering and the other is problem solving. Over the last few years, we've seen a lot of creative problem-solving. We've seen a lot of police thinking outside the box, asking questions about how to solve the underlying causes of a problem and prevent its reoccurrence rather than just being incident-focused.

I don't think, though, that we're seeing a lot of real, genuine partnering, particularly where victims are concerned. We've made great strides with police understanding the importance of treating victims with sensitivity, referring them to services and listening to them. But I think police, given the community policing philosophy, can begin to see victims of crime as resources as well. They're not just people who need help and need referrals, which they are. They're more than that, they're also resources. They're people who can help solve the problem with you. That's part of where we have to go with community policing. Remember that our survey showed that victims view police most favorably of all parts of the system, but that's not saying things couldn't be better.

LEN: One would have to assume that an improved partnership in this regard would lead to better reporting of crimes....

HERMAN: You want to do whatever you can to encourage victims of crime to report, both because they will then hear about all kinds of assistance that's available to them and because by reporting it's more likely that their offender will be caught, and that maybe it will prevent future crimes. So you want to encourage reporting.

LEN: Is there anything specific in the way of training that can be provided to officers to improve their response to, and partnership with crime victims?

HERMAN: Oh, there's lots of training going on around the country. There are victims' advocates who are doing roll-call training around the country; there's all kinds of special training at conferences about the importance of listening carefully, responding with empathy, responding with information that's helpful. Victims say all the time: "If only I had been told that there was a place that would help me; no one told me." And for the most part, that responsibility falls on the shoulders of the police officer.

LEN: But do you think the necessary training is occurring in police academies?

HERMAN: I'm not saying that we're doing all the training that we need to do. There's a lot that's out there, but we need to do more. Every police academy, every POST board in the country should be training police officers in how to respond to victims. And one of the most effective ways of doing that is to invite victims of crime into the training academy to speak about their experience and the importance of helpful response. That's the most convincing way to reach officers—and victims are willing to do it.

UNIT 3
The Police

Unit Selections

Key Points to Consider

- Is there "community policing" in your community? If not, why? If so, is it working? Explain.

- Should the police be involved in community problems not directly concerned with crime? Explain your response.

- Do women police officer candidates face special problems?

 **Links: www.dushkin.com/online/**
These sites are annotated in the World Wide Web pages.

ACLU Criminal Justice Home Page
http://aclu.org/issues/criminal/hmcj.html

Violent Criminal Apprehension Program (VICAP)
http://www.state.ma.us/msp/unitpage/vicap.htm

Introduction to American Justice
http://www.uaa.alaska.edu/just/just110/home.html

Law Enforcement Guide to the World Wide Web
http://leolinks.com/

National Institute of Justice (NIJ)
http://www.ojp.usdoj.gov/nij/lawedocs.htm

Police officers are the guardians of our freedoms under the Constitution and the law, and as such they have an awesome task. They are asked to prevent crime, protect citizens, arrest wrongdoers, preserve the peace, aid the sick, control juveniles, control traffic, and provide emergency services on a moment's notice. They are also asked to be ready to lay down their lives, if necessary.

In recent years the job of the police officer has become even more complex and dangerous. Illegal drug use and trafficking are at epidemic levels, racial tensions are explosive, and terrorism continues to increase at alarming rates.

The role of the police in America is a difficult one, and as the police deal with a growing, diverse population, their job becomes even more difficult. Thus, the need for a more professional, well-trained police officer is obvious.

The lead article in this section, "Ethics and Criminal Justice: Some Observations on Police Misconduct," discusses police misconduct in terms of ethical violations. This is followed by "On-the-Job Stress in Policing—Reducing It, Preventing It" which looks at some sources of job-related stress and the effects it can have on officers.Then, the use of new technology in community policing is treated in "Crime Story: The Digital Age." In "Policing the Police," Kenneth Jost deals with such issues as excessive use of force, the Supreme Court's *Miranda* ruling (and the attempt to overturn it by congressional legislation), and racial profiling.This article is followed by "Police Officer Candidate Assessment and Selection," which talks about the methods of assessment and selection of police officer candidates used by various local and state law enforcement agencies.The New York State Police are making efforts to increase the number of women applicants, as discussed in the final article in this unit, "Improving the Recruitment of Women in Policing."

Ethics and Criminal Justice: Some Observations on Police Misconduct

by Bryan Byers
Ball State University

One need not look far to see evidence of the societal importance placed on ethics in criminal justice. Ethics has been a hot topic in the 1990s and promises to be equally important as we venture into the new millennium. Often, the issue of ethics in criminal justice is considered synonymous with police ethics. However, ethics touches all of the main branches of criminal justice practice as well as the academic realm. Due to the high profile nature of policing in our society, however, ethics is commonly connected with policing. Therefore, particular focus is given to this dimension in the following discussion. Within this essay the topic of ethics is addressed by first examining a general understanding of this concept. Second, a brief discussion of our societal concern over ethics and criminal justice practice is examined. Third, the discussion centers on selected scholarship in criminal justice ethics. Finally, some concluding remarks are offered.

ETHICS AND ETHICAL ISSUES: A PRIMER

According to the Merriam-Webster Dictionary, "ethics" is defined as (1) "a discipline dealing with good and evil and with moral duty" or (2) "moral principles or practice." The first definition suggests that ethics is a discipline or area of study. This certainly has been the case when we examine the academic field of Philosophy. Criminal justice is, admittedly, a hybrid discipline drawing from many academic fields—one being Philosophy. Interestingly, a good portion of the published academic scholarship in criminal justice ethics is philosophical in nature and can be found in the journal *Criminal Justice Ethics*. The other part of the definition suggests that ethics is a combination of cognition ('moral principles') and behavior ('practice'). Therefore, we might conclude that ethics is the study of the principle and practice of good, evil, and moral duty.

As we consider the nature of criminal justice, and in particular policing, within contemporary society, the behavior of law enforcement officers is continually the target of ethical evaluation. The field of law enforcement has been under scrutiny during various historical epochs for behavior that has been called into question on ethical grounds. Whether it be search and seizure "fishing expeditions" prior to *Mapp v. Ohio*, the fallout from the Knapp Commission report (*à la Serpico*) or the latest instance of police misconduct to flood the media, essentially the concern is over conduct or behavior. Cognitive processes and the socialization that reinforces unprofessional and unethical conduct influence the onset and proliferation of undesirable behavior. Thus, while one must be concerned with psychological and sociological forces that help to produce police unprofessionalism and unethical behavior, we should not lose sight of the role choice has in police misconduct.

One would be hard pressed to produce credible evidence to suggest that policing has not become more professional over the past several decades. It seems equally unreasonable to suggest that the entire field of policing is corrupt and permeated with graft. However, and as most readers will know, such an explanation has been offered. The venerable "rotten barrel theory"[1] of police corruption suggests such permeation within a police department. As most readers know, the rotten barrel theory of police corruption suggests that unethical and illegal behavior not only occurs at the individual officer level but is pervasive enough within a police department that unethical conduct may be traced to top administrative officials.

Another interpretation of police corruption is the "rotten apple theory."[2] This approach does not suggest that corruption and unethical conduct is so pervasive that it spreads to the highest ranks and throughout the organization. This approach, rather, suggests that there are a few "rotten apples" in a police department and inappropriate behavior is isolated to a few individuals. Police administrators have been keen on this explanation in the wake of police corruption because it avoids suggestion of wholesale departmental corruption, allows for a tidy response (e.g., fire the offending officer), and does not necessarily have to result in a tarnished image of an entire department.

An additional form of police misconduct has also been identified. In addition to the rotten apple and the rotten barrel, there may also be a "rotten group theory" of police corruption. According to a 1998 report by the General Accounting Office on police corruption in the United States, "The most commonly identified pattern of drug-related police corruption involved small groups of officers who protected and assisted each other in criminal activities, rather than the traditional patterns of non-drug-related police corruption that involved just a few isolated individuals or systemic corruption pervading an entire police department or precinct."[3]

Whether unethical behavior is systematic, small group, or individual, one cannot deny the importance placed on the intellectual process that allows for such conduct to take place. One might still be left wondering what it is about policing that produces opportunities to engage in unethical behavior. That is, what is it about the policing profession that affords officers the opportunity to engage in unethical conduct? The answer might be found in the concepts of "authority" and "power." Police wield a tremendous amount of power and authority within society. The powers to arrest, question and detain are entrusted with the police. The authority given to the police to protect our belongings and persons is unmatched by any other profession. Unethical or illegal behavior results when a law enforcement officer makes a conscious decision to abuse authority or wield power that is not appropriate to the situation. What is fundamental to unethical behavior by police is the conscious decision to abuse authority or power and circumstances, peer pressure, socialization, loyalty, and individual psychology are secondary in their ability to explain the behavior.

It might be best to interpret the role played by factors such as circumstances, peer pressure, socialization, loyalty, and individual psychology as a means of excusing or justifying the unethical or illegal act committed by an officer. That is, while the individual officer makes a decision to violate the public's trust and engage in unethical behavior, one might suggest that the officer's loyalty to his peers was a justification for the conduct. Let us examine this dynamic by way of an ethical dilemma. Assume that Officer X has just pulled over a drunk driver and realizes that the suspect is a fellow officer and friend. In fact, the driver has helped Officer X out of a few "tight spots" over the years. Instead of placing the colleague through a field sobriety test, Officer X helps his buddy park the car and then drives him home with the understanding from his friend that he will "sleep it off." What was the ethical dilemma? The choice between doing what was appropriate (the field sobriety test and subsequent arrest if appropriate) and being loyal to his friend. This situation, at the very least, describes a scenario ripe for abuse of discretion. Since discretion is a power that police have, it can be abused. Thus, many might examine this situation and suggest that the officer abused his discretionary authority. The officer made a decision to abuse his power but did so out of loyalty to the friend that is promoted through socialization behind the "blue curtain."

CONCERN OVER ETHICS: CAN WE CALL IT A TREND?

Media reports of police misconduct pepper us whenever there is an incident of alleged misbehavior or corruption. It might be the nightly newscaster reporting on the Rodney King incident at the start of the 1990s. It could be the recent case of the Philadelphia Police Department officers viewed on tape kicking a downed felony crime suspect at the birth of the twenty-first century. Whatever the instance, the topic of ethics and ethical behavior within the criminal justice profession grabs headlines. The media likes to report on such "ethical misadventures" because it sells. Some of the public, and powerful leaders, use such instances to legitimize their negative attitudes toward police. The police loathe the "bad press" in the wake of their self-perception of "doing good" for the community.

The media might be the only winner in the wake of police misconduct. However, the public loses and so do the fields of policing and criminal justice, in general. Even the academic field of criminal justice loses because policing is so closely linked in the public mind to it. I am reminded of this reality when recalling my flight back from the 1991 Academy of Criminal Justice Sciences meeting in Nashville. As plane passengers do, I began a conversation with the person seated next to me. We engaged in the typical small talk of "where are you from" and "where are you going." When my fellow passenger heard that I was returning from a "criminal justice" meeting, his response was immediate and unequivocal. He said, "why are cops such jerks?" The conversation occurred in the wake of the Rodney King incident and he was referring to the behavior of the L.A. police officers captured on tape. Admittedly taken aback, I was speechless. Part of the reason was personal, given my experiences in the field as a practitioner and those of close family members and friends. The other part of my speechlessness was professional and social scientific in nature, given how astounding it was to me to find a person willing to generalize so broadly from one highly celebrated incident. This seemingly innocuous exchange had an indelible impression on me. It made me think about the impact the field of criminal justice might have in the topic of ethics.

There is little doubt that real world events and their impact on the collective conscience influence the academic field. In fact, one could reasonably argue that societal events drive research agendas and define, to some degree, what is popular to investigate criminologically and what is not. Ethics may be no exception. For instance, the Rodney King incident, one might argue, had a tremendous impact not only on the practical dimensions of policing and police-community relations but also on the academic field of criminal justice. For instance, the book jacket for *Above the Law: Police and the Excessive Use of Force* by Jerome Skolnick and James Fyfe has a frame from the Rodney King video just below the title. The impact goes beyond one book, however.

Using 1991 as a pivotal year, given that the Rodney King beating occurred then, the author decided to conduct a computer search for articles on ethics in criminal justice. The findings, albeit not scientific, are interesting nonetheless. Using Periodical Abstracts, an on-line search method at my institution and offered through the university library, a search was conducted for "criminal justice" + "ethics" comparing the years 1986–1990 to 1991–1999. What I wanted to find out is this: were there more publications in criminal justice ethics prior to Rodney King or after? Since the incident occurred relatively early in 1991, that year was placed in the "post-Rodney King" group of years. From 1986 (the first year the index covers) through 1990, there were 28 "hits" or publications on criminal justice ethics. From 1991 through 1999 there were 152 publications. Admittedly, the "post" period encompassed nine years and the "pre" period only contained five years. However, it is still rather telling that such a difference exists.

Only time will tell if the aforementioned suggests a trend for the discipline. However, there is certainly every indication that criminal justice scholarship and practice will continue with an emphasis on ethics. A key reason why ethics promises to have a strong future presence has less to do with the lasting impact of Rodney King and more to do with constant reminders that ethical misadventures keep occurring. For example, during the past ten years, the cities of New Orleans, Chicago, New York, Miami, and Los Angeles, to name a few, have all reeled in the aftermath of ethical transgressions among their sworn law enforcement officers.

ETHICS AND CRIMINAL JUSTICE PRACTICE

In addition to the Rodney King case, there have been many other instances in which law enforcement officers have been found in ethically compromising or illegal positions. Every major city police force in the United States has experienced some form of unethical or illegal behavior within its ranks. Some of the situations in recent history have involved drugs and drug units. A few examples are listed below:

- A 1998 report by the General Accounting Office cites examples of publicly disclosed drug-related police corruption in the following cities: Atlanta, Chicago, Cleveland, Detroit, Los Angeles, Miami, New Orleans, New York, Philadelphia, Savannah, and Washington, DC. [4]

- On average, half of all police officers convicted as a result of FBI-led corruption cases between 1993 and 1997 were convicted for drug-related offenses. [5]

- A 1998 report by the General Accounting Office notes, "… several studies and investigations of drug-related police corruption found on-duty police officers engaged in serious criminal activities, such as (1) conducting unconstitutional searches and seizures; (2) stealing money and/or drugs from drug dealers; (3) selling stolen drugs; (4) protecting drug operations; (5) providing false testimony; and (6) submitting false crime reports." [6]

- A 1998 report by the General Accounting Office notes, "Although profit was found to be a motive common to traditional and drug-related police corruption, New York City's Mollen Commission identified power and vigilante justice as two additional motives for drug-related police corruption." [7]

- As an example of police corruption, the GAO cites Philadelphia, where "Since 1995, 10 police officers from Philadelphia's 39th District have been charged with planting drugs on suspects, shaking down drug dealers for hundreds of thousands of dollars, and breaking into homes to steal drugs and cash." [8]

- In New Orleans, 11 police officers were convicted of accepting nearly $100,000 from undercover agents to protect a cocaine supply warehouse containing 286 pounds of cocaine. The undercover portion of the investigation was terminated when a witness was killed under orders from a New Orleans police officer. [9]

Part of the fallout from a major finding of unethical or illegal behavior within a police department is a call to "clean up" the agency. As a result, departments in the af-

termath of such an embarrassing situation might become more open to citizen review panels, pledge to re-examine their internal affairs division, require officers to participate in "ethics training," or reinforce the importance of "ethics codes."

The concept of citizen review panels has been in existence for several decades; the first panel may have been formed in Philadelphia around 1958. Citizen review panels, sometimes also called civilian review boards, are in place in some jurisdictions for the purpose of assisting with the investigation of citizen complaints that police officers within the jurisdiction engaged in the unfair treatment of civilians. Review panels can help to build or repair strained police-community relations. However, officers sometimes respond to such efforts with a defensive posture and resentment over "civilians trying to tell them how to do their job."

A department might also pledge to examine its own internal affairs division, the policy and procedure for investigating complaints and cases against officers, and typical responses to officers who have violated departmental policy and/or who have violated the law. It is important to note from the onset that a police department internal affairs division runs the risk of being considered "suspect" from officers and a community's citizenry alike. Officers can view internal affair or "I.A." as the "enemy" and a division that is bent on punishing officers who are risking their lives on the streets every day. From the community, there might be the perception that the police department cannot possibly take on the task of investigating itself. At the very least, this cannot be done "ethically." Thus, I.A. can find itself in a no-win situation. Whether a division in a large department or an officer charged with this responsibility in a smaller department, the I.A. role is critical. However, internal remedies are effective only if they are meted out in a fair and just fashion. I.A. recommendations that are carried out by police administration must bolster the respect of line officers. If perceptions exist that an officer has been treated unfairly, the department will lose any deterrent effect I.A. recommendations might produce.

Yet another response is the concept of "ethics training" for police officers and recruits. The notion of "ethics *training*" (with an emphasis on 'training') is an interesting one given that the concept of 'training' assumes that what a person is being "trained in" can be taught. In this case, the term 'ethics training' suggests, either correctly

or incorrectly, that ethics can somehow be taught to people. I prefer the term "Ethics Awareness Training" in lieu of the aforementioned. Why? The reason is rather elementary. Is it possible to teach someone to be ethical as "ethics training" might suggest? This seems far-fetched, at best. If a department has an officer who has a propensity toward unethical behavior, and this person was not weeded out during the hiring process, the best one might hope for is a heightened awareness and sensitivity for ethical issues and dilemmas. Emphasizing codes of ethics, common today in most disciplines and professions, [10] is another avenue for police departments in the wake of ethical scandal. However, if a code of ethics [11] is printed in the departmental policy and procedure manual, never to be referred to again, it will have very little impact. A code of ethics for any department or organization must be a "living document" that is referenced often and held in high esteem. The code should be a document that officers have pride in and believe to be relevant to their lives as law enforcement officers. Otherwise, the code will have little, if any, impact on officer decision making and conduct.

THE SCHOLARS WEIGH IN

As mentioned above, a large portion of the academic scholarship in criminal justice ethics is philosophical in nature. However, a few academicians have attempted to examine ethics in criminal justice empirically and quantitatively. When discussing scholarship in criminal justice ethics, a few names immediately come to mind, including James Fyfe, Herman Goldstein, Victor Keppeler, Carl Klockars, Joycelyn Pollock, Lawrence Sherman, Jerome Skolnick and Sam Souryal. This is certainly not an exhaustive list, and we cannot possibly survey all of the literature in this field here. However, I would like to spend a few moments discussing two major studies funded by NIJ. The studies are *The Measurement of Police Integrity* by Klockars, Ivkovitch, Harver, and Haberfeld [12] and *Police Attitudes Toward Abuse of Authority: Findings from a National Study* by Weisburd and Greenspan. [13] Both studies were published in May of 2000. While the two studies do not represent the entire literature on police ethics, both studies are national in scope, recent and empirical.

The Klockars et al. study used 3,235 police officer respondents from 30 police agencies within the United States. The respondents were given 11 vignettes describing various types of possible police misconduct. In response to each vignette, officers were asked to answer six questions intended to measure "… the normative inclination of police to resist temptations to abuse the rights and privileges of their occupation." While the results indicate vast differences from agency to agency regarding the "environment of integrity," one finding is consistent with the protections afforded members of the police subculture. The survey revealed that most officers would not report a fellow officer who was engaged in "less serious" types of misconduct (e.g., running a security business on the side, receiving free meals and gifts, or even leaving a minor traffic accident while under the influence). What this suggests, even though the survey revealed little tolerance for what was defined as "serious" police misconduct, is that there is a culture of acceptance within police ranks for some forms of misconduct. While such conduct is typically referred to as "grass eating" (less serious forms of police misconduct) as opposed to "meat eating" (more serious forms of police misconduct), many members of society would find the behavior unacceptable. James W. Birch in *Reflections on Police Corruption*[14] makes an interesting observation regarding such behavior. He states that the public creates an environment for "grass eating" that makes it difficult to not accept the "discount" or the free meal. It would appear that there may be a different definition of what constitutes "misconduct" depending on whether a person is a member of the police subculture or an outsider looking in.

The second NIJ study, by Weisburd and Greenspan, entitled "*Police Attitudes Toward Abuse of Authority: Findings From a National Study*" is the result of the Police Foundation's national telephone survey of over 900 officers from various agencies across the country and addresses police attitudes concerning excessive force. The results indicate that the majority of respondents believed it was not acceptable to use more force than was legally permissible to effect control over a person who had assaulted an officer. However, respondents reported that "… it is not unusual for officers to ignore improper conduct by their fellow officers." Other

findings suggest that the majority of officers/respondents believed that serious instances of abuse were rare and that their department maintained a 'tough stand' on police abuse of citizenry. What about possible solutions to the problem of police abuse? Officers report two fruitful avenues for addressing police abuse. First, it was reported police administrators could have an impact on the occurrence of police abuse by "taking a stand" against abuse and through better supervision. Second, officers believed that training in ethics, interpersonal skills and cultural diversity would be effective in preventing abuse. What about turning fellow officers in for abuse? This was perceived as risky. While the majority of officers maintained that the "code of silence" was not essential to good policing, the majority also maintained that whistle blowing was not worth the consequences within the police subculture.

TOWARD A CONCLUSION

It is difficult to conclude this discussion because there is so much more to say about the topic of ethics in criminal justice. However, I will attempt to make a few concluding observations to make closure on this discussion. First, ethics is an important area within criminal justice practice and scholarship since criminal justice practitioners, especially the police, are continually under scrutiny. Therefore, the discipline has an obligation to remain interested in this topic and to promote the study of ethics. Second, scholars can be of assistance to practitioners by studying the sociological and psychological forces that impact ethical and unethical behavior. There is much the academy can offer criminal justice agencies in the form of research within organizations and training pertinent to ethics. Third, unethical behavior is the result of a conscious decision-making process to abuse one's authority while in a position of public trust. However, one must still take into account social forces that help to perpetuate, excuse, and justify unethical behavior. Fourth, there has been a proliferation of ethics scholarship in criminal justice since the Rodney King case but there is a need for more research of an empirical nature much like the two studies profiled in this

essay. While qualitative and philosophical literature is important to our understanding of ethics in criminal justice there is a need for additional research of a quantitative nature. With more study of ethics and ethical dilemmas faced by police, we might better understand the dynamics that propel officers into the dark side of policing and the factors that serve to justify misbehavior.

ENDNOTES

1. Police Deviance and Ethics. http://faculty.ncwc.edu/toconnor/205/205lec11.htm.

2. Knapp Commission Report. (1973). New York: George Braziller.

3. Government Accounting Office. Report to the Honorable Charles B. Rangel, House of Representatives, Law Enforcement: Information on Drug-Related Police Corruption. Washington, DC: USGPO (1998 May), p. 3.

4. Ibid. p. 36–37.

5. Ibid. p. 35.

6. Ibid. p. 8.

7. Ibid. p. 3.

8. Ibid. p. 37.

9. Ibid. p. 36.

10. The Academy of Criminal Justice Sciences (ACJS) recently adopted a code of ethics modeled after the American Sociological Association's (ASA) code.

11. The International Association of Chiefs of Police (IACP) has a model code of ethics and also publishes a training key on ethics and policing.

12. Klockars, C.B., S.K. Ivkovich, W.E. Harver, and M.R. Haberfeld. (2000, May). "The Measurement of Police Integrity." National Institute of Justice, Research in Brief. U.S. Government Printing Office: Washington, DC.

13. Weisburd, D. and R. Greenspan. (2000, May). "Police Attitudes Toward Abuse of Authority: Findings from a National Study." National Institute of Justice, Research in Brief. U.S. Government Printing Office: Washington, DC.

14. Birch, James W. (1983). "Reflections on Police Corruption." *Criminal Justice Ethics*, Volume 2.

From *Academy of Criminal Justice Sciences (ACJS) Today,* September/October 2000, pp. 1, 4-7. Reprinted with permission of the Academy of Criminal Justice Sciences.

On-the-Job Stress in Policing— *Reducing It, Preventing It*

Police officers and members of their families consider their job to be one of the most stressful. It is hard to disagree with that assessment, as officers themselves report high rates of divorce, alcoholism, suicide, and other emotional and health problems.[1] No job is immune from stress, but for the law enforcement officer, the strains and tensions experienced at work are unique, often extreme, and sometimes unavoidable.

Fortunately, many law enforcement agencies, recognizing the high toll exacted by stress on officers and their families, are tackling it with an array of creative prevention and reduction strategies. Through the CLEFS (Corrections and Law Enforcement Family Support) program of the National Institute of Justice, several of these agencies are receiving support.

This article summarizes an NIJ report that documented the causes and effects of job-related stress affecting law enforcement officers and their families. Much of the information was drawn from interviews, conducted as part of the study, with officers themselves and their family members.[2] Also included in this article are highlights of some stress prevention and reduction programs reported in the study and of some of the CLEFS projects.

Sources of Stress

Exposure to violence, suffering, and death is inherent to the profession of law enforcement officer.

There are other sources of stress as well. Officers who deal with offenders on a daily basis may view some sentences as too lenient; they may perceive the public's opinion of police performance to be unfavorable; they often are required to work mandatory, rotating shifts; and they may not have enough time to spend with their families. Police officers also face unusual, often highly disturbing, situations, such as dealing with a child homicide victim or the survivors of vehicle crashes.

The nature of the organizations in which officers work may also be a source of stress. Police departments historically have been structured along military lines and as a result often have been rigidly hierarchical and highly bureaucratic, with management styles that can be inflexible. Although in many instances police culture is changing, in many others the leadership remains predominately white and male, opportunities for advancement are limited, and despite the ubiquity of the personal computer, a large amount of paperwork still is required.

Is Stress Getting Worse?

Officers may increasingly view stress as a normal part of their job, but they also see themselves as being under considerably more pressure than they or their colleagues were 10 or 20 years ago. They see new sources of stress in the high level of violent crime and in what they perceive as greater public scrutiny and adverse

publicity. They also feel that police camaraderie has declined; they fear contracting air- and blood-borne diseases such as TB and HIV/AIDS; and they see themselves as having to deal with such relatively new issues as cultural diversity and the imperative of "political correctness."

Even widely accepted changes in law enforcement can lead to more stress for some officers. Although community policing may mean more job satisfaction, greater overall department efficiency, and higher morale, the transition to it can cause apprehension on the part of the officers who on a day-to-day basis must operationalize this fundamental shift in the philosophy of policing. Performance expectations are new and perhaps not fully understood by all officers. Whether or not stress is increasing, identifying the causes is a first step toward reducing and preventing it. (See "How One Agency Pinpointed Stress.")

Counting the Ways: The Effects of Stress

The physical and emotional effects of stress are numerous and often severe. Any one of them can impair job performance. The consequences of job-related stress commonly reported by police officers are:
- Cynicism and suspiciousness.
- Emotional detachment from various aspects of daily life.
- Reduced efficiency.
- Absenteeism and early retirement.

How One Agency Pinpointed Stress

When the Baltimore Police Department decided to seek out the sources of stress in the agency, they turned for assistance to public health researchers at nearby Johns Hopkins University. With the Fraternal Order of Police as the third partner, the Department created Project SHIELDS to take on this task as well as to develop response strategies.

The sources of stress were identified by means of a survey, conducted by the researchers, among line officers and spouses/life partners. Some of the results were surprising. For example, fully two-thirds of the officers said they considered media reports of alleged police wrongdoing to be stressful to them. The same proportion said that what they view as lack of administrative support for officers in trouble was a major source of stress. Almost one-fourth reported low energy or chronic back pain, which they believed was related to job stress.

After the Hopkins researchers complete their analysis of the survey data, they and the project's advisory board (officers and family members) will help the Department develop a response. Total quality management (TQM) teams will be established to focus on selected issue drawn from the research findings. Consisting of officers from all ranks, the TQM teams will develop strategies to address aspects of organizational stress identified in the survey as particularly problematic.*

*Unpublished progress report of "Law Enforcement Work Stress and Family Support (Project SHIELDS)," Johns Hopkins University School of Hygiene and Public Health, Baltimore, submitted to the National Institute of Justice, U.S. Department of Justice, by Robyn Gershon, Principal Investigator, March 31, 1999.

- Excessive aggressiveness (which may trigger an increase in citizen complaints).

- Alcoholism and other substance abuse problems.

- Marital or other family problems (for example, extramarital affairs, divorce, or domestic violence).

- Post-traumatic stress disorder.

- Heart attacks, ulcers, weight gain, and other health problems.
- Suicide.

According to many counselors who work with police officers, difficulties with intimate relationships are the most common problem they treat.

Families Feel Stress, Too

If the effects on officers are severe, they can be similarly serious for officers' family members. In one survey of the spouses of police officers, a very large percentage said they experienced unusually high levels of stress because of their spouse's job.[3]

Stress felt by spouses is a concern in and of itself and also because a stressful home environment can adversely affect the officer's job performance. Even conditions, situations, or incidents that may not trouble the officers themselves—or that they may even enjoy, such as shift work or undercover work—can mean severe problems for their families. Sources of stress commonly cited by officers' spouses include:

- Shift work and overtime.
- Concern over the spouse's cynicism, need to feel in control in the home, or inability or unwillingness to express feelings.
- Fear that the spouse will be hurt or killed in the line of duty.
- Officers' and others' excessively high expectations of their children.
- Avoidance, teasing, or harassment of the officer's children by other children because of the parent's job.
- Presence of a gun in the home.
- The officer's 24-hour role as a law enforcer.
- Perception that the officer prefers to spend time with coworkers rather than with his of her family.
- Too much or too little discussion of the job.
- Family members' perception of the officer as paranoid or excessively vigilant and overprotective of them.
- Problems in helping the officer cope with work-related problems
- "Critical incidents," or the officer's injury or death on the job.[4]

Because stress affects family members, they are often the first to recognize the officer's need for help, and they can play a crucial role by encouraging him or her to seek assistance before the problem becomes worse. This is the concept behind the Spousal Academy, a component of the comprehensive officer and family support program offered by the Collier County (Florida) Sheriff's Office.

The Academy offers training to spouses and other domestic partners of deputies and recruits who are enrolled in the Office's training academy. The 10-hour program involves an introduction to the nature of law enforcement work and an opportunity to discuss expectations about the effect the spouses' occupation will have on family life. Participants learn about the structure of the Sheriff's Office, about such human resource issues as employee benefits (health insurance, for example), and about stress management and conflict resolution. Two related programs in the development stage are peer support groups for spouses and life partners and for deputies' adolescent children.[5]

Soliciting feedback from participants is part of the program. Several noted the program's effectiveness in conveying the reality of what an officer does on the job. In the words of one spouse, "I now realize some of what my husband goes through." One of the comments heard most frequently concerns the value of simply meeting and interacting with other spouses. As one participant characterized the spouse's role, "Sometimes, this can be a lonely job."[6]

Countering Domestic Violence

There is some belief that a relatively large proportion of law enforcement officers may be involved in domestic violence, in part because of the stressful nature of the job.[7] Many law enforcement agencies have begun to turn their attention to the issue and devise ways to respond.

One agency, the Los Angeles (County) Sheriff's Department (LASD), has adopted a zero-tolerance policy toward domestic violence, with a full range of disciplinary actions that could include dismissal from the force. To reduce the number of domestic violence incidents among the LASD's 8,000 sworn officers, the Department bolstered the policy with a training program for all supervisory personnel; a vigorous information dissemination campaign (which included development of an educational video to be shown to all staff); and counseling services for individuals, couples, and families. The Department has trained more than 1,200 supervisors to spot signs of stress and domestic violence.[8]

Why Start or Expand a Stress Program?

Why should law enforcement agencies spend time and money on a law enforcement stress program and perhaps set aside space for it? The answer has to do with the implications of stress for the department. Essentially, stress reduces the quality of departmental performance.

Stress Affects Agency Performance

The cumulative negative effects of stress on officers and their families typically affect the agency through impaired officer performance and the related problems of tardiness, absenteeism, and low morale. The consequence for the department is lower productivity. Stress-related performance inadequacies also may generate labor-management friction and lead to civil suits. There may be adverse public reaction as a result of stress-related incidents, such as an officer's suicide or a case of police brutality. Even problems that are confined to only a few individuals or that occur rarely can have major repercussions. For instance, a single incident in which a handful of officers abuse alcohol or other drugs can lower public confidence in the entire agency.[9]

Though establishing and operating a stress reduction program requires a financial outlay, it can mean cost savings in the long term. That is because stress affects the bottom line. Agencies can find it enormously costly when employee turnover increases as a result of stress-related early retirement or long-term disability. Robert Peppler, Assistant

Sheriff of the San Bernardino (California) Sheriff's Department noted the cost to his agency: "We have a tremendous investment in cops," he said, "and if they leave after one traumatic incident, we have lost a tremendous amount. A dollar in psychological services now can save us hundreds of thousands down the road."[10]

Why Not an EAP?

Many agencies have access to city- or countywide employee assistance programs (EAP's). Law enforcement staff and their families may be eligible for services from additional providers. These may include police chaplains, wellness programs, support groups, and local private service providers. This prompts the question: Why shouldn't an agency rely on other existing programs rather than develop its own stress reduction program?

The fact that a service is available does not necessarily mean it is meeting—or can meet—the distinctive needs of police officers. Mental health practitioners, police administrators, and others, when asked about city or county EAP's, said police officers do not use them because these programs do not provide enough confidentiality, because EAP staff usually do not understand law enforcement, and because the officers feared the stigma that might be attached to using an EAP.

What Stress Reduction Programs Look Like

Approaches to reduce or prevent stress can take many forms, among them:

- Services provided by a private mental health practice or an individual therapist working with one or more law enforcement agencies.
- Peer support and referrals from specially trained police officers.
- Psychological services set up in the agency through the union, chaplaincy, or employee assistance program.
- A combination of these arrangements.

Almost all programs are geared primarily to line officers, because they constitute the largest group in

A Little Help From Your Friends—Peer Support in New York City

Sometimes it takes a tragedy or critical incident to prompt a law enforcement agency or related organization to develop or expand a stress reduction program for police officers.

That was the case in New York City, where 26 police officers committed suicide in the 2-year period from 1994 through 1995. The unusually high number was the result of such factors as perceived pressure from the media and allegations of corruption. The crisis spurred the Patrolmen's Benevolent Association, supported by the city council, to establish a peer support program by officers for officers. The Members Assistance Program (MAP) trained 150 officer volunteers to aid fellow officers and an additional 26 to aid their families. The peer support officers staff a 24-hour hotline, serve as a point of first contact and screening for officers who report stress-related difficulties, and encourage individuals who need more intensive help to seek it.

MAP also trained 60 mental health practitioners in law enforcement stress, and these practitioners began taking referrals from the peer support officers. Between 1996, the year the program started, and 1998, the hotline received some 1,500 calls, resulting in more than 650 referrals.*

*NYC Patrolmen's Benevolent Association Members Assistance Program. Program for the Reduction of Stress for New York City Police Officers and Their Families," final report submitted to the National Institute of Justice, U.S. Department of Justice, grant 96-FS-VX-007, December 1998.

any law enforcement agency, they deal with the public on a day-to-day basis, they are widely believed to experience high levels of stress, and they may have limited means to pay for extended counseling. Most programs also provide at least minimal services (that is, referral to other treatment providers) to nonsworn personnel and former employees, as well as to officers' and other employees' family members and close friends.

Services typically include assessment and referral to mental health or other practitioners; critical incident debriefing; intervention for other types of crises; short-term counseling for both individuals and families; and long-term counseling and other services, including treatment for substance abuse.

Most mental health practitioners emphasize the importance of involving family members, when possible, in all these services. To varying extents, all programs include referrals to outside sources of assistance. For some programs that operate with limited resources, referral to outside services is the primary component. That is often the case with programs staffed largely by peers. (See "A Little Help From Your Friends—Peer Support in New York City.")

Preventing Stress

The most common method for preventing stress is to train officers to recognize its signs and sources and to develop individual coping strategies. Training helps encourage officers and nonsworn personnel to use stress reduction techniques and services and dispels the stigma frequently attached to seeking assistance.

One period during which officers could be taught about stress is when they are at the academy, according to most of the police officers, program administrators, and independent mental health practitioners who were asked about this issue. They felt that the initial training period was a possibility because recruits are a captive audience and because the information may remain with them throughout their entire police career. There is some thinking that "inoculation" during recruit training is not the best approach, because most recruits are not experienced enough to recognize that stress comes with the job. The optimal time to reach them may be 6 to 8 months into the job, after they have experienced on-the-job stress. Some agencies offer inservice training not only for line officers but also for midlevel managers and command staff, prospective retirees, and nonsworn personnel.

Because, as noted above, the structure and management of the agency can be a significant source of stress, mental health professionals should consider working with departmental management and unions to play and implement organizational change. This can be done in a number of ways, all of which fall within the domain of management:

- Training command staff in effective supervision.
- Training field training officers to constructively supervise rookies.
- Eliminating rotating shift work.
- Improving the match between officers' capabilities and the demands of specific assignments.

What NIJ Is Doing

The issue of job-related stress for law enforcement officers and their families has received attention at the highest levels of government. In the 1994 Omnibus Crime Act, the President and Congress recognized the severity of the problem and mandated a Federal Government response. The National Institute of Justice was assigned the task of sponsoring research, establishing pilot programs, and conducting program evaluations that support State and local efforts.

Research and Development

Since the start of the Corrections and Law Enforcement Family Support program, NIJ has sponsored research and program development in some 30 agencies and related organizations (labor unions and employee professional organizations, for example). These projects include the development of innovation treatment and training programs as well as research into the nature and causes of stress.

In one study now under way, NIJ is exploring the nature and extent of job-related stress for police in a single geographic region. And to improve access to service, NIJ provided support to the Metro Nashville Police Department in creating an online resource of information for the families of law enforcement officers, particularly those in underserved communities. Available on the Internet, the resource is a new type of service delivery system.[11] The Web site contains, among other things, materials developed by psychologists for preparing workshops on stress, message boards, a chat room, links to related Web sites, recommended readings, and postings from police psychologists and consultants.

From LEFS to CLEFS

Originally geared solely to law enforcement, the NIJ program has expanded to include corrections officers. In some cases, corrections officers experience more intense stress-generating incidents than do law enforcement officers. They may, for example, encounter violent behavior by inmates more often and over longer periods of time.

NIJ support for research and development is given to corrections agencies as well as law enforcement agencies. A study of programs to reduce and prevent stress among corrections staff is under development.

Notes

1. Burke, R. J., "Career Stages, Satisfaction, and Well-Being Among Police Officers," *Psychological Reports* 65 (1989): 3–12; and Delprino, R. P., K. O'Quin, and C. Kennedy, "Identification of Work and Family Services for Law Enforcement Personnel," final report submitted to the National Institute of Justice, 1997 (NIJ grant 95-IJ-CX-0113).

2. The NIJ report is *Developing a Law Enforcement Stress Program for Officers and Their Families*, by Peter Finn and Julie Esselman Tomz, Issues and Practices, Washington, D.C.: U.S. Department of Justice, National Institute of Justice, March 1997 (NCJ 163175).

3. The survey was conducted as part of a study by Leanor Boulin-Johnson, professor of African-American Studies and Family Studies at Arizona State University. See "On the Front Lines: Police Stress and Family Well-Being," testimony of Leanor Boulin-Johnson before the Select Committee on Children, Youth, and Families, U.S. House of Representatives, 102nd Congress, 1st Session, May 20, 1991, Washing-

ton, D.C.: U.S. Government Printing Office, 1991: 32.

4. Borum, R., and C. Philpot, "Therapy With Law Enforcement Couples: Clinical Management of the 'High-Risk Lifestyle,'" *American Journal of Family Therapy* 21 (1993): 122–135.

5. Ferguson, Edward T., and Acey L. Edgemon, "Collier County Sheriff's Office Law Enforcement Family Support Initiative," draft executive summary, report submitted to the National Institute of Justice, U.S. Department of Justice, April 1, 1999.

6. Unpublished program evaluations by participants in Spousal Academy, Collier County (Florida) Sheriff's Office, no date.

7. "On the Front Lines: Police Stress and Family Well-Being," testimony of B. J. Anderson before the Select Committee on Children, Youth, and Families, U.S. House of Representatives, 102nd Congress, 1st Session, May 20, 1991, Washington, D.C.: U.S. Government Printing Office, 1991: 61–63.

8. Unpublished progress report of the Family Violence Prevention and Recovery Project (FVPRP), Los Angeles County Sheriff's Department, submitted to the National Institute of Justice, U.S. Department of Justice, by Audrey L. Honig, Principal Investigator, FVPRP, and Steven E. Sultan, Project Coordinator, FVPRP, for period September 1, 1998, through March 3, 1999.

9. Springer, K., "When the Helper Needs Help: Stress and the Law Enforcement Employee," *EAP Association Exchange* 25 (1995): 6–11.

10. Finn and Tomz, *Developing a Law Enforcement Stress Program for Officers and Their Families:* 3.

11. The site address is http:// policefamilies. com.

Peter Finn, coauthor of the report on which this summary is based, contributed to the preparation of this article. Mr. Finn is an Associate with Abt Associates Inc., a public-policy and business research and consulting firm headquartered in Cambridge, Massachusetts. He also serves as a special police officer with the Belmont, Massachusetts, Police Department. Vincent Talucci, manager of the CLEFS portfolio of grants of NIJ, and Jenifer Wood, a former manager of CLEFS grants, also contributed.

Crime Story:
The Digital Age

Harnessing new technologies to community policing.

by John D. Cohen, Adam Gelb, and Robert Wasserman

The crime news these days is mostly good. Over the last eight years, crime rates have plummeted to the lowest levels in decades. Sustained economic growth, reduction in the use of crack cocaine, tougher gun laws and enforcement, and more cops on the beat have combined to make America's streets safer than at any time since the first reliable statistics were collected in the 1960s. Many of these improvements can be attributed to a surge of community policing techniques around the country that have fundamentally altered the philosophy of how many police departments work and the way they interact with their communities.

Yet for all the good news there are troubling signs on the horizon. Crime numbers are not continuing to plummet everywhere (for example, in Dallas and Houston, Texas, and Tampa, Fla.). New drugs such as ecstasy may reinvigorate the narcotics trade. Racial profiling and a perception of unequal law enforcement has cast a pall over improved rela-

tions in areas where community policing was beginning to make a difference. And, perhaps most worrisome, demographers forecast by 2010 a bubble of 4.4 million more youths in the crime-prone 15-to-24-year age group.

What does this mean for the new administration in Washington? It means that an aggressive new crime-fighting strategy—and appropriate funding—must emerge from Congress to help cities and states get a handle on coming crime problems before they spin back into pre-1990s numbers. This anti-crime agenda should build on the new view of community-based crime fighting developed in the last decade and focus on three key priorities:

1. harnessing the new information and communications technologies to give law enforcement agencies new crime-fighting tools;
2. expanding community policing programs with strategies aimed at dangerous people in dangerous places;
3. replacing racial profiling with criminal targeting.

How We Got Here

To understand the choices we face today in crime fighting, it's important to understand how we got where we are. In the early 1990s the nation was mired in an ideological impasse on crime fighting, in which liberals demanded more money to attack social inequities and conservatives insisted on harsher punishment for criminals. President Clinton proposed a Third Way: a new focus on preventing crime by expanding the number of police and deploying them in more creative ways.

The cornerstone of the Clinton administration's anti-crime policy was the establishment of the Office of Community Oriented Policing Services (COPS) within the Department of Justice. COPS provided funding for 100,000 new police officers both to help undermanned police departments around the country and to encourage them to adopt the new, community-oriented policing strategies that had shown great promise in San Diego and other communities. Since its inception, the COPS office has provided more than $6 billion in grants to state and local agencies for technology and new police officers. The COPS office reports that because of its efforts, 109,139 new police officers are working with community members to make neighborhoods safer.

BEATING BAD GUYS: Digital equipment and updated software helps pinpoint hot spots and repeat offenders better than old-fashioned hunches and random police cruising.

While the "100,000 cops" initiative grabbed most of the headlines, the most important accomplishment of the COPS program has been strategic: It has shifted the basic policing approach away from the old "911" model known as calls-for-service. This reactive approach is now moving toward community collaboration and preemptive problem solving. Instead of driving around randomly in cars and responding to emergency calls, police are now on foot and on bicycles so that they become visible fixtures in neighborhoods. They work with community leaders to identify conditions that breed disorder; they share information about potential problems; and they forge common strategies for preventing crime, not simply catching criminals after the fact.

In short, community-oriented policing has reconnected police with the communities they serve. It has also breached the bureaucratic barriers that prevented multiagency responses to the quality-of-life problems that facili-

tate crime, such as broken streetlights and abandoned buildings. Effective crime prevention requires that lights be repaired so that crimes aren't cloaked in darkness and that abandoned houses be condemned and razed so that they cannot be used for prostitution and drug trafficking. Thus, "broken windows" environments are eliminated before they begin attracting or reinforcing criminal activity. Even filling potholes is good policing policy—it frees officers from directing traffic to catching criminals.

Community-oriented policing also helps break down the stovepipe mentality of public agencies. It allows government and citizens to work together to tailor solutions that fit the crime problems in individual neighborhoods. It is supported by emerging information technologies such as wireless data and the Internet to improve the delivery of government services.

Agenda for the Future

Building on these successes, the new administration should pursue a technology-driven agenda for the future that breaks into three key parts—increasing COPS funding for technology tools, targeting hot spots and repeat offenders, and replacing racial profiling with criminal targeting.

1) Boost the technology budget of the COPS program. The federal government should push crime fighting into the digital age by providing national standards that support the deployment of cutting-edge information and communication systems. Through the COPS office, it should funnel seed money to state and local governments.

"Most police, parole officers, and courts are operating with 20-year-old information technology. Even though high-speed digital technology is already available, many cops must still wait 20 minutes for basic information about a vehicle or person they've stopped."

Rapidly collecting and disseminating good information about the people who commit crime and the places where crime occurs is the key. Yet most police, parole officers, and courts are operating with 20-year-old information technology. Even though high-speed digital technology is already available, many cops must still wait 20 minutes for basic information about a vehicle or person they've stopped (digital technology can obtain and transmit a car's record in 10 seconds). Days or weeks can pass before criminal warrants find their way into computers, leaving dangerous criminals on the street and police unaware they are wanted. Judges sentence offenders without seeing their criminal history records.

Some states, such as Pennsylvania, Maryland, and North Carolina, are working to establish statewide networks that improve information sharing and voice communication between the various components of the criminal justice community. These networks will link state and local law enforcement efforts and non-law enforcement agencies.

In addition to these initiatives, the criminal justice community must adjust to the new phenomenon of cybercrime. As criminals use communications and information technologies to commit traditional crimes in new ways (forgery, identification theft, drug trafficking, child pornography) and to devise entirely new types of crime such as cyberterrorism, law enforcement agencies need to make a techno-leap in crime fighting. This will require substantial new funds and training in areas about which police today have little knowledge.

2) Hit the bad guys where they work. Research on crime convincingly demonstrates two central facts: that crime is highly concentrated in geographic areas, with as much as 50 percent of offenses occurring at just 3 percent of locations; and that a small subset of criminals is responsible for a vastly disproportionate share of crime, with an estimated 5 percent to 7 percent of offenders committing from 50 percent to 70 percent of total offenses. To take advantage of this research, the Justice Department should establish a grant program to support local efforts to target crime hot spots and high-risk offenders.

Other research tells us that certain programs work. True community policing can shut down a drug market and keep it shut down while a traditional street-corner sweep would simply move dealers down the block. A strict regimen of drug testing and treatment, backed up by escalating penalties for violations, can dramatically cut drug use among offenders. Structured after-school activities linked to students' schoolwork can reduce juvenile crime and gangs, as well as drug use and teen pregnancy.

When well managed, each of these efforts can produce results. But used alone, no single approach can hope to turn a blighted neighborhood around, so they must be combined. Crime mapping technology can identify these crime-ridden areas and be used to track, in real time, shifting and emerging patterns so police can get a jump on new trends. Local leaders must coordinate a comprehensive effort with all government resources—policing, parole, prosecution, prevention, drug treatment, nuisance abatement, housing, and business development.

3) Eliminate racial profiling and develop criminal targeting. Racial profiling is the single greatest threat to the progress we've made in crime reduction. To counter the practice, a number of states have passed legislation that requires police departments to track traffic stops with an eye

to patterns of profiling. Some police departments are under scrutiny by the U.S. Justice Department because of allegations of racial profiling and brutality. Yet tensions between police and minority communities continue to increase—to the point that some police chiefs fear they are just one nasty incident away from an outbreak of civil disobedience. Law enforcement action, whether stopping a motorist, prosecuting a case, or sentencing an offender, must be based on more than statistical probabilities. Police executives must support anti-profiling policies by collecting verifiable data on the contacts that their officers have with citizens and by taking appropriate action against those who exhibit prejudice.

DRIVING WHILE BLACK: Racial profiling drives a wedge between aggrieved citizens and the police. Besides being unjust, it is also poor police work. Digitally-based criminal targeting is far more effective.

Law enforcement officials must also become more much sophisticated about the nature of our cultural prejudice. They should develop a deep and meaningful appreciation of how practices based on invalid assumptions can be perceived as discriminatory by people of color. Then they can become effective and impartial enforcers of the law. They must also understand that racial profiling is ineffective as a crime prevention tool because when police devote time targeting innocent people, criminals are free to commit crimes. Finally, they must understand that racial profiling breeds distrust in the very communities that need aggressive policing, reinforcing racial stereotypes.

Among the tools necessary for color-blind law enforcement are technologies to collect data on traffic and subject stops. But data collection is not enough. The widespread belief that police routinely engage in racial profiling has more to do with outmoded reactive and random crime control techniques traditionally used by police than with overt bias. Ironically, the very Justice Department that is now at the forefront of ending racial profiling promoted the use of profiling as a tool to interdict drug shipments.

The federal government should take a leadership role in eliminating racial profiling and replacing it with criminal targeting based on faster access to good information. Washington must make it a priority to provide police officers the needed technology so that they no longer rely on hunches; then they can target the people who are actually involved in criminal activity. With real time access to information that targets people who have committed crimes as opposed to members of racial and ethnic minorities, police can do a more effective job.

Conclusion

Sixty years ago, advances in technology—the patrol car and the two-way radio - offered great promise to improve the effectiveness of law enforcement. Unwittingly, these advances separated police from the citizens they are sworn to serve.

The recent movement toward community policing has started to rebuild those bonds. Now, the technology boom must be aggressively used to exchange information and establish stronger ties between all government agencies and citizens.

Police action alone can never free neighborhoods from crime and violence. Nor by itself can it reduce fear. Only when law enforcement is viewed as an integral part of a fully accountable government structure will we be able to systematically create strong communities resistant to disorder, decline, and crime.

John D. Cohen is president and CEO of PSComm, LLC, and executive director of the Progressive Policy Institute's Community Crime Fighting Project. Adam Gelb is chief operating officer of PSComm, LLC, and a former policy adviser to Maryland Lt. Gov. Kathleen Kennedy Townsend. Robert Wasserman is chairman of PSComm, LLC, and former chief of staff of the White House Office of National Drug Control Policy.

From *Blueprint* magazine, Winter 2001, pp. 56-59. © 2001 by Blueprint. Reprinted by permission.

Policing the Police

BY KENNETH JOST

THE ISSUES

Rafael Perez had wanted to be a policeman since childhood. After four years in the Marines, he joined the Los Angeles Police Department in 1989. He did well and was assigned to a special anti-gang squad in the Rampart Division, just west of downtown.

The densely populated Rampart area is home to many Asian and Hispanic immigrants and to some of the city's most feared street gangs. When Perez started in the elite squad, Rampart had one of the highest murder rates among the city's 18 police divisions. Today, violent crime has declined there—perhaps a credit to the LAPD's aggressive anti-gang and anti-drug efforts.

The Rampart Division, however, is taking no bows for its work these days. Instead, Rampart has become the name of a stunning scandal of police misconduct ranging from manufacturing evidence and committing perjury to stealing drugs and shooting unarmed suspects. The spreading scandal threatens hundreds, perhaps thousands, of criminal convictions and deals a body blow to the LAPD's efforts to regain public confidence after a troubled decade marked by the Rodney King beating and the O. J. Simpson murder trial.

Perez was once in the middle of the corruption but is now the source of the scandal's most damning disclosures. Facing trial in September on charges of stealing 6 pounds of cocaine from a police evidence room, Perez negotiated a plea bargain by promising to tell all he knew about misconduct in the Rampart Division.

"There's a lot of crooked stuff going on in the LAPD," Perez told authorities, according to transcripts of the interviews obtained by the *Los Angeles Times*.[1]

The Rampart scandal emerged as law enforcement agencies around the country were coming under renewed scrutiny on a variety of issues. The New York City Police Department was still reeling from the brutal sodomizing of a Haitian immigrant in 1997 when four white officers last year shot and killed an unarmed West African immigrant, Amadou Diallo, in the vestibule of his Bronx apartment building. Their trial, moved to Albany because of massive local publicity about the case, ended last month with the officers' acquittal on all counts—a verdict that served only to renew the debate over police tactics and racial attitudes.

Meanwhile, civil-rights and civil-liberties organizations were mounting attacks on "racial profiling," the practice of making traffic or other investigative stops on the basis of an individual's race or ethnicity. Two states, Maryland and New Jersey, have signed federal court consent decrees agreeing to end the practice after lawyers from the American Civil Liberties Union (ACLU) gathered evidence showing racial patterns in highway stops by state police. Other suits are pending. Critics also want to require police to collect racial data on traffic stops in other states to determine the extent of the practice—which law enforcement officials insist is not widespread.

The public focus on police practices comes at a time of declining crime rates and generally increasing police professionalism. A recent survey of both rank-and-file police personnel and officers suggests that the vast majority of police recognize legal constraints on their conduct, try to stay within the law and disapprove of colleagues who do not.

Still, policing the police—either through internal management or external review—remains a difficult job. "Cops and teachers exercise the most unsupervised discretion of any government employees in living up to the public trust or not," says Edwin Delattre, dean of Boston University's School of Education and author of a book on police ethics. "If you look at a cop on the street, there's nobody immediately looking over the cop's shoulder."

"The gap between the best and worse police departments is bigger than ever," says Samuel Walker, a professor of criminal justice at the University of Nebraska in Omaha and author of a history of U.S. law

Black Motorists on I-95 Still Targeted

*T*he state of Maryland settled a racial-profiling suit in January 1995 by agreeing to halt the practice and to furnish racial data on traffic stops to the American Civil Liberties Union of Maryland to monitor the agreement. Despite the settlement, the data showed that a disproportionate number of motorists stopped since then along the I-95 corridor in Maryland—more than two-thirds—were people of color.

Detentions and Searches January 1995-June 1999

	Number of Stops	Percent
African-Americans	1,205	60.7%
Hispanics	117	5.9
Whites	641	32.3
Other	23	1.2
Total non-white	1,322	67.8
Total searches	**1,986**	

Note: Total does not add to 100 percent due to rounding

Source: American Civil Liberties Union of Maryland

enforcement. "In places like San Diego and Charlotte, there is good discipline. They care about their citizens. That's simply not true in New York and Los Angeles."

Police officials tend to simultaneously minimize the extent of abusive practices while insisting they are taking steps to prevent them. Abuse-of-force cases are "insignificant arithmetically," says James Powers, chief of the Fredericksburg, Va., police department and an adviser to an International Association of Chiefs of Police (IACP) study on the use of force. "But perception-wise, it's very significant. One misuse of force to us is catastrophic. And for a long, long time, we've been taking every step we know to restrict or prohibit the improper use of force."

"There is no excuse for stopping someone because they're black or Hispanic or because they're a black person in a white neighborhood," says Earl Sweeney, director of the New Hampshire Police Standards and Training Council and chair of the IACP's highway safety committee. But Sweeney says racial-profiling abuses "have been perpetrated by a minority of individuals, in some cases well-motivated but poorly

trained. We really think the answer is in policy, training and supervision."

Many of the most volatile police controversies—such as the two recent New York City cases—are racially charged. Public mistrust of police remains high in many minority communities.

"Given the large numbers of African-Americans today in prison or under the jurisdiction of the criminal justice system, there are questions in the black community whether this has resulted from discriminatory practices on the part of the police," says Hubert Williams, president of the Police Foundation, a Washington-based research organization.

In Los Angeles, however, many of the officers implicated so far, including Perez, are Hispanics who were targeting Hispanic offenders and suspects.

"This is not a black-white or white-brown incident," says Elizabeth Schroeder, associate director of the ACLU of Southern California. "You've got minority cops who are beating up minorities."

The efforts to control police conduct from the outside began in earnest in the 1960s, when the U.S. Supreme Court, under Chief Justice

Earl Warren, handed down a series of decisions aimed at protecting the rights of suspects and criminal defendants. The best known of those rulings—the so-called *Miranda* decision in 1966—required police to advise suspects after their arrest of their right to remain silent and to have a lawyer present during any questioning.

At around the same time, efforts were being made to increase the number of minority officers on urban police forces. In addition, police critics sought to establish civilian review boards to receive and in some cases adjudicate complaints regarding police conduct.

Today, those changes are widely, but not universally, accepted. In particular, the *Miranda* rule has become an ingrained police practice—and universally known through three decades of police stories on television and film. But law enforcement groups are lining up behind an effort to relax the *Miranda* decision by breathing life into a 1968 law that sought to partly lift its enforcement in federal courts.

The Justice Department has generally refused to invoke the law—known as Section 3501—because of doubts about its constitutionality. But the Supreme Court will consider a case next month in which a federal appeals court invoked the law to turn back a defendant's challenge to a confession that he claimed police obtained before giving him his *Miranda* warnings.

"We do not want to be in a situation where officers know that they can torture a suspect to get a confession" says Gene Voegtlin, legislative counsel for the IACP, which filed a brief urging the court to uphold Section 3501. "But we believe you need to have some flexibility so that society is not punished for small oversights by having confessions thrown out and convictions lost."

But Williams says there is no need to relax or overturn *Miranda*. "Why would we—at a time when the crime rate is spiraling down, when we're trying to focus on community policing—why open up the door for inappropriate practices by some officers that in the past have vastly colored the reputation of the whole force?" Williams asks.

As the justices prepare to hear the *Miranda* case, here are some of the questions being debated by police and their critics:

Should the Miranda *rule regarding police interrogation be relaxed?*

Charles Dickerson was not physically mishandled or psychologically coerced when an FBI agent and an Alexandria, Va., police detective questioned him about a 1997 bank robbery. But a federal judge found that Dickerson—contrary to the FBI agent's testimony—had not been "Mirandized" before he gave a statement linking himself to the getaway vehicle used in the holdup. On that basis, the judge blocked the government from using Dickerson's statement in his scheduled trial.

Three years later, Dickerson has yet to be tried. Instead, his case goes before the U.S. Supreme Court next month in a crucial test of the federal law aimed at partially overturning

Miranda—Section 3501. Critics of *Miranda* hope the court will use the case to relax the application of a decision that they say has hurt law enforcement by making confessions harder to get and allowing some defendants to avoid conviction because of technical mistakes unrelated to any improper conduct by police.

"When you have technical errors or inadvertent oversights—good-faith mistakes—you end up punishing society by excluding evidence that could be used to keep dangerous people off the streets," says Voegtlin of the police chiefs' association.

Supporters of the *Miranda* decision deny that the ruling has greatly hampered law enforcement, but also insist that the mandatory warnings are essential to protect suspects' rights in police interrogation.

"It's ridiculous to think that a lay person understands their rights under the Fifth Amendment," says Lisa Kemler, co-author of a brief in the case on behalf of the National Association of Criminal Defense Lawyers. "The police setting is inherently coercive. All of the things that the [Supreme Court] talked about in the *Miranda* decision are still true today."

The effects of the *Miranda* decision have been debated ever since the Supreme Court handed down its decision on June 13, 1966. In recent years, an academic critic of the decision, University of Utah law professor Paul G. Cassell, has sought to prove the ruling's adverse effects on law enforcement in voluminous scholarly articles as well as in court briefs.

The Supreme Court case, however, does not directly concern the pros and cons of the *Miranda* ruling. Instead, the case tests Congress' power to pass a law to change a decision that the Supreme Court itself indicated might be subject to legislative revision.

Section 3501 of the federal Criminal Code provides that any "voluntary" confession can be introduced in federal courts. The law lists the giving of warnings as two out of five factors for a court to consider in de-

termining whether a statement was voluntary.

The defenders of Section 3501 note that the court itself said that the procedures laid out in the *Miranda* decision might not be the only way to protect suspects' rights.

"*Miranda* itself is not a constitutional mandate," says Kent Scheidegger, legal director of the California-based Criminal Justice Legal Foundation. "The court created some rules for the implementation of constitutional rights that are not themselves constitutionally required, and those rules are subject to revision by Congress."

Critics of the law, however, insist that Congress had no power to overturn a decision defining constitutional rights. "If Congress can overrule *Miranda* by legislation, then it can overrule anything," says Yale Kamisar, a University of Michigan law professor and longtime defender of the ruling.

"The *Miranda* opinion says that these warnings aren't the only solution as long as you come up with an alternative that is equally effective," Kamisar adds. "The proponents of the statute never mention the [court's] statement that you'd have to come up with an alternative that is equally effective."

Cassell, who will present the arguments in defense of the law before the Supreme Court next month, says that police will "absolutely" continue to give the warnings even if the statute is upheld. "The warnings aren't the problems," Cassell says. "The problems are the vast procedural apparatus that's been erected around the warnings."

In fact, some pro-law enforcement observers say *Miranda* has actually benefited police. "*Miranda* is probably the best thing that's ever happened to police, even though they may not know it," says Craig Bradley, a law professor at Indiana University in Bloomington and former federal prosecutor and Justice Department official.

The ruling "gives police something very easy to comply with,"

Bradley continues. And compliance with the warnings typically limits further inquiry into police conduct.

"In *Miranda*, the court condemned a number of techniques" such as psychological pressure and deceptive tactics, Bradley says. "After *Miranda*, no one looks into that any more. There's very little examination of police tactics short of outright brutality."

Voegtlin agrees on some of the benefits of the ruling. "The *Miranda* decision gave law enforcement some valuable guidelines," he says. "It put policies and procedures into place to protect officers as well as suspects. Once it was certified that the warnings were given, there wasn't a question of the voluntariness of the confession."

Still, the police chiefs' group is joining other law enforcement organizations in urging the court to uphold the law limiting *Miranda* impact. "For someone to go free because of a technical oversight is wrong," Voegtlin says, "and that's what we're trying to remedy."

Are stronger measures needed to prevent use of excessive force by police officers?

Public confidence in New York City's finest was still recovering from the brutal sodomizing of Haitian immigrant Abner Louima in 1997 when it was shaken again a year ago by the Amadou Diallo shooting. But NYPD officials say that the controversy over Diallo's death and the prosecution of four white police officers for the shooting obscures an encouraging trend: a decline in police shootings and civilians killed or wounded by police fire.

In all, New York City police shot and killed 11 civilians in 1999. That figure is sharply down from the previous year's total of 19. Moreover, the number has been declining steadily since 1990, when 41 civilians were killed. The number of wounded also fell to 31 last year

from 43 in 1998, and the number of incidents dropped to 155 from 249 in the same period.

"Generally, when it comes to the use of firearms, we are the most restrained large city police department in the United States," New York City Police Commissioner Howard Safir told a *New York Times* columnist last month.[2]

Police organizations nationwide are also trying to reassure the public about improper use of force by officers. A study released by the IACP in January showed that police used force fewer than 3.5 times per 10,000 calls for service, and suspects were injured in fewer than 3 percent of the instances when force was used.

"The incidence of use of force is minuscule compared to the number of citizen contacts, and the incidence of use of improper force is also minuscule in relation to that number," Fredericksburg Police Chief Powers said.[3]

Outside critics and observers, however, see no cause for complacency. "Excessive force has long been and continues to be a serious problem with enormous racial overtones in New York City," says Norman Siegel, executive director of the New York Civil Liberties Union. "And it will probably continue as long as mayors and police commissioners continue to deny the painful problem of police brutality, until civilian review boards become more effective, until police departments such as New York City's become more racially representative of the people they police and until they get better training."

"Whenever police abuse their authority, it's a social problem that needs to be controlled," says Geoffrey Alpert, a professor at the University of South Carolina's College of Criminal Justice in Columbia and an adviser to police departments on use of force. "It's a very powerful tool that they're given, and to abuse it flies in the face of why we give it to them."

Civil-rights and civil-liberties organizations often emphasize exter-

nal mechanisms to try to control use of excessive force by police, such as civilian review boards, civil damage suits and criminal prosecutions. The effectiveness of civilian-review mechanisms is a subject of sharp dispute between civil-rights advocates and police unions and public officials in many cities. In New York, for example, Mayor Rudolph Giuliani is strongly opposed to the city's civilian review board, although the City Council voted overwhelmingly several years ago to keep it in existence.

"A number of them are very successful and have documented records of achievements," says the University of Nebraska's Walker, author of a forthcoming book on police accountability. "A number of them are abject failures. It's a question of determining which ones work, and why."

"Civilian review can be useful if it's a cooperative venture that doesn't just have to do with problems," Delattre says. "If the only time they're engaged is over some type of crisis, or if it has inordinate power, you're not going to have anything except a higher wall of resistance and silence [from police]."

Legal actions also have mixed results on officer conduct, experts say. Alpert says civil damage suits don't radically affect police behavior. "A lot of that information stays in the legal offices and never filters back to the police department," he says.

As for criminal prosecutions of questionable police behavior—which are relatively few in number in any event—Alpert says officers on patrol often respond by becoming more reluctant to initiate investigations of suspicious circumstances. "For a lot of these shootings that are relatively close calls, they're likely to say 'the system is just punishing us for doing our jobs' and become more careful in not going out on a limb," he says.

Police officials are more likely to emphasize improved recruitment and training as ways to prevent excessive use of force. "We now give psychological tests and do extensive interviews before hiring," says Fredericksburg Police Chief Powers. "We take every step we can to make sure that officers are not predisposed to that. And we do extensive training and talk about what is the proper use of force."

Categorical rules on use of force also may reduce civilian injuries, according to Carl Klockars, a professor of criminal justice at the University of Delaware in Newark. Departments that specifically prohibit high-speed chases or the use of warning shots, for example, appear to have few civilians killed or injured by police conduct, Klockars says.

"Excessive force has been with us forever, and it's still with us," says the Police Foundation's Williams. "It has not abated significantly at all. But you've got to understand the environment police are working in. It's a very tough job, and in many instances they're just trying to do the best they can do."

Should the use of "racial profiling" be prohibited?

Christopher Darden and Johnnie Cochran squared off against each other in a Los Angeles courtroom as prosecutor and defense lawyer in the O. J. Simpson murder case. But the two African-American attorneys had something in common before the trail. Both had been victims of what they regarded as racially motivated traffic stops by police while working for the Los Angeles district attorney's office.[4]

Darden and Cochran are just two of the many African-Americans from all walks of life who have stepped forward during recent years to complain about being stopped for the not-so-fictitious offense of DWB—"driving while black." Minority groups representing blacks as well as Hispanics complain that police use racial or ethnic stereotypes in traffic enforcement or other investigative stops.

"This is not a new thing, by any means," says David Harris, a law professor at the University of Toledo who has studied the issue for the ACLU. "What is new is that we have begun over the last few years to see the collection of some of the data to substantiate what blacks and other minorities have been saying for a long time."

Some police officials acknowledge the practice while also expressing strong disapproval. "Whether racial profiling is existent in the United States—I'm sure that it probably is," says Jack Grant, manager of the Division of State and Provincial Police at the police chiefs' association. "We discourage it. Responsible police administrators do everything they can to prevent it. It cannot be tolerated as a practice in police work."

Many police officials and law enforcement supporters, however, also insist that race can sometimes be a legitimate factor for officers to consider in police investigations. "Racial profiling is wrong," says Cornelius Behan, retired police chief in Baltimore County, Md., "but it gets confused with sensible police procedures. It's wise to try to develop a profile of who the offenders are, and sometimes a legitimate profile would have race in it."

"The distinction is between profiling and discriminatory profiling," Delattre says. "Anybody who says you can enforce the law and protect public safety without profiling is trying to sell you a pipe dream. What you need are clear statements of policy about how to justify responsible profiling from profiling that's based on bigotry and that has the effect that bigotry has."

Racial and ethnic minorities have long been accustomed to being regarded with suspicion when they frequent "white" neighborhoods, whether on foot or in vehicles. The "driving while black" issue has become more visible in recent years because of stepped-up traffic enforcement aimed in large part at detecting drug offenses. "These pretext stops are about drugs," Harris says. "That's what the

federal government has trained local law enforcement to use them for."

Harris and other critics of racial profiling say police who target blacks or other minorities in drug-interdiction efforts are operating on a false assumption that use of drugs is highest among African-Americans. "Police are focused on the drug market in the inner city, and that's in African-American communities and other minority communities," the Police Foundation's Williams explains. "They look at the people they're arresting, and that's where they get their profile. So it always winds up with a heavy representation of African-Americans and Hispanics."

Critics also question the value of using traffic stops for drug enforcement, noting that the vast majority of people stopped in drug-related patrolling end up not being charged with any drug offenses. John Crew, director of the ACLU of Northern California's Police Practices Project, says data gathered for a class-action suit against the California Highway Patrol indicate that the CHP stopped about 33,000 motorists in 1997 in drug-related investigations but had a "hit rate" of less than 2 percent. "If you use a tactic that fails 98 percent of the time," Crew says, "normally that's not something that you would view as successful."

But Sweeney, who oversees training for all of New Hampshire's state and local police, defends the use of traffic enforcement for other anti-crime purposes. "Aggressive enforcement of the traffic laws keeps crime down," Sweeney says. "You have a tendency to detect people who are violating the laws."

"People who have been arrested tell you that they stay away from communities and areas where there is intensive enforcement of traffic laws," Sweeney continues. "If they're carrying drugs, carrying burglary tools, they're likely to be stopped while driving along that stretch of the highway."

While condemning racial profiling, police officials generally contend the problem is relatively isolated. Critics insist the practice is more widespread. To try to substantiate their beliefs, the ACLU and other critics favor legislation—passed in two states and pending in Congress and at least 18 other states—to require state and local law enforcement agencies to gather data on the race of persons stopped for traffic violations. Police groups generally oppose such proposals as unnecessary and expensive.

But Crew also notes that many police leaders have become more attuned to the problem, in part because of the effect that the perception of racial profiling has on public confidence in law enforcement.

"It's interesting to hear law enforcement groups talk about this not just as a civil-rights issue, not just a justice issue, but as an effective-policing issue," Crew says. "If they're going to be effective, they can't afford to have a large segment of the American population, people of color, disaffected from police."

BACKGROUND

A Checkered Past

The creation of the first full-time police departments in the United States in Philadelphia and Boston in the 1830s came not long after Sir Robert Peel established what is regarded as the first modern force, the London Metropolitan Police, in 1829. The London police quickly gained a reputation for professionalism, but urban police departments in the United States were beset by continuing scandals through the 19th century. Police departments were guilty of "pervasive brutality and corruption," according to historian Walker, and "did little to prevent crime or provide public services."[5]

A police-reform movement developed in the early 20th century. The reformers sought to rid-police departments of political influence and

cronyism and turn them into efficient, nonpartisan agencies committed to public service. They wanted police departments to be run by trained experts with job tenure to insulate them from political interference. They also wanted to improve the recruitment and training of officers and to centralize a command structure for better accountability. Some progress was made on all of those goals. Still, a federal crime commission—reported in 1931 that physical brutality was "extensively practiced" by police departments around the country.[6]

The Supreme Court first stepped in to police the interrogation process in 1936 in a flagrant case in which three black tenant farmers "confessed" to the murder of a white farmer after being brutally tortured by local sheriff's deputies in Mississippi. An involuntary confession was unreliable, the court reasoned, and its use in court would violate the 14th Amendment's prohibition against depriving anyone of life or liberty without due process of law. In a second confession case six years later, the court shifted its focus by declaring that the Due Process Clause prohibited the use of any evidence—whether true or false—that police obtained through techniques that "shocked the conscience" of the community or violated fundamental standards of fairness.[7]

The high court ruled on more than 30 confession cases between 1936 and 1964, deciding whether a confession was voluntary by looking at the totality of the circumstances in each case.[8] In some cases, the court established that certain interrogation methods—including physical force, threats of harm or punishment, lengthy or incommunicado questioning, solitary confinement, denial of food or sleep and promises of leniency—were presumptively coercive and therefore constitutionally impermissible. But the court did not attempt to set out a specific checklist of procedures for police to assure that a suspect's statement would be

deemed voluntary and therefore admissible in court.

Police professionalism "continued to make steady advances" during this period, according to historian Walker.[9] A "new generation" of police chiefs provided better leadership, while officers became more productive because of technological advances, such as patrol cars with sophisticated communications systems.

At the same time, racial flareups foreshadowed the crisis in police-community relations that fully developed in the 1960s. Racial disturbances in Detroit and New York City's Harlem in 1943 produced accusations of discriminatory enforcement against the cities' African-American populations, while the "Zoot Suit" riots in Los Angeles exposed tensions between blacks, Hispanics and the city's over whelmingly white police force.

Some police chiefs and national organizations responded with programs to improve race relations. But, as Walker notes, recruitment of black police officers lagged, and the "pioneering efforts" in improving police-community relations did not keep pace with the rapidly changing context of race relations in the decades after World War II.

By the mid-1960s, the Supreme Court had a liberal majority that was determined to continue the civil-rights revolution it had launched with the landmark school-desegregation rulings of the 1950s. The court also was determined to bring about a due-process revolution in the administration of criminal justice across the country. In 1961 the court ruled that illegally obtained evidence could not be used in state trials; two years later it ruled that the states had to provide lawyers for indigent criminal defendants in felony trials if they could not afford to pay for one themselves.[10]

Then in 1964 the court held in *Escobedo v. Illinois* that a suspect has a right under the Sixth Amendment to consult with his lawyer during police interrogation once an investigation had moved from a general inquiry to

Chronology

Before 1900

Corruption and brutality are pervasive in U.S. police forces.

1900–1960

Police reform movements advance; Supreme Court begins to review confession cases.

1936

First Supreme Court decision to bar confession as involuntary.

1960s

Warren Court seeks to control police conduct.

1961

Supreme Court rules illegally seized evidence cannot be used in state court trials.

1966

Supreme Court in *Miranda v. Arizona* requires police to advise suspects of rights.

1968

Kerner Commission warns of deep mistrust of police by African-Americans; Congress passes law aimed at overturning *Miranda* in federal courts.

1970s

Burger Court restricts **Miranda,** *but does not overturn it.*

1971

Confession obtained in violation of *Miranda* can be used to impeach defendant's testimony at trial, Supreme Court rules.

1980s

Conservative era in law enforcement.

1986

Justice Department unit proposes effort to overturn *Miranda*, but plan is not pursued.

1990s

Police brutality and racial profiling emerge as major issues.

1991

Black motorist Rodney King is kicked and beaten by white Los Angeles police officers; they are acquitted in state trial in 1992, but two are convicted a year later of civil-rights violations.

1993

Black lawyer Robert Wilkins files anti-racial profiling suit after being stopped by Maryland state troopers; state settles suit in 1995 by agreeing to end racial profiling and provide racial data on traffic stops to ACLU.

1996

Supreme Court upholds pretextual traffic stops for drug enforcement.

1997

Black immigrant Abner Louima is sodomized by white New York police officers; Justin Volpe pleads guilty in 1999 and draws 30-year prison term.

February 1999

Black immigrant Amadou Diallo is fatally shot by four white NYPD officers; murder trial moved to Albany because of publicity in New York City.

April 1999

New Jersey attorney general issues report acknowledging racial profiling by state police; state settles Justice Department suit in December by agreeing to end practice.

September 1999

Rafael Perez implicates himself and other LAPD anti-gang officers in city's Rampart Division in widespread abuse, including planting evidence and shooting suspects.

December 1999

Supreme Court agrees to review appeals court ruling upholding 1968 law aimed at overturning *Miranda* in federal courts.

2000s

Racial profiling, police brutality continue as high-profile issues.

January 2000

Democratic presidential candidates Al Gore and Bill Bradley oppose racial profiling; GOP front-runner George W. Bush is ambiguous.

Feb. 25, 2000

NYPD officers are acquitted in Diallo shooting; former LAPD officer Perez gets five years in prison for stealing cocaine from police evidence room.

March 1, 2000

LAPD report blames Rampart scandal on lax supervision and "culture of mediocrity."

April 19, 2000

Supreme Court set to hear arguments on anti-*Miranda* law.

---

focus specifically on him. The implications of the decision were unclear; one reading suggested that it applied only to suspects like Escobedo who already had an attorney.

But two years later the court made clear it had a broader interest in po-

lice interrogations by scheduling argument in four consolidated cases in which defendants challenged their convictions by claiming that police had obtained confessions from them in violation of their constitutional rights.

Miranda's Rights

Ernest Miranda confessed to the kidnap-rape of a Phoenix, Ariz., teenager in 1963 after an interrogation session with no overt indications of coercion. Police found

Miranda, a 23-year-old laborer, after tracking the license plate of a truck driven by the assailant. Detectives went to his home, asked him to accompany them to the police station and there began questioning him about the crime. A line-up was inconclusive, but police told Miranda he had been identified. At that point, he admitted that he had raped the girl.[11]

The Supreme Court heard arguments in Miranda's effort to reverse his state court conviction and in three other confession cases on March 2 and 3, 1966. When he announced the decision in the cases on June 13, Chief Justice Warren acknowledged that Miranda's statement might not be deemed involuntary "in traditional terms." But Warren, a former district attorney in California, said that "incommunicado interrogation" and such recognized police techniques of undermining a suspect's will through flattery, isolation or trickery were inherently compulsive and violated the Fifth Amendment's "cherished" principle against self-incrimination.

To protect that right, Warren continued, police must advise a suspect of the right to remain silent, the right to an attorney and the right to have an attorney appointed if he cannot afford one, and must warn that any statement given after waiving those rights could be used in court against him. Warren acknowledged that the Constitution might not require this particular set of safeguards. But unless equally effective safeguards were established, police had to give those warnings for a suspect's statement to be admissible later in court.

The 5–4 decision stopped short of the most restrictive position urged in arguments: an absolute requirement to have an attorney present during any police interrogation. The dissenting justices nonetheless forcefully criticized the ruling. They argued for retaining what Justice Byron White called the "more pliable" method of testing confessions on the totality of the circumstances. And each of the four dissenters warned of a likely adverse effect on law en-

forcement. "We do know that some crimes cannot be solved without confessions," Justice John Marshall Harlan wrote, "and that the Court is taking a real risk with society's welfare in imposing its new regime on the country."

Those warnings were quickly picked up and amplified by police, prosecutors and politicians. The court, critics said, had "handcuffed" the police. Congress responded in 1968 with a provision in the Omnibus Crime Control and Safe Streets Act seeking to overturn Miranda in federal courts and return to a voluntariness test. The main sponsor, Sen. John McClellan, D-Ark., had proposed a constitutional amendment shortly after the decision was announced, but turned to the easier legislative route instead.

Also in 1968, Republican presidential nominee Richard M. Nixon made the Supreme Court's criminal-procedure decisions a major focus on his campaign and promised to appoint law-and-order justices to the court if elected. The next year, as president, Nixon chose Warren E. Burger, a conservative judge from the federal appeals court in Washington, D.C., to succeed Warren as chief justice.

During Burger's 17 years as chief justice, both supporters and critics of Miranda found cause for disappointment. Initially, the court somewhat expanded the ruling—for example, to cover custodial interrogation outside a police station. In 1971, however, Burger and the four Miranda dissenters joined in a 6–3 decision carving out a major exception that allowed prosecutors to use a statement obtained in violation of the decision to cross-examine a defendant at trial. Other exceptions and restrictions followed.

Still, the Burger Court stopped short of overturning Miranda. And police attitudes toward Miranda changed from hostility to acceptance. By the late 1980s, an American Bar Association survey found that "a very strong majority" of police, prosecutors and judges believed Miranda

"does not present serious problems for law enforcement."[12]

Critics of the Warren Court's criminal-procedure rulings saw a better chance for undoing some of the decisions after President Ronald Reagan chose William H. Rehnquist to succeed Burger as chief justice in 1986. Within the Justice Department, the Office of Legal Policy proposed a direct challenge to Miranda, but Solicitor General Charles Fried largely rebuffed the idea.

"Most experienced federal prosecutors in and out of my office were opposed to the project, as was I," Fried wrote in his memoir.[13] Cassell points to cases in which federal prosecutors did try to use Section 3501, and their efforts were supported by the department on appeal.

Still, Justice Antonin Scalia, writing in a 1994 case, complained about the government's "repeated refusal" to invoke the provision in confession cases.[14] And a year earlier, the Rehnquist Court signaled a sort of acceptance of by reaffirming—on a 5–4 vote with Rehnquist in dissent—that federal courts can set aside state court convictions if police violated a suspect's Miranda rights during questioning.[15]

Use of Force

Police came under intense, renewed criticism in the 1990s despite the easing of the controversy over interrogation practices. The issue was police use of force—a problem that flared up most dramatically in the beating of black motorist King in Los Angeles in 1991 and the sodomizing of Haitian immigrant Louima in New York City in 1997.[16] The incidents provoked new accusations of racism against both police departments from minority and civil rights groups and new concerns among police executives and government officials about how to control use of excessive force by police.

Police shootings of black civilians had touched off several of the racial disturbances that had erupted in the

Controversial *Miranda* Ruling Still Stands

The U.S. Supreme Court's 1966 *Miranda* decision requiring police to advise suspects of their constitutional rights against self-incrimination before interrogation has been narrowed over the years by subsequent high court decisions but not overturned.

Case	Vote	Ruling
Miranda v. Arizona (1966)	5-4	Police must advise suspect before interrogation of right to remain silent, right to a lawyer, right to have lawyer appointed, and give warning that any statement can be used against him; police cannot use any statement obtained without such warnings.
Orozco v. Texas (1969)	6-2	Police must give *Miranda* warnings whenever a suspect is effectively in custody--in this case, in his home.
Harris v. New York (1971)	6-3	Statement obtained in violation of *Miranda* can be used to cross-examine defendant or impeach testimony at trial.
Michigan v. Tucker (1974)	8-1	Police can use statement in violation of *Miranda* as a lead for obtaining other evidence; Rehnquist opinion emphasizes *Miranda* not constitutionally required.
Michigan v. Mosley (1975)	7-2	Police did not violate *Miranda* by questioning suspect who invoked his right to silence about a second offense after they gave a second warning.
United States v. Mandujano (1976)	8-0	No *Miranda* warning needed for grand jury witness.
Brewer v. Williams (1977)	5-4	Police officer's speech pleading for "Christian burial" of child murder victim was "tantamount to interrogation" and violated suspect's *Miranda* rights.
Fare v. Michael C. (1979)	5-4	Probation officer need not give Miranda warnings before questioning juvenile suspect.
Rhode Island v. Innis (1980)	6-3	Police appeal to suspect's conscience did not amount to interrogation in violation of *Miranda*.
Edwards v. Arizona (1981)	9-0	Police must stop interrogation after suspect asks for lawyer.
Minnesota v. Murphy (1984)	5-4	No *Miranda* warning needed before interview with probation officer.
New York v. Quarles (1984)	5-4	Police did not violate *Miranda* by asking suspect, "Where's the gun?" before giving warnings; suspect's answer could be used as evidence at trial ("public safety exception").
Withrow v. Williams (1993)	5-4	*Miranda* violation can be basis for challenging state court conviction in federal habeas corpus proceeding.

nation's big cities three decades earlier. The 1968 report by a presidential panel appointed to study the cause of the riots—the so-called Kerner Commission—found "deep hostility between police and ghetto communities" to have been a "primary cause" of the disorders.

Historian Walker also blames the lack of controls on the use of force by police. "Even the best departments had no meaningful rules on deadly force," Walker writes, "offering their officers many hours of training on how to shoot but not on when to use their weapons."[17]

Much progress was made over the next 25 years, according to Walker. Civilian review boards—favored by groups seeking to hold police accountable—gradually achieved a measure of acceptance after having been stoutly resisted by police unions, local politicians and some segments of the public. By the 1990s, Walker reports, more than three-fourths of the police departments in the nation's biggest cities had some form of external or civilian review of complaints.

In addition, local police departments began adopting rules to guide officers in the use of force. The rules

Law OKs 'Voluntary' Confessions

Section 3501 of the federal Criminal Code (Title 18) attempts to partly overturn the *Miranda* decision as used in federal courts. The law provides that a confession "shall be admissible in evidence" in any federal prosecution "if it is voluntarily given." The law lists five situations—some of which track the four warnings required under *Miranda*—that a judge should consider in determining whether a confession was voluntary:

• The time between the defendant's arrest and arraignment in court.*

• Whether the defendant knew the nature of the offense with which he was being charged when he confessed.**

• Whether the defendant "was advised or knew that he was not required to make any statement and that any such statement could be used against him."

• Whether the defendant "had been advised prior to questioning of his right to the assistance of counsel."

• Whether the defendant "was without the assistance of counsel when questioned."

This recognizes that the longer a suspect is held without charges the greater the possibility that mistreatment prompted the confession.
**This recognizes the possibility that police sometimes threaten to hold suspects incommunicado until they confess.*

appeared to bring results. New York City Police Commissioner Patrick Murphy instituted a rule in 1972 allowing officers to shoot only in "the defense of life" and requiring reports and reviews of any weapons discharge. Officer-involved shootings declined 30 percent over the next three years, according to research by James Fyfe, a professor of criminal

justice at Temple University in Philadelphia and an expert on use-of-force issues.[18]

The beating of King by four white Los Angeles police officers after a high-speed car chase on March 3, 1991, put the issue of police brutality back on the national agenda. An 81-second videotape shot by a resident of a nearby apartment—broadcast countless times around the world over the next two years—showed the officers repeatedly kicking King and hitting him 56 times with their batons as he lay on the ground.

The episode produced a national outcry, but criminal prosecutions of the officers ended with mixed results. A predominantly white jury in a neighboring county acquitted the officers of state charges in April 1992; two officers were convicted of violating King's civil rights in a federal court trial in April 1993, but they were given relatively light sentences of 30 months each.

Meanwhile, though, a special commission appointed by Los Angeles Mayor Tom Bradley concluded that the incident was merely one example of what it described as "a tolerance within the LAPD of attitudes condoning violence against the public."[19]

Six years after the King beating, police brutality again became a national issue with an episode in New York that had none of the ambiguity or arguable justifications of the Los Angeles incident. New York police officers arrested Louima on Aug. 9, 1997, following an altercation outside a Brooklyn nightclub. Officer Justin Volpe later acknowledged that he struck Louima while taking him to the patrol car. Once at the station house, Volpe took Louima into a restroom and plunged a broken broomstick handle into the Haitian's rectum. Volpe pleaded guilty to six federal charges in May 1999 and was later sentenced to 30 years in prison; a second officer, Charles Schwarz, was convicted of beating Louima and holding him down during the sodomizing.*

The incident produced universal revulsion, even among sympathetic police observers. "This was clearly a case of sadism and racism," says Boston University's Delattre. Nonetheless, New York Mayor Giuliani, a strong police supporter, saw a positive sign in the willingness of Volpe's fellow officers to aid investigators in uncovering the incident and to testify against him. The trial, Giuliani said, "destroys the myth of the blue wall of silence" among police officers.

For his part, though, Walker says the King and Louima cases represented a setback for public perceptions of police accountability.

"All of the positive developments have been obscured by these horrific examples in New York and Los Angeles, which make it appear to the average citizen that nothing has changed, and maybe things have gotten worse," Walker says.

'Driving While Black'

Racial profiling became the new flashpoint of police-community relations during the 1990s. African-Americans from many walks of life testified to their experiences of having been stopped and questioned by police seemingly for no reason other than their race.

By the end of the decade, the leading law enforcement groups were joining civil-rights and civil-liberties groups in saying that race alone should never be the basis for a traffic stop or other police investigation. But police were also continuing to defend the use of race as one factor in criminal profiling, particularly in anti-drug enforcement.

Police explained their use of race in deciding what drivers or pedestrians to stop for investigation by pointing to the statistics showing that African-Americans are more likely than whites to be arrested or convicted of many of the most common crimes, especially drug offenses and so-called street crimes. Courts up to and including the U.S. Supreme Court sanctioned the practice.

Race Colors Attitudes About Police Conduct

Most Americans—including a majority of blacks and a substantial majority of whites—have a favorable opinion of their local police. African-Americans are nearly four times as likely as whites to feel they are treated unfairly by local police, according to a recent Gallup Poll. Among blacks, younger men were nearly twice as likely as younger women to feel unfairly treated. Here are some questions from the poll:

Do you have a favorable or unfavorable opinion of your local police?

	Favorable	Unfavorable	Don't know
Blacks	58%	36%	6%
Whites	85%	13%	2%

Do you feel you're treated fairly by the local police in your area?

	Fairly	Not Fairly	Not Applicable/Did not answer
Blacks	66%	27%	7%
Whites	91%	7%	2%

Do you feel you're treated fairly by the local police in your area?

Black men	Treated Fairly	Not Treated Fairly
Ages:		
18-34	43%	53%
35-49	71%	23%
50+	68%	22%
Black women	**Treated Fairly**	**Not Treated Fairly**
Ages:		
18-34	67%	26%
35-49	75%	19%
50+	71%	18%

Source: The Gallup Organization. The survey is based on 2,006 phone interviews with a random sample of adults in the continental U.S. from Sept. 24, to Nov. 16, 1999.

In one representative case, the Arizona Supreme Court in 1975 upheld a police officer's decision to question a Mexican male because he was sitting in a parked car in a predominantly white neighborhood. The use of race, the court said, was "a practical aspect of good law enforcement."[20]

Two decades later, the Supreme Court in 1996 gave police a blank check to use traffic violations as a pretext for stopping motorists for suspected drug violations. The ruling in *Whren v. United States* turned aside the plea by two black defendants that they had been stopped because of their race.

By the 1990s, though, racial profiling was being challenged not only by convicted defendants but also by the innocent victims of the practice—people who were stopped, questioned, perhaps searched and then allowed to go on their way when police found no evidence of crime. The first major victory for critics of the practice came in a case brought by Robert Wilkins, a public defender in Washington, D.C., who was stopped by Maryland state police in May 1992 while driving with his family back to Washington. When Wilkins refused to consent to a search of his car troopers called for a trained narcotics dog to try to detect drugs, but no drugs were found.

Wilkins, represented by the ACLU of Maryland and two private Washington lawyers, filed a federal civil rights damage suit in May 1993 contending that the use of a racial profile violated his constitutional rights. The state agreed to settle the suit in January 1995. The state said it would adopt an official policy prohibiting racial profiling and, significantly, maintain detailed records of motorist stops to be provided to the ACLU to monitor any patterns of discrimination. Wilkins and his family were also awarded $50,000 plus attorney fees.

Critics of racial profiling won another settlement late last year after New Jersey officials acknowledged that some state troopers had singled out black and Hispanic motorists for anti-drug enforcement. The long-simmering issue recently erupted in the state when the head of the state police, Carl Williams, was quoted as saying it was "most likely a minority group" that was involved with marijuana or cocaine. The state's Republican governor, Christine Todd Whitman, fired Williams on Feb. 28.

Less than two months later, Whitman appeared with the state's attorney general at a news conference on April 20 to release a two-month study that confirmed a stark racial pattern in traffic stops by troopers at some stations. At year's end, the state signed an agreement with the U.S. Justice Department mandating an overhaul of the state police to end racial profiling and agreeing to the appointment of a federal monitor to oversee implementation of the accord.

The shift of opinion on the issue could be seen in comments by candidates in the 2000 presidential campaign. The two leading Democrats—Vice President Al Gore and former New Jersey Sen. Bill Bradley—both spoke out against racial profiling in a Jan.17 debate in Iowa. Bradley drew blood on the issue by challenging Gore to "walk down that hallway" in the White House and get President Clinton to sign an executive order barring racial profiling by federal law enforcement agents. Gore aides later noted that Clinton has ordered federal agencies to collect data on the practice.

For his part, the Republican front-runner, Texas Gov. George W. Bush, also criticized racial profiling in a Jan. 10 campaign debate in Michigan. "No one wants racial profiling to take place in any state," Bush said. But Bush also said, "It's not the federal government's role to run state police departments." The ACLU criticized what it called Bush's "vague" statements and challenged him to issue an executive order in Texas barring the practice.

NOTES

1. Scott Glover and Matt Lait, "L.A. Police Group Often Broke Law, Transcripts Say," *Los Angeles Times*, February 10, 2000, p. A1. For other articles, see the Times' Web site: www.latimes.com/rampart.
2. Clyde Haberman, "Despite Diallo, Data Show Gun Restraint," *The New York Times*, Feb. 4, 2000, p. B1.
3. International Association of Chiefs of Police, "Police Use of Force in America," October 1999.
4. See Christopher A. Darden, *In Contempt* (1996), p. 110; "Cochran & Grace," "Johnnie Cochran: Driving While Black," Court TV, March 23, 1997, cited in David A. Harris, "The Stories, the Statistics, and the Law: Why 'Driving While Black' Matters," *Minnesota Law Review*, Vol. 84 (1999), pp. 265–266.
5. Samuel Walker, *Popular Justice: A History of American Criminal Justice* (1980), p. 61. Other historical background is also drawn from this first edition and from a revised and updated edition published in 1998.
6. National Commission on Law Observance and Enforcement, *Lawless in Law Enforcement* (1931), p. 103, cited in Walker, op. cit., p. 174.
7. The case of *Brown v. Mississippi* (1936) and *Lisenba V. California* (1941).
8. Background drawn from Yale Kamisar *et al.*, *Modern Criminal Procedure: Cases, Comments, and Questions* (8th ed. 1994), as summarized in Richard A. Leo, "The Impact of Miranda Revisited," *Journal of Criminal Law and Criminology*, Vol. 86, No. 3 (1996), pp. 624–625.
9. Walker, *op. cit.*, pp. 194–199.
10. The cases of *Mapp v. Ohio* (1961) and *Gideon v. Wainwright* (1963).
11. Account of interrogation taken from Paul G. Cassell, "The Statute That Time Forgot: 18 U.S.C. Section 3501 and the Overhauling of Miranda," *Iowa Law Review*, Vol. 85 (1999), pp. 183–191. The teenaged victim said she thought Miranda could be the assailant, but could not be positive. After the line-up, Miranda asked if the teenager and a second assault victim had identified him. "Yes, Ernie, they did," a detective replied.
12. ABA Special Commission on Criminal Justice in a Free Society, Criminal Justice in Crisis (1988), p. 28.
13. Charles Fried, *Order and Law* (1990), p. 46.
14. The case is *Davis v. United States* (1994).
15. The case is *Withrow v. Williams* (1993).
16. For background, see Richard L. Worsnop, "Police Brutality," *The CQ Researchers*, Sept. 6, 1991, pp. 633–656.
17. Walker, *op. cit.* (2d ed.), p. 197.
18. See *Ibid.*, pp. 232–234.
19. Cited in Worsnop, *op. cit.*, p. 644.
20. Cases cited in Randall Kennedy, *Race, Crime, and the Law* (1997), p. 152.

Kenneth Jost is a veteran legal-affairs journalist and CQ Researcher staff writer. He holds a law degree from Georgetown University, where he was editor of the Georgetown Law Journal. He is author of The Supreme Court Yearbook and a contributor to several legal periodicals.

From *Congressional Quarterly*, March 17, 2000, pp. 211-230. © 2000 by Congressional Quarterly, Inc. Reprinted by permission.

Police Officer Candidate Assessment and Selection

By DAVID A. DECICCO

For some individuals, the mere sight of a law enforcement officer can elicit feelings of excitement, curiosity, or fear; however, these are mild effects that citizens can experience from afar. Yet, the officers themselves often experience long periods of boredom, peppered with moments of excitement and even sheer terror. In the lives of many officers, adrenalin becomes a drug and adversity becomes part of their daily lives. Handling feelings of separation, uselessness, and frustration becomes a ritual habit. Some officers handle the stress of the job adequately, while for others it can prove hazardous, if not debilitating.

Police officer misconduct may arise as a result of the various pressures this profession exerts, from officers' inappropriate management of the ensuing stress. The departments and governments that police officers represent frequently incur lawsuits as a result of the officers' reaction to stress. In addition, the actions of individual officers can impact civilian and officer safety, and more generally, public opinion of a department or of law enforcement as a whole. Police officers are entrusted with a tremendous amount of authority. They make quick decisions and seldom make them under direct supervision. Improper actions can prove very costly, not only with regard to monetary judgements, but also in terms of investigative costs, personnel costs (i.e., staff shortages due to suspensions, dismissals, and temporary reassignments), and morale.[1]

"... the assessment center approach is... designed to simulate actual police officer responsibilities and working conditions."

Officer DeCicco serves with the Clarkstown Police Department in Rockland County, New York.

"... the selection of entry-level officers greatly affects the future leadership of a department."

Some experts believe that more or improved training will sufficiently manage the risks associated with police officer misconduct. However, departments rarely make improvements in the selection process of candidates prior to training. Police managers should direct critical emphasis in this initial phase in order to effectively combat the problem. The New York City Police Department estimated that each new officer costs approximately $500,000, which includes expenses incurred from recruitment through the end of an officer's probationary period.[2] Many benefits of weeding out potentially hazardous officers exist. These can include the financial savings of training and possible litigation as well as the influence that "bad" officers could have on their peers. Moreover, because supervisory and managerial positions generally are filled from within, the selection of entry-level officers greatly affects the future leadership of a department.[3] Police managers often assert that recruiters place too much emphasis on obtaining a large applicant pool, rather than quality applicants who have prepared for this type of career. Therefore, in order to have better patrol officer performance, departments should scrutinize the selection of candidates before attempting improvements in officer training.

A COMPREHENSIVE APPROACH

Although methods of assessment and selection of candidates vary among the approximate 12,000 local and state law

One Department's Assessment Method

The Appleton, Wisconsin, Police Department uses various exercises to assess their police officer candidates.

- *Group discussion*—A leaderless interaction regarding a law enforcement topic that an entry-level candidate can understand that will elicit information on a candidate's interpersonal and communication skills.
- *Situational response*—Observation of a department-prepared video tape requiring a written response regarding the situations presented that will obtain information to help gauge a candidate's problem-solving and written communication skills.
- *Oral presentation*—Assignment of a topic for a candidate to present, with a limited preparation time to stimulate stress. Topics should elicit information on how well a candidate can adapt and react to adverse situations.
- *Background/achievement report*—Response to questions that develop information about each candidate's life history and preparation for a law enforcement career.
- *Observational response*—Analysis of a crime scene or prepared room, with instructions to document observations or find clues, which illustrates a candidate's information-gathering and problem-solving skills.

Source: B. D. Kolpack, "The Assessment Center Approach to Police Officer Selection," Police Chief, September 1991, 44–46.

enforcement agencies in the United States, many similarities exist between the longstanding departments. Some of the tactics used may include written tests, a background investigation, physical exam, and an interview. The majority of agencies must follow state civil service regulations. For example, the New York State Civil Service Commission administers the preliminary police officer exam and then reports the results to departments who supervise subsequent stages of selection and assessment within the regulations set by the Civil Service Commission. However, many larger city jurisdictions can administer their own exam while adhering to both city and state civil service directives.

A typical candidate will express their interest in becoming a police officer by either applying directly for employment or taking a scheduled exam, usually given by the county or city personnel office. Administrators should remember that agencies hire less than 4 percent of those who apply to become police officers.[4] In the next phase, the personnel officer administers a group exam designed to test candidates' verbal skills, math aptitude and reasoning, clerical, and related perceptual abilities.[5] After grading this exam, which generally takes a few months, jurisdictions with openings will receive a list of the top-scoring candidates. Often, these candidates will have qualified already on a physical fitness test, which requires minimum performance on such exercises as sit-ups, pull-ups, squat thrusts, and a 50-yard dash.

Once applicants pass the first phase, agencies may use a variety of tests to further determine qualified candidates. For example, departments may use all or a combination of various methods, such as field background investigations, medical examinations, physical strength and agility tests, situational tests, psychological examinations, polygraph tests, and assessment centers.

Background Investigation

Research has shown that all departments use background investigations and medical examinations. Generally, departments place emphasis on the background investigation because an intensive background investigation can help to ensure agencies recruit only the most qualified individuals and also can indicate an applicant's competency, motivation, and personal ethics.[6] During this process, a candidate usually will complete a background questionnaire covering a breadth of data, including all places of residence, level of education, identities of family members and friends, and personal references. The questionnaire will ask an applicant to provide an employment record, credit history, criminal history, and any alcohol or other drug use. This document then serves as a basis for the investigation.

The investigator will confirm the veracity of each piece of information submitted by personally visiting all high schools and colleges that the candidate has attended, as well as interviewing past employers to discuss a candidate's work ethic, performance, honesty, and sociability. A candidate's credit history can serve as a cross-check of information on previous employers, addresses, creditors, history of credit payments, and any civil action taken against the candidate. Investigators can obtain driving and criminal records from state and federal authorities to determine if an applicant has any disqualifying offenses. In addition, the investigator should interview neighbors, spouses, and personal references to provide more details on the applicant's background and lifestyle. Finally, to complete this phase, a formal board interview should ask candidates to discuss current events, their interest in law enforcement, personal and professional backgrounds, and any discrepancies discovered by the investigating officer.[7]

Medical Exam

This section of the hiring process requires that the candidate visit a physician, appointed by the department or certifying personnel agency, for a complete physical examination. The physician should attest that the candidate is generally in good health and meets certain minimum standards such as a height to weight ratio, 20/20 eyesight (corrected), and adequate hearing.

Physical Strength and Agility Tests

Research revealed that 80 percent of departments require applicants to take a physical fitness test.[8] The state civil service commission may require this type of test, which departments may administer subsequent to the written exam. Most agencies hold this test in the gymnasium of a local high school and often include pull-ups, to test strength; sit-ups, to test endurance; a run, to measure aerobic endurance; and an obstacle course, squat thrusts, or side lunges, to test agility. The exam also may include a test of hand strength to verify an applicant's ability to pull the trigger of a gun.

Although these exercises remain typical among many departments, some individuals often criticize the process as having a disparate impact on women. As a result, some applicants who fail this part of the process sue law enforcement agencies alleging that the tests do not assess job-related skills. If a physical agility test has a disparate impact on female applicants then such a test violates Title VII of the 1964 Civil Rights Act. The only justification for a disparate impact is proof that the standards tested are required for the job. Police agencies often have lost legal challenges in such cases unless they could show that these standards apply to all of their on-board sworn personnel. The argument is that if the standard is required for the job then it is necessary for people who already have the job. Because few police agencies are willing to fire employees who cannot meet such standards the courts have not upheld them. Only when the standard can be related to a public safety issue and is applied to on-board personnel, will such standards be upheld.

Some departments have developed a newer battery of tests to assess specific characteristics needed for police officers, but less simulative in nature than other tests and scaled based on age and sex. This new test uses push-ups or a bench press to test absolute strength, sit-ups for muscular endurance, a 1.5- to 2-mile run for aerobic capacity, and a "sit-and-reach" for flexibility. In one department, a male, age 20 to 29, would need to complete a minimum of 38 sit-ups in 1 minute, reach 1.5 inches past his toes, bench press 99 percent of his body weight, and complete 1.5 miles in less than 12 minutes and 51 seconds.[9]

Situational Tests

Fifty-eight percent of departments use some type of real-life, simulated test-ing.[10] These tests may include mock crime scenes, simulated traffic stops, shoot/don't shoot decisions, leaderless group discussions, or role-playing scenarios. Assessment centers also use these types of exercises that incorporate many of the traditional techniques of selection with the addition and emphasis on situational exercises. Some individuals view this approach as an increasingly promising method of selection.

Psychological Testing

Candidates disqualified from employment based on psychological findings also can file lawsuits against the police agency. Fortunately, adjustments to the methods used and the way the findings are reported can reduce the expense of defending such decisions.

Departments use these screens to determine that a police officer candidate is mature, emotionally stable, independent, sociable, and capable of functioning in stressful situations. A certified psychologist, with experience in psychological assessment for law enforcement, should direct this screening process.

Initially, the candidate should take a personality inventory test. Of the exams used in police testing circles, the most popular are the Minnesota Multiphasic Personality Inventory, used by 60 percent of departments, and the California Personality Inventory, used by 19 percent of departments.[11]

Agencies must use the results in conjunction with other components of a psychological assessment in order for these test results to prove most useful. The psychologist should use the test results to indicate areas that investigators should probe further during an interview. The interview should follow a standardized format and elicit information relevant to a candidate's characteristics suitable for employment as a police officer.

The psychologist then should formulate a decision whether to permit or withhold employment of a candidate and prepare a written conclusive summary that completely articulates the assessment process and the reasoning behind the decision. In order to provide a legally defensible report, the assessor also should include specific examples of a

candidate's character pathology (e.g., behavior, promptness, and dress).

Of all the phases in the selection process, administrators should consider the psychological exam with particular caution and meticulous planning. The psychological testing must accurately predict an applicant's performance as a police officer before departments can use it as a basis to disqualify an individual.[12]

Polygraph Tests

Although prohibited from use in most private sectors by the Employee Protection Act of 1988, government organizations can use polygraph testing. Approximately 56 percent of police departments use this test, based on measures of a person's respiration, heart rate, and galvanic skin response.[13] A qualified polygrapher will inquire about the information applicants provide on their background questionnaire in order to verify accuracy and completeness and to note any significant physiological irregularities.

A great deal of controversy has arisen as to the validity of polygraph measurements; therefore, departments should look at the results as a small part of a candidate's assessment process. Law enforcement professionals and polygraph administrators should use the machine to deter lying, rather than to detect it. The U.S. Court of Appeals for the Third Circuit decided that "…in the absence of scientific consensus, reasonable law enforcement administrators may choose to include a polygraph requirement in their hiring process without offending the equal protection clause."[14]

Assessment Centers

First, police administrators must realize the difference between an assessment center and an assessment center approach. An assessment center is a place where a series of events or exercises will occur; however, the assessment center approach is a method that supplements the traditional assessment and selection procedures with situational exercises designed to simulate actual police officer responsibilities and working conditions.

Use of Testing Procedures		
Type of Procedure	Number of Agencies	Percentage
Field Background Investigation	62	100.0
Medical Exam	62	100.0
Physical Strength and Agility Tests	49	79.6
Situational Tests	36	58.1
Polygraph	35	56.5
Psychiatric Exam	35	56.5
Assessment Centers	14	22.6
Agency Usage (N=62)		

Source: P. Ash, K.B. Siora, and C.F. Britton, "Police Agency Officer Selection Practices," *Journal of Police Science and Administration*, 17, no. 4 (1990): 258-69.

First used in its basic form by the Cincinnati, Ohio, Police Department in 1961, today, nearly 35 percent of police agencies use the assessment center approach in some form.[15] Some individuals predict this number to increase steadily, as the legal defensibility of this method becomes more widely appreciated. However, the relatively high cost of implementation has hindered the employment of this approach by more departments. Additionally, the fact that the exercises used do not require the candidate to have knowledge about police procedure raises another concern.

A department using the assessment center approach should follow a general outline. The first phase, where the candidates take the police officer exam, remains unchanged. Next, test administrators contact the individuals who scored highest on the exam to notify them of the date and time to report for the assessment test. Generally, this test occurs in a 1-day session, during which assessors rank all of the candidates. Most departments hold assessment centers in a local school or a large facility that offers a variety of rooms suitable for each phase of the testing.

Each candidate participates alternately in a series of five to eight exercises, each designed to assess a particular "dimension" necessary for a police officer. For example, the exercises ensure a candidate's ability to deal with the public, maintain emotional stability in stressful situations, work in teams, communicate adequately, and demonstrate the proper use of force.[16] Additionally, administrators should ensure that the tests—

• remain standardized;
• prove relevant and realistic to situations police officers might expect to face in the line of duty;
• have several alternative solutions;
• remain complex enough to engage the candidate;
• prove stressful enough to elicit a number of possible emotional responses; and
• not require specialized abilities.[17]

Individuals specifically selected and trained to serve as assessors will rate the performance of each candidate. Some experts suggest departments use one assessor for every two candidates and that the assessment panel include a police administrator, a psychologist, and a local citizen with a background in social work or community service.[18] Assessors should remain thoroughly trained and familiar with the methodology of the process and the exercises used and the dimensions being tested. They also should practice performing such ratings. Assessors should develop an overall rating of each candidate by discussing individual performance on the exercises and then come to an agreement with other assessors on each dimension.

CONCLUSION

Law enforcement agencies throughout the United States have a diverse choice of methods to assess and select their officers. The actual assessment and selection procedures prove critical in that process and present a prime opportunity to scrutinize those who will hold an enormous amount of authority. The performance of these officers likely will undergo strict criticism by a more-watchful-than-ever public.

The courts have encouraged the use of assessment centers as the most fair and job-related method of assessing police officer candidates. No other assessment tool can better extract behavior from candidates that would parallel their performance on the job. When properly executed, the assessment center approach will raise emotions and stress that cannot be roused with other traditional testing methods.

Administrators should place the assessment center method as an integral part of a comprehensive selection procedure. In doing so, they can confidently make new officer hires, and more important, ensure residents that the highest quality police officers serve and protect their communities.

NOTES

1. G. F. Coulton and H. S. Feild, "Using Assessment Centers in Selecting Entry-Level Police Officers: Extravagance or Justified Expense?" *Public Personnel Management*, 1995, 2: 223–243.

2. E. Fitzsimmons, "N.Y.P.D. Psychological Screening of Police Candidates: The Screening Process, Issues and Criteria in Rejection," *Psychological Services for Law Enforcement*, Library of Congress No. 85-60053 8 (Washington, DC: Government Printing Office, 1986).

3. Supra note 1.

4. M. Hyams, "Recruitment, Selection, and Retention: A Matter of Commitment," *Police Chief*, September 1991, 24–27.

5. P. Ash, K. B. Slora, and C. F. Britton, "Police Agency Officer Selection Practices," *Journal of Police Science and Administration*, 17, no. 4 (1990): 258–269.

6. T. H. Wright, "Pre-employment Background Investigations," *FBI Law Enforcement Bulletin*, November 1991, 16–21.

7. D. Bradford, "Police Officer Candidate Background Investigation: Law Enforcement Management's Most Effective Tool for Employing the Most Qualified Candidate," *Public Personnel Management*, 27, no. 1 (1998): 423–424.

8. Supra note 5, 27, no. 1 (1998). The Americans With Disabilities Act (ADA) prohibits inquiries into disabilities until an agency has made a conditional offer of employment. This has the effect of prohibiting broad physical examinations prior to such an offer being made.

9. As published in Suffolk County, New York, Police Officer Examination Announcement, given May 1999.

10. Supra note 5.

11. Supra note 5.

12. D. Schofield, "Hiring Standards: Ensuring Fitness for Duty," *FBI Law Enforcement Bulletin*, November 1993, 27–32.

13. Supra note 5.

14. *Anderson v. City of Philadelphia*, 845 F.2d 1225 (3rd Cir. 1988).

15. Supra note 1.

16. J. Pynes, and H. J. Bemardin, "Entry-level Police Selection: The Assessment Center Is an Alternative," *Journal of Criminal Justice*, 1992, 20: 41–52.

17. Supra note 1.

18. Supra note 1.

Improving the Recruitment of Women in Policing

An Investigation of Women's Attitudes and Job Preferences

By Lieutenant Colonel Deborah J. Campbell and Lieutenant Bryon D. Christman, New York State Police, Albany, New York, and Melissa E. Feigelson, Student, Industrial Organizational Psychology Department, University at Albany, New York

One goal of any recruitment program is attracting an applicant pool that is diverse enough to meet the organization's objectives. Many law enforcement agencies, however, find it difficult to attract a sufficient number of female applicants. Consistent with this trend, the position of New York State Trooper has historically not been sought after by a large number of female applicants. Although the number of women taking the New York State Trooper exam has increased over the past decade, less than eight percent of the agency's sworn force is female. The desire of the New York State Police to increase the number of women in the agency has led to the development of a human resources project aimed at improving the recruitment of women.

To address this issue, the agency conducted a programmatic investigation of the recruitment of women. The scope of this investigation included four different survey instruments, administered to approximately 3,500 individuals. While this research focused exclusively on residents of New York State and their perceptions of the New York State Police, its findings may prove useful to police chiefs and executives from other departments who wish to recruit more women to the field of policing.

The recruitment message, as portrayed by recruitment literature, posters, and even by recruiters themselves, must be carefully evaluated.

The investigators set out to answer a number of research questions. First, what are women's perceptions of careers in law enforcement? Researchers sought to identify aspects of the job that women find attractive, as well as those that deter women from applying. Second, what job characteristics are important to women, including women who have chosen careers in law enforcement? To attract women, knowledge about what they are looking for in a profession is very important. For example, do salary and benefits outweigh other aspects, such as good co-worker relations? Third, which characteristics of a state trooper's job are most likely to attract women? In other words, how closely does the trooper position match what women desire in a job?

Person-Environment Fit Theory

The person-environment (P-E) fit theory, which has been explored in the fields of psychology, sociology, and vocational studies, states that individuals will be more attracted to an organization that provides an environment that closely matches their own wishes, values, personalities, and interests.[1] P-E fit is thought to be a good predictor of job selection, job satisfaction, and employee retention. Organizational attractiveness is likely to influence each job decision an individual makes—to obtain information about the job opening, to apply for the job or take an entrance exam, to accept the job offer, to complete training, and to remain on the job. In general, when jobs provide an environmental match to personal characteristics, ratings of organization attractiveness are high.

Therefore, one approach to attracting female applicants to law enforcement is to emphasize those aspects of the officer's job that are characteristic of what females are looking for in a career—to illustrate, in other words, that there is good P-E fit. But which characteristics of the job will females desire?

Job Characteristics Desired by Females

Of particular interest to vocational psychologists is the study of gender differences in work values and job preferences. In one influential study, published in 1978, researchers asked 57,000 individuals, who had applied to a public utility company during a 30-year period, to rank a list of inducements according to their importance.[2] The inducements included advancement potential, benefits, favorable impression of the company, pleasant and agreeable co-workers, work hours, working conditions, pay, job security, considerate and fair supervisors, and type of work. The results of the study suggested that women were far less interested in pay and security than were men. Instead, women ranked type of work as the most important factor.

The results of more recent studies suggest some additional gender differences. Women consistently indicated a higher level of interest in job enrichment factors such as development of knowledge and skills, intellectual stimulation, rewards for good performance, personal challenge, and opportunity for advancement.[3] Women also consistently rated items associated with a supportive work climate, including working with congenial associates, and comfortable working conditions as important.[4] Both men and women viewed job security, salary, and opportunity for advancement among the most important job factors. But when job factors relating specifically to the relationship between work and family were included, there were significant gender differences. Women rated items related to family-friendly flexibility

in scheduling and maternity leave more important than did men.[5] However, family-friendly flexibility in scheduling and maternity leave ranked much lower than factors pertaining to job enrichment and salary for both women and men. In one study, women rated the opportunity to help others more highly than did their male counterparts.[6]

One important strategy, based on the survey results, is for police agencies to emphasize programs and policies that are designed to accommodate work-family issues.

Women's Perceptions of Law Enforcement Jobs

Critical to this research project was identifying women's perceptions of the characteristics of a job in law enforcement. The fit regarding the match between job characteristics important to women and those perceived as prevalent in a law enforcement job is reported and assessed. It is important to note that perceptions of the job of trooper are just as important as actual job characteristics, since it is the perceptions of the job that will affect the decision-making processes. The core hypothesis is that recruitment efforts will be more successful if these efforts incorporate the message that law enforcement jobs offer women a good P-E fit. Therefore, the survey instruments were designed to obtain information about perceptions of the job of trooper and importance ratings of different job characteristics.

Research Design

The New York State Police, in conjunction with the University at Albany, investigated the project research questions using four different surveys. Each survey instrument

was designed successively based on the findings of the prior survey. The surveys were administered to four samples of respondents: college students; New York State Police recruits; New York State Troopers of all ranks; and a general sample of New York State residents between the ages of 19 and 29. While males were included in the samples for comparative analysis, females were overrepresented in the survey of the general population. Completed surveys were obtained from just over 1,000 individuals.

The average respondent to the New York State resident survey was a white female from a rural area who had at least some college education. Single women with no children made up the largest percentage, followed by single women with children. A very small percentage of urban women and women of color responded to the survey, despite the fact that each group received roughly the same number of surveys. Rural communities typically have more contact with the New York State Police because they are the primary policing agency for those areas. On the other hand, urban areas are typically policed by municipal departments. Consequently, since rural areas tend to be less ethnically diverse, the sample is also less ethnically diverse.

Research Findings

Perceptions of the Job of New York State Trooper. One of the primary objectives of this investigation was to determine public perceptions of the job of a New York State Trooper. Perceptions of the job were measured both in terms of general impressions of the agency and specific job attributes. An assessment of the respondent data from all surveys identified the respondents' perceptions of a state trooper's job attributes. These items were factor-analyzed to statistically index their relationship with one another, yielding the job characteristics described in Table 1.

TABLE 1

Job Characteristic (Listed in Order of Strength of Perceptions)	Items Used to Measure Factor
Professionalism and Para-Military Structure	Clear-cut rules and procedures to follow, physical fitness and strength requirements, highly specialized skills required, a feeling of protocol and structure at work
Social Contribution	Helping others, critical and important work, interpersonal and social interaction, authority and responsibility for high-risk situations, opportunity to protect those who are more vulnerable then others
Job Enrichment	Job challenge, skill variety, the ability to learn new things, advancement opportunities, intellectual stimulation
Good Coworker Relations and Camaraderie	Camaraderie among fellow troopers, attitude of co-workers, a sense of belonging, good working relationship with co-workers
Compensation and Benefits	Salary, benefits, job security
Occupational Prestige and Personal Respect	High status and respect from others; occupational prestige
Job Danger	Potential to use deadly force; potential situation that could threaten personal safety, dangerous job
Working Conditions	Working alone, working at night
Possibility of Relocation	Rotating shifts, time away from family, and travel associated with promotional opportunities
Family-Related Job Flexibility	Flexibility in arrangement of work schedule to meet family obligations

Figures 1 and 2 present the average ratings for each of these identified job factors. The graph in Figure 1 represents perceptions of the job of a New York State Trooper as reported by the general population of New York State, while the graph in Figure 2 reflects perceptions of the job of state trooper as reported by incumbents. Factors followed by an asterisk (*) indicate a statistically significant difference between females and males. For example, females rated family-friendly policies as significantly less characteristic of the job of trooper than did males (F = 4.41 and M = 4.87).

Important Job Attributes

This next section presents the important job characteristics identified by females and males surveyed from the general public in seeking any employment opportunity. It is interesting to note that regardless of their current career, women seemed to

FIGURE 1

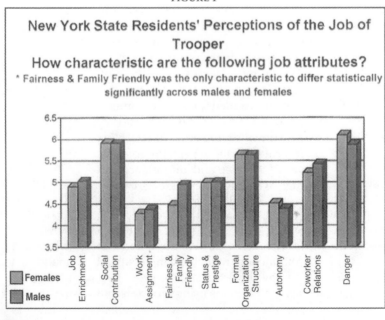

FIGURE 2

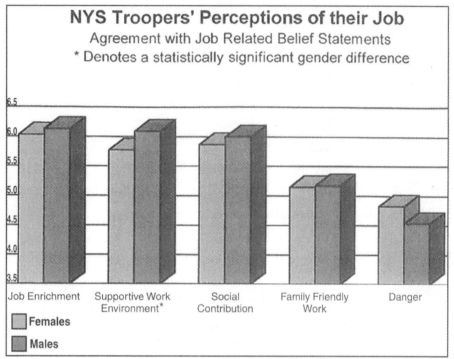

value the same job attributes. The following job attributes are reported in order of importance; factors that received the highest importance ratings are presented first. Importance ratings for New York State residents are presented in Figure 3.

The job attribute that received the highest importance rating across both males and females was Financial and Job Security. The average importance rating for females in the general public was 6.17 out of 7, where a rating of 7 indicates "extremely important." The second most important job attribute for females was a Supportive Work Climate. This attribute pertains to a job where co-workers are easy to work with, working conditions are comfortable, supervisors are considerate and fair, the work atmosphere is welcoming, and employees feel safe on the job. This job attribute was rated, statistically, significantly higher by females (average rating of 6.1) than by males (average rating of 5.5). In other words, this attribute is more important to females than males. The third most important job attribute was Job Enrichment. This job attribute is characterized by interesting work, skill variety, performance feedback, feelings of achievement, intellectual stimulation, and challenging work. The average rating by females was 5.82 out of 7.

FIGURE 3

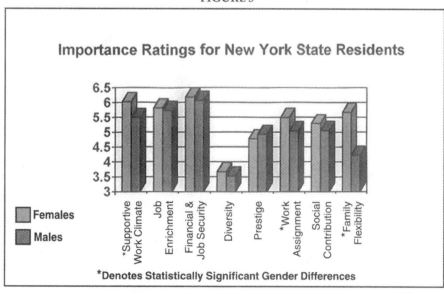

Family-friendly work policies was the next most important job attribute and was, statistically, significantly more important to females than males. Family-friendly work policies referred to the flexibility offered to employees regarding maternity and childcare issues. Females perceived this to be more important than males ($F = 5.68$ and males = 5.04). It must be noted that there are many potential definitions of family-friendly work policies; however, the items in these surveys referred to maternity and the scheduling of hours to meet family-related responsibilities.

Another job attribute that was rated as statistically significantly more important to females than males was the Choice of Work Assignment, which concerned starting and quitting time; number of hours per day, week or shift worked; autonomy; control over scheduling and flexibility of hours; and job location. The average female rating was 5.49 and the average male rating was 5.04 out of 7. According to the sample of troopers surveyed, working shift-work was also of greater concern to female troopers than to male troopers.

Social Contribution is a job attribute that covers meeting and speaking with many people, making a social contribution to the community, and having the opportunity to help others. This factor was rated as being either moderately or somewhat important to females. The average importance rating for females was 5.29 out of 7. It is important to note that a score of 4 on the 7-point scale indicates that the item is "somewhat" important, or true "to some extent," while a score of 7 indicates great importance.

Assessment of P-E Fit

The assessment of P-E fit is crucial to this investigation because it addresses one of the primary research questions: Which characteristics of the job of trooper are most attractive to women?

Overall, it appears that there is a moderate to good fit between what women want in a job and what the job of a New York State Trooper offers. Qualitative analyses suggest that women are looking for a supportive work environment, job enrichment, and family-friendly work policies (replicating the results of previous research). These are all attributes that women perceive to be true of the job of a trooper. It is perplexing, then, that the number of female applicants for the position of trooper remains low. One might conclude that women fail to realize just how close the match is between what they desire in a career and what the job of a New York State Trooper offers them.

One area where P-E fit seemed poor involved perceptions of danger associated with a policing job. Females, particularly, perceived the job of a trooper to hold inherent danger. However, female troopers reported feeling that danger was only a slight concern for them. Anecdotal evidence suggests that women may misperceive the level of violence and danger on the job to such a degree that it negatively influences their overall perception of the job. This lack of fit, between the general public's concerns over safety and the reality that women and men employed as troopers do not perceive the same level of danger, should be addressed in future recruitment programs. Agencies may be well served by emphasizing their safety training programs and the high level of preparation that candidates receive prior to being assigned to road patrol. This reassurance may help to address candidates' concerns about the job's level of danger. The implications of the P-E fit analysis will be discussed further in the conclusion of this article.

Another factor that is important to the analysis of P-E fit is that of financial inducements. Evident from the data is that P-E fit is geographically specific. In some cases, the starting salary of a New York State Trooper was perceived to be a positive attribute. However, perceptions of favorability changed according to the cost of living in each location. Nonetheless, it must be recognized that starting salary was rated by both males and females as one of the most important job attributes, so importance must be given to presentation of this information in any recruitment campaign.

Secondary Analyses

Although the primary focus of this investigation was to explain why more females are not attracted to the position of New York State Trooper, there were secondary questions also addressed in the study. One secondary research question for the New York State Police was to learn what interests and activities are most attractive to women who would be interested in pursuing a career in law enforcement. An important aspect of the project involved utilizing the findings of the study to develop future marketing strategies or recruitment techniques.

Favorite Activities and Their Relation to Intentions

One section of the survey required respondents to rate their favorite activities. A comprehensive list of 35 activities was provided. The responses were analyzed to determine if there is a relationship between the individual's intentions to consider a career with the New York State Police and whether or not they participate in one of the listed activities. The activity with the most significant correlation with female intentions to pursue a job in law enforcement was "Home and auto-repairs/do it yourself projects."

However, only 43 people reported participating in this activity. The small number of individuals that reported engaging in hunting and fishing also indicated having favorable perceptions of the job of trooper and intentions of joining the New York State Police. Activities that a larger number of females reported participating in, which were statistically significantly correlated with intentions to join, were team athletics (r = .167, number of participants [n] = 97), continuing education (r = .238, n = 89); volunteer work (r = .145, n = 79), and computers (r = .148, n = 132).

Recruitment Tactics

Law enforcement agencies employ a number of different recruitment tactics aimed at enticing candidates to consider a career in the field. These strategies may range from advertisement on television, radio, and publications to attendance at career fairs to personal contact by members of the organization. It is both useful and cost effective to be able to determine which of these strategies are most likely to influence a candidate to apply to join their organization. Item-level analyses conducted for data from the last three surveys provide some indication of important influences on potential job applicants. In the second survey, recruits were asked to report the factors that were most influential in their decision to join the New York State Police.

Qualitative assessments indicated that the most frequently reported factors by recruits were

a. a relative or friend in the agency
b. the opportunity to help others
c. community service

The trooper survey incorporated the responses of the recruits as well as subject matter experts to comprise a comprehensive list of potential influences, including many popular recruitment tactics such as full-time recruitment officers, attendance at career fairs, and exposure to the profession through an in-school program.

Factors that influenced troopers decisions to join the New York State Police were

a. the opportunity to help and protect others

b. the opportunity to do non-routine and exciting work
c. advice from a family member
d. advice from a trooper acquaintance

The last survey included a similar list of recruitment tactics for which respondents were asked to indicate the likelihood that they would respond positively to each strategy. The sample of New York State residents reported the following recruitment tactics as most likely to elicit a favorable response:

a. contact by trooper you know
b. attendance at a career fair
c. contact by trooper you do not know (such as a recruitment officer)

The combined data from these surveys suggest that contact by a trooper may be the single most important influence on people's intentions to consider a career with the agency. Chiefs and executives of departments may benefit from finding ways to actively involve all sworn officers within their departments in recruiting potential candidates.

The main objective of this study was to obtain information that would be useful for enhancing recruitment programs so that more women would be attracted to the job of trooper. Three research questions were asked and answered as a result of this investigation. The first question asked what perceptions women have of careers in law enforcement. To summarize, women viewed the job of trooper as one that provides job enrichment, status and prestige, and opportunities to help others, and one that has a formal organizational structure and is somewhat dangerous. The second question raised was what job attributes are important to women in considering a career. The results of this study suggest that financial and job security is the most important factor, followed in importance by a supportive work climate, job enrichment, and family-friendly work policies. In ad-

dition, women rated choice of work assignment and opportunity for social contribution as important. The third question of interest referred to the characteristics of the job of trooper that are most likely to attract women. To answer this question, the person-environment fit was assessed. In the sample of women that responded to the study, the attractive characteristics of the job of trooper are the diversity of tasks and skills required on the job, the challenging nature of the job, the camaraderie among troopers, and the retirement and pension plans. Further, the agency's implementation of policies relevant to the flexibility required to meet family obligations may also be attractive to future female applicants.

Policy Implications

The following are recommendations for the use of these findings in future recruitment programs. These recommendations should prove beneficial for any agency looking to increase the numbers of female applicants for police officer positions. Primarily, it is suggested that the recruitment messages focus on the job attributes that were rated as most important to women.

- Emphasize challenging nature of the job, the diverse activities and skills required, the camaraderie among police officers, and the positive work atmosphere within the agency.
- Emphasize programs/policies designed to accommodate work-family issues.
- Emphasize community service aspect, as well as the quality of police training, to minimize the effects of the media's over-glamorized portrayal of the potential dangerous aspects of the job.
- Emphasize value of retirement and pension plans.

In addition to modifying the recruitment message, certain specific aspects of a recruitment program can be enhanced. Survey respondents reported that meeting a trooper they did not know would have an influence on their decision to join. For this reason, any contact between agency members and potential applicants should be considered a recruitment strategy. As a result, each agency member should be made aware of the potential impact he or she may have on future applicants. Incentive programs for officers who successfully recruit applicants for the entrance exam may help officers understand the importance to recruitment efforts of their contacts with the general public. Some agencies have reportedly used such incentives as monetary rewards and provision of time off for officers who are successful at bringing in future applicants.

Another strategy is to focus recruitment efforts in locations where women that participate in certain activities are likely to be found. For example, women who participated in high school athletics or team activities had more favorable opinions of a career in policing. Based on this finding, efforts should be made to attract young women at the high school and college level by meeting with varsity athletic teams and by placing recruitment literature in places frequented by those young women. Other suggestions are to place recruitment literature in facilities where women exercise or participate in physical fitness activities, such as local gyms, and to actively recruit at road races

frequented by female runners. In addition, individuals who reported an interest in home improvement activities and do-it-yourself projects also had favorable opinions of the policing profession. In response, home improvement stores should be considered as potential sources for the recruitment of women. Sources for hunting and fishing licenses may also provide a useful avenue of expanding the traditional approach to recruitment.

Overall, the recruitment message as portrayed by recruitment literature, posters, and even by recruiters themselves, must be carefully evaluated. Evidence suggests that individuals evaluate information about potential job opportunities according to their own preferences and beliefs. Every effort should be made to create recruitment posters that focus on the preferred job attributes by the targeted applicants. To enhance the attractiveness of policing to women, the recruitment message should focus on those job characteristics important to women, such as information about the positive social climate and work atmosphere, the flexibility of scheduling to meet family obligations, and aspects that enhance job enrichment. It is the premise of this research that when individuals perceive prospective job opportunities to have characteristics that are important to them, they will be more likely to continue with the application process. Clearly, the information collected by the New York State Police should be

important to chiefs and police executives seeking to increase the number of female applicants within their agencies. A comprehensive recruitment program that includes strategies outlined in this study should favorably impact the number of women seeking to join a police agency.

For more information regarding this research project, contact Lieutenant Colonel Deborah J. Campbell, director of human resources for the New York State Police, at (518) 485-0854 or send an e-mail to dcampbel@troopers.state.ny.us.

Notes

1. R. D. Caplan, "Person-Environment Fit Theory and Organizations: Commensurate Dimensions, Time Perspectives, and Mechanisms," *Journal of Vocational Behavior* 31 (1987): 248–267.
2. C. E. Jurgensen, "Job Preferences (What Makes a Job Good or Bad?)," *Journal of Applied Psychology* 63 (1978): 267–276.
3. N. J. Beutell and O. C. Brenner, "Sex Differences in Work Values," *Journal of Vocational Behavior* 28 (1986): 29–41; J. S. Bridges, "Sex Differences in Occupational Values," *Sex Roles* 29 (1989); 205–211; P. P. Scozzaro and L. Mezydio-Subich, "Gender and Occupational Sex-Type Differences in Job Outcome Factor Perceptions," *Journal of Vocational Behavior* 36 (1990): 109–119.
4. N. J. Beutell and O. C. Brenner, "Sex Differences in Work Values."
5. J. S. Bridges, "Sex Differences in Occupational Values."
6. J. S. Bridges, "Sex Differences in Occupational Values."

UNIT 4
The Judicial System

Unit Selections

Key Points to Consider

- Is the American jury system in trouble? Defend your answer.

- In your view, is "jury nullification" ever justified? Why or why not?

- Is there an alternative to "getting tough on crime?"

 **Links: www.dushkin.com/online/**
These sites are annotated in the World Wide Web pages.

Center for Rational Correctional Policy
http://www.correctionalpolicy.com
Justice Information Center (JIC)
http://www.ncjrs.org
National Center for Policy Analysis (NCPA)
http://www.public-policy.org/~ncpa/pd/law/index3.html
U.S. Department of Justice (DOJ)
http://www.usdoj.gov

The courts are an equal partner in the American justice system. Just as the police have the responsibility of guarding our liberties by enforcing the law, the courts play an important role in defending these liberties by applying the law. The courts are where civilized "wars" are fought, individual rights are protected, and disputes are peacefully settled.

The articles in this unit discuss several issues concerning the judicial process. Ours is an adversary system of justice, and the protagonists—the state and the defendant—are usually represented by counsel.

Noting deficiencies in jury trials, the authors of "How to Improve the Jury System" recommend allowing jurors to take notes and submit written questions for witnesses. Focusing again on the jury, "Q: Should Juries Nullify Laws They Consider Unjust or Excessively Punitive?" explores the pros and cons of this issue. In "Looking Askance at Eyewitness Testimony," the problem of unreliable eyewitness evidence is examined, and a much more dependable source of identification, DNA, is looked at in "The Creeping Expansion of DNA Data Banking." Finally, some problems that prosecutors may face are explored in "Community Prosecution."

COMMENTARY

How to Improve the Jury System

by Thomas F. Hogan, Gregory E. Mize, and Kathleen Clark

The subject of the American jury system raises conflicting cultural sentiments. While the jury trial is revered as the most democratic institution in our society, a summons for jury service is dreaded as an unwelcome intrusion into our lives. Jury verdicts, respected because they are reached by a group of peers, are also ridiculed in recent high-profile trials.

Amid this cultural cognitive disconnect, however, there is no major movement to abolish the right to a trial by jury. Rather, across the country, communities and their courts are joining forces to fix the system. Recent efforts in Washington, D.C., Arizona, California, Colorado, New York, and other states have all focused on modernizing the jury system by making it more convenient, democratic, and educational for the jurors.

The ongoing jury reform experience in Washington, D.C., provides a look at jury service through the eyes of the juror and reveals that community-wide collaboration may be the most effective way to reconnect our actions and our values about the duty to serve.

In late 1996, the Council for Court Excellence assembled a committee and charged it with recommending improvements to the jury systems in Washington, D.C. Then, in February 1998, after a full year of study, the D.C. Jury Project published its comprehensive research report, which includes 32 specific recommendations to the bench and bar on how to modernize jury trials in the local and federal courts.

In the District of Columbia, where well-intentioned committees addressing worthy problems are hardly uncommon, nothing unusual has happened. Or has it? This report, entitled *Juries for the Year 2000 and Beyond*, may not become another denizen of the library shelf after all.

What makes the D.C. Jury Project's recommendations worthy of thoughtful consideration by the local and national legal communities? First and foremost, the quality of analysis regarding an impressive number of important issues in *Juries for the Year 2000 and Beyond* renders it both readable and well worth reading.

The revered constitutional institution of the jury trial, under recent media attack, deserves a renewed opportunity to thrive. Modernization efforts such as this could be a good opportunity. Besides offering rather mundane and unexceptionable recommendations, such as improving the quality and scope of the juror source list and providing comfortable facilities for jurors, the report probes deep into the history of the jury selection process and takes a stand on the complex issue of peremptory challenges.

Second, the courts and the bar should consider the message in this report because of who the authors are. The 36 diverse members of the D.C. Jury Project, collaborating in a way not previously experienced by these authors, were able to avoid the typical chasm that exists between the legal and civic communities. When jurors, lawyers, and judges take the time to actually listen to one another, then their conclusions deserve special attention.

Substantive recommendations aside for a moment, one of the most gratifying and productive aspects of the D.C. Jury Project was the makeup of the committee. Instead of assembling a generic group composed entirely of like-minded lawyers and judges, the Council for Court Excellence actively recruited citizens with jury service experience as well as academicians with an interest in the field. Additionally, attorneys and businesspeople from a variety of backgrounds and viewpoints were called upon. Federal and local trial judges were included. Court administrators and jury officers rounded out the group.

The diversity of professional experience and personal background among Jury Project members was not an effort to have token representatives on the committee. Rather, the wide range of viewpoints enhanced the effectiveness of the collaborative effort. Each member was respected for his own perspective, but everyone understood that the purpose was to reach common/higher ground for the good of the overall system.

Improving the Jury System

There is a national movement to modernize the jury system and reconnect our actions and our values about the duty to serve.

Recommendations include improving the quality and scope of the juror source list and providing comfortable facilities for jurors.

Jurors need practical training and easier access to information about the particulars of the cases before them.

Not unlike a jury deliberation, we went about our work methodically, setting aside, when our convictions allowed, personal interests or biases that would impede true progress. It was clear at the outset that the citizen-juror members of the group were the real experts among us.

Also like deliberating jurors, committee members accepted the challenge with honesty and integrity. They struggled at times with controversial issues and differences of opinion yet continued to search for the right answers—overcoming the destructive chasm that so often divides the civic and the legal communities. Because this uncommon level of commitment and vision came from such a diverse committee and because former jurors contributed so significantly to the conclusions, the bench and bar need to listen to their consumers by giving careful consideration to all of the recommendations in *Jurors for the Year 2000 and Beyond*.

PEREMPTORY CHALLENGES

One lesson learned from this collaborative effort involves group dynamics. Since the committee comprised people who often sit opposite one another in the courtroom, perspectives and theories were bound to collide. Over time, though, committee members developed a sense of trust and respect for one another. Improper gamesmanship, cynicism, and distrust were replaced by year's end with a refreshing dose of candor and a willingness to listen. At no point in the process was this lesson in group dynamics more evident than in our discussion of jury selection and peremptory challenges.

Many members of the D.C. Jury Project believe that peremptory challenges should be abolished, and an overwhelming majority believe that if not eliminated, they should be drastically reduced.

Several two- or three-hour meetings were devoted to this topic, and the discussions were both enlightened and forthright. After much study, soul-searching, and listening to our juror colleagues, a majority of the Jury Project reached the conclusion that the peremptory challenge is inconsistent with the fundamental precepts of an impartial jury.

In *Batson v. Kentucky* (1986) and subsequent decisions over the past decade, the Supreme Court has affirmed the constitutional principle that peremptory strikes of jurors may not be exercised in our nation's trial courts to discriminate against jurors based on their race or gender, and that parties are not constitutionally entitled to peremptory strikes. Justice Thurgood Marshall, concurring in the *Batson* decision, forcefully advocated ridding trials of peremptory strikes. "The decision today will not end the racial discrimination that peremptories inject into the jury-selection process," he wrote. "That goal can be accomplished only by eliminating peremptory challenges entirely. Misuse of the peremptory challenge to exclude black jurors has become both common and flagrant."

Indeed, in the experience of most trial judges on the Jury Project, attorneys in both civil and criminal cases continue to exercise peremptory strikes in a manner that, at a minimum, suggests the appearance that prospective jurors are being peremptorily stricken on the grounds of race, gender, or both. The District of Columbia Court of Appeals, as well as numerous state and federal appellate courts throughout the nation, repeatedly have found that such discrimination routinely occurs.

It is important to note that the use and abuse of peremptory challenges leaves prospective jurors and the public in general with the perception that people are being arbitrarily and discriminatorily denied the opportunity for jury service. Such a perception inevitably undermines confidence in our courts and the administration of justice.

In *The Future of Peremptory Challenges*, the Court Manager 16 (1997), G. Thomas Munsterman, director of the Center for Jury Studies of the National Center for State Courts, writes:

> The peremptory challenge is a curious feature of our jury system. Starting with randomly selected names from broadbased lists, we work hard to assemble a demographically representative panel from which to select a jury. We defend every step of the process used to arrive at that point. Then comes the swift sword of the peremptory challenge, cutting jurors from the panel with nary an explanation.

No one has recently written more thoroughly or compellingly of the need to eliminate peremptory challenges than Judge Morris Hoffman, a state trial judge in Denver, Colorado.

In *Peremptory Challenges Should Be Abolished: A Trial Judge's Perspective*, 64 U. Chi. L. Rev. 809 (1997), Hoffman carefully traces the history of the peremptory challenge and demonstrates that it is not rooted in principles of fairness, impartiality, or protection of the rights of the accused; rather, it stems from "the now meaningless and quite undemocratic concept of royal infallibility," having been "invented two hundred years before the notion of jury impartiality" was conceived.

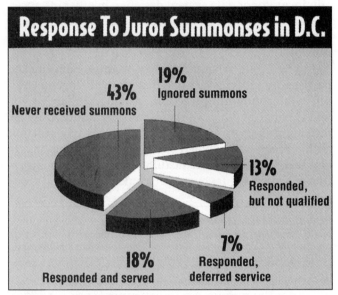

Source: Council for Court Excellence, Civic Apathy or Governmental Deficiency? An Examination of Low Juror Yield in the District of Columbia, Richard Seltzer (December 1997)

He also observes that "the Supreme Court has consistently and unflinchingly held that the peremptory challenge is neither a constitutionally necessary component of a defendant's right to an impartial jury, nor even so fundamental as to be part of federal common law."

Indeed, there was no discussion whatsoever of peremptory challenges in the *Federalist* papers or during the Constitutional Convention, and the Constitution is "utterly silent" on the matter. As Hoffman forcefully demonstrates, efforts to subvert constitutional rights, *not* to defend them, have invigorated and sustained the practice of peremptory challenges as the "last best tool of Jim Crow" in American trials. Such challenges provide "an incredibly efficient final racial filter" to keep African Americans off juries in the South and throughout the United States.

Against this background, Hoffman shows that peremptory challenges have never had a legitimate purpose and have none today. Their genesis in England was to serve as a basis to excuse jurors for *cause*. Peremptory challenges are "decidedly undemocratic," are "susceptible to significant abuse by authorities," and are "inherently irrational." There is evidence that, notwithstanding

the *Batson* decision and its progeny, they are used "in the same old way" they always have been used, "save for some nominal and meaningless extra hoops now required by *Batson*."

Judge Hoffman concludes, as do many members of the D.C. Jury Project, that the peremptory challenge is inconsistent with fundamental precepts of an impartial jury because (1) it reflects an inappropriate distrust of jurors, causing "perfectly acceptable, perfectly fair and perfectly impartial prospective jurors to be excluded in droves" and to become frustrated and cynical about the justice system; (2) it improperly shifts the focus on jury selection from the individual to the group; and (3) it injects an inappropriate level of adversariness into the jury selection process, tending to result in the selection not of impartial jurors but of jurors who are biased for one side or the other.

The foregoing considerations have persuaded a substantial majority of the D.C. Jury Project that peremptory strikes should be eliminated or drastically reduced in the District of Columbia. The project is also persuaded, however, that if peremptory strikes are eliminated, it is vital to improve the ability to ascertain grounds for strikes of jurors for cause. Relevant information about jurors should be obtained by (1) using a written questionnaire completed by all jurors and given to the court and parties upon the jury panel's arrival in the courtroom and (2) requiring that each juror be examined at least once during the voir dire process and attorneys be given a meaningful opportunity to ask follow-up questions of all jurors.

The process should be conducted so that no jurors will be called to the bench more than once. Moreover, to assure to the extent possible that prospective jurors who may be biased or partial are in fact stricken for cause, an expanded legal standard governing for-cause strikes should be established. It should mandate that when a prospective juror's demeanor or substantive response to a question during voir dire presents *any* reasonable doubt as to whether the juror can be fair and impartial, the trial judge shall strike the juror for cause at the request of any party, or on the court's own motion.

Throughout the report, the primary theme is that jurors need more institutionalized respect. When jurors arrive in a courtroom, we thank them for coming and remind them of their importance in the trial process. They are, we say with sincerity, the "other judges." Then, in more than a handful of instances, jurors and their needs are promptly forgotten. Our other actions—from the jury selection process throughout deliberations—send quite a different message about how important jurors really are.

No longer treated like judges, jurors are expected to endure a jury selection process that insults their intelligence and infects the entire judicial process with the stench of unfairness. They will likely spend countless hours waiting in the lounge or the jury room, often with no word of when they will be needed. During trial, we ask them to absorb complex and contradictory information, many times without the appropriate tools they need to fully understand and retain such information.

As Stephen Adler wrote in *The Jury*, "To build a better jury system, we need to grant jurors the perquisites of power: reasonable creature comforts, practical training in the nature of their endeavor, and easier access to information about the particulars of the cases before them." Fortunately, many judges in the District of Columbia and around the country have found ways to do this. In searching for ways to enhance the jury service experience and improve the quality of justice, the Jury Project learned from these judges.

For years, jurors have been viewed as passive recipients of often complex information. Recently, however, increasing numbers of judges and attorneys across the nation have recognized the juror education that takes place during trial.

Jurors, like students, need appropriate tools to make informed and rational decisions. We wouldn't send our children to school without pencils and paper. Why should jurors not have basic tools to do their important job? The Jury Project recommends that jurors be allowed to take notes and submit written questions for witnesses, that judges minimize sidebar conferences while the jury is in the room, that the court provide exhibit notebooks and interim summations in extended trials, and that judges offer to assist a jury that reports itself at an impasse.

How to efficiently incorporate these procedures into trials can be a part of every judge's training. What jurors want and need to do their job effectively is for such practices to be uniform throughout the court system. A citizen should have the same treatment no matter whose courtroom he reports to for jury service.

We recognize that receptivity to these recommendations will vary among those who read and ponder their contents. A recommendation may strike one person as unremarkable and a long-accepted custom, while another recommendation may appear radical or unreachable. The prime audience for one recommendation may be a juror administrator or data system designer. In other instances, a recommendation will be most relevant to a newer member of the bench or to a continuing legal education coordinator.

In any event, whether you are a jurist, policymaker, barrister, or citizen, we hope that you will engage yourself in this continuing project. In so doing, we believe, you will experience what we have: an opportunity to revisit important first principles of our jury system, join hands with a broad and talented spectrum of Washingtonians, and seek to make a genuine difference in the administration of justice in our courts. Welcome aboard.

Judge Thomas F. Hogan, of the U.S. District Court for the District of Columbia, and Judge Gregory E. Mize, of the D.C. Superior Court, are co-chairs of the D.C. Jury Project. Kathleen Clark is a senior analyst for the D.C. Jury Project and is on the Council for Court Excellence.

Q: Should juries nullify laws they consider unjust or excessively punitive?

Yes: Juries can and should correct the overly broad use of criminal sanctions.

BY CLAY S. CONRAD

Jury nullification occurs when a criminal-trial jury refuses to convict a defendant despite proof of guilt because the jurors believe the law is unjust or is being unjustly applied. According to studies, 3 to 4 percent of jury criminal trials involve jury nullification. There is no way to prevent jury nullification because juries never can be ordered to convict or be punished for acquitting someone. A jury acquittal, under the Constitution, is final.

Juries rarely nullify irresponsibly. Consider the acquittal of Sam Skinner, a California AIDS patient prosecuted for using marijuana. The marijuana helped counteract the devastating side effects of the drug AZT and kept Skinner from wasting away. Although Skinner admitted to the facts, the jury found him not guilty because they believed the prosecution was fundamentally unjust.

Sometimes juries find defendants guilty only of lesser offenses when they believe the punishment for the charged offense is excessive. In earlier times, British law made theft of 40 shillings or more a capital offense. Juries often undervalued property so as to spare the life of the accused—including one case in which a jury found ten £10 notes to be worth 39 shillings. Jack Kevorkian's latest trial involved just that sort of amelioration. The jury found him guilty of second-degree murder despite the facts because they believed a conviction for first-degree murder would be too great.

Alternatively, it often is argued that race and prejudice lead to jury nullification more often than do considerations of justice. As common as that argument is, it doesn't hold

water. During the 1960s in the trials of some who participated in crimes against civil-rights workers in the Deep South, it is true that juries returned "not guilty" verdicts. However, it also is true that sometimes prosecutors regularly refused to pursue those cases, police refused to investigate or testify honestly in them and judges eviscerated the cases through discretionary rulings. The juries rarely were given cases justifying conviction—and then were scapegoated for failings elsewhere in the system.

These contentions are proved by the fact that federal prosecutions for violations of civil-rights laws, involving the same cases, regularly ended in convictions—before juries selected from the same communities. Different judges, prosecutors and investigators—but the same jury pool. Obviously, any racist acquittals must be explained by something other than the juries.

A recent *National Law Journal* poll revealed that three in four Americans would nullify if they believed the court's instructions would lead to injustice. That only 3 to 4 percent of jury trials end in nullification verdicts shows that, in most cases, the law is just and justly applied. In exceptional, marginal or divisive cases, however, jurors often acquit in the interests of justice—just as the Founders of this country intended.

The Founders on both sides of the ratification debate believed trial by jury was necessary to prevent governmental overreaching. Thomas Jefferson said it was the only way to anchor government to constitutional principles. Alexander

Hamilton said it was the surest protection of the people's liberties. Theophilus Parsons, first chief justice of Massachusetts, said in the Constitutional Convention: "The people themselves have it in their power effectually to resist usurpation, without being driven to an appeal to arms. An act of usurpation is not obligatory; it is not law; and any man may be justified in his resistance. Let him be considered as a criminal by the general government, yet only his fellow-citizens can convict him; they are his jury, and if they pronounce him innocent, not all the powers of Congress can hurt him; and innocent they certainly will pronounce him, if the supposed law he resisted was an act of usurpation."

A just society has to have just rules. Juries, by refusing to enforce unjust rules, can help improve the law and the society that it governs.

Many important colonial trials ended in nullification. American jurors knew they could refuse to enforce unjust laws. Early jurors routinely were informed by courts of their right to try the law as well as the fact, and lawyers regularly argued the merits of the law to the jury. The independent role of juries was well-accepted in early American law.

It was not until the mid-19th century that courts began to question the jury's independent voice. Judges attempted to bind juries to their instructions and began prohibiting lawyers from arguing law to the jury. The Supreme Court allowed such practices to stand, and today many judges wrongly believe they are forbidden to allow jury nullification to be discussed in court.

American courts have not always been so reluctant to trust the conscientious judgments of juries. In the early years of this country, the Supreme Court itself occasionally heard cases with a jury. In 1794, Justice John Jay, for a unanimous Supreme Court, instructed a jury: "It may not be amiss, here, gentlemen, to remind you of the good old rule, that on questions of fact, it is the province of the jury, on questions of law, it is the province of the court to decide. But it must be observed that by the same law, which recognizes this reasonable distribution of jurisdiction, you have nevertheless a right to take upon yourselves to judge of both, and to determine the law as well as the fact in controversy. On this, and on every other occasion, however, we have no doubt, you will pay that respect, which is due to the opinion of the court: For, as on the one hand, it is presumed, that juries are the best judges of fact; it is, on the other hand, presumable, that the courts are the best judges of the law. But still both objects are lawfully within your power of decision."

These instructions meticulously delineate the roles of bench and jury. The court instructed the jury on a general rule, which allowed for exceptions. They admonished the jury to take their instructions with respect, yet acknowledged that the jury could not be bound by them. These instructions fostered juror independence and responsibility, not jury lawlessness or wanton disregard for the rights of the parties. Similar instructions could assist jurors in delivering fair, just verdicts today—making sure the law is applied in a manner in which the citizens of this country approve and giving us a legal system of which again we could be proud. The Fully Informed Jury Association, a Section 501(c)(3) [tax-exempt] educational organization with a mission to inform potential jurors of their right to nullify unjust laws, has provided model initiatives to allow for just such instructions. These initiatives have been introduced by legislators in more than a dozen states.

What would be the result of informing jurors about their power to nullify the law in the interests of justice? Perhaps better questions would be: Is the criminal law applied more or less fairly in 1999 than it was in 1799? Is it more or less a source of social divisiveness and tension? Has the criminal sanction been wrested from providing social protection to become a tool for social engineering?

Criminal law often is a divisive factor in society. The nonsensical distinctions between powder and crack cocaine; enormous penalties for many minor crimes; unfair sentencing favoritism given to snitches (who serve a small fraction of the time given their underlings); criminalization of "wetlands" violations; regulatory, licensing and administrative infractions; and the often-mechanical application of law favored by prosecutors have resulted in a hodgepodge of injustices strung together without rhyme or reason. Apologists who claim a society must have rules miss the point—a just society has to have just rules. Juries, by refusing to enforce unjust rules, can help improve the law and the society it governs.

Courts usually pretend injustices under law cannot occur. They can and too often do. As Judge Thomas Wiseman noted, "Congress is not yet an infallible body incapable of passing tyrannical laws." Occasionally, jurors follow their instructions, then leave court in tears, ashamed of their verdict.

This sort of thing is not supposed to happen in America. It isn't justice. If being a juror means anything, it should mean never having to say you're sorry. If the law is just and justly applied, jurors should be proud of their verdict and confident that any sentences meted out are well-deserved. Then we will engender respect for the law because, as Justice Louis Brandeis observed, for the law to be respected it first must be respectable.

What happens when a jury nullifies a law? One factually guilty person is acquitted in the interests of justice. If a particular law frequently is nullified, the legislature should bring the law into conformity with the judgment of the community. If the law is being misapplied, the legislature may make the law more specific or prosecutors may quit applying it overbroadly. The law is improved, and injustices are prevented.

Does jury nullification lead to anarchy—or is it democracy in action, allowing citizens to participate in the administration of justice? The concept that jury nullification is anarchy has been bandied about without analysis or justification in the face of juries being given nullification instructions for the first century of this country's existence without collapse into anarchy. Jury nullification does not eliminate law—it regulates it, allowing the people's perception of justice, not the government's, to prevail. It takes a true authoritarian to call such vital citizen participation in governmental decisionmaking "anarchy."

Trial by jury, according to the Supreme Court, exists to prevent oppression by government. It is easy to see that an occasionally oppressive government does not like to have its powers limited. However, those of us who someday may find ourselves on the other side of the equation should be grateful that the Founders of this country had the foresight and wisdom to install this safety valve, this elegant and time-tested mechanism to anchor our government to the principles of its Constitution. It would be a disgrace to those same Founders to be unwilling to utilize this safety valve today, when circumstances indicate it would be appropriate to do so.

Conrad is an appellate attorney in Houston, on the board of the Fully Informed Jury Association and author of Jury Nullification: The Evolution of a Doctrine.

No: Don't give society's mavericks another tool to subvert the will of the people.

By Nancy King

Inviting jurors to acquit regardless of what the law says is attempting cure-all for the law's ills. But cultivating jury nullification is a mistake. Like the peddler's elixir, jury nullification is just as likely to produce unpleasant side effects as it is to bring relief. The most compelling reasons to be wary of the practice of jury nullification are the very arguments its advocates trot out in its defense—history, democracy, fairness, political change and the Constitution itself.

One does not have to look back far into history to find a good reason for discouraging jury nullification. True, the colonists embraced the jury's power as a weapon against the king's oppressive laws. And, we're reminded, juries bravely blocked prosecutions of those who resisted the Fugitives Slave Act, Prohibition and the Vietnam War draft. But jury nullification has not been neatly confined to the rejection of "bad" law or the release of "good" defendants. A much less appealing pattern of jury lawlessness is also prominent in our nation's history. For generations juries have refused to convict or punish those who clearly are guilty of violence against unpopular victims, particularly African-Americans. The Klan Act, barring Ku Klux Klan sympathizers from juries after the Civil War, was passed because juries were exercising their "independence" to ignore civil-rights statutes. In Texas after the Civil War, prosecutors had to strike from juries those who "believe, morally, socially, politically, or religiously, that it is not murder for a white man to take the life of a [N]egro with malice aforethought." This is not a proud legacy. We should not assume that refusal to punish those who harm members of less popular groups is entirely behind us just because some juries, in some places, are more racially diverse than they used to be.

Racism, of course, is not the only risk. To invite nullification is to invite jurors to devise their own defenses to criminal charge. All three branches of government may have labored to eliminate similar considerations from the assessment of guilt. Juries have acquitted defendants in rape cases after concluding that the victims deserved to be raped because of the way they dressed or acted. Jurors may acquit protesters who trespass, damage property or harm others if they conclude the defendants were right to bypass lawful means of redress. Jurors may believe that reasonable doubt is not a strong-enough burden of proof and require fingerprints or eyewitnesses before convicting. They may decide that certain conduct by the police should be a complete defense, oblivious of efforts by legislators and judges to craft remedies and regulations for police misconduct. Now, as in the past, encouraging "good" nullification inevitably means encouraging "bad" nullification as well, because there is no way to second guess a jury's acquittal once delivered.

It is not feasible to try to separate "good" nullification from "bad." Even nullification advocates cannot agree on what type of nullification is acceptable. One supporter would require nullification instructions only in cases involving non-violent acts of civil disobedience where the defendant had "given serious thought" to legal means of accomplishing the same objective. Another would encourage jury pronouncements on the law only when the issue was the constitutionality of a criminal statute. A third insists that "true" nullification is limited to decisions "based on conscientious grounds." In a recent survey, college students were asked whether jury nullification included any combination of a set of possible reasons for acquittal, all of which the researchers believed were valid reasons for juries to nullify, such as,"The police wrongfully assaulted the defendant after he was arrested." When only 13 percent of those surveyed agreed that nullification included all of the reasons listed, the researchers concluded their subjects had a lot to learn about nullification. The response should suggest something else—that it is wishful thinking to assume that legislators or judges will be able to agree when jurors should ignore the law and when they should not.

One might support expanding the lawmaking role of the jury if one believes juries are an essential feature of our democracy, better at assessing whether a law is "just" or "unjust" than democratically elected legislators. But juries probably are much worse at this task. Unlike legislators or electors, jurors have no opportunity to investigate or research the merits of legislation. Carefully stripped of those who know anything about the type of case or conduct at stake, juries are insulated from the information they would need to make reliable judgments about the costs and benefits, the justice or the injustices, of a particular criminal prohibition. Nor can jurors seek out information during the case. The so-called "safety valve" of jury nullification, which exempts a defendant here and there from the reach of a controversial law, actually reduces the pressure for those opposed to a truly flawed statute to lobby for its repeal or amendment and deprives appellate courts of opportunities to declare its flaws.

Our democratic process should not be jettisoned so arbitrarily by an unelected group of citizens who need never to explain themselves.

Nullification's supporters point out that legislatures cannot anticipate unfair applications of the laws they enact, so jury nullification is needed for "fine-tuning." But jurors are not in any better position than judges or prosecutors to decide which defendants should be exempted from a law's reach. Again, jurors probably are much worse at this function because they lack critical information. Any juror who actually knows the defendant is excused from the jury. Jurors only can speculate on the penalty that would follow from their verdict: Unless the defendant testifies (and most defendants do not), the jury will never hear him explain his side of the story nor learn whether he has a prior record. They may never learn, of evidence suppressed because it was illegally obtained or because of other errors on the part of the prosecution. More importantly, because jurors decide only one case, they cannot compare the culpability of

different defendants or assess the relative importance of enforcing a particular prohibition against a particular defendant. No doubt about it: Juries are excellent fact finders and lie detectors. But when facts are not in issue and guilt is clear, the ability of jurors to reach sound decisions about when the law should be suspended and when it should be applied is questionable at best.

Jury nullification sometimes is touted as an effective political tool for those who have failed at the voting booth and on the legislative floor. There are two problems with this argument. First, if a group is not influential enough to obtain favorable legislation, it is not likely to secure a majority in the jury box. At most, jurors with dissenting views succeed in hanging the jury. But hung juries are a political dead end.The defendant is not spared; he can be tried again and convicted. More importantly, as a recent recommendation in California demonstrates, rising hung-jury rates inevitably lead to proposals to eliminate the unanimity requirement, proposals that if adopted would shut down minority viewpoints more effectively than any instruction against nullification ever could.

Even if a politically unsuccessful group finds strength in some local jury boxes, should we really be heartened by the prospect of being stuck with the decision of 12 people who have been encouraged to ignore the pronouncements of the state or nation's elected representatives? If there is a concentrated population of homophobes, racists or anti-Semites in my state, I, for one, do not want judges and lawyers encouraging jurors drawn from these communities to apply their own standards—standards that may vary with the victim's sexual orientation, race or religion. Local dissent, of course, is not limited to group-based views. People disagree strongly about a variety of laws—laws against possessing weapons, euthanasia, driving after a couple of drinks, the use of marijuana, slapping one's wife or children around or the dumping of paint or oil. There are places well-suited for resolving these disagreements: the legislature and the polling booth. Our democratic process should not be jettisoned arbitrarily by an unelected group of citizens who need never explain themselves.

Finally, the Constitution does not support an enhanced law-making role for juries. Jurors have no personal constitutional right to disregard the law—otherwise, they would not be required to take an oath to obey it. Nor do defendants have constitutional right to insist that jurors be given the opportunity to disregard the law. True, judges cannot overturn a conviction or acquittal without the consent of the defendant (through appeal, motion or otherwise). But this rule is in place not because the Constitution considers the jury a superior lawmaker but because the Fifth Amendment prohibits the government from putting the defendant in jeopardy of life or limb more than once for the same offense. Judges also are barred from directing verdicts of guilt, but only because the Sixth Amendment guarantees to the defendant a jury's assessment of the facts.

Beyond what is necessary to protect these important interests of the accused, our refusal to tolerate jury nullification must not stray. Judges, for example, should continue to avoid seating jurors who cannot or will not promise to follow the judge's instructions; continue to prohibit argument and deny instructions concerning defenses not supported by the evidence; continue to instruct jurors about the law and require them to follow these instructions; and continue to prohibit nullification advocates from approaching jurors with nullification propaganda (just as they bar prosecution sympathizers from lobbying the jury for conviction). Although each of these practices is designed to prevent jury nullification, each is constitutional because the Constitution does not protect jury nullification itself. It protects a defendant's right to fact-finding by a jury and to the finality of a verdict.

Legislators and judges so far steadfastly have rejected repeated proposals to lower barriers to jury nullification because they understand that the costs of such changes would far outweigh any benefits they may bring. Other fundamental changes in our jury system, such as the Supreme Court's decision to ban race-based peremptory challenges as a violation of the equal-protection rights of potential jurors, have been preceded by sustained social, political and legal critique of the status quo. A similar groundswell to cede more power to those who sit in jury boxes in criminal cases has never existed and, fortunately, probably never will.

King teaches law at Vanderbilt University and is author of the article, "Silencing Nullification Advocacy Inside the Jury Room and Outside the Courtroom."

Looking Askance at Eyewitness Testimony

Psychologists, showing how errors reach the courts, offer advice on handling such evidence

BY D. W. MILLER

RONNIE BULLOCK was sentenced to 60 years in jail for kidnapping and raping a young Illinois girl. Edward Honaker spent a decade in a Virginia prison for sexually assaulting a woman at gunpoint. Kirk Bloodsworth was shipped off to Maryland's death row for raping and strangling a 9-year-old girl.

All three of those men were convicted in part because eyewitnesses or victims firmly placed them at the scene of the crime. But not one of them was guilty. They were among the first convicts to be exonerated by DNA tests proving that someone else was responsible.

Some psychologists believe that such mistakes happen in thousands of courtrooms every year. But most crimes leave no DNA traces to rule out the innocent. For more than two decades, psychological researchers have asked, How could so many witnesses be wrong, and what can be done about it? Only recently have they seen their findings influence the way the criminal-justice system handles eyewitness testimony.

Psychologists have conducted hundreds of studies on errors in eyewitness identification. In some cases, of course, witnesses simply lie. But research has shown that flawed police procedures and the vagaries of memory often lead witnesses to identify the wrong person, and that credulous jurors too easily credit their testimony.

To those familiar with the mountain of evidence about the way the human mind works, that comes as no surprise. "Why should people make good eyewitnesses?" asks Gary L. Wells, a psychologist at Iowa State University who is widely considered the dean of eyewitness research. In the presence of danger, he says, "we're wired for fight or flight. What helped for survival was not a quick recall of details."

The findings of Mr. Wells and his colleagues are finally gaining currency in the halls of criminal justice. In part

that is due to the gradual acceptance of expert testimony on eyewitness identification.

Far more crucial, however, is the growing roster of convicts cleared by DNA evidence. In 1996, the U.S. Department of Justice released a report on the first 28 known cases of DNA exoneration. After studying those and 12 subsequent cases, Mr. Wells discovered that mistaken eyewitness testimony had played a part in about 90 percent of the convictions.

MISSING THE KEY DETAILS

Concerned about the high rate of eyewitness error in the DNA cases, U.S. Attorney General Janet Reno invited him to a meeting in early 1997. As a result of their conversation, the department's National Institute of Justice asked Mr. Wells and five fellow scholars to join a panel of law-enforcement officials, criminal-defense lawyers, and prosecutors created to write guidelines for handling eyewitness testimony.

The guide, published in October, gave scholars the opportunity to show that human memory is not a highly reliable tool for determining guilt in the courtroom. For example, contrary to popular belief, people under stress remember events no better than, and often less well than, they do under ordinary circumstances. Witnesses also perceive time as moving more slowly during traumatic events. That, in turn, leads them to overestimate how much time they had to notice details, a key factor of their credibility in court. And studies have found that witnesses to a crime are so distracted by the presence of a weapon—a phenomenon called "weapon focus"—that they remember little else with accuracy.

Researchers cannot ethically recreate the trauma of real crimes. But plenty of field research suggests that witnesses are apt to misidentify people.

Gary L. Wells: "Why should people make good eyewitnesses?" In times of danger, "we're wired for fight or flight. What helped for survival was not a quick recall of details."

For example, many studies have tested the ability of convenience-store clerks and bank tellers to recall customers they encountered in non-stressful situations. Around a third of the time, the employees wrongly identified faces from "lineups" that did not include the person they had actually met.

THE DETERIORATION OF MEMORY

In addition, all sorts of factors inhibit our ability to recognize and recall facial detail. For instance, psychologists have established that most of us have more difficulty recognizing people of a different race. And memory deteriorates very quickly over time.

Elizabeth F. Loftus, a psychologist at the University of Washington and a pioneer in research on false memory, has discovered that it's remarkably easy to alter one's recollection without realizing it. Human beings are highly susceptible to incorporating "post-event information"—newspaper articles, comments by police, conversations with other witnesses—into their recollections.

Witnesses also have been known to identify as criminals people they recognized from some other encounter, a process called "transference." In one bizarre example, an Australian psychologist and memory researcher named Donald Thomson was himself once identified by a rape victim as her attacker. Not only was his alibi airtight—he was being interviewed on live television at the time—but she had mistaken him for the rapist because she had seen his face on her television screen during the assault.

IMPROVING POLICE PROCEDURES

Of course, policymakers can't do much to improve the flaws in our memories. So scholars like Mr. Wells, who wanted to reduce eyewitness mistakes, began to focus on things that the justice system can control—particularly police procedures.

One of the biggest problems with eyewitness identification, researchers have found, is that uncertain witnesses are often prompted to finger the person whom police have detained, even when the suspect is not the same person they spotted at the scene. Witnesses viewing a lineup tend to assume that police have caught the person they saw. So they think their job is to find the face that most resembles the description they gave to police.

The police sometimes exacerbate that tendency by designing lineups poorly. Imagine a witness to a liquor-store robbery who says the robber was white, stocky, and bearded. Based on that description, the police identify a suspect and ask the witness to look at a lineup of live individuals or at a spread of photos (known as a "six-pack").

Too often, say researchers, the "distractor" faces used by police do not closely match the witness's description, or the suspect's photo looks different from the others. If the suspect stands out in any way—if his is the only color photo in the six-pack, for instance—the witness is far more likely to say, "That's the guy."

Lineups are also fraught with the possibility of mistaken identity, researchers report, because of our tendency to overlook differences in facial appearance among people not of our race. Not only are white witnesses, say, more likely to mistake one black suspect for another (and vice versa), but police officers may overestimate the degree to which the distractors they choose match the suspect's description.

Recently, Mr. Wells has raised the alarm about the way a witness's confidence can be manipulated. Witnesses are easily influenced during and after the lineup—by talking with other witnesses or police interviewers—to be more certain of their choice than their recall warrants. Police investigators, for example, may praise a witness for "picking the right guy" out of the lineup.

That taint frequently makes its way to the jury box. Understandably, jurors put a lot of stock in a witness who can point to the defendant and say, "He's the one. I'll never forget his face." But scholars have learned that the degree of confidence during trial is a poor predictor of a witness's accuracy. And, they warn, jurors ought to be particularly skeptical if they learn that a witness professed more confidence on the witness stand than in the squad room. Recall, they say, doesn't improve over time.

ASKING THE RIGHT QUESTIONS

Until recently, the criminal-justice system made little use of those findings. Defense lawyers, of course, have embraced and exploited them at least since the 1980's. But according to Brian L. Cutler, a psychologist at Florida International University, they have rarely been able to use the research to cross-examine eyewitnesses or police.

"Defense lawyers have no special training—they don't know what questions to ask," says Mr. Cutler. "If they do ask the right questions, how well-equipped are jurors to

As Expert Witnesses, Psychologists Have an Impact —but Only a Case at a Time

UNTIL a few years ago, when the U.S. Department of Justice invited six psychologists to help reshape police procedures for eyewitness identification, scholars had only one way to influence criminal justice: one defendant at a time. Many have themselves testified to educate juries about the pitfalls of witness memory.

Like a lot of his colleagues, Gary L. Wells, a psychologist at Iowa State University who testifies four or five times a year, got into that line of research in part to save innocent defendants from false imprisonment, and to force police to improve methods for interviewing witnesses and identifying suspects. "There was a time 20 years ago when I was so naive as to think that all I had to do was document the problem and the police would change their procedures," he says. But eventually he decided that "the courtroom was never the place to have that kind of impact."

"Judges are reluctant to tell police how to do their jobs," he says. And judges tend to hew to the established view that juries are the arbiters of witness credibility.

That has been changing slowly. In 1993, the U.S. Supreme court ruled in *Daubert* v. *Merrell Dow Pharmaceuticals, Inc.* that new federal rules of evidence permitted a broader standard for allowing expert psychological testimony. Since then, says Solomon Fulero, a psychologist at Sinclair Community College, in Dayton, Ohio, several convictions have been overturned because the trial judge had not allowed such experts to testify.

Still, there's a limit to the broad change that scholars can effect by testifying. According to Mr. Wells, there just aren't that many experts: About 50 to 75 psychologists testify in court regularly, and only about 25 of them actually do original research in the field.

Furthermore, their services can be pricey. While rates vary widely, the psychologists themselves report fees of up to $3,500 a case, although most will take some clients *pro bono.*

WITNESS CREDIBILITY

In general, the experts try to avoid challenging the credibility of individual witnesses or the conduct of the police officers who worked with them. "The goal of the defense is to cast doubt on the credibility of a particular witness. But that's not my job," says Mr. Fulero, who was invited to join the Justice Department's eyewitness-testimony panel because of his courtroom experience, not his scholarly *vitae.* What he can testify to, he explains, is that "eyewitnesses are not as accurate, over all, as the jurors believe them to be."

Unfortunately for defendants, that means the research doesn't always help their cause.

"The deep problem," says James M. Doyle, a Boston defense lawyer who served on the panel, "is that the research is all statistical and probabilistic, but the trial process is clinical and diagnostic." In other words, a jury expects the experts to say whether a witness is right or wrong, when all an expert can really do is explain how to assess the odds.

Mr. Wells echoes many of his colleagues when he says that he's not really in it for the money. He was among the half-dozen scholars who helped to fashion the new Justice Department guidelines for handling eyewitness testimony. If they are widely adopted, he says, "we have no business in the courtroom on this issue. My purpose is to make expert testimony unnecessary."

He may get his wish. According to participants, prosecutors on the Justice Department panel were concerned that quick-witted defense lawyers would use the new guidelines to impeach eyewitness testimony.

Mr. Doyle, who has co-written a lawyer's guide to the research, *Eyewitness Testimony,* calls that a reasonable fear. In the past, his colleagues have had difficulty incorporating the science into their cross-examination techniques, because they haven't taken the trouble to understand the research methods, he says. Now they won't have to.

On the other hand, he doubts that's a bad thing. "One thing police and defense lawyers share is that we don't really want to deal with innocent people. It's not necessarily easier or better for me to represent innocent people. I would just as soon the police did their jobs."

—D. W. MILLER

evaluate the questions?" Unfortunately, jurors cling to a belief that "the way memory works is a matter of common sense," he says. "It just isn't so."

"People expect it's like videotape, that we attend equally well to everything out there," says Roy S. Malpass, a psychologist at the University of Texas at El Paso who served on the Justice Department panel. In fact, he says, "we're highly selective."

No one knows how often eyewitness error leads to false convictions, but some scholars have taken a stab at the question. In their book *Mistaken Identification: The Eye-witness, Psychology, and the Law* (Cambridge University Press, 1995), Mr. Cutler and Steven D. Penrod, of the University of Nebraska at Lincoln, do some courtroom calculations: If just 0.5 percent of America's yearly 1.5 million convictions for serious crimes are erroneous—a rate suggested by some studies—then other research allows the authors to infer that well over half of those defendants, or around 4,500 innocent people, are convicted on false eyewitness testimony.

All that may change now that the nation's top law-enforcement officials have created new guidelines for police conduct. The Justice Department report, "Eyewitness Evidence: A Guide for Law Enforcement," reads like a primer on eyewitness research. Among other things, it instructs investigators who assemble a lineup to:

- Select "distractors" that match the witness's description, even simulating tattoos or other unusual features if necessary.
- Remind the witness that the suspect they saw may not even be in the lineup, and that the lineup is intended to clear the innocent as much as it is to identify the guilty.
- Avoid any comments that might influence the witness's selection.
- Ask for and record the witness's degree of certainty immediately.
- Photograph or film lineups to make the police more accountable to the defense.

Before they can take their new influence for granted, psychologists say, there is more to be done. For one thing, police officers and prosecutors need to be educated about the guidelines, which do not have the force of law. But Mr. Wells and others believe that both groups will embrace them once defense lawyers in the courtroom begin to hold the guidelines up as the gold standard of diligent police work.

NO DOUBLE-BLIND LINEUPS

The social scientists didn't win every battle. Despite their urgings, law-enforcement officials on the Justice Department panel batted down two key suggestions for improving police lineups. Research suggests that lineups are more accurate when they are double-blind—in other words, when the investigator in charge doesn't know which person is the suspect—and sequential—when the witness sees faces one at a time.

According to participants, police representatives nixed the former idea, because logistically it would be difficult to round up investigators who didn't know who the suspect was. More important, they said, it would be a tough sell to their fellow cops, because it smacks of mistrust and requires them to cede control of an investigation to someone else.

After scholars lost the battle to include double-blind procedures, participants say, they gave up on demanding sequential lineups. Without the first precaution, they explained, sequential lineups might be even more vulnerable to manipulation than simultaneous lineups are.

John Turtle, a panel member and a psychologist at the Ryerson Polytechnic Institute, in Toronto, believes that he has a high-tech solution to all those concerns. He has developed computer software that purports to take the bias out of the photo-spread lineups, which constitute about 80 percent of those in the United States and virtually all of those in Canada.

All a police investigator would need to do is scan a photo of the suspect into a computer and sit the witness down in front of the screen. The machine would then automatically choose photos of others who match the witness's description from a large database, and offer standardized, neutral instructions that wouldn't nudge the witness toward a particular response.

Psychologists deny they are imputing bad faith to police investigators. It's human nature, they say, to want your results to match your expectations. The scholars are simply urging police officers to treat their procedures for handling witnesses with all the care of scientific experiments. "Human memory is a form of trace evidence, like blood or semen or hair, except the trace exists inside the witness's head," says Mr. Wells. "How you go about collecting that evidence and preserving it and analyzing it is absolutely vital."

The Creeping Expansion of DNA Data Banking

By Barry Steinhardt

I want to explain my fears about the creeping expansion of DNA data banking and the uses that this information will be put to. I want to explain what those fears are based on and to challenge those who advocate the use of DNA evidence in the criminal justice system to prove me wrong—to demonstrate that the lid can be firmly kept on Pandora's box.

Let me start with a point that I hope we can all agree on. Drawing a DNA sample is not the same as taking a fingerprint. Fingerprints are two-dimensional representations of the physical attributes of our fingertips. They are useful only as a form of identification. DNA profiling may be used for identification purposes, but the DNA itself represents far more than a fingerprint. Indeed, it trivializes DNA data banking to call it a genetic fingerprint; in Massachusetts, lawmakers have specifically rejected that term.[1]

I understand that the CODIS system[2] contains only a limited amount of genetic information compiled for identification purposes. But the amount of personal and private data contained in a DNA specimen makes its seizure extraordinary in both its nature and scope. The DNA samples that are being held by state and local governments can provide insights into the most personal family relationships and the most intimate workings of the human body, including the likelihood of the occurrence of over 4,000 types of genetic conditions and diseases. DNA may reveal private information such as legitimacy at birth and there are many who will claim that there are genetic markers for aggression, substance addiction, criminal tendencies and sexual orientation.

And because genetic information pertains not only to the individual whose DNA is sampled, but to everyone who shares in that person's blood line, potential threats to genetic privacy posed by their collection extend well beyond the millions of people whose samples are currently on file.

It is worth bearing in mind, too, that there is a long, unfortunate history of despicable behavior by governments toward people whose genetic composition has been considered "abnormal" under the prevailing societal standards of the day.

Genetic discrimination by the government is not merely an artifact of the distant past. During the 1970s, the Air Force refused to allow healthy individuals who carried one copy of the sickle-cell gene to engage in flight training, even though two copies of the gene are needed for symptoms of sickle-cell disease to develop. This restriction was based upon the then untested (and now known to be incorrect) belief that people with a single such gene could display symptoms of sickle-cell disease under low oxygen conditions, even though they would not actually have sickle-cell disease.[3]

Genetic discrimination by private industry is becoming increasingly commonplace as well. A 1997 survey conducted by the American Management Association found that six to ten percent of responding employers (well over 6,000 companies) used genetic testing for employment purposes.[4] The Council for Responsible Genetics, a nonprofit advocacy group based in Cambridge, Mass., has documented hundreds of cases in which healthy people have been denied insurance or a job based on genetic "predictions."

In short, there is a frightening potential for a brave new world where genetic information is routinely collected and its use results in abuse and discrimination.

Now, I am certainly aware that the primary purpose of forensic DNA databases like CODIS is identification and that the profiles are of 13 loci that currently provide no other information. However, I reject the term "junk DNA" because as the Human Genome Project and other studies continue those loci may well turn out to contain other useful genetic information.

The question then is why I am skeptical that we can hold the line and ward off the brave new world of genetic determinism?

In general, I am skeptical because of the long history of function creep. Of databases, which are created for one discrete purpose and, which despite the initial promises of the their creators, eventually take on new functions and purposes. In the 1930s promises were made that the Social Security numbers would only be used as an aid for the new retirement program, but over the past 60 years they have gradually become the universal identifier which their creators claimed they would not be.

Similarly, census records created for general statistical purposes were used during World War II to round up innocent Japanese Americans and to place them in internment camps.

We are already beginning to see that function creep in DNA databases. In a very short time, we have witnessed the ever-widening scope of the target groups from whom law enforcement collects DNA and rapid fire proposals to expand the target populations to new and ever greater numbers of persons.

In a less than a decade, we have gone from collecting DNA from convicted sex offenders—on the theory that they are likely to be recidivists and that they frequently leave biological evidence—to data banks of all violent offenders; to all persons convicted of a crime; to juvenile offenders in 29 states and now to proposals to DNA test all arrestees.

I am skeptical because too many state statutes allow evidence which has been purportedly collected only for identification purposes, to be used for a variety of other purposes. The Massachusetts law that the ACLU is challenging, for example, contains an open-ended authorization for any disclosure that is or may be required as a condition of federal funding and allows for the disclosure of information, including personally identifiable information for "advancing other humanitarian purposes."[5]

I am skeptical because there are proponents of these DNA database laws who continue to cling to notions of a genetic cause of crime. In 1996, the year before the Legislature's enactment of the law authorizing the Massachusetts DNA database, the Legislature commissioned a study to research the biological origins of crime that focused on the genetic causes.

That report specifically focused on genes as the basis for criminal behavior, stating: The report foresaw a future where "genetics begin… to play a role in the effort to evaluate the causes of crime," and even cited two articles regarding the debunked "XYY syndrome."[6]

I am skeptical too because too many holders of DNA data refuse to destroy or return that data even after the purported purpose has been satisfied.

The Department of Defense, for example, has three million biological samples it has collected from service personnel for the stated purpose of identifying remains or body parts of a soldier killed on duty. But it keeps those samples for information for *50 years*—long after the subjects have left the military. And the DOD refuses to promulgate regulations which assure that no third parties will have access to the records. Isn't it likely that once the genetic information is collected and banked, pressures will mount to use it for other purposes than the ones for which it was gathered, such as the identification of criminal suspects or medical research? In fact, on several occasions, the FBI has already requested access to this data for purposes of criminal investigations near military bases.

Similarly, many state laws do not require the destruction of a DNA record and/or sample after a conviction has been overturned or—in the case of Louisiana's incipient law—do not require that a person arrested for a crime of which he is not convicted automatically has his DNA records expunged.

The existence of private DNA databases in testing laboratories and government offices, that operate outside the relatively strict CODIS framework, also gives me reason for concern and skepticism.

I am also skeptical, when I hear from Professor Barry Scheck of discussions he has had with law enforcement officials who are considering DNA "dragnets" of neighborhoods or classes of people without informed consent. And I am particularly distressed by the trumpeting of the British model, with its expansive testing and where in one case all the young male inhabitants of a whole village were required to submit to blood or saliva tests.

And I am made more skeptical by sloppy practices that indicate that too few jurisdictions take seriously their obligations under the data bank regime to carefully preserve and test the samples that they do have. Only two state statutes, for example, mandate outside proficiency testing of DNA labs.

In short, the trend is away from limited-purpose forensic data banks. The purposes and target populations are growing and the trend is ominous.

Compounding this problem is that there are few laws, and certainly none at the federal level, which prohibit genetic discrimination by employers, insurers or medical care providers. More and more DNA is being collected, and with the advances in genetic research that make that DNA more and more valuable, instances of discrimination and misuse will grow as well.

Now let me turn to the specific question of DNA data collection from arrestees. Aside from supporting my suspicions that we will see an ever-widening circle of DNA surveillance, these proposals are fundamentally unfair, they violate the Constitution and even from a law enforcement perspective they are not practical—at least not at the moment.

Let's start with what I thought would be the obvious. Arrest does not equal guilt and you shouldn't suffer the consequences of guilt until after you have been convicted. The fact is that many arrests do not result in a conviction.

For example, a national survey of the adjudication outcomes for felony defendants in the 75 largest counties in the country revealed that in felony assault cases, half the charges were dismissed outright, and in 14 percent of cases, the charges were reduced to a misdemeanor.

A study released by the California State Assembly's Commission on the Status of African American Males in the early 1990s revealed that 64 percent of the drug arrests of whites and 81 percent of Latinos were not sustainable, and that an astonishing 92 percent of the black men arrested by police on drug charges were subsequently released for lack of evidence or inadmissible evidence.

Indeed, there is a disturbing element of racial disparity that runs throughout our criminal justice system that can only be compounded by the creation of databases of persons arrested but not convicted of crimes.

Racial profiling and stereotyping is a reality of our criminal justice system. One study of police stops on a strip of interstate in Maryland gives some insight into the nature of the problem. Over several months in 1995, a survey found that 73 percent of the cars stopped and searched were driven by African-Americans, while they made up only 14 percent of the people driving along the interstate. While the arrests rates were about the same for whites and persons of color (approximately 28 percent), the disproportionate number of stops of minorities resulted in a disproportionate number of persons of color being arrested.

Now I make no secret of the ACLU's opposition to DNA data banking, even for convicted felons. We have argued and will continue to argue in cases like *Landry*[7] in Massachusetts that these are intrusive, unreasonable searches made without the individualized suspicion required by the Fourth Amendment and analogous provisions of state constitutions. But even if you accept the rulings that DNA data banking for convicted felons is permissible, either because a special need is present where persons have been convicted of crimes with high recidivism rates and the presence of biological evidence like sexual assaults, or that convicted felons have a diminished expectation of privacy, neither of those circumstances apply to persons who have simply been arrested.

To find otherwise is to equate arrest with guilt and to empower police officers, rather than judges and juries, with the power to force persons to provide the state with evidence that harbors many of their most intimate secrets and those of their blood relatives. Under the current circumstances of mistrust, that is an especially chilling notion for a New Yorker.

Take, for example, the "diminished expectations" argument on which most of the post-conviction DNA testing cases rest. Under this doctrine, the rights of persons who have been convicted of crimes become "diminished," only to the extent that those rights are "fundamentally inconsistent"[8] with the "needs and exigencies" of "the regime to which they have been lawfully committed."[9]

It cannot be argued that forcing arrestees to provide blood samples serves any legitimate security concern, even if they are in pre-trial detention. There are ample other means of confirming their identity. Nor by definition can DNA samples be used to insure compliance with any specified term of post-conviction supervised release. Put simply, these persons have not been convicted of any crime and may never be.

The only possible justification is investigatory and if law enforcement has reason to suspect an individual arrestee then it can and should seek a warrant.

If the special-exception doctrine makes any sense in the context of the post-convicted, it is based on the assumption that they have been found to have committed a crime where the recidivist rate is high and the presence of biological evidence is likely. How can you justify forced testing of a person arrested for jaywalking, or taking part in a political demonstration under that doctrine?

Now let me turn to the most practical of considerations—indeed the only consideration that gives me reason to hope that we will not move further down the path of DNA surveillance. As I read the literature, the single greatest obstacle to implementation of existing DNA data bank regimes is the large backlog of unprocessed samples. If I read the literature correctly, there is a backlog of 450,000 unprocessed samples and only 38,000 have been processed.[10]

There were 15 million arrests last year. From the law enforcement perspective does it really make sense to put the next dollars into collecting and processing samples for persons who have never been convicted of a crime; let alone a crime of the sort where DNA evidence is most likely to be probative. Wouldn't it make more sense to put scarce resources into processing the samples you already have and will generate in the future under the existing programs.

Let me say that I would love to be proved wrong. I would be more than happy to find that my fears are misplaced and that the civil liberties community is wrong about the likely future. If the advocates of DNA data banking can, in fact, restrict the uses of the data to forensic identification, if the data banks only cover persons convicted of a small number of crimes like sexual assault, if testing practices and data security are improved, all to the better. I won't mind being wrong. Pandora's box can be closed.

But the stakes are high and the risks are great. Every expansion of the data banks and every new use for the data increases those risks. The Commission has an obligation not just to assist law enforcement, but to protect the privacy interests of all Americans.

We may not agree on what has come before, but I hope you will agree that if the line is not held here, it may never be held at all.

Notes

1. *Commonwealth v. Curnin,* 409 Mass. 218, 219 n. 2 (1991) (rejecting the use of the phrase "'DNA fingerprinting' because (1) it tends to trivialize the intricacies of the processes by which information for DNA comparisons is obtained (when compared to the process of fingerprinting) and (2) the word fingerprinting tends to suggest erroneously that DNA testing of the type involved in this case will identify conclusively, like real fingerprinting, the one person in the world who could have left the identifying evidence at the crime scene.").

2. Combined DNA Index System, "[a] collection of databases of DNA profiles obtained from evidence samples from unsolved crimes and from known individuals convicted of particular crimes. Contributions to this database are made through State crime laboratories and the data are maintained by the FBI." Jeremy Travis & Christopher Asplen, National Commission on the Future of DNA Evidence, NCJ Pub. No. 177626, Postconviction DNA Testing: Recommendations for Handling Requests 67 (1999).

3. F. Donald Shapiro & Michelle L. Weinberg, *DNA Data Banking: The Dangerous Erosion of Privacy,* 38 Clev. St. L. Rev. 455, 480 n. 132 (1990).

4. American Management Association, Workplace Testing & Monitoring (1997), *quoted in* Rosemary Orthmann, *Three-Fourths of Major Employers Conduct Medical and Drug Tests,* Employment Testing—Law & Policy Reporter (Jul. 1997).

5. Mass. Gen. Laws Ann. ch. 22E, 10 (West 1999).

6. "Questions Concerning Biological Risk Factors for Criminal Behavior" (1996), *cited in* Brief of Amicus Curiae, Council for Responsible Genetics, *Landry v. Harshbarger* (No. SJC-07899), http://www.aclu.org/court/landry/harshbarger_crg.html.

7. *Landry v. Attorney General,* 429 Mass. 336 (1999) *cert. denied,* 68 U.S.L.W. 3153 (U.S.Mass. Jan 10, 2000) (No. 99–359) (holding that involuntary collection of DNA samples from persons subject to Massachusetts' DNA statute did not result in unreasonable search and seizure under the 4th Amendment and the State Constitution).

8. *Hudson v. Palmer,* 468 U.S. 517, 523 (1984).

9. *Wolff v. McDonnell,* 418 U.S. at 555–556 (1974).

10. National Commission on the Future of DNA Evidence, *CODIS Offender Database Backlog Reduction Discussion* (last modified Jan. 17, 2000) http://www.ojp.usdoj.gov/nij/dnamtgtrans3/trans-k.html.

Barry Steinhardt, Esq., is the Associate Director, American Civil Liberties Union.

This article is based on the author's testimony before the National Commission on the Future of DNA Evidence on Monday, March 1, 1999. Transcripts of his and other testimony before the Commission are available on line at http://www.ojp.usdoj.gov/nij/dna.

Community Prosecution

By Sarah Glazer

THE ISSUES

The young mother facing the judge in Winston-Salem, N.C. had been ticketed for driving her child without a car seat.

But when Judge Loretta Biggs asked why she had neglected her child's safety, the woman explained that she didn't have enough money for a child-seat. She had scraped together enough to pay her fine, though.

Biggs had an unusual solution. She ordered the woman to use the money to buy a car seat—and to bring it back to court to show she had made the purchase.

"Traditionally, we would find the person guilty and send her on her way," Biggs recalls. "I thought the better result was to have that child in a car seat."

Biggs' car-seat solution typifies the "problem-solving" approach to crime that is becoming increasingly popular in courts across the nation.

Yet in her seven years as a judge, Biggs often felt frustrated in her attempts to help people, especially youths. By the time most of them ended up in court, they were "heavily involved in criminal activity. So any problem-solving was too late."

That helps to explain how Biggs found herself sitting across the table from young gang members in High Point, N.C., recently. Biggs' widely admired commitment to finding every legal pathway to keep kids out of crime had caught the attention of U.S. Attorney Walter Horton, who offered her a job in his office in 1994.

High Point, famed for its furniture manufacturing, had been plagued with gang-related shootings, but Biggs felt that just prosecuting the young criminals would not end the violence. So she set up the meeting with gang members and issued a blunt warning: If the violence continues, you will face lengthy federal prison sentences. She backed up the threat by pointing to the daunting sentences her office had recently obtained for other local offenders.

But the federal prosecutor also offered a carrot to the gang members: If they gave up their lucrative drug trade, she'd help them get jobs. After several gang members took up the offer of legitimate work, gang-related gun homicides dropped from eight to zero in the year following the meeting.[1]

In High Point and other cities, prosecutors like Loretta Biggs are stepping beyond their traditional, tough-guy roles and targeting the social conditions that create criminals. That means fighting poor education with after-school tutoring, unemployment with job training and drug addiction with treatment.

"If we don't come up with comprehensive solutions, all we're doing is putting a Band-Aid on it," says Biggs, now Horton's chief assistant.

Biggs has also launched programs to provide social services to families of young offenders and to remove the graffiti and garbage disfiguring high-crime neighborhoods.

The approach espoused by Biggs and other prosecutors, often dubbed problem-solving or community prosecution, attempts to tackle local crime problems strategically, by targeting chronic offenders or prime locations responsible for the most persistent crime in a neighborhood. About half the nation's local district attorneys say they employ some form of "community prosecution—setting up storefront offices and attending neighborhood association meetings on nights and weekends to learn what residents consider their biggest crime problems.[2]

Often that means getting rid of a crime problem without prosecuting a case. In Washington, D.C., local prosecutors helped rid a neighborhood of a drug problem with a call to the city asking it to haul away an abandoned car that was a stash for drugs. In Boston, prosecutors accompanied residents to a liquor-license hearing to help argue for reduced hours for businesses attracting drug-dealing and intimidating crowds of youths. In Palm Beach County, Florida, prosecutors are turning abandoned buildings in drug-ridden neighborhoods into youth community centers.

Biggs says prosecutors traditionally operate more passively—sitting

Tackling Crime in Brooklyn... By Solving People Problems

The young woman at the defendant's table looks disappointed when the case isn't dismissed. In a car accident several weeks before, she had been charged with driving under the influence of drugs—in this case "angel dust" popular with the nightclub set.

Dressed in a bright red turtleneck that matches her fire-engine red fingernail polish, her blonde hair neatly combed, she is the picture of a good citizen gone straight. She has a new job as a receptionist with an oral surgeon, her attorney tells the judge.

Most judges would have dismissed a case this minor long ago if it had come before the busy central court in downtown Brooklyn, groaning under a caseload of far more serious crimes.

But this is the experimental Red Hook Community Justice Center, which aims to tackle the root causes of a crime, not just mete out a penalty. And Presiding Judge Alex M. Calabrese won't let the young defendant go so easily. He has already made her return repeatedly for drug counseling and drug screening.

With a click of the computer at his podium, Calabrese sees that she has not attended all of the drug-counseling sessions he assigned, and her urine has tested "dirty" for drugs. The judge orders her to wear a "sweat patch," which detects drug use through the skin, for several weeks and to return to his courtroom in six weeks for another drug test.

"I want you to understand one thing," he tells the young woman. "This court looks at underlying problems. That can work to your benefit if you test clean long enough. I can talk to the district attorney about reducing the charge so you'll have no criminal record. The bad part is you are going to have to return for a while. While the case may take longer, you may end up with a better result. I'm not going to let the case go until I know you're testing clean."

The court where Judge Calabrese wields his own brand of tough love is one of a dozen "community courts" around the country that try to help offenders overcome their problems.[1] In some cases, that means mandating drug treatment instead of jail time for a chronic offender. But in Red Hook, it often means that low-level crimes, which would normally be dismissed, will come under the scrutiny of social workers and a judge. Conveniently, counseling for drug abuse, domestic violence and job placement share the same courthouse building, along with health services.

Community courts like Red Hook also try to pay attention to the crimes that a specific neighborhood considers most destructive to its quality of life. "If you look at the front-line cases in most courts, what you saw as nothing much happening—the process of arresting and arraigning had become the punishment," says John Feinblatt, director of the Center for Court Innovation, the research arm of the New York state court system that helped plan the Red Hook court.

Prostitution and low-level corner drug dealing are two offenses Feinblatt says often get dismissed after the offender has spent a night in a New York City jail awaiting sentencing. But those are exactly the kinds of persistent crimes residents complained woke them up at night or disturbed their children on the way to school, he says. "We were saying you need more meaningful sentences that send a message that crime has consequences."

Red Hook is a geographically isolated community where 70 percent of the residents live in public housing and drug use is rampant. But even a community so hardened to violence was shocked in 1992 when Patrick Daly, a popular local school principal, was gunned down by a stray bullet fired by a drug dealer in the projects.

The death of Daly, who had been out looking for a missing student, sparked the neighborhood court experiment, according to Anne Swern, deputy district attorney for Brooklyn.[2] The Red Hook court handles low-level felonies such as possession of small amounts of drugs and misdemeanors like minor assaults, shoplifting, fare-beating and quality-of-life offenses like prostitution and vandalism.

It's too early to say whether Red Hook has been successful in preventing chronic offenders from getting in trouble again. But those who work at the court, which opened in June, agree that it at least supplies drug treatment and other services far more quickly than the conventional system.

It can take at least six weeks before a defendant in Brooklyn's downtown court can get drug treatment—a waiting time that often discourages them from showing up at all. For a person with a drug problem arraigned in Red Hook, it's customary for a court employee to escort the defendant to drug treatment, often starting with counseling in the building that day.

"We'll have a person in a bed in treatment that night," says Adam J. Mansky, Red Hook's project coordinator.

W. Brett Taylor, a staff attorney with the Criminal Defense Division at Red Hook, says that his clients sentenced downtown often did not show up for drug treatment when handed an address and appointment date on a slip of paper. "These are people who have had problems dealing with the rules of society to begin with," he says. "And by making it difficult for them to access these services, you're not really giving them the help they need."

At Manhattan's Midtown Community Court, the first community court started in New York City (in 1993), offenders were more likely to complete mandated one-day drug counseling and community service than at the central downtown court, an evaluation of its first two years found.[3] Drug offenders who completed 90 days or more of treatment mandated by the Midtown court cut their annual arrest days by half, according to Michele Sviridoff, deputy director of the Center for Court Innovation, which helped plan the Midtown court.[4]

(continued on next page)

in their offices waiting for the police to bring them cases. But like Biggs, prosecutors around the country say they are frustrated by a revolving door of repeat criminals. For every drug dealer imprisoned on a particu-

(continued from previous page)

Public defender Taylor says he sometimes get criticism from other defense attorneys for agreeing to mandated drug counseling for a client who could walk out of the downtown courthouse with a dismissal. "In the regular system, we could have gotten rid of the case," he says of a typical first-time drug possession, "but in six months they're back because we haven't resolved the underlying problem—it's like putting a Band-Aid on a splinter."

Some legal experts question whether defense lawyers should be recommending what amounts to longer sentences for their client—even if it's time spent in treatment. "If you can walk your client out the door, don't you have an obligation to do that?" asks Anthony Thompson, a professor of clinical law at New York University School of Law. "My question is: To what extent are we sacrificing aggressive representation for this notion of participating in the community?" Critics of community courts say the extra services the courts provide make them so expensive that it is unlikely they will be replicated to handle most of a city's cases. Some consider that unfair favoritism for certain neighborhoods. Manhattan District Attorney Robert M. Morganthau has argued that the money spent at Midtown could be better used to improve conditions at Manhattan's main Criminal Court.[5]

Advocates of community courts respond that if fulfilled, the benefits of community courts—fewer prisoners filling jails, fewer addicts committing crimes and safer streets—would outweigh the additional costs.

---

1. Twelve community courts are in operation nationwide and another 12 will be established in the next 12 months, according to the Center for Court Innovation in New York City.
2. The Red Hook Court handles cases that would normally be dealt with in three separate courts in downtown Brooklyn: Criminal Court, Family Court and Housing Court.
3. Michele Sviridoff *et al., Dispensing Justice Locally: The Implementation and Effects of the Midtown Community Court* (1997), pp. 174, 177. Arrests for prostitution and illegal vending also dropped after the Midtown Community Court opened, according to the evaluation.
4. Preliminary findings from the second phase of evaluation on the Midtown Community Court.
5. See Joseph P. Fried, "Court is Moving Back into the Neighborhood," *The New York Times,* Oct. 10, 1999.

---

lar corner, for example, another rises to take his place.[3]

Community prosecution relies heavily on community leaders to identify local concerns and to carry out a message of deterrence. In some cases, historic barriers of distrust between low-income communities and the justice system are demolished. In High Point, for example, Biggs invited prominent African-American clergy, longstanding critics of the police, to the table along with local police.

At first, Biggs met resistance. The Rev. Williams S. Sails of the Greater First United Baptist Church in High Point said he initially turned down Biggs' invitation because of his own distrust of the police.

Yet Sails and other black community leaders eventually became allies of the police. Sails and gang members who told him they could make more money selling drugs than in dead-end jobs persuaded him of a central tenet of the new prosecution strategy—that some criminals will stop committing crimes if given an alternative.

"I can tell you of a ton of cases where we prosecuted drug dealer after drug dealer and made no appreciable impact on the way people were living in that community," Biggs says. "We weren't getting the right one." By contrast, an intensive undercover investigation in High Point conducted by federal investigators and local police was able to target the individuals responsible for most of the gang-related crime. So far, 40 people have been indicted on drug, firearms and other federal charges.

Roger L. Conner, an attorney who has studied community-prosecution approaches for the Department of Justice, says the alliance achieved in racially polarized High Point demonstrates that prosecutor-led efforts can create a new level of trust in even the most estranged communities.[4]

"The prosecutor can play the role of convener. If you get the police and community groups in conflict, almost no one else can get them to the table," says Conner, a former visiting fellow at the National Institute of Justice and currently executive director of Search for Common Ground in America, a conflict-resolution organization in Washington, D.C.

Despite the claims of advocates, it's still not clear whether community prosecution can take credit for local improvements in crime statistics or whether prosecutors are simply benefiting from a nationwide decline in crime. In Palm Beach County, crime actually went up in areas where community prosecution was introduced, because prosecutors went after crimes that hadn't been reported or investigated before, according to James L. Martz, chief of the county's community-prosecution unit.

"It's hard to allocate resources to programs that don't have a tangible result," he says. "Community prosecution is difficult to evaluate." A neighborhood improvement like the removal of an abandoned building harboring prostitutes may not show up right away as an improvement in crime statistics even though Martz believes more-livable communities eventually have less crime.

"Community prosecution has become a catch phrase that includes a

Getting Tough With Boston's Gangs

One of the most widely hailed efforts in problem-solving prosecution took place in Boston during the mid-1990s. Operation Ceasefire, as it is known, pioneered face-to-face meetings with gang members at a time of unprecedented youth violence in the city.

Caught in a spiral of gang warfare, Boston had averaged 44 youth homicides a year between 1991 and 1995, before federal and local prosecutors and law-enforcement officials faced down Boston gangs at a meeting on May 15, 1996. At the meeting, gang members were told they would be hit with federal charges—which brought tougher sentences than state charges—if they continued the gun violence.

Also seated at the long table facing gang members were street outreach workers, probation officers and clergy, who offered gang members the alternative of summer jobs and other help. The gang members were told the story of Freddie Cardozo, a Boston gang member who had been prosecuted in federal court for possession of a single bullet—an offense that normally would have been handled in state court. Cardozo's 20-year federal prison sentence became a symbol on the street that the Ceasefire team "meant business."[1]

In 1996, the number of Boston youth homicides (age 24 and under) decreased to 26 and the following year dropped to 15—an average monthly decline of 63 percent.[2] The impact on crime has been so impressive that several cities, including High Point, N.C., and Indianapolis, have received federal grants to copy Boston's approach of facing gang members directly with a carrot (social services) and stick (federal convictions) approach.

Impressive though these drops are, cities across New England and the nation were also experiencing drops in youth gun violence during the same time, some without taking on any new crime-fighting initiative, argues Jeffrey Fagan, a professor at the Columbia University School of Public Health. Also at around the same time, Boston mounted an intense effort to crack down on illegal guns finding their way to youths on the street, and black clergymen became actively involved in offering mainstream alternatives to gang participation.

"It raises the question of whether what they observed in Boston was simply part of a long national trend or whether it was unique," Fagan says. As for the movement of other cities to copy Boston, Fagan says, "I think there's a rush to judgment here."

Indeed, says Brian Forst, a professor of criminal-justice policy at American University, there were so many anti-crime initiatives going on in Boston at the same time it's virtually impossible to say which had an effect. In addition to the community-prosecution effort known as Boston's Safe Neighborhood Initiative, police stepped up enforcement of quality-of-life crimes like graffiti and noise. Around the same time Boston formed a Youth Violence Strike Force composed of prosecutors and police and employed civil-forfeiture laws to take over drug dens and renovate them for housing.

"We don't know which of the interventions done in Boston were most responsible for the reduction in crime," he says. "Some may have been counterproductive."

Operation Ceasefire was based on the research of David M. Kennedy, a senior researcher at Harvard University's John F. Kennedy School of Government, indicating that shootings were being fueled by beefs among a relatively small number of youths caught in a cycle of feuding.[3] Kennedy helped design both Operation Ceasefire and the gun-interdiction effort.

Answering skeptics, Kennedy says, "The drops in Boston were larger than the rest of the country, they coincided precisely with Ceasefire going operational and they were felt precisely in the kinds of age groups at which Ceasefire was directed." Other possible influences like the improving economy and the work of black ministers happened later or were too small to account for the shifts, Kennedy maintains.

Moreover, he notes, "We're starting to see similar results in North Carolina and Indianapolis."

---

1. Jeremy Travis, "New Challenges in Evaluating Our Sentencing Policy: Exploring the Public Safety Nexus," Address to the National Workshop on Sentencing and Corrections, Hilton Head, S.C., June 1, 2000, p. 5.
2. Anthony A. Braga and David M. Kennedy et al., *Problem-Oriented Policing Deterrence, and Youth Violence: An Evaluation of Boston's Operation Ceasefire* (Unpublished paper), June 12, 2000, p. 13.
3. About 1,300 gang members—less than 1 percent of youths citywide—concentrated in 61 gangs were responsible for at least 60 percent of all youth homicide in the city, Kennedy found. See Braga and Kennedy *op. cit.*, p. 5.

whole variety of interventions," but it's not clear which if any of these efforts works, says Brian Forst, a professor of criminal-justice policy at American University.

It's almost impossible to tell what effect community prosecution is having on a given office since most prosecutors' offices don't publicly

report how they dispose of the cases brought to them by police or even their rate of conviction, Forst says. "Even the best of programs lack systematic bottom-line public accountability," he wrote recently.[5]

For some prosecutors, more convictions may result because a neighborhood DA handles a case from

arrest to courtroom instead of bouncing it from one prosecutor to another in the typical assembly-line treatment given run-of-the-mill crimes.

But that's a reform that could be implemented independently of community prosecutions in an effort to deter schoolchildren from crime. The effort is similar to DARE, a program where police officers lecture to schoolchildren on the dangers of drugs, "though there's not a shred of evidence it works," Forst says.

Many critics of community prosecution believe that prosecutors should not be trying to solve underlying social problems. "If you turn prosecutors into social workers, you have poor prosecutors and poor social workers," says Otto G. Obermaier, a former U.S. attorney in New York appointed by former President George Bush. Obermaier doubts whether prosecutors can succeed where President Lyndon Johnson's anti-poverty programs failed. And he questions whether federal prosecutors have the manpower to spare working on social programs instead of focusing on their central function—locking up the worst criminals.

"There is concern you won't be able to prosecute other types of crimes that may well justify greater attention," says Obermaier, now in private practice.

Harvard Law School Professor Philip B. Heymann, a former deputy U.S. attorney general, opposes the increasing involvement of federal prosecutors in gang violence and other local problems. The trend, Heymann observed recently, has been accompanied by a reduction in uniquely federal prosecutions, notably of officials charged with corruption. Moreover, he says, the skyrocketing number of federal drug prosecutions over the last decade has not reduced drug availability.[6]

Similarly, some critics question whether federal prosecutors will get so cozy with local police that they will lose the detachment needed to prosecute a police-brutality case.[7] For that matter, they ask, how does a prosecutor who has worked closely with a local tenant association leader handle the prosecution of the tenant leader's son for drug trafficking?

Forst has urged prosecutors to become more familiar with community concerns. But he says the millions of dollars in federal grants for community prosecution have just become a "new pork barrel" for elected district attorneys. "My cynical fear is they're realizing there's a political payoff there—it gets votes," he says.

He also questions whether time spent in the streets could actually hurt crime-fighting efforts. Community prosecution "may reduce convictions," Forst warns, "because when prosecutors are spending time in the community there may be cases they're not getting convictions on."

As criminal-justice officials consider community-prosecution strategies, these are some of the questions being raised:

Does community prosecution reduce or prevent crime?

In 1997, residents of the Grove Hall section of Boston's Roxbury neighborhood complained that hundreds of young people were congregating on weekend nights, blasting boom boxes and intimidating motorists. At meetings with police and prosecutors, residents in the predominantly black neighborhood expressed fear that the crowds could explode into violence.

Yet very few crimes were being committed beyond public drinking and drug violations. The corner's main draw appeared to be all-night fast-food businesses. When local police were unable to get rid of the crowds, prosecutors who had been assigned to the neighborhood in 1995 helped residents petition the city to close the restaurants earlier. Three were required to close by 1 a.m.; the remaining businesses agreed to close earlier. Within two months, the crowds had disappeared.[8]

In 1994, Grove Hall had the highest rate of violent crime in Boston, according to Catherine Coles, a researcher at Rutgers University in Newark, N.J. By 1999, violent crime in Grove Hall had dropped 36 percent from its 1996 levels, compared with the city's overall 24 percent decrease in crime.[9]

While community-prosecution efforts around the country vary according to a particular neighborhood's needs, they often share three basic elements of the Grove Hall incident. Residents tell local prosecutors they are more concerned about threats to their daily quality of life than violent crimes. Prosecutors must develop imaginative ways to solve problems that may have nothing to do with prosecuting cases. The improvements are obvious to residents and prosecutors but may not show up in crime statistics.

Even when prosecutors can point to decreases in crime, it is often difficult to determine how much is due to community prosecution rather than broader trends like an improving economy or a decline in citywide crime. Moreover, the initiatives are often accompanied by community policing, which also involves listening to residents and finding solutions that improve the quality of life. Cole is convinced community prosecution makes a difference despite the complicating factors.[10]

"The police tell us—and we've observed—that once you bring prosecutors into the equation, the [decreases in crime] become really noticeable," Coles reports. "There's a certain status prosecutors bring that makes them effective and powerful." But, Cole adds, "I don't know if we can ever get to the point where we can isolate community prosecution's contribution alone."

In a landmark 1982 article putting forward their now famous "Broken Windows" theory, ex-cop George Kelling and criminologist James Q. Wilson argued that the first broken window—or intimidating panhandler—in a neighborhood can start a cycle of abandonment, crime and, ultimately, fear among residents.[11]

"We're moving away from the focus on individual cases and trying to recognize that the community itself can be a victim of violent crime," Coles says. "The community can suffer when you begin the spiral into decay: Young people can't play freely outside; old people can't go out of their houses at night; people move out of the neighborhood." She adds, "It's been tough to bring prosecutors around to a broader outlook."

An increased sense of trust between residents and law enforcers has been another benefit of the community-prosecution effort known as the Safe Neighborhood Initiative in Roxbury, according to Coles. "Citizens now feel the initiative has brought equal justice to their community," Coles says. "They say, 'Our kids are more likely to get treated the same way your [white] kids are.'"

Boston and High Point are not the only cities where crime reductions have followed community-prosecution efforts. After two community prosecutors were assigned in 1996 to a Northeast Washington, D.C., neighborhood plagued by open-air drug markets, violent crime plummeted over a three-year period.[12] Deputy U.S. Attorney General Eric Holder, who started the program when he was U.S. attorney for the District of Columbia, has cited the program as a national model.

In Austin, Texas, prosecutors obtained a controversial civil injunction in 1998 to prohibit five gang members from associating with each other in a two-block area. Residents there had complained they were afraid to go out at night because of gang activity, robberies, loitering and drug dealing. Gang-related crime in the area dropped 46 percent from 1998 to 1999.[13]

Skeptics say that most of the dramatic success stories are told by prosecutors promoting their own programs, not objective researchers. Claims of crime reductions should be regarded with caution, warns Lawrence W. Sherman, a criminologist at the University of Pennsylvania. "Since 1993, crime has been dropping throughout the country," he says. "So for almost anything [that happens] during that period, you'd expect crime to go down."

Even the concept of sending out prosecutors—who are typically elected—to listen to the concerns of community leaders is not new, points out University of Wisconsin law Professor Michael Smith. "It's what politically savvy prosecutors have done forever," he says. And, he adds, "A lot of the practice is shallow, it's not real; it's rhetoric."

Indianapolis experienced record-setting levels of homicides throughout the mid-1990s, even as large East and West Coast cities were enjoying declining crime rates.[*] In late 1998, an anti-violence task force modeled on Boston's coalition of prosecutors, police and social service workers started meeting with parolees and probationers involved in the drug trade in Indianapolis. As in Boston, the task force threatened federal prosecution for gun violence.

Edmund McGarrell, director of the Crime Control Policy Center at the Hudson Institute in Indianapolis, says the city's violent crime started to drop dramatically after the so-called Brightwood gang was successfully prosecuted for drug trafficking and firearms charges in 1999.[14] By October 2000, homicides had dropped 40 percent from 1997 levels, according to McGarrell. If the declines had simply been part of the national trend, as some skeptics have suggested, McGarrell says the declines would have been smaller—on the order of 10 percent.

"People who attend these meetings have long criminal records, so you'd think they'd be [blasé] about threats," McGarrell says. "But they seem to sit up in their seats and listen when the federal prosecutors talk about how you'll serve 85 percent of your time, you won't be eligible for bail before trial and you'll serve your sentence not in the state of Indiana but anywhere around the country."[15]

For gang members who view state prisons as a picnic—a familiar nearby venue to hang out with their friends and gain a tough-guy reputation on the street—federal penitentiaries and federal sentences pose the threat of something unfamiliar and intimidating, agrees the Rev. Sails of High Point. "You're talking about ending up in San Antonio, Texas, where your mother or sister can't come and bring you a box of cookies."

McGarrell credits the threat of federal prosecution with helping to reduce the crime and violence. The fact that federal sentences offer no parole and that time served is usually close to the actual sentence also differentiates federal sentences from state sentences, which many gang members have experience with.

"People stand up all the time and say, 'We won't tolerate gang violence in our society,' and nothing happens," says David M. Kennedy, a senior researcher at Harvard University's John F. Kennedy School of Government. And he says gang members don't find the message believable. "You're speaking to a population that has seen their friends hurt and nothing done about it," he says. Most crimes go unreported, the majority of crimes that are reported do not result in an arrest and most arrests result in relatively light penalties—probation being the most common sanction.[16]

By contrast, the efforts in Boston delivered a believable deterrence message, Kennedy contends, by increasing the cost of violence in ways visible to gang members. The Operation Ceasefire alliance—as the coalition of law enforcement and social-service agencies was known—disrupted the street drug markets of targeted gangs through crackdowns on normally ignored probation and parole violations, serving outstanding warrants and seeking severe federal sentences.[17]

The approach pioneered by Boston is unusual for a criminal-enforcement campaign in its explicit recognition that while some gang members may be hardened criminals, others follow a path limited by life's choices. Community leaders in both Boston and High Point conveyed a strong moral message that they wanted the violence to stop, Kennedy says—recognizing that some gang members were reachable with something beyond punishment.

"What [community leaders] don't want is a scorched-earth law-enforcement policy," he says. After burying several victims of High Point's gang warfare, the Rev. Sails agrees. He came to realize that the assailants as well as the victims in the High Point shootings "were the children of my parishioners."

Is community prosecution an appropriate role for prosecutors to play?

Critics of community prosecution charge that prosecutors may represent one segment of a community —often their political constituency— while neglecting others with less political clout. An effort by neighborhood DA's in Portland, Ore., to exclude repeat drug dealers from crime-ridden neighborhoods represents a microcosm of the dilemma. The initiative has won kudos from community groups but has come under fire from lawyers for the homeless and indigent, who say it violates their clients' constitutional rights.[18]

In the early 1990s, merchants and residents in Portland complained that within hours of arrest, drug dealers were often back on the street. In response, the City Council passed a trespassing ordinance in 1992 drafted by neighborhood prosecutors that permitted police to exclude an individual arrested on drug charges from a neighborhood designated as a drug-free zone for 90 days. Upon conviction, the individual can be excluded for an additional year.

According to the Multnomah County DA, drug trafficking was eradicated in the area of town where the ordinance was first enforced, drug arrests were cut in half for the first two years it was tried in a second neighborhood and arrests dropped by more than 20 percent in a third.

Richard Brown, co-chair of the Portland Black United Front, says the drug-free zone approach transformed his neighborhood from an open-air drug market to one where property values are rising.

"It was hell in this community before the drug-free zone. Living hell," Brown says. At a local housing complex, an elderly resident told Brown she slept in her bathtub because of stray bullets. "Prior to the drug-free zone, folks would get picked up [for drug selling] and beat the cops back to the neighborhood," Brown recalls. "Now, once they trespass, they don't pass go, they go directly to jail. It makes an impression on them."

But Kelly Skye, a Portland public defender, says the ordinance "has allowed police a lot of leeway for harassment." She charges that some of her clients have been excluded from the drug-free zone even when no drugs have been found on their person.

"If you have family in the drug-free zone, you can't visit them," Skye says, charging that the ordinance violates basic constitutional rights of association and travel. While the ordinance allows someone to apply for a variance from the exclusion if they live or work in the zone or need to enter it for other reasons, Skye says many of her clients don't have sufficient education or the kinds of identification necessary to apply for a variance.

The ordinance has been the target of court challenges in both state and federal courts. In a federal lawsuit in U.S. District Court in Portland, Glenn White contended he had been excluded from the drug-free zone after a drug arrest but had received a variance permitting him back into the zone because he resides there. Police later arrested White for criminal trespass in front of his home because he did not have his variance papers on him at the time, according to his attorney.[19]

An ordinance in Cincinnati modeled after Portland's drug-free ordinance was declared unconstitutional in January by an Ohio district court, which said the ordinance violated citizens' rights.[20] The city has appealed.

James Hayden, the assistant DA assigned to Brown's Portland neighborhood, says the court challenges haven't dampened his enthusiasm for employing drug-free zones.

"I've been to every single neighborhood association, and I know how many people are in favor of it," he says. "Let's not forget who we're talking about. These are people who would degrade their own neighborhood by dealing drugs in it."

He insists that police rarely exclude individuals from the drug-free zone without evidence of drugs on them. The *Portland Oregonian* reported 28 such cases out of 3,700 exclusions issued in 1999.[21]

Michael D. Schrunk, district attorney for Multnomah County, supports Portland's use of drug-free zones, but he says they do not completely satisfy community prosecution's approach of tackling root causes.

"Drug-free zones are interim solutions until you can change the drug culture," he says. "The real problem in the drug-free zone is probably outside the criminal-justice system, but you can work on it," Schrunk says. He cites drug-prevention education and a new community court in Portland that emphasizes drug treatment over punishments.

The Portland controversy raises the question of whether it's fair to bring all the powers of a prosecutor's office—including investigation, indictment and potentially harsher sentencing—to one neighborhood when the same offenses would be dismissed or overlooked in another.

Taking the context of a crime into account makes sense, advocates of community prosecution insist. But that perspective flies in the face of the principle that law students learn early on—"treat like cases alike."

"Here we are saying that where [crime] happens, when it happens and who it happens to matters," says Jeremy Travis, a senior fellow at the Urban Institute.

Conner of Search for Common Ground in America cites the case of a notorious drunk in a low-income Washington neighborhood who would expose himself to children, panhandle aggressively and break car windshields. "Reds" had been arrested 50 times, but he always was released and returned to his usual street corner.

Finally, the neighborhood prosecutor discovered Reds had a pending theft charge that had never been fully investigated. The prosecutor found a witness to the crime and told Reds' attorney he could face the prospect of a year in jail or go into treatment for his alcoholism. Reds chose treatment.[22]

"The neighborhood thought they'd died and gone to heaven," says Conner of Reds' removal from the neighborhood and subsequent sobriety. Yet fellow prosecutors questioned their colleague for spending so much time on one drunk when a similar charge would have been dismissed in any other part of the city, according to Conner.

What the conventional prosecutorial system creates when it continually dismisses petty behavior of this sort, Conner suggests, is inequality of peace of mind between low-income neighborhoods and wealthy neighborhoods. Community prosecution aims to restore peace to low-income neighborhoods threatened by disorder, he argues. "We know peace of mind is important because people pay a lot of money for it by moving to the suburbs."

But do prosecutors' offices, already strained by heavy caseloads, have the manpower to spare from prosecuting serious crimes? "I think they can certainly do more things to prevent crime than prosecute—if their political constituencies will let them," says criminologist Sherman. But he cautions that prosecutors' offices are "always underfunded. They barely have enough staff to handle their caseloads; they plea bargain away lots of cases because they don't have time to take them to trial. They

have to be very conscious of what bang for the buck they're getting."

The close involvement of neighborhood prosecutors in the life of a community also gives them potentially incriminating information, coupled with growing discretion over which cases to prosecute. "Even in some of the best collaborations, some of the community members complain that what they get is longer sentences for the sons and daughters of their neighbors," says Christopher Stone, director of the Vera Institute of Justice in New York City.

Several Washington residents who cooperated with neighborhood prosecutors told Stone they were dismayed by the severity of the sentences their testimony had helped make possible. "While residents accept the need for that, in some cases they would prefer other kinds of solutions," he says.

Some prominent legal authorities have questioned the involvement of federal prosecutors in what are essentially local crimes. Federal prosecutors have enormous discretion to increase the severity of a sentence by choosing to prosecute under federal law a crime that would receive much lighter penalties if prosecuted under state law.

An American Bar Association task force headed by Edwin Meese III, former attorney general under President Ronald Reagan, recently attacked the growing involvement of federal prosecutors in local crime problems. The "current federalization trend presents a troubling picture" capable of undermining local differences and of undermining the local relationships forged by community policing, it said.[23]

Advocates of this school of thought, known as federalism, argue that federal prosecutors need to remain distant from local politics so that they will be able to prosecute police or political corruption dispassionately. But other legal experts note that federal prosecutors are already deeply enmeshed in many local communities by virtue of the

drug and gang prosecutions they pursue.

Activist U.S. attorneys counter that federal prosecutors have always exercised discretion over which cases to prosecute. But traditionally they did so "in a vacuum, not giving much thought to whether we were having an impact on the local community," in the words of North Carolina prosecutor Biggs. "We're saying that's not the best use of our prosecutorial resources," she argues. "I'd rather see an impact—kids not sleeping behind dressers because of gunshots in their neighborhood."

For local prosecutors making their way up the political ladder to higher office, community prosecution poses a similar tension between a DA's professional role and interest in getting re-elected.

"In a strict community-prosecution regime, assistant prosecutors may feel compelled to prosecute relatively minor cases because of their local importance—cases that they would previously have dismissed because of the weakness of the evidence and the lack of resources to pursue further investigation of routine crimes," Stone has cautioned.[24]

BACKGROUND

Prosecutors' Role

In an influential 1992 article, law Professor Ronald Goldstock of New York University argued that prosecutors should view the reduction of crime as one of their central purposes, not just as incidental fallout from prosecuting cases. A historical role for the prosecutor as problem-solver could be traced to the 1930s, Goldstock noted, when New York prosecutors undertook sophisticated investigations in an attempt to wipe out organized crime, official corruption and labor racketeering.

Goldstock suggested that prosecutors were continuing that tradition with their recent experiments in referring juvenile offenders to reading and wilderness programs, for example, instead of prosecuting them.

Why should prosecutors, rather than social workers, undertake such efforts? Goldstock argued that the prosecutors' traditional tough-guy role gives them the public credibility to try softer approaches to crime prevention. "Just as it was once said that only Nixon could go to China, perhaps only prosecutors, generally regarded as conservative, will be given latitude by the public to propose solutions which may appear unconventional," he wrote."[25]

In the past decade, two main influences have been cited for the growing popularity of community prosecution: the widely perceived success of community policing and the crack cocaine epidemic of the 1980s and '90s. Crack convinced some prosecutors that their traditionally reactive stance to prosecuting could not keep up with the cyclical drug markets plaguing neighborhoods.[26]

The widespread adoption of community policing and the subsequent crime declines in major cities that tried it led many observers to credit community policing with reducing crime. Community policing advocated the return of police to walking a beat and emphasized getting to know the residents of a neighborhood in order to understand local crime problems.

In his 1992 campaign, President Clinton advocated community policing. Under the Crime Act of 1994, the largest investment of federal funds in local police departments in U.S. history bore the label of community policing.[27]

In New York and other cities, meetings called by police to listen to a community's problems started to include prosecutors. "Sometimes the local DA would say, 'This is interesting. I should be involved, too.' The environment became more fertile because of community policing, and

prosecutors became more creative," says the Urban Institute's Travis, a former counsel to New York City Police Commission Lee Brown, a community-policing advocate.

The theoretical basis for community policing can be traced in part to Wilson and Kelling's 1982 "Broken Windows" article in *The Atlantic Monthly.* In a foot patrol experiment conducted in the mid-1970s in Newark, N.J., Kelling had observed that although crime was not reduced in neighborhoods where police walked the beat, residents reported feeling safer. They went out more at night and even left their doors unlocked.

Kelling also noticed that foot patrol officers were more likely to ask people with disruptive behavior to stop breaking the community's rules, rather than ignore them. Often, it was enough to ask the person to move on rather than make an arrest.

The two criminologists theorized that disorderly behavior that goes unchecked, like broken windows that never get repaired, sends a signal to would-be criminals that no one cares, inviting more serious crime. Studies of other cities in 1990 supported a causal link between disorderly streets and serious crime.[28]

Solving Local Problems

In 1990, Wayne Pearson, the first prosecutor assigned full time to a Portland neighborhood, discovered what Kelling and other researchers had been writing about for 20 years, according to researcher Barbara Boland.[29]

Pearson's area, the Lloyd district, was slated for a new shopping mall and convention center. But merchants were worried that customers would be scared away by the unsavory street activity, including prostitution, public drinking and drug use and littering. The source of the problem was transients who slept in a nearby railroad gully, Sullivan's

Gulch, and came into the district to buy liquor.

Pearson devised a plan that included a major garbage cleanup of the gulch. Campers were handed garbage bags for their possessions and asked to pack up and move on. Neon-colored "No camping" signs were posted with addresses on the reverse side of the signs listing places that could provide temporary housing to the homeless. Pearson and the police would visit the Gulch several times a day to get people moving. Business owners would drive by and shine their lights on the campers at night.

"All of a sudden, the problem went away," recalls Mike Kuykendall, a former deputy district attorney in Portland. Changing the environment without doing mass arrests became the prototype for community prosecution in Portland. Kuykendall now helps to train other prosecutors in community prosecution as director of the community-prosecution program at the American Prosecutors Research Institute, an affiliate of the National District Attorneys Association.

The local press criticized Pearson as a "hired gun" since local businesses had contributed to his neighborhood office. But to the surprise of District Attorney Schrunk, "the phone rang off the hook with other communities saying, 'Can we buy one too?'" (Actually, citizens no longer have to contribute to the cost of DAs—every neighborhood in Portland gets one.)

Criminologists have long known that a small percentage of the population commits most of the crime. But community prosecutors have extended that insight to locations that spawn continual crime as well. Research conducted by University of Pennsylvania criminologist Sherman in 1986 discovered that 50 percent of the crime calls to police emanated from only 3 percent of the possible addresses.[30]

As Kuykendall notes, a lot of community prosecution consists of going after "recidivist people and recidivist places—but not necessarily with arrests."

In the early 1990s, an apartment building at 165th Street and Broadway in New York City was responsible for the highest number of 911 calls in the precinct, then the homicide capital of Manhattan. About 10 percent of the apartment units had been taken over by drug dealers, who terrorized the neighborhood with gunfire, street transactions and loud noise at night. Despite dozens of arrests at the building, the problem remained intractable.

As counsel to police Commissioner Brown, Travis seized the building in a civil action and had it placed in receivership. The new management company rented out the drug dealers' apartments to new tenants and installed security measures. Within days, shootings and complaints had dropped sharply and "the drug market on the sidewalk virtually ceased to exist," Travis recalled.[31]

Increasingly, local prosecutors find themselves instituting similar civil actions to deal with buildings where repeated arrests have been ineffective. In some cases, the threat of enforcing health and safety codes is enough to get a recalcitrant landlord to evict drug-dealing tenants.

Such civil tactics, says Sherman, have proven effective for reducing mid-level drug dealing in several cities. In Maryland, crime has dropped at twice the rate of the national decrease in areas targeted by the state's Hot Spots program, which identifies high-crime areas and launches local prosecutors and police to fight crime there.[32]

Melinda Haag, one of Indianapolis' first community prosecutors, recalls a neighborhood where drug dealers lived in several rental properties. After residents complained that their calls to police had done nothing, city attorneys put the landlord on notice that his buildings could be taken by the state; he evicted the drug dealers. "It changed the whole neighborhood," says Haag, now director of the Marion County Justice Agency in Indianapolis.

CURRENT SITUATION

Aid From Clinton

In March 1999, President Clinton proposed a five-year, $200 million program to help communities hire as many as 1,000 prosecutors annually to work on community-prosecution strategies. The administration cited Washington, D.C., Portland and Indianapolis as examples of cities where community prosecution has led to strategically oriented, successful crime fighting.[33]

In November, the administration awarded its latest round of grants—$10 million to 61 cities and counties to support community-prosecution efforts in district attorneys' and municipal attorneys' offices. That's on top of close to 40 offices that received community-prosecution grants for fiscal 1999. Legislation awaiting the president's signature would authorize $25 million in additional grants for fiscal 2001, which could bring community prosecution to an estimated 150 cities.

In addition, U.S. attorneys in 10 cities have been chosen to receive Justice Department grants to help them develop problem-solving prosecution strategies modeled after the Operation Ceasefire program in Boston. Harvard's Kennedy is advising the prosecutors on how to use data to understand the underlying cause of a persistent local crime problem. As in Boston, the prosecutors are trying solutions outside their normal realm, often offering alternatives to crime in collaboration with social service agencies. (The 10 cities are Indianapolis, Memphis, Tenn.; New Haven, Conn.; Portland, Ore.; Winston-Salem, N.C.; Atlanta, St. Louis, Rochester, N.Y.; Detroit and Albuquerque, N.M.)[34]

New Strategy

Inspired by Boston's Operation Ceasefire, the U.S. attorney in Mas-

sachusetts is trying out a similar carrot-and-stick approach to tackle two seemingly intractable problems: domestic violence and heroin overdoses. In Brockton, federal prosecutors are singling out individuals with repeat domestic-violence offenses for prosecution on federal charges where guns have been used or where the offender faces another potentially federal charge. As part of the new strategy, probation officers monitor repeat offenders with home visits. Offenders are also offered help with problems that contribute to battering, such as drug/alcohol abuse and unemployment.

In Lynn, where hundreds of people have overdosed from heroin since 1996, some fatally, drug dealers may be slapped with an additional 20-year federal sentence if their drug dealing has resulted in death or injury. The U.S. attorney views overdoses both as an opportunity to trace the drug dealer and to offer the heroin user treatment. Since three-quarters of those who overdosed have a criminal history, the prosecutor can frequently use recovering overdose victims' probation as leverage to pressure them into treatment.

"We see our role as protecting public safety," says Joy Fallon, executive assistant U.S. attorney in Massachusetts, explaining why her office is trying to help illegal-drug users. As for tough penalties for dealers: "We think the cost of doing business for the heroin dealer should not just be 'Oh, I lost a customer,' when that person dies."

A Growing Trend

The popularity of community prosecution has expanded quickly since 1990, when Portland was one of a handful of cities to send prosecutors into the field.[35] At least 85 district attorneys' offices now assign lawyers full time to neighborhoods, and close to half say they do some form of community prosecution, according to Kuykendall of the American Prosecutors Research Institute.

The community-oriented approach, which often makes use of civil remedies, has also seeped into other aspects of law, including city attorneys' offices, police departments, public interest law groups, pro bono law and legal-aid groups.[36] In New York City, for example, the police department now boasts more than 50 precinct-level lawyers, who develop civil remedies along the lines pioneered by the Urban Institute's Travis to attack problems ranging from noisy businesses to car-theft rings. In Baltimore, lawyers in the city's Housing Department use outstanding building-code violations to help clean up neighborhoods.[37]

Skeptics of community prosecution say its combination of listening to neighborhoods and obtaining city services for them is simply political grandstanding, something prosecutors have done as long as they've held elective office. But in its most recent incarnation, community prosecution often aims to help the kind of low-income, minority neighborhood where crime is a fact of life but political sway is not.

Schrunk, the Multnomah County DA, argues that district attorneys can use their political clout with city leaders and agencies to get improvements a neighborhood might not get any other way. Asked why prosecutors should be the ones to tackle the seemingly intractable social problems that spawn crime, he answers, "No one else is doing it."

Both the federal problem-solving approach and the more localized community-prosecution efforts are part of a broader reform trend in the criminal-justice system that aims to solve underlying problems, not just dispose of cases. Pioneering this trend are some 400 drug courts around the country, which leverage criminal penalties to persuade drug offenders to get treatment for their addiction.

"In many ways community prosecution asks, 'Is our goal just to put bad guys away or is our goal to improve public safety?'" says John Feinblatt, director of the Center for Court Innovation, the research arm of the New York state court system. "In some ways, that's what the drug court is saying: 'Is our job just to prosecute street corner buys and busts or is our job to address the addiction so you don't put them in the revolving door?'

"Many of the prosecutors are looking for strategies with more durable results," Feinblatt continues. "What was on their plate before was putting bad guys behind bars. What's on their plate now is improving the health of a community. If that takes putting their weight behind development of a jobs program, you see prosecutors stepping up to the plate and dosing that."

OUTLOOK

Future Support?

Community prosecution has had strong support from Attorney General Janet Reno, who has encouraged prosecutors to seek out community concerns and has supported funding to train prosecutors in this new way of thinking. It's an open question whether the incoming administration will provide the same kind of support to the fledgling movement.

A new Republican attorney general could be hostile to community prosecution, viewing it as a Democratic program because of Clinton's strong support, in the view of some prosecutors who advocate continued funding for the approach. Without federal funding, warns Kuykendall of the American Prosecutors Research Institute, prosecutors are unlikely to divert manpower from offices already spread thin handling growing caseloads.

As president, Texas Gov. George W. Bush would replace the current slate of U.S. attorneys—many of them committed to community-oriented prosecution. Bush appointees are likely to advocate less intervention by the federal government in local crime and more reliance on local law enforcement, some veteran Republican prosecutors predict.

Moreover, community prosecution's philosophy of tackling social problems has a decidedly old-style Democratic tinge in the eyes of some Republican prosecutors. On the other hand, advocates count elected Republic district attorneys among the practitioners of community prosecution, which may lend the movement a less partisan cast under a new administration.

The new skills required of community prosecutors, like making referrals to social service agencies and mediating community disputes, remain foreign to conventionally trained lawyers no matter what their political persuasion, notes Anthony Thompson, a professor of clinical law at New York University Law School. Thompson trains law students in community-prosecution scenarios as part of a prosecution law clinic, but he says many district attorneys' offices are unfamiliar with the concept, or reject it.

"You have the most seasoned prosecutors who say, 'Our job is to lock up the bad guys. That's the beginning and end of our job descriptions.'" Thompson adds, "That attitude will continue until we change the way we teach in law school."

Community prosecution, like community policing, varies so much from place to place that it is hard to predict what shape it will take in the future. "You can ask a city how it spent community-policing funds: One will show you its armored personnel carrier; another will show you its youth center," says the Vera Institute's Stone. Since most communities are internally divided, Stone warns, the success or failure of community prosecution may hinge on which interest group a prosecutor chooses to represent.

Many advocates of community prosecution say the next stage in solving the underlying problems of crime lies with community courts. Modeled on drug courts, which use their sentencing leverage to push addicts toward treatment, community courts try to solve myriad social problems from domestic violence to unemployment that lead to petty crimes.

"I think that is a model that will begin growing around the country," Kuykendall says. He speaks favorably of a new community court being tried in the Red Hook neighborhood of Brooklyn because "they've got the defense bar on board realizing it's not always best to help the client escape on a technicality. The defense can play a role in this too, in terms of getting drug treatment" and other kinds of help for a client.

Skeptics may question this idealized vision in which all sides agree on an offender's underlying problem and the best solution.

But ultimately, what most people want from a changing justice system is a sense that the system can be trusted to be fair to all parties, particularly in a climate of distrust. Whether community prosecution can fulfill that vision remains to be seen.

---

* Criminologists think Midwestern cities were slower to suffer crack epidemics than the two coasts and that the slowdown of the epidemic also took longer to reach them.

Notes

1. Eight criminal homicides with firearms involving gang or drug activity occurred annually in High Point in 1997 and 1998. None occurred in 1999. High Point's Violent Crime Task Force, led by the U.S. attorney, held its first meeting in 1998, shortly after the first sentencing in July 1998 of High Point offenders on federal charges. To date, only 10 of the 156 individuals notified by the task force of potential federal sanctions have been found committing subsequent violent crimes, according to the U.S. attorney's office.

2. Unpublished survey in Roger L. Conner, "Community Oriented Lawyering: An Emerging Approach to Legal Practice," Sept. 19, 2000 (Draft).

3. Mary H. Cooper, "Drug Policy Debate," *The CQ Researcher,* July 28, 2000, pp. 593–616.

4. Conner, *op. cit.*

5. Brian Forst, "Prosecutors Discover the Community," *Judicature,* November–December 2000.

6. Philip B. Heymann, "Cautionary Note on the Expanding Role of the U.S. Attorney's Offices," *Capital University Law Review,* No. 4, 2000, pp. 745–751.

7. Kenneth Jost, "Policing the Police," *The CQ Researcher,* March 17, 2000, pp. 209–240.

8. Catherine Coles *et al,* "Crime Prevention through Community Prosecution and Community Policing: Boston's Grove Hall Safe Neighborhood Initiative," in *Problem-Oriented Policing: Crime-Specific Problems, Critical Issues and Making POP Work,* Vol. 3, Police Executive Research Forum (forthcoming).

9. *Ibid.*

10. Another initiative aimed at reducing youth violence citywide, Operation Ceasefire, overlapped with the Safe Neighborhood Initiative. See also Richard L. Worsnop, "Community Policing," *The CQ Researcher,* Feb. 5, 1993, pp. 97–120.

11. J. Q. Wilson and G. I. Kelling, "Police and Neighborhood Safety: Broken Windows," *The Atlantic Monthly,* March 1982, pp. 29–38.

12. Nancy Zuckerbrod, "Prosecutors Hit the Streets in What Could be National Model," The Associated Press, Aug. 8, 1999.

13. Robert Victor Wolf, "Community Prosecution Profile: Austin, Texas; Using New Tools," Center for Court Innovation.

14. Twenty-one persons were indicted in the investigation. At least six received sentences at or above 20 years. See U.S. Department of Justice Southern District of Indiana Press Release, "Brightwood Defendant Sentenced to Prison Term of 34 Years," Sept. 1, 2000.

15. Under 1998 federal sentencing guidelines, parole was abolished for federal terms. However, prisoners serving federal sentences can earn "good time" credits for good behavior worth a reduction in prison time of up to 15 percent of their sentence. By contrast, state prisoners can serve as little as a third of their sentence or less depending upon the state. Compared with state laws, federal bail laws are more favorable to government prosecutors arguing that a prisoner should be held without bail.

16. See David Kennedy, "Pulling Levers: Getting Deterrence Right," *National Institute of Justice Journal,* July 1998, p. 4.

17. *Ibid.,* p. 5.

18. Robin Franzen, "Drug-Free-Zone Law Challenged in Federal Court," *The Oregonian,* Aug. 12, 2000, D1.

19. Robin Franzen and Scott Learn, "Rights Getting Zoned Out?" *The Oregonian,* July 30, 2000. A10.

20. *Patricia Johnson et al. v. City of Cincinnati,* order by District Judge Susan J. Dlott in the U.S. District Court for the Southern District of Ohio Western District, Jan. 20, 2000.

21. Franzen and Learn, *op. cit.,* July 30, 2000.

22. For description of Washington, D.C., community prosecution, See Roger Conner, "Community Oriented Lawyering: An Emerging Approach to Legal Practice," *National Institute of Justice Journal,* January 2000.

23. The Federalization of Criminal Law, Task Force on the Federalization of Criminal Law, American Bar Association (1998), pp. 41, 43.

24. Christopher Stone and Nicholas Turner, "Politics, Public Service and Professionalism: Conflicting Themes in the Invention and Evaluation of Community Prosecution," prepared for the workshop "What's Changing in Prosecution," sponsored by the National Academy of Sciences, Washington, D.C. July 15, 1999, p. 3.

25. Ronald Goldstock, "The Prosecutor as Problem Solver," *Criminal Justice,* fall 1992. See also Kenneth Jost, "The Federal Judiciary, *The CQ Researcher,* March 13, 1998, pp. 217–240.

26. Coles, *et al., op. cit.,* p. 1.

27. Stone and Turner, *op. cit.,* p. 1.

28. Wesley Skogan, *Disorder and Decline: Crime and the Spiral of Decay in American Cities* (1990).

29. Barbara Boland, "How Portland Does It: Community Prosecution," prepared for the Prosecution in the Community Working Group, April 18–19, 1996, John F. Kennedy School of Government, Harvard University, p. 9.

30. Lawrence W. Sherman, "Hot Spots of Crime and Criminal Careers of Plac-

es," in John E. Eck and David Weisburd, eds., *Crime and Place* (1995).

31. Jeremy Travis, "New Challenges in Evaluating Our Sentencing Policy: Exploring the Public Safety Nexus," Address to the National Workshop on Sentencing and Corrections, Hilton Head, S.C. June 1, 2000.

32. Scott Maxwell, "Democrats Unveil Anti-Crime Bills Based on Md. Programs," The Associated Press, Aug. 31, 1999.

33. The Clinton Administration's Law Enforcement Strategy Combating Crime with Community Policing and Community Prosecution," March 1999.

34. This program, known as Strategic Approaches to Community Safety Initiative (SACSI), is described in Veronica Coleman *et al.*, "Using Knowledge and Teamwork to Reduce Crime," *National Institute of Justice Journal,* October 1999, pp. 17–23.

35. Manhattan began a community-outreach program in 1985 to work with citizens' groups on drugs and crime. See Barbara Boland, "The Manhattan Experiment: Community Prosecution," May 1997. (Unpublished paper)

36. Conner, *op. cit.*, p. 30.

37. *Ibid.*

About the Author

Sarah Glazer is a freelance writer in New York who specializes in health- and social-policy issues. She has written for *The Washington Post* health section and *The Public Interest.* She graduated from the University of Chicago with a degree in American history.

UNIT 5
Juvenile Justice

Unit Selections

Key Points to Consider

- What reform efforts are currently under way in the juvenile justice system?

- What are some recent trends in juvenile delinquency? In what ways will the juvenile justice system be affected by these trends?

- Is the departure of the juvenile justice system from its original purpose warranted? Why or why not?

 **Links: www.dushkin.com/online/**
These sites are annotated in the World Wide Web pages.

Gang Land: The Jerry Capeci Page
http://www.ganglandnews.com

Institute for Intergovernmental Research (IIR)
http://www.iir.com

National Criminal Justice Reference Service (NCJRS)
http://virlib.ncjrs.org/JuvenileJustice.asp

National Network for Family Resiliency
http://www.nnfr.org

Partnership Against Violence Network
http://www.pavnet.org

Although there were variations within specific offense categories, the overall arrest rate for juvenile violent crime remained relatively constant for several decades. Then, in the late 1980s, something changed, bringing more and more juveniles charged with a violent offense into the justice system. The juvenile justice system is a twentieth-century response to the problems of dealing with children in trouble with the law or children who need society's protection.

Juvenile court procedure differs from the procedure in adult courts because juvenile courts are based on the philosophy that their function is to treat and to help, not to punish and abandon the offender. Recently, operations of the juvenile court have received criticism, and a number of significant Supreme Court decisions have changed the way that the courts must approach the rights of children.

Despite these changes, however, the major thrust of the juvenile justice system remains one of diversion and treatment, rather than adjudication and incarceration, although there is a trend toward dealing more punitively with serious juvenile offenders.

This unit's opening essay address the issue of young people becoming killers. In "Why the Young Kill," Sharon Begley maintains that a particular biology leads to tragic results. In the article that follows, "Juvenile Justice: A Century of Experience," Steven Drizin contends that the juvenile court is one of the most important contributions the United States has made to the world. "Juvenile Probation on the Eve of the Next Millennium" cites current trends in juvenile crime and identifies reforms needed to improve the probation experience. In the last essay, "Judging Juveniles," juvenile court judge John Carlin struggles to set kids straight. As Evan Gohr reports, in spite of the judge's efforts, roughly one-third of the boys and girls who pass through his courtroom seem destined for a life of crime.

WHY THE YOUNG KILL

Are certain young brains predisposed to violence? Maybe—but how these kids are raised can either save them or push them over the brink. The biological roots of violence.

BY SHARON BEGLEY

THE TEMPTATION, OF COURSE, IS TO SEIZE on one cause, one single explanation for Littleton, and West Paducah, and Jonesboro and all the other towns that have acquired iconic status the way "Dallas" or "Munich" did for earlier generations. Surely the cause is having access to guns. Or being a victim of abuse at the hands of parents or peers. Or being immersed in a culture that glorifies violence and revenge. But there isn't one cause. And while that makes stemming the tide of youth violence a lot harder, it also makes it less of an unfathomable mystery. Science has a new understanding of the roots of violence that promises to explain why not every child with access to guns becomes an Eric Harris or a Dylan Klebold, and why not *every* child who feels ostracized, or who embraces the Goth esthetic, goes on a murderous rampage. The bottom line: you need a particular environment imposed on a particular biology to turn a child into a killer.

It should be said right off that attempts to trace violence to biology have long been tainted by racism, eugenics and plain old poor science. The turbulence of the 1960s led some physicians to advocate psychosurgery to "treat those people with low violence thresholds," as one 1967 letter to a medical journal put it. In other words, lobotomize the civil-rights and antiwar protesters. And if crimes are disproportionately committed by some ethnic groups, then finding genes or other traits common to that group risks tarring millions of innocent people. At the other end of the political spectrum, many conservatives view biological theories of violence as the mother of all insanity defenses, with biology not merely an explanation but an excuse. The conclusions emerging from interdisciplinary research in neuroscience and psychology, however, are not so simple-minded as to argue that violence is in the genes, or murder in the folds of the brain's frontal lobes. Instead, the picture is more nuanced, based as it is on the discovery that experience rewires the brain. The dawning realization of the constant back-and-forth between nature and nurture has resurrected the search for the biological roots of violence.

Early experiences seem to be especially powerful: a child's brain is more malleable than that of an adult. The dark side of the zero-to-3 movement, which emphasizes the huge potential for learning during this period, is that the young brain also is extra vulnerable to hurt in the first years of life. A child who suffers repeated "hits" of stress—abuse, neglect, terror—experiences physical changes in his brain, finds Dr. Bruce Perry of Baylor College of Medicine. The incessant flood of stress chemicals tends to reset the brain's system of fight-or-flight hormones, putting them on hair-trigger alert. The result is the kid who shows impulsive aggression, the kid who pops the classmate who disses him. For the outcast, hostile confrontations—not necessarily an elbow to the stomach at recess, but merely kids vacating en masse when he sits down in the cafeteria—can increase the level of stress hormones in his brain. And that can have dangerous consequences. "The early environment programs the nervous system to make an individual more or less reactive to stress," says biologist Michael Meaney of McGill University. "If parental care is inadequate or unsupportive, the [brain] may decide that the world stinks—and it better be ready to meet the challenge." This, then, is how having an abusive parent raises the risk of youth violence: it can change a child's brain. Forever after, influences like the mean-spiritedness that schools condone or the humiliation that's standard fare in adolescence pummel the mind of the child whose brain has been made excruciatingly vulnerable to them.

In other children, constant exposure to pain and violence can make their brain's system of stress hormones unresponsive, like a keypad that has been pushed so often it just stops working. These are the kids with antisocial personalities. They typically have low heart rates and impaired emotional sensitivity. Their signature is a lack of empathy, and their sensitivity to the world around them is practically nonexistent. Often they abuse animals: Kip Kinkel, the 15-year-old who killed his parents and shot 24 schoolmates last May, had a history of this; Luke Woodham, who killed three schoolmates and wounded seven at his high school in Pearl, Miss., in 1997, had previously beaten his dog with a club, wrapped it in a bag and set it on fire. These are also the adolescents who do not respond to punishment: nothing hurts. Their ability to feel, to react, has died, and so has their conscience. Hostile, impulsive aggressors usually feel sorry afterward. Antisocial aggressors don't feel at all. Paradoxically, though, they often have a keen sense of injustices aimed at themselves.

Inept parenting encompasses more than outright abuse, however. Parents who are withdrawn and remote, neglectful and passive, are at risk of shaping a child who (absent a compensating source of love and attention) shuts down emotionally. It's important to be clear about this: inadequate parenting short of Dickensian neglect generally has little ill effect on most children. But to a vulnerable baby, the result of neglect can be tragic. Perry finds that neglect impairs the development of the brain's cortex, which controls feelings of belonging and attachment. "When there are experiences in early life that result in an underdeveloped capacity [to form relationships]," says Perry, "kids have a hard time empathizing with people. They tend to be relatively passive and perceive themselves to be stomped on by the outside world."

RISK FACTORS

Having any of the following risk factors doubles a boy's chance of becoming a murderer:

- **Coming from a family with a history of criminal violence**
- **Being abused**
- **Belonging to a gang**
- **Abusing drugs or alcohol**

Having any of these risk factors, in addition to the above, triples the risk of becoming a killer:

- **Using a weapon**
- **Having been arrested**
- **Having a neurological problem that impairs thinking or feeling**
- **Having had problems at school**

These neglected kids are the ones who desperately seek a script, an ideology that fits their sense of being humiliated and ostracized. Today's pop culture offers all too many dangerous ones, from the music of Rammstein to the game of Doom. Historically, most of those scripts have featured males. That may explain, at least in part, why the murderers are Andrews and Dylans rather than Ashleys and Kaitlins, suggests Deborah Prothrow-Smith of the Harvard School of Public Health. "But girls are now 25 percent of the adolescents arrested for violent crime," she notes. "This follows the media portrayal of girl superheroes beating people up," from Power Rangers to Xena. Another reason that the schoolyard murderers are boys is that girls tend to internalize ostracism and shame rather than turning it into anger. And just as girls could be the next wave of killers, so could even younger children. "Increasingly, we're seeing the high-risk population for lethal violence as being the 10- to 14-year-olds," says Richard Lieberman, a school psychologist in Los Angeles. "Developmentally, their concept of death is still magical. They still think it's temporary, like little Kenny in 'South Park'." Of course, there are loads of empty, emotionally unattached girls and boys. The large majority won't become violent. "But if they're in a violent environment," says Perry, "they're more likely to."

There seems to be a genetic component to the vulnerability that can turn into anti-

social-personality disorder. It is only a tiny bend in the twig, but depending on how the child grows up, the bend will be exaggerated or straightened out. Such aspects of temperament as "irritability, impulsivity, hyperactivity and a low sensitivity to emotions in others are all biologically based," says psychologist James Garbarino of Cornell University, author of the upcoming book "Lost Boys: Why Our Sons Turn Violent and How We Can Save Them." A baby who is unreactive to hugs and smiles can be left to go her natural, antisocial way if frustrated parents become exasperated, withdrawn, neglectful or enraged. Or that child can be pushed back toward the land of the feeling by parents who never give up trying to engage and stimulate and form a loving bond with her. The different responses of parents produce different brains, and thus behaviors. "Behavior is the result of a dialogue between your brain and your experiences," concludes Debra Niehoff, author of the recent book "The Biology of Violence." "Although people are born with some biological givens, the brain has many blank pages. From the first moments of childhood the brain acts as a historian, recording our experiences in the language of neurochemistry."

There are some out-and-out brain pathologies that lead to violence. Lesions of the frontal lobe can induce apathy and distort both judgment and emotion. In the brain scans he has done in his Fairfield, Calif., clinic of 50 murderers, psychiatrist Daniel Amen finds several shared patterns. The structure called the cingulate gyrus, curving through the center of the brain, is hyperactive in murderers. The CG acts like the brain's transmission, shifting from one thought to another. When it is impaired, people get stuck on one thought. Also, the prefrontal cortex, which seems to act as the brain's supervisor, is sluggish in the 50 murderers. "If you have violent thoughts that you're stuck on and no supervisor, that's a prescription for trouble," says Amen, author of "Change Your Brain/ Change Your Life." The sort of damage he finds can result from head trauma as well as exposure to toxic substances like alcohol during gestation.

Children who kill are not, with very few exceptions, amoral. But their morality is aberrant. "I killed because people like me are mistreated every day," said pudgy, bespectacled Luke Woodham, who murdered three students. "My whole life I felt outcasted, alone." So do a lot of adolescents. The difference is that at least some of the recent school killers felt emotionally or physically abandoned by those who should love them. Andrew Golden, who was 11 when he and Mitchell Johnson, 13, went on their killing spree in Jonesboro, Ark., was raised mainly by his grandparents while his parents worked. Mitchell mourned the loss of his father to divorce.

Unless they have another source of unconditional love, such boys fail to develop, or lose, the neural circuits that control the capacity to feel and to form healthy relationships. That makes them hypersensitive to perceived injustice. A sense of injustice is often accompanied by a feeling of abject powerlessness. An adult can often see his way to restoring a sense of self-worth, says psychiatrist James Gilligan of Harvard Medical School, through success in work or love. A child usually lacks the emotional skills to do that. As one killer told Garbarino's colleague, "I'd rather be wanted for murder than not wanted at all."

THAT THE LITTLETON MASSACRE ENDED in suicide may not be a coincidence. As Michael Carneal was wrestled to the ground after killing three fellow students in Paducah in 1997, he cried out, "Kill me now!" Kip Kinkel pleaded with the schoolmates who stopped him, "Shoot me!" With suicide "you get immortality," says Michael Flynn of John Jay College of Criminal Justice. "That is a great feeling of power for an adolescent who has no sense that he matters."

The good news is that understanding the roots of violence offers clues on how to prevent it. The bad news is that ever more children are exposed to the influences that, in the already vulnerable, can produce a bent toward murder. Juvenile homicide is twice as common today as it was in the mid-1980s. It isn't the brains kids are born with that has changed in half a generation; what has changed is the ubiquity of vio-

lence, the easy access to guns and the glorification of revenge in real life and in entertainment. To deny the role of these influences is like denying that air pollution triggers childhood asthma. Yes, to develop asthma a child needs a specific, biological vulnerability. But as long as some children have this respiratory vulnerability—and some always will— then allowing pollution to fill our air will make some children wheeze, and cough, and die. And as long as some children have a neurological vulnerability—and some always will—then turning a blind eye to bad parenting, bullying and the gun culture will make other children seethe, and withdraw, and kill.

With ADAM ROGERS, PAT WINGERT *and* THOMAS HAYDEN

JUVENILE JUSTICE
A CENTURY OF EXPERIENCE

STEVEN A. DRIZIN

On July 3, 1999, the first juvenile court in the world, founded in Chicago, Illinois, celebrated its 100th birthday. While few outside of Chicago marked this anniversary, I raised a glass to toast the court. For in the past year, as I have worked on activities to commemorate the Chicago court's centennial and immersed myself in its history, I have learned that the juvenile court is one of the most important and enduring contributions the United States has made to the world.

That my enthusiasm is not widely shared outside of Chicago is perhaps understandable. The juvenile court is among the most maligned of American institutions. Attacks on its legitimacy have accompanied it since its inception. Until recently, the court has managed to absorb these assaults and repeatedly transform itself to meet the concerns of critics. In the past 10 years, however, the relentless and heightened pounding of the court by its critics, notably politicians and prosecutors, has begun to take its toll.

Whether the court is able to reassert its legitimacy as it enters its second century is anybody's guess. But if history has proven anything, this much maligned institution has a strong self-preservation instinct. In fact, the court can draw on the lessons from its history as a source of strength in these seemingly desperate times.

LESSONS OF HISTORY

In order to understand the historical importance of the juvenile court, turn your mind's eye back to the turn of the twentieth century for a moment. Imagine what life was like for a small immigrant child, one of millions of such children who along with their parents came to the United States in great waves from Europe. Many lived in abject poverty, crammed in ghettoes and tenement houses. From about the age of seven or eight, they were forced to work to help supplement the family's income.

Children often worked long hours in sweatshops, performing menial tasks for many hours at a time when environmentally hazardous factory conditions dotted the urban landscape.

School was a luxury most poor children simply could not afford. Time spent in the classroom meant time away from work and less food on the family table. When not at work or in school, they played in the alleys and the streets on which they lived; there were few if any parks and other public spaces specifically designed for children.

For many years, there was little outcry about these conditions because the world viewed children very differently from the way we've come to think of them. Children had no "rights." They were considered the "property" of their parents (in particular, their fathers) or, if orphaned, the "property" of the state. From about the age of 10 or 11, they were viewed simply as little adults. They even dressed the part. Photographs of children at the turn of the century show young boys in suits with caps and young girls in dresses and skirts—miniaturized versions of their parents.

When children got into trouble, the law treated them no differently than adults. Although children between the ages of 7 and 13 were presumed to be incapable of forming criminal intent, this presumption did not prevent authorities from locking them in adult jails pending trial.

John Altgeld, an aspiring young lawyer who would later become governor of Illinois, observed the prevailing treatment of juveniles in 1882 when he toured the House of Corrections in Chicago, also known as Bridewell. There, he discovered hundreds of children, including some as young as 8 years old, jailed alongside adults. All told, children under 18 made up slightly less than 10 percent of Bridewell's population.

The plight of these children outraged Altgeld. His lectures and writings inspired Jane Addams, Lucy Flower, Julia Lathrop, and others associated with Addams's Hull

House to establish a better and more humane justice system for children. Their community organizing and coalition building led to the first juvenile court act in 1899 and the creation of a separate justice system for children, one premised on rehabilitation and individualized justice rather than the crippling punishments and one-size-fits-all sentencing policies of criminal court.

REDEFINING "CHILDHOOD"

The juvenile court was only the start of a remarkable run of child-centered reforms spearheaded by the Hull House women. Soon to follow were such other universal reforms as the child-labor laws; compulsory education laws; the construction of playgrounds, recreation centers, and parks for children; and pioneering work in the area of early childhood education.

These reforms helped redefine "childhood," creating an unprecedented and uniquely American vision of childhood as a sacred period in human life in which children and adolescents required the care and guidance of responsible adults. No longer did society view children as "mini-adults"; it accepted that they were qualitatively and developmentally different, which made them both less culpable for their actions and more amenable to intervention.

To the Chicago reformers, the last thing a civilized society should do to its children was to process and punish them like adults. They believed that government had a moral responsibility to act as "kind and just parents." In the context of a court system, this meant that children should receive individualized attention, under the watchful eyes of trained and sensitive judges and probation officers.

In addition to focusing on delinquent children, the first juvenile court catered to the needs of abused, neglected, and dependent children. Court proceedings were informal, non-adversarial, and closed to the public. The focus on the proceedings was less on whether the child had offended than on "why" and on "what" could be done to prevent reoffending. There were lawyers for neither the state nor the child—only a probation officer who functioned as the "eyes and ears of the court" and whose job was to put into action the treatment plans developed by the court and its experts. The stigmatizing language of the criminal court was rejected, and court records were eventually made confidential to protect children from long-term damage to their future prospects.

The reformers' ideas spread like wildfire, leading to the development of juvenile courts in 46 states, three territories, and the District of Columbia by 1925. Even more remarkable, in the days when there were few highways, let alone superinformation highways, and boat travel still surpassed air travel, the juvenile court movement quickly spread throughout the world. By 1925, Great Britain, Canada, Switzerland, France, Belgium, Hungary, Croatia, Argentina, Austria, India, the Netherlands, Madagascar, Japan, Germany, Brazil, and Spain had all established separate court systems for children. Today, every state has a separate court system for children, as do most nations throughout the world.

CRITICS LEFT AND RIGHT

America's juvenile court system remained largely unchanged throughout the first half of the twentieth century—except that the service functions of the court were gradually taken over by trained professionals rather than the volunteers and untrained staff who served the early courts. And first prosecutors and then defense attorneys began to make appearances in the court.

Then, in the mid 1960s, the juvenile court underwent a radical transformation. Critics from the right attacked the court for its inability to deal with a new breed of delinquent youth, a familiar refrain that would rear its head time and time again throughout the court's history. Critics from the left, caught up in the due process revolution of the 1960s, raised concerns that juvenile court proceedings were arbitrary and unfair and that the court was ignoring the rights of the children who appeared before it.

In a series of decisions in the late 1960s, beginning with the landmark *Kent v. United States* (1966) and *In re Gault* (1967) decisions, the U.S. Supreme Court ordered the juvenile court to protect children's due process rights and provide them with notice of the nature of the charges against them, attorneys to represent them in delinquency proceedings, the right to confront and cross-examine witnesses, and the privilege against self-incrimination.

One effect of the Court's rulings was the replacement of informal, non-adversarial court proceedings with more formal proceedings. After the dust had cleared, the juvenile court more closely resembled the adult criminal court—with the exception that juveniles did not have a constitutional right to a jury trial. Yet many of the protective trappings of the old court remained. Proceedings were largely closed to the public, juvenile records remained confidential, punishments were less severe than in the adult court, and the "best interests of the child" was still as paramount a concern as the "protection of the public."

In the last 20 years, however, particularly during the last decade, the juvenile court has undergone yet another radical transformation. First, critics from the left have zeroed in on the post-*Gault* juvenile court, decrying the "due process" afforded juveniles and calling for the abolishment of the juvenile court. Barry Feld, a University of Minnesota law professor, has led this charge, repeatedly pointing out that even after *Gault* many juveniles do not receive counsel or routinely waive the right to counsel, that the Supreme Court's refusal in *McKeiver v. Pennsylvania* (1971) to give juveniles the right to a jury trial has resulted in less accurate and often biased fact-finding, and that recent trends to criminalize the juvenile court have transformed the court from "its original model as a social service agency into a deficient criminal court that provides people with neither the positive treatment nor criminal procedural justice."

A PROBLEM OF PERCEPTION

In the late 1980s and early 1990s, an alarming increase in the number of juvenile homicides spurred academics like John DiIulio of Princeton and James Alan Fox of Northeastern University to predict a coming tidal wave of "remorseless and morally impoverished youth" because of projected increases in the youth population. These predictions, in turn, resurrected age-old concerns that the court was ill-equipped to deal with this new "breed" of delinquent. The new breed was even given a name: the "juvenile superpredator."

In response, state and federal politicians began to dismantle systematically the remaining protective elements of the juvenile court. Between 1992 and 1995, 41 states passed laws to make it easier to prosecute juveniles as adults. Language in juvenile codes stressing "rehabilitation" and "the best interests of the child" was replaced or augmented with language stressing "punishment" and the "protection of the public." Juvenile records, previously confidential, were made widely accessible, and juvenile proceedings, previously closed to the public, were opened in certain cases. Discretion was taken out of the hands of judges and given to prosecutors, resulting in less individualized justice and more decisions based solely on the nature of the charged offense.

These "reforms" have continued unabated despite the fact that juvenile crime has declined significantly in each of the past six years at the same time that the number of juveniles in the population has increased. These trends have completely discredited the "superpredator" theory and have caused some of the academics who supported it to back away from their earlier predictions.

But politicians continue to demagogue the juvenile crime issue, fueling public perception that there is still an epidemic and that the only way to stem the crime wave is to punish children ever more harshly. In the past three years, 43 states have tinkered further with their transfer laws, increasing the numbers of children tried as adults and housed in adult prisons. According to Amnesty International, some 200,000 children under the age of 18 were tried as adults last year. And some 18,000 children were housed in adult prisons, 3,500 of whom shared living spaces with adults. In defending his pending bill, which would allow 13-year-olds to be jailed with adults, Congressman Bill McCollum recently said of America's children, "They're the predators out there, they're not children anymore. They're the most violent criminals on the face of the earth."

The media are also partly responsible for this perception. Between 1993 and 1996, there was a 30 percent decline in homicides in America. You'd never know it if you watched the evening news. During that same period of time, there was a 721 percent increase in the number of homicides reported on the ABC, CBS, and NBC evening news. Less than one-half of one percent of America's kids were arrested for violent offenses in 1996. Yet two-thirds of the times children are depicted on the evening news, it is in connection with violence.

Factor in the proliferation of crime shows like "Cops" and "America's Most Wanted," entertainment "news" shows, talk radio, and other outlets pounding the steady drumbeat of kids and violence, and you have the makings of a massive misinformation campaign. It's no wonder that Americans believe that juveniles are responsible for 43 percent of all homicides when they're actually responsible for about 10 percent and that 84 percent of adults surveyed in 1996 believed that U.S. teens had committed more crimes that year than during the previous year.

The recent heightened assaults clearly have shaken the court to its roots. So much of the juvenile court founders' unique vision of children as possibility has been discarded—not because children have changed but because adults are no longer willing to devote the time, energy, and resources to guide children through adolescence and because it has become fashionable and politically advantageous to scapegoat all teens based on the actions of a disturbed few.

SAVING AN ENDANGERED SPECIES

How then can admirers and defenders of the court stop history from repeating itself? What can be learned from the court's history, and how can that be applied to get the court off the endangered species list?

Supporters of the court, including judges and court administrators, must do a better job marketing its successes to the public. The simple fact is that juvenile court success stories greatly outnumber its failures. Most children who get into trouble with the law never reoffend, and most whose crimes are so serious that they are referred to the court never come back after court intervention. The juvenile court is also more likely to impose sanctions on violent offenders than the adult court, although adult sanctions are more severe. Both of these statistics rebut the commonly held perception that public safety is not a priority for the juvenile court.

In commemoration of the court's centennial, the Justice Policy Institute and the Children and Family Justice Center of Northwestern University School of Law's Legal Clinic are telling the stories of 25 people who turned their lives around after getting arrested as kids in a new book, *Second Chance: 100 Years of The Children's Court*. In addition to the book, the two groups have jointly produced and disseminated two public service announcements featuring former offenders' success stories and highlighting the importance of giving children second chances.

Success stories are essential in this age of negative campaigning, when publicity about the court's failures [is] guaranteed to be front page news. For every Willie Horton, there are many more Bob Beamons. Supporters of the court must find ways to publicize these successes even though they may be harder to sell to the mainstream media than their negative counterparts.

But publicizing success stories is not a panacea for the court's poor public image. The court and its supporters must also fight the misinformation campaign with good, solid empirical research that refutes the claims of the court's opponents. Court officials and supporters rarely tell the public, for example, that juveniles who are kept in juvenile court rather than transferred to adult court are less likely to recidivate. But it's true.

Nor do they inform the public about the horrors of putting children in adult prison: that children are eight times more likely to commit suicide, five times more likely to be sexually assaulted, and twice as likely to be assaulted by staff than if kept in a juvenile facility. Such information is out there and easily available, much of it from the government's own Office of Juvenile Justice and Delinquency Prevention. In order to ensure the court's survival, supporters must fight fire with fire and return every volley from the court's critics.

In addition to repairing its public image, the court must make sure to provide meaningful due process to the children and families it serves. The criticisms of the "abolitionists" must be addressed rather than ignored. Rather than decreasing due process protections for children, the court must provide enhanced protections. The right to counsel for children must be mandatory and nonwaivable, both in the stationhouses and in the courtrooms. The court should employ the best staff—including judges, mental health professionals, prosecutors, defenders, and probation officers—and must demand a first-class, rather than second-class justice for children. All who work at the court must rededicate themselves to the court's historic mission of holding children accountable for their actions in ways that will not cripple their life chances.

And the court must reach out to the communities that it serves—especially the poor and minority communities who make up the bulk of its constituents in urban centers—and find ways for community members to have a voice in the quality of justice dispensed by the court, whether as volunteer mentors or as trained mediators, peer jurors, or community panelists.

In 1925, at a conference marking the 25th anniversary of Cook County's Juvenile Court, Julia Lathrop, one of the Hull House women most responsible for the court's creation, wrote:

Perhaps it is not out of place to remind ourselves that it has been clear from the beginning that the great business of the court is intimately involved in the most delicate and complicated question of social life. The court cannot serve its end unless it is sustained by intelligent public interest and cooperation.

Part of the juvenile court's demise is attributable to misinformation about its failures, but part of it is due to its own inertia. If the court is to survive and flourish into the next century, its supporters must educate the public about its successes and begin not only to court but to shape the public's opinion about its continuing worth.

Mr. Drizin is a professor at Northwestern University School of Law. From "The Juvenile Court at 100" by Steven A. Drizin, *Judicature,* July/August 1999.

Juvenile Probation on the Eve of the Next Millennium

BY RONALD P CORBETT JR.

JUDGE JUDITH SHEINDLIN, supervising judge for the Manhattan Family Court, published in 1996 her perspective on the state of affairs in juvenile justice, titled *Don't Pee on My Leg and Tell Me It's Raining.* Judge Sheindlin's views, graphically implied in the title, include a repudiation of the social causation approach to juvenile delinquency and a call for a return to an ethic of self-discipline and individual accountability. From the vantage point of over twenty years experience as a juvenile judge, Sheindlin sees a system that can "barely function" (p. 5), trading in empty threats and broken promises. Juvenile courts in her view have avoided assigning blame for wrongdoing and have thereby encouraged a lack of individual responsibility, leaving young offenders with ready excuses for their predatory behavior and completely without fear of any consequences. The system must "cut through the baloney and tell the truth," starting with the "total elimination of probation" (p. 61) in favor of a greater reliance on police surveillance and increased incarceration.

While more extreme than most, Sheindlin's damning critique of the juvenile justice system is of a piece with a number of recent treatments of the system, both journalistic and academic. A brief synopsis of each suggests a system in a severe state of crises:

- In *No Matter How Loud I Shout,* Edward Humes (1996), a Pulitzer prize winning author, presents an inside view of the workings of the Los Angeles Juvenile Court. Describing the system generally as "broken, battered and outgunned" (p. 371), Humes echoes

Sheindlin's theme of a widespread sense of immunity among juvenile offenders, perpetuated by a system that dispenses wrist slaps and apple bites in lieu of real sanctions. Facing continuous delays instead of prompt justice, and infrequent phone contact from probation officers instead of the close supervision needed, the young offenders in Los Angeles quickly learn that they are beyond the reach of the law:

> That's how the system programs you. They let you go and they know that just encourages you, and then they can get you on something worse later on. It's like, they set you up. Of course, I'm to blame, too, for going along with it. I didn't have to do those things, I know that. But the system didn't have to make it so goddamn easy (Humes, 1996, p. 333).

- In *The State of Violent Crime in America,* the first report of the newly formed Council on Crime in America (1996), the juvenile system is portrayed as a revolving door where again the theme of the lack of consequences and the consequent emboldening of young offenders is struck. Chaired by former Attorney General Griffin Bell and well-known conservative intellectual William Bennett, the report illustrates the success of one jurisdiction (Jacksonville, Florida) with the increased use of adult punishments for serious juvenile offenders and generally calls for a sober realization that the juvenile justice system's traditional reliance on treatment interventions must give way to strategies based on incapacitation and punishment.

- Finally, in *Screwing the System and Making It Work,* an ethnographic study of an unnamed juvenile court system, sociologist Mark Jacobs (1990) depicts a system whose principal intervention—community supervision—is demonstrably failing and whose state of disorganization and administrative weakness undermines any attempt at effective solutions. The few successes that Jacobs finds are accomplished in spite of the system by creatively evading the rules and regulations which otherwise frustrate all reasonable efforts. In the end, Jacobs concludes that the juvenile justice system fails because it attempts to solve problems of social breakdown through the largely ineffectual means of individual treatment plans.

Even granting that exposes will always earn publication more quickly than positive coverage, these four notable publications have such convergent findings that a conclusion regarding a crisis state for juvenile justice generally and juvenile probation specifically, seems inescapable. What then should be done? What initiatives might be undertaken in probation that would set juvenile justice on a more promising course, earning it back a measure of public trust and genuine impact on the lives of young offenders? This article will attempt an answer to those questions by first reviewing the scope of the work of juvenile probation and current trends in juvenile crime, then reviewing what has been learned about successful correctional interventions and how those lessons can be applied to juvenile probation, concluding with an examination of a new model for juvenile justice that can incorporate the findings of research in a context that values the rights and expectations of offenders, victims and society.

"Trends within the juvenile probation system are ominous. The number of delinquency petitions increased 23 percent between 1989 and 1993, leading to a 21 percent increase in probation caseloads."

Juvenile Probation in the United States

In a review of juvenile probation nationally published in March 1996 by the Office of Juvenile Justice and Delinquency Prevention, Torbet reports an annual caseflow of nearly 1.5 million delinquency cases, resulting in some 500,000 juveniles under probation at any one time. Juvenile probation officers have caseloads averaging 41 offenders, with much higher numbers typifying urban locations.

Duties of juvenile probation officers are multiple but chiefly fall into the following three categories:

- **Intake, Screening and Assessment**—Juvenile probation officers are charged with the responsibility in many jurisdictions of determining which juveniles under arrest will proceed to a formal court process or instead be diverted to an informal process, if the offense involved is minor. In making this recommendation, the officer will obtain from the offender, his/her family and any social agencies involved with the juvenile at least a threshold amount of current status and background information involving such factors as school attendance, behavior at home and in the community, family relationships, peers, etc. A great deal of emphasis in screening will be placed on the circumstances of the offense and the previous record, if any. In addition to recommending for or against diversion, this intake process will yield pertinent information for the juvenile judge to utilize in making decisions regarding detention, bail, conditions of release, appointment of counsel and other matters.
- **Pre-Sentence Investigations**—Probation officers play a crucial role in determining the most appropriate sentence or disposition to be imposed on the juvenile before the court. In preparing such reports, probation officers will begin by expanding information gathered at intake as well as reaching out to other officials, treatment personnel and family that may have useful information or perspectives bearing on the issue of an appropriate disposition. Pre-sentence reports will typically include as major sections a detailed examination of the facts and circumstances surrounding the offense and the juvenile's role in the incident; an elaborate social history, including any professional evaluations undertaken at the request of the court or the family; a summary of the impact of the delinquency on the victim(s) and their views regarding an appropriate disposition; and a discussion of the elements of an ideal disposition, including the alternatives available along with the probation officer's recommendation (National Center for Juvenile Justice, 1991).
- **Supervision**—The bulk of the work of juvenile probation officers is consumed in supervising youth placed by the courts on probation. This supervision includes both direct and regular contact with the offender (where resources permit) as well as collateral work with parents, schools, employers and agency personnel. It is the probation officer's responsibility to enforce the orders of the court in the form of victim restitution or curfews, to oversee the activities of the offender as much as possible, to uncover any lapses in behavior or company, and to insure that the juvenile

takes advantage of all opportunities for addressing personal problems such as substance abuse or school failings. While the ideal is to insure full compliance with all the conditions of probation and to see that the juvenile leaves probation better equipped for a law abiding life than when supervision began, probation officers must also respond quickly to non-compliance and must move for revocation of probation and a more serious sentence when circumstances warrant.

In discharging this core function of supervision, effective probation must play many roles—police officer, counselor, family therapist, educator, mentor, and disciplinarian. It is the successful juggling of these multiple roles, assessing which is most appropriate in a given situation, that leads to the most effective practice.

Recent Trends

Trends within the juvenile probation system are ominous. The number of delinquency petitions increased 23 percent between 1989 and 1993, leading to a 21 percent increase in probation caseloads. At the same time, there has been no concomitant increase in resources provided to the juvenile courts, though the public demand for accountability and hard-nosed, intensive treatment of juveniles before the court has become most pronounced (Torbet, 1996).

More worrisome still is the worsening profile of the juveniles coming before the court. Even though most youth placed on probation are adjudicated for property offenses, the percent placed on probation for violent offenses has increased significantly in the last years. In 1989, 17 percent of those youth on probation were adjudicated for violent offenses; by 1993, that percentage had increased to 21 percent, which translates into nearly a 25 percent growth in the proportion of violent offenders on juvenile probation (Torbet, 1996).

This trend has changed the character of probation work for many juvenile officers, who now must reckon with safety issues of a new dimension. A Justice Department survey found that one-third of officers polled had been assaulted in the line of duty and that 42 percent reported themselves as being either usually or always concerned for their safety (Torbet, 1996).

This problem is amplified by the generally held view that today's juveniles have a degree of unprecedented cold-bloodedness and remorselessness. While difficult to quantify in terms of traditional research, it has been this author's experience that, pervading discussions within both probation and police circles, has been the theme of a growing and alarming lack of concern and emotion among young offenders for both the consequences to their victims or even themselves of their involvement in serious violence. This is the new face of juvenile crime and it is a major departure from past experience, leaving few reliable blueprints for action available to concerned officials. In this connection,

James Q. Wilson, a professor of public policy at UCLA, has referred to "Youngsters who afterwards show us the blank, unremorseful stare of a feral, presocial being" (as quoted in DiIulio, 1996).

The Coming Plague—Juvenile Violence

In a column appearing in the New York Times in the summer of 1996, Princeton criminologist John DiIulio described the juvenile violence problems as "grave and growing" (p. A15). The following trends underline DiIulio's concern and provide further evidence of an explosion of juvenile violence that has the potential to overwhelm America's big cities.

- The number of juveniles murdered grew by 82 percent between 1984 and 1994;
- While most trends in adult arrests for violent crime are down since 1990, juvenile arrests for serious violence increased 26 percent by 1994, including a 15 percent increase in murder;
- Juvenile arrest rates for weapons violations nearly doubled between 1987 and 1994;
- In 1980, the number of juveniles murdered by firearm was 47 percent. By 1994, that percentage had increased to 67 percent (Snyder, et al., 1996).

Researchers have been able to attribute the greatest part of the increase in juvenile homicides to firearm-related murders. Al Blumstein (1996) has offered an analysis of this increase that traces its origins to the emergence of the crack cocaine trade in the mid 1980s and the acquisition of firearms that was a unique aspect of that emerging criminal enterprise. Young people who obtained guns originally for business purposes would also have them available in the event of other, more conventional types of conflicts among youth. The wider circulation and possession of firearms by the "players" caused other youth not involved in the drug trade to pick up guns for self-protection, as they did not wish to leave themselves at a tactical disadvantage.

"Murders by young people are still alarmingly high and, as the number of teenagers increases over the next several years, it will take hard work and good fortune to sustain the currently hopeful trend."

Related research confirms that though firearm related deaths among youth may be commonly seen as related to drug trade, in fact most such homicides are a byproduct of a violent argument rather than an event occurring during the commission of a crime (Pacific Center, 1994). It becomes plain then that strategies to reduce the most serious juvenile crime must address the issue of reducing gun possessions, an issue to be taken up later in this paper.

Two additional observations help frame in the future of juvenile violence. It is commonly accepted that rates of juvenile crime, including violence, are driven by a demographic imperative. That is, as the number of people in the crime-prone age bracket—the teens and early twenties—ebbs and flows, so generally does the crime rate (Fox, 1996). The bad news in this respect is that America is entering a 10–15 year span when the crime-prone age cohort will increase substantially. For example, by the year 2000, there will be a million more people between the ages of 14–17 than there were in 1995, of which roughly half will be male (Wilson, 1995a). By the year 2010, there will be 74 million juveniles under age 17 (Dilulio, 1996). These estimates have left Dilulio and others to project that juvenile participation in murder, rape and robbery will more than double by 2010.

However, the most recent data, while limited, is promising. During 1995, for the first time in ten years, the rate of juvenile homicide decreased for the second year in a row, by 15.2 percent (Butterfield, 1996). In a report issued by the U.S. Department of Justice, data gathered by the FBI revealed that the juvenile homicide rate, which reached an all time high in 1993, declined over the following two years by 22.8 percent. While a two-year trend is certainly encouraging, it is too soon to predict that the demographical forecast is inoperative. Murders by young people are still alarmingly high and, as the number of teenagers increases over the next several years, it will take hard work and good fortune to sustain the currently hopeful trend.

Lessons Learned About Effective Interventions

While one could hardly guess it from the current tone of relentless punitiveness pervading the debates on criminal justice policy, there has been a near exponential increase over the last 15 years in what is known with some significant confidence about the characteristics of effective correctional interventions. While the amount of public funds devoted to criminal research pales in comparison with that devoted to other forms of basic research (e.g., health issues), researchers have nonetheless made important advances in our understanding of the ingredients necessary to purposefully impact criminal and delinquent careers (Petersilia 1990).

Canadian criminologists Don Andrews and Paul Gendreau have been at the leading edge of this research. By employing the relatively new statistical technique of mega-analysis, which allows for combining the results of multiple studies of a similar type to test the aggregate strength of a given intervention, Andrews and Gendreau (1990) have

been able to identify key factors that can be utilized in the construction of correctional programs, factors which when used in combination can reduce recidivism by as much as 50 percent. Their research looked equally at juvenile and adult programs and found commonalities across the two groups. Effective programs had the following features:

- They were intensive and behavioral. Intensity was measured by both the absorption of the offenders' daily schedule and the duration of the program over time. Appropriate services in this respect will occupy 40–70 percent of the offenders' time and last an average of six months. Behavioral programs will establish a regimen of positive reinforcements for pro-social behavior and will incorporate a modeling approach including demonstrations of positive behavior that offenders are then encouraged to imitate;

- They target high risk offenders and criminogenic needs. Somewhat surprisingly, effective programs worked best with offenders classified as high-risk. This effect is strengthened if the program first identifies the presence of individual needs known to be predictive of recidivism (e.g. substance abuse, poor self-control) and then focuses on eliminating the problem. Targeting needs not proven to be related to criminal behavior (e.g. self-esteem) will not produce favorable results;

- Treatment modalities and counselors must be matched with individual offender types, a principle Andrews and Gendreau refer to as "responsivity." The program approach must be matched with the learning style and personality of the offender—a one-size-fits-all approach will fail. Taking care to compare the style of any therapist/counselor with the personality of the offender (e.g., anxious offenders should be matched with especially sensitive counselors) also is critical;

- They provide pro-social contexts and activities and emphasize advocacy and brokerage. Effective programs will replace the normal offender networks with new circles of peers and contacts who are involved in law abiding lifestyles. Success will be enhanced by aggressive efforts to link offenders with community agencies offering needed services. Most offenders will be unfamiliar with strategies for working the community and effective programs can serve as a bridge to facilitate a kind of mainstreaming of offenders (Gendreau, 1996).

Lipsey (1991) undertook a mega-analysis of some 400 juvenile programs and reached findings similar to those of Andrews and Gendreau. Lipsey's findings are impressive due to the much greater number of programs included in the analysis and the fact that he restricted his study to juvenile programs. In addition to those findings that parallel earlier results, Lipsey further discovered that skill building programs and those that were closely monitored, usually by a research team, for program implementation and integrity, were successful.

Effectiveness of Specific Programs

Traditional Probation

Despite the fact that it is clearly the treatment of choice for most juvenile offenders, there has been amazingly little major research on the effectiveness of regular probation (Clear and Braga, 1995). Targeted at only a small percentage of the overall probation population, researchers' monies and efforts have more commonly been devoted to more recent innovations such as intensive supervision, electronic monitoring or boot camps.

One noteworthy exception to this trend is a study published in 1988 by Wooldredge, in which he analyzed the impact of four different types of dispositions—including traditional probation—imposed by Illinois juvenile courts. This study of the subsequent recidivism of over two thousand delinquents found that lengthy probation supervision if combined with community treatment had the greatest effect in suppressing later recidivism, particularly when compared with incarceration or outright dismissal. Wooldredge concludes as follows:

"While it appears that 'doing something' is [usually] better than 'doing nothing' for eliminating recidivism, this study suggests that differences in 'something' may also yield differences in recidivism rates. Specifically, two years of court supervision with community treatment is superior to any other sentence examined in this study for eliminating and [delaying] recidivism. On the other hand, sentences involving detention should be carefully considered in relating the types of delinquents they may be effective on" (Wooldredge, 1988, pp. 281, 293).

Juvenile Intensive Supervision

The concept of intensive probation supervision (IPS) was one of a new generation of strategies to emerge from the intermediate sanctions movement. First developed for adult offenders, IPS programs were intended to both provide an alternative to incarceration for appropriate offenders as well as to enhance the impact of supervision on high-risk probationers.

The concept spread to the juvenile domain quickly and spawned similar experimentation, though not nearly on the same scale as the adult programs. The program models emphasized reduced caseloads and, in contrast to similar efforts in the 1960s, put a premium on closer surveillance and monitoring, with reduced attention to treatment (Armstrong, 1991).

As with so much else in the juvenile correctional field, little reliable scientific evidence is available on program impact. The National Council on Crime and Delinquency (NCCD) undertook in the late '80s a review of some 41 programs and found that evaluative data of program sites was "generally nonexistent" (Krisberg, et. al., 1989, p. 40). A similar conclusion was reached by Armstrong (1991) who found only five scientifically acceptable program evaluations and further criticized the absence of any apparent theoretical base for the programs.

Though useful research on juvenile IPS programs is scarce, two studies produced at least minimally reliable results. In the New Pride Replication Project conducted between 1980 and 1984, ten newly established juvenile IPS programs located in both medium and large cities. The program, comprised of two six-month phases, was the first involving nearly daily contact which gradually decreased during the second phase. The programs supplemented this intensive supervision with heavy doses of alternative schooling, vocational training and job placement.

After gathering three years of outcome data, findings revealed no significant differences between the experiment and control groups (Palmer, 1992). A similar study by Barton and Butts (1990) on three juvenile IPS programs using random assignment found comparable results, though it was asserted that the IPS cost less than one-third the expense of incarceration.

More recently, an experiment was undertaken by the Toledo Juvenile Court in using IPS as a diversion from commitment to the state youth authority. Employing a mix of surveillance and treatment techniques, the program extended over six months and the research employed an 18 month follow-up period. Results found that there was no difference in subsequent recidivism between the IPS youth and a matched group committed to the Ohio Department of Youth Services. Researchers concluded that the IPS program posed no greater threat to public safety, at approximately 20 percent of the cost of incarcerating the same youth (Weibush, 1993).

Violent Offenders

In light of the prospect of a growing number of violent juveniles, information specific to intervening with this particular offender is especially critical. Recent research includes one major evaluation of intensive supervision for violent juveniles, though it must be said that this program *followed* commitment to a small, secure juvenile facility for subsequent stays in community programs for several months. Consequently, it would be difficult to compare the population and prior experience to that of most juvenile probationers. The supervision focused on job placement, education, and to some lesser extent, family counseling and peer support.

In a two-year follow-up measuring for subsequent felony or violent arrests, no significant differences were found between program youth and a control group who were institutionalized for eight months and then placed on standard juvenile parole. Some evidence was found that sites which had stronger and/or consistently implemented treatment components produced better results (Palmer, 1992).

Juvenile Boot Camp

Boot camps have become a popular option on the continuum of sanctions for adult offenders so—as with IPS programs—it is not surprising that juvenile agencies have implemented their own versions. Such programs emphasize strong discipline, modeled on military programs and a strict physical conditioning regimen. The typical program is aimed at non-violent offenders, and involves a three month commitment followed by after-care (Peterson, 1996).

In 1992, the U.S. Justice Department's Office of Juvenile Justice and Delinquency Prevention (OJJDP) funded three new juvenile boot camps and undertook impact evaluations. The subsequent reports included the following findings:

- most participants completed the program;
- academic skills were significantly improved;
- a significant number of participants found jobs during aftercare; and
- no reduction in recidivism was found compared to a control group of youth who were institutionalized or placed on probation. (Peterson, 1996).

How Intensive is Intensive?

All of the programs reviewed above represent the characteristic efforts at recent reform in juvenile corrections and are alike in their emphasis on increased oversight of offenders, coupled in some instances (the more effective experiments) with increased rehabilitative services. They are also alike in having largely failed by the most important measure—recidivism.

Why has there been so little success? Ted Palmer, arguably the Dean of research in juvenile corrections, argues that their "intensive" programs have not been intensive enough, in light of the multiple needs presented by high risk offenders:

"...given the interrelatedness of most serious, multiple offenders' difficulties and deficits, it is perhaps overly optimistic to expect fairly short-term programs to help most such individuals sort out and settle these matters once and for all, even if the programs are intensive." (Palmer, 1992, p. 112).

It may be that the system has been attempting to generate success on the cheap. To create expectations of turning very troubled youth from confirmed pathways of negative and predatory behavior—patterns developed over perhaps a decade of poor if not harmful rearing—through the application of concentrated service for a 6–12 month period, may be entirely unrealistic. To do the impossible, we have generally spent less than one-third the cost of institutionalizing these same youth.

Rather than congratulate ourselves for the short-term cost savings represented by diversion from incarceration to an intermediate sanction, we should think of making a substantial investment in the near term—something, let us say, more equivalent to the cost of a year's incarceration—in order to increase the chances of long-term significant savings represented by future imprisonments avoided. Americans, it has been often observed, are congenitally drawn to short-term strategies and addicted to quick returns on their investment. What has been found not to work in other domains (business, personal investment, etc.) may similarly prove self-defeating in juvenile justice.

Juvenile Transfer to Adult Court

One clear result of the growing violence committed by youth is an increased reliance on the "transfer" option—that is, the power of the system to move jurisdiction over juvenile offenders into adult court, to take advantage of the greater penalties available on the adult level. The popularity of the transfer option is reflected in both an increased number of cases where jurisdiction is waived (a 41 percent increase from 1989–1993) as well as legislative reforms aimed at making waivers more automated than discretionary (Howell, et al, 1996).

Studies conducted on the comparative effectiveness of handling similar offenders in adult versus juvenile court give the advantage to juvenile court where recidivism is the measure. Most studies indicate that juveniles imprisoned in adult facilities were more likely to be arrested following release.

In the making of criminal or juvenile justice policy, frequently political and ideological considerations will override (if not totally ignore) the available empirical data. The move to transfer a greater number of juvenile offenders to adult court is not likely to abate; it is a specific reform that has become captive of the "get tough" philosophy that unquestionably holds sway in the current climate.

Five Steps Toward a Reformed Juvenile Probation

#1 Let Research Drive Policy

Despite an ever-growing body of research relevant to the formation of criminal justice policy, it remains remarkable how little empirical findings inform the design of programs in juvenile justice. As a result of this rather willful ignorance, the juvenile probation field can be found to embrace existing models for intervention (e.g. juvenile IPS) with scant if any evidence that such models work (Blumstein and Petersilia, 1995).

The field too often becomes enthralled by the latest fad and rushes to adopt it, irrespective of the evidence that it has or can work. Finkenauer (1982) has referred to this as the "panacea phenomenon" and it seems no less common fifteen years after he first identified this tendency.

This myopia on the part of correctional administrators has multiple explanations. Practitioners typically value the wisdom imparted by experience more than that contained in criminological journals. They prefer to consult their own intuition and gut instincts, more than any hard data. Secondly, the pertinent research is not as accessible as it might be. This is a product of the conventions of the academy, which rewards publication in criminological journals more so than writing done for the publications practitioners would read or consult. Thirdly, administrators and policy makers live and work in a politically charged atmosphere where consideration of "what works" is only one of the relevant considerations in developing policy. In the administrator's world, that which is congruent with the current political climate may indeed depart from what makes sense empirically.

Even allowing for the burden to survive the ideological wars, juvenile probation administrators could do a much better job of incorporating a research perspective into their decision making. This research-sensitive approach would take two forms: first, managers must realize that policy rarely needs to be created in a vacuum; that is, in setting policy in any particular direction, there will usually be some data bearing on the decision to be made. Becoming familiar with the techniques for adequately researching the literature and accessing the federal information services is crucial, which implies the staffing of at least a modest research division.

Secondly, all new initiatives should include a strong evaluation component. We have missed opportunities to learn from much previous experimentation because data was not kept in a way that facilitated any useful analysis (Palmer, 1992). All new programs should be seen as experiments, with clearly demonstrated time lines and methodologies for assessing impact. Juvenile probation agencies must become "learning organizations" (Senge, 1990) in which no course of action becomes institutionalized until its value is proven and feedback loops become a regular feature of the informational architecture of an agency.

Instead of viewing decisions about future programs as primarily a choice between hard or soft, tough or lenient, probation administrators should train themselves to think more in terms of smart versus dumb. "Smart" programs are those built on existing research with strong evaluation components. While not all programs sponsored by juvenile probation must meet this test absolutely (restitution programs are vital, irrespective of their impact on recidivism), juvenile probation will gain in credibility and impact as it gets "smarter."

#2 Emphasize Early Intervention

If juvenile probation were analogized to an investment strategy, the enterprise would be facing bankruptcy. In many respects, resources are allocated to that area (older, chronic offenders) where they are least likely to gain an impressive return. First offenders, by contrast, are all but ignored. Demonstrated incapacity for reform—not amenability

to change—is what earns attention from the system. That must change.

Much has been learned in the past twenty years about the early precursors for chronic delinquency (Greenwood, 1995). We have learned for example, that children whose parents are cold, cruel and inconsistent in their parenting skills are at greatly increased risk for becoming enmeshed in the juvenile justice system.

So what? Is there anything that can be done about it? Yes! Models have been developed that work dramatically in training parents to more effectively supervise their own children themselves, reducing significantly their later delinquencies. In a report released in the spring of 1996, Rand Corporation researchers identified this form of parent training as being among the two or three most cost-effective strategies in terms of reduction in crime and delinquency (Greenwood, et al., 1996). An elaborate and highly tested model for this training, developed by the Oregon Social Learning Center, has been supported by repeated evaluations (Wilson, 1995b).

One collateral finding from this research, in fact from nearly all research on prevention, is that intervening earlier (in or before the primary grades) yields stronger results. Most delinquents enter the juvenile court in their early teens. Can they be reached earlier?

Quite apart from what schools and other communities can do with younger children, juvenile courts have access to young children encountered either as the subject of abuse and neglect petitions or as younger siblings of older delinquents. By reconceptualizing their mandate as intervening with families instead of solely with the convicted juvenile, courts can truly enter the prevention business in a viable way. The Rand report strongly suggests that a small amount spent on young children and their families earlier can save much more substantial costs later.

Intervening aggressively with abusive families would very likely repay itself many times over. Juveniles found guilty of the more serious crimes typically have long histories of abuse. A National Institute of Justice study found that an abused or neglected child has a 40 percent greater chance of becoming delinquent than other children (DiIulio, 1996).

Assessment instruments are now available to determine the ongoing risk for abuse within families as well as to predict the likelihood that patterns of abuse will change once an intervention has commenced (Gelles, 1996). Focusing attention on abusive families will pay off both in terms of child protection and delinquency prevention.

The Los Angeles Juvenile Court has undertaken a special project with first offenders who have the hallmarks of chronic delinquents. Instead of waiting for several arrests before intensive services are provided, the notion now will be that a greater investment earlier on targeted youth makes more sense (Humes, 1996). This preventive approach promises to work better and cost less.

#3 Emphasize the Paying of Just Debts

The public image of the juvenile court has been marred for decades now by the impression that it coddles vicious children and "treats" kids who are more deserving of punishment.

Probation administrators ignore this perception at their peril, as it undermines their credibility and diminishes their support. Both as a matter of justice and good correctional practice, juveniles should get their "just deserts" for harm done. Restitution and community service programs repay and restore victims and harmed communities and counter the prevalent notion that juvenile offenders are immune from any real penalties, an impression certainly re-enforced by Humes (1996) recent study of the Los Angeles Juvenile Court.

In his otherwise bleak and discouraging account, Humes relates the story of a program that places juvenile probationers in a school for disabled children where the probationer must discharge their community service responsibilities by caring for and feeding young children with major disabilities. A juvenile prosecutor describes the impact of the program as follows:

These are street thugs, serious offenders, some of the worst kids who come through here. Most of them have served time in camp or at the Youth Authority, and they're harder than ever. Then they end up feeding and bathing autistic and wheelchair-bound kids, working with them intensively, having these handicapped folks depending on them utterly. It works a kind of magic. It softens them. For the first time in their lives, someone is dependent on them. And it changes them. It's been going for four years, there's never been a problem, never anyone neglected or hurt. Rival gang members go there and work together side by side. Sometimes it seems like a miracle (p. 173).

One of the most promising new paradigms in juvenile justice is the "Balanced and Restorative Justice Mode" developed by Gordon Bazermore of Florida Atlantic University and his colleagues. In a compelling design that attempts to simultaneously serve the just expectations of victim, community and offender alike, the following principle is enunciated: "When an offense occurs by the offender, an obligation incurs by the offender to the victim that must be fulfilled" (Maloney et al., 1995 p. 43).

All juvenile probationers—in the interests of justice, for the sake of any injured victims or communities, and, not insignificantly, for their own moral education—must be compelled to pay their just debts. In doing so, wounds heal, losses are restored, and the moral sentiments of the community are assuaged.

#4 Make Probation Character Building

In the parlance of traditional clinical assessments, most delinquents have been labeled as "character disordered." To many observers, this was a kind of "default" diagnosis that filled in the blank when no other form of mental illness seemed present.

Indeed, delinquents do seem lacking in what we refer to commonly as character, by which we generally mean habits of thought and action that reveal a fidelity to principles of integrity, good comportment, concern for others and self-control (Wilson, 1995b).

Neo-conservative perspectives on crime have brought the issue of character defects among delinquents and criminals to the foreground, in contrast to the medical model which attributed various "problems" and "illnesses" to offenders, deficiencies presumably beyond their control and therefore beyond their responsibility (Wilson, 1995a). Imparting bad character to delinquents would seem to imply greater responsibility for wrong-doing while also pointing to a different type of remediation.

Can a term of juvenile probation build character? As Wilson (1995b) suggests, we know little about how to inculcate character. Yet we have some clues. According to Aristotle, character is reflected not in some inner quality or virtue, but in a pattern of commendable actions which, in the doing, both build and reveal character.

In the Aristotelian sense then, juvenile courts can attempt to build character by compelling probationers to complete actions that youth of high character would undertake. Compensating for harm done, discussed above, is surely part of this. Regular attendance and good behavior at school would also reflect character in action. Obeying the reasonable requests of parents and respectable conduct at home and in the neighborhood would further exemplify character. If Aristotle was right that we become good, by doing good, requiring juvenile probationers to do good even though they may not seem or yet be good could, over time, build what we call character.

As Andrews and Kiessling (1980) found, effective probation officers model pro-social behavior. Juvenile probation officers must then see themselves as moral educators, who must constantly look for opportunities to exemplify good character to those they supervise. Every occasion where self-restraint is exercised in the face of a probationer's provocation, where kindness and courtesy is extended to a probationer's family in defiance of the juvenile's expectation, and every effort by the officer to insure fair treatment in dispositional and revocational proceedings are opportunities for character building and moral education.

If character is revealed in making moral decisions, then juvenile probation agencies could undertake more explicit strategies for moral development. Though more employed in educational than correctional settings, techniques for instilling a heightened moral sense have been used successfully in advancing the moral reasoning powers of young children (Lickona, 1992). Based on Lawrence Kohlberg's highly regarded theory of moral development, participants in the program are led through discussions of moral dilemmas where they must reconcile competing interests and reach just solutions. Research has shown that subjects can elevate their moral reasoning away from more selfish egocentric perspectives to broader, more altruistic and emphatic thinking.

This psychoeducational strategy would lend itself readily to the probation environment. In lieu of what is too often a rather mechanical and vacuous exchange with a probation officer once or twice each month, young offenders could participate in discussion groups led by trained probation officers with both offenders and staff likely feeling that they are engaged in a more productive experience.

#5 Prioritize Violence Prevention

In light of the growing rates of serious juvenile violence and with this trend expected to continue into the next decade (Fox, 1996), juvenile probation must focus on efforts it can undertake to suppress violent behavior.

As mentioned earlier, there is scant evidence that the more punitive strategies will have long term impact (It must be said that there are independent "just deserts" rationales for punishing seriously violent offenders, but this does not account for first offenders showing aggressive tendencies). Again drawing from efforts more commonly found in schools, some juvenile probation departments have undertaken violence prevention programs with juvenile probationers (Office of the Commissioner of Probation, 1995). These programs employ curricula designed to improve the social, problem-solving and anger-management skills of young offenders. While curricula vary, most employ an interactive, exercise-based, skill-building model that extends over an average of 10–15 sessions of an hour or so duration (Brewer, et al., 1996).

Evaluations conducted on such programs indicate that they are generally effective in improving social skills and as measured by their response to hypothetical conflict solutions (Brewer, et al., 1996). An evaluation of a program undertaken with juvenile probationers in Massachusetts demonstrated significant reductions in subsequent juvenile violence (Romano, 1996). More importantly, this program, sponsored by the Boston Juvenile Court for several years now, attests to the viability of such programming within the juvenile probation context.

Given the aforementioned growth in juvenile violence attributed to firearms, prevention programs targeted on this area warrant consideration. Unfortunately, very little has been done: "Programs that intervene with young people who use guns or have been caught with guns unfortunately are rare and in dire need of further development" (Office of Juvenile Justice and Delinquency Prevention, 1996, p. 16).

Nonetheless, initiating more efforts in this area make sense. Studies of handgun possession by youth indicate that handguns are more likely to be owned by individuals with a prior record of violent behavior, particularly where the gun is illegal (OJJDP, 1996). This suggests a real potential pay-off in targeting juvenile probationers.

Firearm prevention programs have been undertaken in several juvenile jurisdictions, though thus far, little evaluative information is available. Pima County Arizona Juvenile Court, for example, operates a course for youth who, though not chronic offenders, are before the court for offenses involving the carrying or firing of a gun or youth who have been identified as being at risk for firearm use. Parents are required to attend these educational sessions, where the law governing gun use and the dangers implicit in unauthorized use are explained (OJJDP, 1996).

Given the extent of the violence problem, further experimentation and evolution seems highly warranted. Moreover, a greater reliance on substantive group-work modalities offers a common-sense alternative to the traditional and exhausted model of one-on-one contact, cynically derided within the profession as "fifteen-minutes-of-avoiding-eye-contact-once-a-month."

The Prospects Ahead

The five reforms recommended above constitute a modest and therefore doable agenda, not one that would likely entail additional large expenditures but would rely on reallocating existing resources and redeploying current staff. Implementing them will not deliver utopian, crime-free communities in the next millennium, but we have reason to believe they would be worth the effort.

Progressive administrators will no doubt consider such initiatives, as well as others. As to the rest, a changing climate in governmental circles may compel the reluctant and unimaginative to undertake steps toward building a system both more effective and more congruent with public attitudes and expectations (Corbett, 1996). In the face of disturbing projections for future rates of youthful violence, immediate action would not seem premature.

References

Andrews, D., Kiessling, J., Robinson, D., & Mickus, S. (1986). The risk principle of case classification: An outcome evaluation with young adult probationers. Canadian Journal of Criminology, 28, 377–384

Blumstein, Alfred Ph.D., 1996. "Youth Violence, Guns, and Illicit Drug Markets." National Institute of Justice, January 1996.

Butterfield, Fox. (1996, August 9). After 10 years, juvenile crime begins to drop. The New York Times.

Council on Crime in America, The. 1996. The State of Violent Crime in America. Washington, D.C.

DiIulio, John J. Jr. (1996, July 31). Stop crime where it starts. The New York Times.

Finckenauer, J. (1982). Scared straight! and the panacea phenomenon. Englewood Cliffs, NJ: Prentice Hall.

Fox, James Alan. 1996. Trends In Juvenile Violence—A Report to the United States Attorney General on Current and Future Rates of Juvenile Offending. Washington, D.C.: Bureau of Justice Statistics, United States Department of Justice.

Gelles, Richard J. 1996. The Book of David. New York: Basic Books.

Gendreau, Paul. 1996. "The Principles of Effective Intervention With Offenders." In *Choosing Correctional Options That Work,* ed. Alan T. Harland, California: Sage Publications, 117–130.

Greenwood, Peter W., K. Model, C.P. Rydell, J. Chiesa. 1996. *Diverting Children From A Life of Crime.* California: RAND.

Humes, Edward. 1996. *No Matter How Loud I Shout.* New York: Simon & Schuster.

Jacobs, Mark D. 1990. *Screwing the System and Making It Work.* Chicago: The University of Chicago Press.

Lickona, Thomas. 1991. *Educating for Character.* New York: Bantam Books

Krisberg, B., Rodriguez, O., Baake, A., Nuenfeldt, D., & Steele, P. (1989). Demonstration of post-adjudication, non-residential intensive supervision programs: Assessment report. San Francisco: National Council on Crime and Delinquency.

Maloney, Dennis M. and Mark S. Umbreit. 1995. "Managing Change: Toward A Balanced and Restorative Justice Model." *Perspectives,* Spring 1995, 43–46.

National Center for Juvenile Justice. 1991. Desktop Guide to Good Juvenile Probation Practice. Pittsburgh: National Juvenile Court Services Association.

Office of Juvenile Justice and Delinquency. "Reducing Youth Gun Violence: An Overview of Programs and Initiatives." Washington, D.C.: Office of Justice Programs: May 1996.

Palmer, Ted. 1992. *The Re-Emergence of Correctional Intervention.* California: Sage Publications.

Petersilia, Joan. 1991. "Policy Relevance and the Future of Criminology." Criminology, Vol. 29, 1–15.

Peterson, Eric. "Juvenile Boot Camps: Lessons Learned". *Juvenile Justice Bulletin.* Washington, D.C.: Office of Juvenile Justice and Delinquency Prevention: June 1996.

Romano, Linda. 1996. *Preliminary Evaluation Report: Violence Prevention Groups.* Newton: Romano & Associates.

Senge, Peter M. 1990. *The Fifth Discipline.* New York: Double-Day Currency.

Sheindlin, Judy. 1996. *Don't Pee On My Leg and Tell Me It's Raining.* New York: Harper Collins Publishers, Inc.

Snyder, Howard N., M. Sickmund, E. Poe-Yamagata. 1996. "Juvenile Offenders and Victims: 1996 Update on Violence." Washington, D.C.: Office of Juvenile Justice and Delinquency.

Torbet, Patricia McFall. "Juvenile Probation: The Workhorse of the Juvenile Justice System." *Juvenile Justice Bulletin.* Washington, D.C.: Office of Juvenile Justice and Delinquency Prevention.

Wiebush, Richard G. 1993. "Juvenile Intensive Supervision: The Impact on Felony Offenders Diverted From Institutional Placement." *Crime & Delinquency 39:68–89.*

Wilson, James Q. 1995a. "Crime and Public Policy." In Crime, eds. James Q. Wilson, and Joan Petersilia. San Francisco: CS Press.

Wilson, James Q. 1995b. *On Character.* Washington: The AEI Press.

Wooldredge, J. (1988). Differentiating the effects of juvenile court sentences on eliminating recidivism. Journal of Research in Crime and Delinquency, 25 (3), 264–300.

Ron Corbett, Jr. *is the Deputy Commissioner, Massachusetts Probation Department.*

From *Perspectives,* Fall 2000, pp. 22-30. Reprinted with permission from the American Probation and Parole Association.

Judging Juveniles

Evan Gahr

It's barely past nine o'clock on a crisp Wednesday morning in Fort Myers, Florida. On the fifth floor of the Lee County Justice Center, defendants, their family members and lawyers are squeezed into Courtroom C. Soon the bailiff will instruct this motley crew to "all rise" for the honorable Judge John Carlin. Meanwhile, a court clerk pops her head inside the blond wood courtroom. Surveying the scene, she says to nobody in particular, "All the old-timers are here."

Whether handcuffed in orange prison-style jumpsuits or squeezed onto the spectator benches, the defendants seem a weary, almost blasé lot. A few may hang their heads in shame, but most appear to look down in boredom as they wait to huddle with defense lawyers and enter a plea. Some defendants whisper and snicker among themselves with the insouciance of schoolhouse smartalecks. Other[s] doze off. Are they weary with age? Hardly. Many of the "old-timers" assembled for this juvenile court don't look old enough to shave. The one-quarter who are girls never will. Most of them stare blankly as Judge Carlin struggles to find a program that, he emphasizes, will "meet their needs."

Don't let that touchy-feely language fool you. Elected in 1996 as judge for the Twentieth Judicial Circuit, which includes Fort Myers and its suburb Cape Coral, Carlin is bereft of liberal sentimentality. From extensive interviews and two days in his courtroom, it looks like Carlin does most everything right. That's why watching him is profoundly disheartening. Just how much can a good judge do? Is he ultimately an ineffectual paper-pusher? Faced with young criminals who almost universally come from broken families, can he really set them straight?

This Court is ground zero for the decline of the two-parent home. One memorable mother-and-daughter team appeared in Judge Carlin's court, both in tight jeans and thick make-up. Mom and the young woman she's raising alone each had a previous offense for assaulting the mother's live-in boyfriend. If that's what goes on inside the home, is it any surprise the girl gets in trouble outside?

Carlin struggles to be judge, jury, uncle, and father to these kids. As they teeter on the point of no return, he tries to rescue them from a lifetime of criminality. The juvenile justice system in Florida, he says, is ultimately geared toward rehabilitation. "Juvenile court is still aimed at figuring out what can we do to punish this child so he won't continue in a life of crime. The system has to let them know there are consequences for their bad choices," Carlin explains. "My job is to help those children."

Televised court battles may give viewers the impression that justice is meted out at an excruciatingly slow and deliberative pace. Carlin's courtroom reveals the opposite. The sheer volume of cases means each one can't take more than a few minutes. Starting at roughly 10:30 a.m., Carlin heard about 50 cases in two hours. This is not so much revolving-door justice as bakery-style justice: Fidgety "clients" and their relatives sit restlessly in the court waiting area. A bailiff keeps the process moving by calling out names of defendants "on deck" and justice is served as quickly as possible.

When defendants finally stand before Judge Carlin he swears them in at rapid fire; often, swearing to tell the truth is the only time the juvenile stands up straight. The judge always asks the defendant if his or her plea was entered without coercion. He repeats certain phrases by rote, almost like an auctioneer, asks a few general questions, or mentions that he remembers the kid from a previous appearance. "Each child has a story to tell" he says later. "But that doesn't excuse their behavior."

The story is painfully obvious even before the defendant enters his or her plea. Most, judging by their mannerisms and slouch, act not so much guilty as indifferent. The racial mix looks like, well, America—black, Caucasian, Hispanic, Asian. Their parents and family members are dressed in everything from cut-off blue jeans to business suits. Others wear uniforms for hotel or chain restaurant jobs.

Despite the diversity, however, the defendants start to look and sound alike. When their names are called they shuffle forward, usually with head down. Few speak above a whisper, and complete sentences are even rarer.

"Do you have gum in your mouth?" Carlin asks one youngster. He signals to the bailiff to bring a trash can so the kid can spit it out.

Charges run the gamut from trespass to aggravated battery; car theft is the most common. (For more serious crimes, prosecutors generally have kids tried as adults.) As they enter their plea, Carlin scans the computer print-outs with information on each kid. Sometimes there is no need to consult the paper work. "My memory is you had a bad attitude" Carlin tells a kid accused of trespass. One of the youngest defendants, a black boy well under five feet, is 13. Accused of aggravated battery and possession of drug paraphernalia, he stands silently before the judge. His mother (presumably), dressed in jeans and a pink sweater, stands expressionless by his side. The plea is entered, and like all other defendants, the pint-sized miscreant walks off to receive the required paperwork from a bailiff seated to Carlin's left. He and his mother are given instructions on when to return to court for sentencing.

Most "clients" decide upon a plea after consultations with their lawyer inside the courtroom or in the drab corridors outside. A few clients have hired their own lawyers, but most are from the public defender's office. The lawyers, like the judge, serve several roles. "So he needs to go to school tomorrow?" one mother asks a defense lawyer outside the courtroom as her son stands by. "He needs to go every day" the lawyer explains patiently. "I better find you in school today" the lawyer says, shifting his attention to the kid. "You've done this to yourself, landing in trouble"

This court is ground-zero for the decline of the two-parent family.

Occasionally, adults actually discipline their own kids. Outside the courtroom, a middle-aged man tells a probation officer that his nearby son—or is it grandson?—"has to learn to grow up and shut up." The defense attorney, however, focuses on the judicial question only. Arrested for brandishing a weapon on school grounds, the boy has a good chance to beat the rap. "I don't think you should plead guilty, because of an illegal search" the lawyer says, promising to have an investigator from his office build a case against the cops.

One floor above Courtroom C is Robert Jacobs' office. The veteran defense attorney is Public Defender for the Twentieth Judicial Circuit. Even his own grandmother still asks, "How can you defend these people?" But vigorously defend he does, from literally the moment they enter the office. In the reception area, handy blue cards order criminal suspects not to talk to cops and list their Miranda rights in English and Spanish.

But Jacobs is no William Kuntsler. When interviewed, he resists several invitations either to blame society for the kids' crimes or to accuse police of railroading innocent victims. Asked about the alarming increase in juvenile crime, he simply replies, "You've got to start prevention at an early age." Still, Jacobs is unapologetic about "zealously defending" the rights of the accused.

Even in the public defender's office, however, rights don't make right. Asked if she helps to spring accused criminals on what many call "technicalities," Angelique Agoston, an assistant public defender who specializes in youth cases, says she has a firm duty to protect her clients' rights. But, she adds candidly, "I've had cases where clients commit crimes, and I file motions to suppress the evidence, and it's dropped. I try to explain to them" she says, "that next time they might not be so lucky. I may be the only person telling them that. I try to give counsel and explain there are other ways to behave."

There is a big audience for such advice. In the latest year, 104,176 Florida juveniles were arrested for delinquency; they were charged with committing 150,747 crimes. Good news for feminists: The gender gap is closing. Girls are now one of every four juvenile offenders in Florida; five years ago, it was one out of five.

Juvenile crime is decreasing in some categories—like auto theft—and rising in others. Aggravated assault and battery by juveniles increased 25 percent over the last half decade. The Department of Juvenile Justice (DJJ) speculates this is mostly domestic violence—a rather literal sign of growing family breakdown.

The total rate of juvenile crime in Florida peaked in the mid '90s, coinciding with the state's decision to toughen sentences and build more holding facilities for delinquents. About 5,000 sentenced juveniles are incarcerated in residential facilities on any given day. Facilities are divided into four categories. Maximum Risk is toughest and resembles a maximum security adult prison, the Department says. Juveniles stay there from 18 months to 3 years. The next level down is "High Risk" with average stays of 15 months. Sex offenders are confined to these places.

If your crime is less severe, you go to a moderate risk facility, which include boot camps, wilderness camps, and vocational work programs. The least serious offenses can land you in "Low-Risk" residential facilities, like family group homes and short-term wilderness programs. Some first-time offenders avoid all these facilities if they and prosecutors agree to a "diversion program." In such cases, the youngster avoids any court record. Instead, the Department of Juvenile Justice, through private subcontractors, arranges for him to receive counseling.

Thursday afternoon is disposition time for cases tried earlier. Four lawyers from the Public Defender's Office handle a total of 95 cases on the docket (some are no-shows). They congregate on the left side of the courtroom; prosecutors and a representative from the Department of Juvenile Justice gather on the right side. When the defendant is called for sentencing, he approaches the bench with any adults accompanying him.

Judge Carlin often issues a tougher sentence than the DJJ recommends. "Why is the Department recommending probation when he was already on probation?" Carlin asks at one point. The DJJ representative scans the chart and promises to provide an explanation.

At sentencing, Judge Carlin becomes a cross between Oprah and a strict school principal.

At sentencing, Judge Carlin becomes a cross between Oprah and a strict school principal. He seems quite empathetic. At the same time, he won't tolerate excuses from either parent or child. On Thursday afternoon, for example, a father in cut off-jeans and a bowling shirt admits he hasn't started homeschooling his son as promised. When Carlin presses for an explanation of the delay, the father resorts to a tortuous answer about the difficulty of obtaining supplies. "He needs an education," the judge almost pleads. "He has not been in school in two months."

A similar scenario plays out when a teenage girl and her similarly dressed mother stand before Carlin. The mother sheepishly admits she has not followed through on her promises to tutor her daughter at home. Under pressure from the judge, she promises to begin with all deliberate speed. Carlin then turns to the defendant. "You are skating on thin ice," he tells the girl before placing her on probation. "You have no more room for any more bad choices."

One bad choice in this courtroom is to cross the judge or not admit your mistakes. When a defendant tells Carlin he didn't really steal from his victim, the judge replies sar-castically, "He wanted you to have his money?" Exceeding the DJJ's recommendation for probation, Carlin says the boy needs the "structured program" provided by residential facilities. Later, when a hulking teenager appears before the judge, he remembers the boy and his mother (not present this time) all too well from a previous trial. "Bobby was disruptive. And the mother was causing more trouble than he was" Carlin says. "I don't think probation will meet his needs." Bobby, a high school senior, does not understand why a little robbery should stand between him and the basketball team. It was a "little mistake," he explains. "I should not go to no program."

Carlin decides that's exactly where he belongs. "You are an habitual offender. And I want to make sure you don't go to [adult] prison."

But can he? Can anyone? According to the Department of Juvenile Justice, approximately 55 percent of the youths "who commit crimes, when tracked over a three-year period, do not receive additional charges. Recidivism remains a problem, however; overall about two out of three juvenile offenders within a year of release from a day treatment or residential program have subsequent delinquency referrals or arrests, and about 35 percent have subsequent commitments to a juvenile program or land in adult prison or probation."

The plain reading of these numbers is that Judge Carlin and so many other men and women who struggle to set these kids straight are often tilting at windmills. Roughly one-third of the boys and girls who pass through his courtroom seem destined for a life of crime. Sadly, until family deterioration is reversed, "old-timers" are likely to remain a permanent fixture of juvenile court.

Evan Gahr is a senior fellow at the Hudson Institute.

UNIT 6
Punishment and Corrections

Unit Selections

Key Points to Consider

- What issues and trends are most likely to be faced by corrections administrators at the beginning of this new century?

- How does probation differ from parole? Are there similarities?

- Discuss reasons for favoring and for opposing the death penalty.

 **Links: www.dushkin.com/online/**
These sites are annotated in the World Wide Web pages.

American Probation and Parole Association (APPA)
http://www.appa-net.org

The Corrections Connection
http://www.corrections.com

Critical Criminology Division of the ASC
http://www.critcrim.org/

David Willshire's Forensic Psychology & Psychiatry Links
http://members.optushome.com.au/dwillsh/index.html

Oregon Department of Corrections
http://www.doc.state.or.us/links/welcome.htm

Prison Law Page
http://www.prisonwall.org

In the American system of criminal justice, the term "corrections" has a special meaning. It designates programs and agencies that have legal authority over the custody or supervision of people who have been convicted of a criminal act by the courts. The correctional process begins with the sentencing of the convicted offender. The predominant sentencing pattern in the United States encourages maximum judicial discretion and offers a range of alternatives from probation (supervised, conditional freedom within the community) through imprisonment, to the death penalty.

Selections in this unit focus on the current condition of the U.S. penal system and the effects that sentencing, probation, imprisonment, and parole have on the rehabilitation of criminals. The lead essay, "The Past and Future of U.S. Prison Policy: Twenty-Five Years After the Stanford Prison Experiment," contains a reflection on lessons learned in the famous Stanford Prison Experiment. It also includes suggested reforms for American corrections. The article that follows, "Bringing College Back to Bedford Hills," describes efforts made by volunteers and movie stars to revive college education in prison. Are there viable options other than imprisonment to control criminals and to keep communities safe? Cait Murphy, author of "Crime and Punishment," maintains that there are. The next essay discusses ex-offenders with nowhere to go when they are released from jail. They are the subject of Jeff Glasser's article, "Ex-Cons on the Street." He contends that the nation's get-tough-on-crime laws are fueling this phenomenon.

Next the death penalty is under scrutiny in the next selection, "The Death Penalty on Trial." The author identifies severe problems with the administration of the ultimate penalty.

The Past and Future of U.S. Prison Policy

Twenty-Five Years After the Stanford Prison Experiment

Craig Haney
University of California, Santa Cruz

Philip Zimbardo
Stanford University

In this article, the authors reflect on the lessons of their Stanford Prison Experiment, some 25 years after conducting it. They review the quarter century of change in criminal justice and correctional policies that has transpired since the Stanford Prison Experiment and then develop a series of reform-oriented proposals drawn from this and related studies on the power of social situations and institutional settings that can be applied to the current crisis in American corrections.

Twenty-five years ago, a group of psychologically healthy, normal college students (and several presumably mentally sound experimenters) were temporarily but dramatically transformed in the course of six days spent in a prison-like environment, in research that came to be known as the Stanford Prison Experiment (SPE; Haney, Banks, & Zimbardo, 1973). The outcome of our study was shocking and unexpected to us, our professional colleagues, and the general public. Otherwise emotionally strong college students who were randomly assigned to be mock-prisoners suffered acute psychological trauma and breakdowns. Some of the students begged to be released from the intense pains of less than a week of merely simulated imprisonment, whereas others adapted by becoming blindly obedient to the unjust authority of the guards. The guards, too—who also had been carefully chosen on the basis of their normal–average scores on a variety of personality measures—quickly internalized their randomly assigned role. Many of these seemingly gentle and caring young men, some of whom had described themselves as pacifists or Vietnam War "doves," soon began mistreating their peers and were indifferent to the obvious suffering that their actions produced. Several of them devised sadistically inventive ways to harass and degrade the prisoners, and none of the less actively cruel mock-guards ever intervened or complained about the abuses they witnessed. Most of the worst prisoner treatment came on the night shifts and other occasions when the guards thought they could avoid the surveillance and interference of the research team. Our planned two-week experiment had to be aborted after only six days because the experience dramatically and painfully transformed most of the participants in ways we did not anticipate, prepare for, or predict.

These shocking results attracted an enormous amount of public and media attention and became the focus of much academic writing and commentary. For example, in addition to our own analyses of the outcome of the study itself (e.g., Haney et al., 1973; Haney & Zimbardo, 1977; Zimbardo, 1975; Zimbardo, Haney, Banks, & Jaffe, 1974) and the various methodological and ethical issues that it raised (e.g., Haney, 1976; Zimbardo, 1973), the SPE was hailed by former American Psychological Association president George Miller (1980) as an exemplar of the way in which psychological research could and should be "given away" to the public because its important lessons could be readily understood and appreciated by nonprofessionals. On the 25th anniversary of this study, we reflect on its continuing message for contemporary prison policy in light of the quarter century of criminal justice history that has transpired since we concluded the experiment.

When we conceived of the SPE, the discipline of psychology was in the midst of what has been called a "situational revolution." Our study was one of the "host of celebrated laboratory and field studies" that Ross and Nisbett (1991) referred to as having demonstrated the ways in which "the immediate social situation can overwhelm in importance the type of individual differences in personal traits or dispositions that people normally think of as being determinative of social behavior." Along with much other research conducted over the past two and one-half decades illustrating the enormous power of situations, the SPE is often cited in textbooks and journal articles as a demonstration of the way in which social contexts can influence, alter, shape, and transform human behavior.

Our goal in conducting the SPE was to extend that basic perspective—one emphasizing the potency of social situations—into a relatively unexplored area of social psychology. Specifically, our study represented an experimental demonstration of the extraordinary power of *institutional* environments to influence those who passed through them. In contrast to the companion research of Stanley Milgram (1974) that focused on individual compliance in the face of an authority figure's increasingly extreme and unjust demands, the SPE examined the conformity pressures brought to bear on groups of people functioning within the same institutional setting (see Carr 1995). Our "institution" rapidly developed sufficient power to bend and twist human behavior in ways that confounded expert predictions and violated the expectations of those who created and participated in it. And, because the unique design of the study allowed us to minimize the role of personality or dispositional variables, the SPE yielded especially clear psychological insights about the nature and dynamics of social and institutional control.

The behavior of prisoners and guards in our simulated environment bore a remarkable similarity to patterns found in actual prisons. As we wrote, "Despite the fact that guards and prisoners were essentially free to engage in any form of interaction... the characteristic nature of their encounters tended to be negative, hostile, affrontive and dehumanising" (Haney et al., 1973, p. 80). Specifically, verbal interactions were pervaded by threats, insults, and deindividuating references that were most commonly directed by guards against prisoners. The environment we had fashioned in the basement hallway of Stanford University's Department of Psychology became so real for the participants that it completely dominated their day-to-day existence (e.g., 90% of prisoners' in-cell

conversations focused on "prison"-related topics), dramatically affected their moods and emotional states (e.g., prisoners expressed three times as much negative affect as did guards), and at least temporarily undermined their sense of self (e.g., both groups expressed increasingly more deprecating self-evaluations over time). Behaviorally, guards most often gave commands and engaged in confrontive or aggressive acts toward prisoners, whereas the prisoners initiated increasingly less behavior; failed to support each other more often than not; negatively evaluated each other in ways that were consistent with the guards' views of them; and as the experiment progressed, more frequently expressed intentions to do harm to others (even as they became increasingly more docile and conforming to the whims of the guards). We concluded,

The negative, anti-social reactions observed were not the product of an environment created by combining a collection of deviant personalities, but rather the result of an intrinsically pathological situation, which could distort and rechannel the behaviour of essentially normal individuals. The abnormality here resided in the psychological nature of the situation and not in those who passed through it. (Haney et al., 1973, p. 90)

In much of the research and writing we have done since then, the SPE has served as an inspiration and intellectual platform from which to extend the conceptual relevance of situational variables into two very different domains. One of us examined the coercive power of legal institutions in general and prisons in particular (e.g., Haney, 1993a, 1997b. 1997c, 1997d, 1998; Haney & Lynch, 1997), as well as the importance of situational factors in explaining and reducing crime (e.g., Haney, 1983, 1994, 1995, 1997a). The other of us explored the dimensions of intrapsychic "psychological prisons" that constrict human experience and undermine human potential (e.g., Brodt & Zimbardo, 1981; Zimbardo, 1977; Zimbardo, Pilkonis, & Norwood, 1975) and the ways in which "mind-altering" social psychological dynamics can distort individual judgment and negatively influence behavior (e.g., Zimbardo, 1979a; Zimbardo & Andersen, 1993). Because the SPE was intended as a critical demonstration of the negative effects of extreme institutional environments, much of the work that grew out of this original study was change-oriented and explored the ways in which social and legal institutions and practices might be transformed to make them more responsive to humane psychological imperatives (e.g., Haney, 1993b; Haney & Pettigrew, 1986; Haney & Zimbardo, 1977; Zimbardo, 1975; Zimbardo et al., 1974).

In this article, we return to the core issue that guided the original study (Haney et al., 1973)—the implications of situational models of behavior for criminal justice institutions. We use the SPE as a point of historical departure to briefly examine the ways in which policies concerning crime and punishment have been transformed over the intervening 25 years. We argue that a series of psychological insights derived from the SPE and related studies, and the broad perspective that they advanced, still can contribute to the resolution of many of the critical problems that currently plague correctional policy in the United States.

Crime and Punishment a Quarter Century Ago

The story of how the nature and purpose of imprisonment have been transformed over the past 25 years is very different from the one that we once hoped and expected we would be able to tell. At the time we conducted the SPE—in 1971—there was widespread concern about the fairness and the efficacy of the criminal justice system. Scholars, politicians, and members of the public wondered aloud whether prisons were too harsh, whether they adequately rehabilitated prisoners, and whether there were alternatives to incarceration that would better serve correctional needs and interests. Many states were already alarmed about increased levels of overcrowding. Indeed, in those days, prisons that operated at close to 90% of capacity were thought to be dangerously overcrowded. It was widely understood by legislators and penologists alike that under such conditions, programming resources were stretched too thin, and prison administrators were left with increasingly fewer degrees of freedom with which to respond to interpersonal conflicts and a range of other inmate problems.

Despite these concerns about overcrowding, there was a functional moratorium on prison construction in place in most parts of the country. Whatever else it represented, the moratorium reflected a genuine skepticism at some of the very highest levels of government about the viability of prison as a solution to the crime problem. Indeed, the report of the National Advisory Commission on Criminal Justice Standards and Goals (1973), published at around the same time we published the results of the SPE, concluded that prisons, juvenile reformatories, and jails had achieved what it characterized as a "shocking record of failure" (p. 597), suggested that these institutions may have been responsible for creating more crime than they prevented, and recommended that the moratorium on prison construction last at least another 10 years.

To be sure, there was a fiscal undercurrent to otherwise humanitarian attempts to avoid the overuse of imprisonment. Prisons are expensive, and without clear evidence that they worked very well, it was difficult to justify building and running more of them (cf. Scull, 1977). But there was also a fair amount of genuine concern among the general public about what was being done to prisoners behind prison walls and what the long-term effects would be (e.g., Mitford, 1973; Yee, 1973). The SPE and its attendant publicity added to that skepticism, but the real challenge came from other deeper currents in the larger society.

The late 1960s saw the beginning of a prisoners' rights movement that eventually raised the political consciousness of large numbers of prisoners, some of whom became effective spokespersons for their cause (e.g., American Friends Service Committee, 1971; Jackson, 1970; Smith, 1993). Widely publicized, tragic events in several prisons in different parts of the country vividly illustrated how prisoners could be badly mistreated by prison authorities and underscored the potentially serious drawbacks of relying on prisons as the centerpiece in a national strategy of crime control. For example, just a few weeks after the SPE was concluded, prisoners in Attica, New York, held a number of correctional officers hostage in a vain effort to secure more humane treatment. Although national celebrities attempted to peaceably mediate the standoff, an armed assault to retake the prison ended tragically with the deaths of many hostages and prisoners. Subsequent revelations about the use of excessive force and an official cover-up contributed to public skepticism about prisons and doubts about the wisdom and integrity of some of their administrators (e.g., Wicker, 1975).

Legal developments also helped to shape the prevailing national Zeitgeist on crime and punishment. More than a decade before we conducted the SPE, the U.S. Supreme Court had defined the Eighth Amendment's ban on cruel and unusual punishment as one that drew its meaning from what Chief Justice Warren called "the evolving standards of decency that mark the progress of a maturing society" (*Trop v. Dulles*, 1958, p. 101). It is probably fair to say that most academics and other informed citizens anticipated that these standards *were* evolving and in such a way that the institution of prison—as the major organ of state-sanctioned punishment in American society—would be scrutinized carefully and honestly in an effort to apply contemporary humane views, including those that were emerging from the discipline of psychology.

Psychologists Stanley Brodsky, Carl Clements, and Raymond Fowler were engaged in just such a legal effort to reform the Alabama prison system in the early 1970s (*Pugh v. Locke*, 1976; Yackle, 1989). The optimism with which Fowler (1976) wrote about the results of that litigation was characteristic of the time: "The practice of psychology in the nation's correctional systems, long a neglected byway, could gain new significance and visibility as a result [of the court's ruling]" (p. 15). The same sentiments prevailed in a similar effort in which we participated along with psychologist Thomas Hilliard (1976) in litigation that was designed to improve conditions in a special solitary confinement unit at San Quentin (*Spain v. Procunier*, 1976). Along with other psychologists interested in correctional and legal reform, we were confident that psychology and other social scientific disciplines could be put to effective use in the creation and application of evolving standards inside the nation's prisons (see Haney & Zimbardo, 1977).

And then, almost without warning, all of this critical reappraisal and constructive optimism about humane standards and alternatives to incarceration was replaced with something else. The counterrevolution in crime and punishment began slowly and imperceptibly at first and then pushed forward with a consistency of direction and effect that could not be overlooked. It moved so forcefully and seemingly inexorably during the 1980s that it resembled nothing so much as a runaway punishment train, driven by political steam and fueled by media-induced fears of crime. Now, many years after the SPE and that early optimism about psychologically based prison reform, our nation finds itself in the midst of arguably the worst corrections crisis in U.S. history, with every indication that it will get worse before it can possibly get better. For the first time in the 200-year history of imprisonment in the United States, there appear to be no limits on the amount of prison pain the public is willing to inflict in the name of crime control (cf. Haney, 1997b, 1998). Retired judge Lois Forer (1994), in her denunciation of some of these recent trends, warned of the dire consequences of what she called the "rage to punish." But this rage has been indulged so completely that it threatens to override any of the competing concerns for humane justice that once served to make this system more compassionate and fair. The United States has entered what another commentator called the "mean season" of corrections, one in which penal philosophy amounts to little more than devising "creative strategies to make offenders suffer" (Cullen, 1995, p. 340).

The Radical Transformation of "Corrections"

We briefly recount the series of wrenching transformations that laid the groundwork for the mean season of corrections that the nation has now entered—the some 25 years of correctional policy that have transpired since the SPE was conducted. Whatever the social and political forces that caused these transformations, they collectively altered the correctional landscape of the country. The criminal justice system not only has become increasingly harsh and punitive but also has obscured many of the psychological insights on which the SPE and numerous other empirical studies were based—insights about the power of social situations and contexts to influence and control behavior. Specifically, over a very short period of time, the following series of transformations occurred to radically change the shape and direction of corrections in the United States.

The Death of Rehabilitation

A dramatic shift in correctional philosophy was pivotal to the series of changes that followed. Almost overnight, the concept that had served as the intellectual cornerstone of corrections policy for nearly a century—rehabilitation—was publicly and politically discredited. The country moved abruptly in the mid-1970s from a society that jus-

tified putting people in prison on the basis of the belief that their incarceration would somehow facilitate their productive reentry into the free world to one that used imprisonment merely to disable criminal offenders ("incapacitation") or to keep them far away from the rest of society ("containment"). At a more philosophical level, imprisonment was now said to further something called "just desserts"—locking people up for no other reason than they deserved it and for no other purpose than to punish them (e.g., von Hirsch, 1976). In fact, prison punishment soon came to be thought of as its own reward, serving only the goal of inflicting pain.

Determinate Sentencing and the Politicizing of Prison Pain

Almost simultaneously—and, in essence, as a consequence of the abandonment of rehabilitation—many states moved from indeterminate to determinate models of prison sentencing. Because indeterminate sentencing had been devised as a mechanism to allow for the release of prisoners who were rehabilitated early—and the retention of those whose in-prison change took longer—it simply did not fit with the new goals of incarceration. This shift to determinate sentencing did have the intended consequence of removing discretion from the hands of prison administrators and even judges who, studies showed, from time to time abused it (e.g., American Friends Service Committee, 1971). However, it also had the likely unintended consequence of bringing prison sentencing into an openly political arena. Once largely the province of presumably expert judicial decision makers, prison administrators, or parole authorities who operated largely out of the public view, prison sentencing had remained relatively free from at least the most obvious and explicit forms of political influence. They no longer were. Moreover, determinate sentencing and the use of rigid sentencing guidelines or "grids" undermined the role of situation and context in the allocation of punishment (cf. Freed, 1992).

The Imprisoning of America

The moratorium on new prison construction that was in place at the time of the SPE was ended by the confluence of several separate, powerful forces. For one, legislators continued to vie for the mantle of "toughest on crime" by regularly increasing the lengths of prison sentences. Of course, this meant that prisoners were incarcerated for progressively longer periods of time. In addition, the sentencing discretion of judges was almost completely subjugated to the various aforementioned legislative grids, formulas, and guidelines. Moreover, the advent of determinate sentencing meant that prison administrators had no outlets at the other end of this flow of prisoners to relieve population pressures (which, under indeterminate sentencing, had been discretionary). Finally, federal district court judges began to enter judicial orders that prohibited states from, among other things, cramming two and three or more prisoners into one-person (typically six feet by nine feet) cells (e.g., *Burks v. Walsh*, 1978; *Capps v. Atiyeh*, 1980). Eventually even long-time opponents of new prisons agreed that prisoners could no longer be housed in these shockingly inadequate spaces and reluctantly faced the inevitable: Prison construction began on an unprecedented scale across the country.

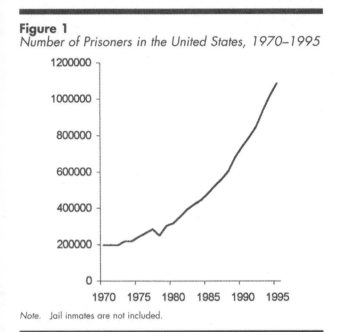

Figure 1
Number of Prisoners in the United States, 1970–1995

Note. Jail inmates are not included.

Although this rapid prison construction briefly eased the overcrowding problem, prisoner populations continued to grow at unprecedented rates (see Figure 1). It soon became clear that even dramatic increases in the number of new prisons could not keep pace. In fact, almost continuously over the past 25 years, penologists have described U.S. prisons as "in crisis" and have characterized each new level of overcrowding as "unprecedented." As the decade of the 1980s came to a close, the United States was imprisoning more people for longer periods of time than ever before in our history, far surpassing other industrialized democracies in the use of incarceration as a crime control measure (Mauer, 1992, 1995). As of June 1997, the most recent date for which figures are available, the total number of persons incarcerated in the United States exceeded 1.7 million (Bureau of Justice Statistics, 1998), which continues the upward trend of the previous 11 years, from 1985 to 1996, when the number rose from 744,208 to 1,630,940. Indeed, 10 years ago, long before today's record rates were attained, one scholar concluded, "It is easily demonstrable that America's use of prison is excessive to the point of barbarity, with a prison rate several times higher than that of other similarly developed Western countries" (Newman, 1988, p. 346). A year later, a reviewer wrote in the pages of *Contemporary Psychology*:

American prison and jail populations have reached historically high levels.... It is noteworthy that, although in several recent years the levels of reported crime declined, the prison and jail populations continued to rise. The desire for punishment seems to have taken on a life of its own. (McConville, 1989, p. 928)

The push to higher rates and lengths of incarceration has only intensified since then. Most state and federal prisons now operate well above their rated capacities, with many overcrowded to nearly twice their design limits. At the start of the 1990s, the United States incarcerated more persons per capita than any other modern nation in the world. The international disparities are most striking when the U.S. incarceration rate is contrasted to those of other nations with which the United States is often compared, such as Japan, The Netherlands, Australia, and the United Kingdom; throughout most of the present decade, the U.S. rates have consistently been between four and eight times as high as those of these other nations (e.g., Christie, 1994; Mauer, 1992, 1995). In fact, rates of incarceration have continued to climb in the United States, reaching the unprecedented levels of more than 500 per 100,000 in 1992 and then 600 per 100,000 in 1996. Although in 1990 the United States incarcerated a higher proportion of its population than any other nation on earth (Mauer, 1992), as of 1995, political and economic upheaval in Russia was associated with an abrupt increase in rate of incarceration, and Russia surpassed the United States. (Additional data on the abrupt growth in the U.S. prison population and international comparisons of incarceration rates can be found in the Appendix, Tables A1 and A2.)

The increase in U.S. prison populations during these years was not produced by a disproportionate increase in the incarceration of violent offenders. In 1995, only one quarter of persons sentenced to state prisons were convicted of a violent offense, whereas three quarters were sent for property or drug offenses or other nonviolent crimes such as receiving stolen property or immigration violations (Bureau of Justice Statistics, 1996). Nor was the increased use of imprisonment related to increased levels of crime. In fact, according to the National Crime Victimization Survey, conducted by the Bureau of the Census, a survey of 94,000 U.S. residents found that many fewer of them were the victims of crime during the calendar year 1995–1996, the year our incarceration rate reached an all-time high (Bureau of Justice Statistics, 1997b).

The Racialization of Prison Pain

The aggregate statistics describing the extraordinary punitiveness of the U.S. criminal justice system mask an important fact: The pains of imprisonment have been inflicted disproportionately on minorities, especially Black men. Indeed, for many years, the rate of incarceration of White men in the United States compared favorably with those in most Western European nations, including countries regarded as the most progressive and least punitive (e.g., Dunbaugh, 1979). Although in recent years the rate of incarceration for Whites in the United States has also increased and no longer compares favorably with other Western European nations, it still does not begin to approximate the rate for African Americans. Thus, although they represent less than 6% of the general U.S. population, African American men constitute 48% of those confined to state prisons. Statistics collected at the beginning of this decade indicated that Blacks were more than six times more likely to be imprisoned than their White counterparts (Mauer, 1992). By 1995, that disproportion had grown to seven and one-half times (Bureau of Justice Statistics, 1996). In fact, the United States incarcerates African American men at a rate that is approximately four times the rate of incarceration of Black men in South Africa (King, 1993).

All races and ethnic groups and both sexes are being negatively affected by the increases in the incarcerated population, but the racial comparisons are most telling. The rate of incarceration for White men almost doubled between 1985 and 1995, growing from a rate of 528 per 100,000 in 1985 to a rate of 919 per 100,000 in 1995. The impact of incarceration on African American men, Hispanics, and women of all racial and ethnic groups is greater than that for White men, with African American men being the most profoundly affected. The number of African American men who are incarcerated rose from a rate of 3,544 per 100,000 in 1985 to an astonishing rate of 6,926 per 100,000 in 1995. Also, between 1985 and 1995, the number of Hispanic prisoners rose by an average of 12% annually (Mumola & Beck, 1997). (Additional data on some of the disparities in imprisonment between Whites and Blacks in the United States can be found in the Appendix, Tables A3 and A4, and Figure A1.)

The Overincarceration of Drug Offenders

The increasingly disproportionate number of African American men who are being sent to prison seems to be related to the dramatic increase in the number of persons incarcerated for drug-related offenses, combined with the greater tendency to imprison Black drug offenders as compared with their White counterparts. Thus, although Blacks and Whites use drugs at approximately the same rate (Bureau of Justice Statistics, 1991), African Americans were arrested for drug offenses during the so-called war on drugs at a much higher rate than were Whites (Blumstein, 1993). The most recent data show that between 1985 and 1995, the number of African Americans incarcerated in state prisons due to drug violations (which were their only or their most serious offense) rose 707% (see Table 1). In contrast, the number of Whites incarcerated in state prisons for drug offenses (as their only or most serious offense) underwent a 306% change. In 1986, for example, only 7% of Black prison inmates in the United States had

been convicted of drug crimes, compared with 8% of Whites. By 1991, however, the Black percentage had more than tripled to 25%, whereas the percentage of White inmates incarcerated for drug crimes had increased by only half to 12% (Tonry, 1995). In the federal prison system, the numbers of African Americans incarcerated for drug violations are shockingly high: Fully 64% of male and 71% of female Black prisoners incarcerated in federal institutions in 1995 had been sent there for drug offenses (Bureau of Justice Statistics, 1996).

Table 1
Change in Estimated Number of Sentenced Prisoners, by Most Serious Offense and Race, Between 1985 and 1995

Most serious offense	Total % change, 1985–1995	White % change, 1985–1995	Black % change, 1985–1995
Total	119	109	132
Violent offenses	86	92	83
Property offenses	69	74	65
Drug offenses	478	306	707
Public-order offenses[a]	187	162	229
Other/unspecified[b]	–6	–72	64

Note. Adapted from *Prisoners in 1996* (Bureau of Justice Statistics Bulletin NCJ 164619, p. 10), by C.J. Mumola and A.J. Beck, 1997, Rockville, MD: Bureau of Justice Statistics. In the public domain.
[a]Includes weapons, drunk driving, escape, court offenses, obstruction, commercialized vice, morals and decency charges, liquor law violations, and other public-order offenses.
[b]Includes juvenile offenses and unspecified felonies.

According to a historical report done for the Bureau of Justice Statistics (Cahalan, 1986), the offense distribution of federal and state prisoners—a measure of the types of crimes for which people are incarcerated—remained stable from 1910 to 1984. The classification of some offenses changed. For example, robbery is now included in the category of violent crime rather than being classified with property crimes, as it was in the past. Public order offenses, also called morals charges, used to include vagrancy, liquor law violations, and drug offenses. Drug offenses are no longer classified with public order crimes. Of course, not only have drug offenses been elevated to the status of their own crime category in national statistical compilations and their own especially severe legislated penalties, but there is also a "Drug Czar" in the executive branch and a large federal agency devoted exclusively to enforcing laws against drug-related crimes.

As we noted, the types and proportions of offenses for which people were incarcerated in the United States were highly consistent for the 75 years prior to 1984. For most of the 20th century, the U.S. prison population consisted of around 60–70% offenders against property, 13–24% of-

Figure 2
Distribution of Offenses: State and Federal Prisons, 1985 and 1995

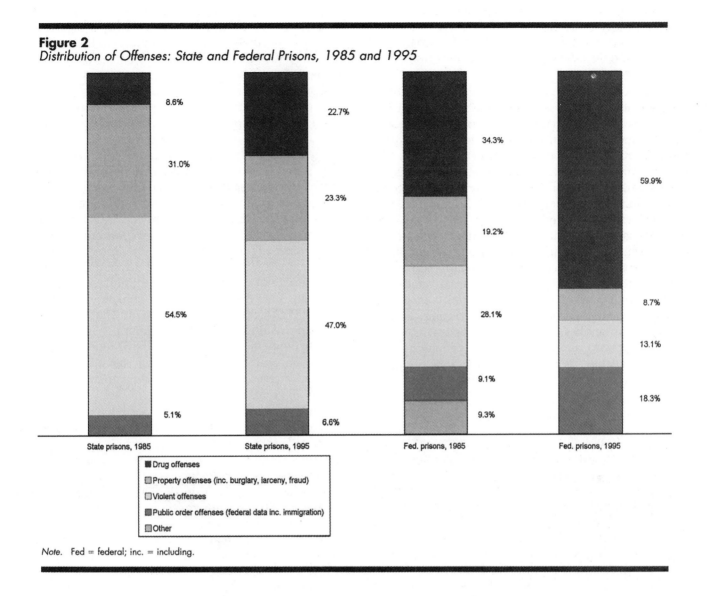

State prisons, 1985: 8.6%, 31.0%, 54.5%, 5.1%

State prisons, 1995: 22.7%, 23.3%, 47.0%, 6.6%

Fed. prisons, 1985: 34.3%, 19.2%, 28.1%, 9.1%, 9.3%

Fed. prisons, 1995: 59.9%, 8.7%, 13.1%, 18.3%

- ■ Drug offenses
- ▨ Property offenses (inc. burglary, larceny, fraud)
- ☐ Violent offenses
- ▦ Public order offenses (federal data inc. immigration)
- ▨ Other

Note. Fed = federal; inc. = including.

fenders against persons (now called violent crime), around 20% public order–morals violations (which included drug offenses), and 10% other types of offenders (Cahalan, 1986).

However, these distributions have changed dramatically during the past 10 to 15 years. The federal government is now willing to incarcerate people for a wider range of criminal violations, and both state and federal prisoners remain incarcerated for longer periods of time. The number of violent offenders who are incarcerated has risen but not as steeply as the number of drug offenders who are now sent to prison. In 1995, 23% of state prisoners were incarcerated for drug offenses in contrast to 9% of drug offenders in state prisons in 1986. In fact, the proportion of drug offenders in the state prison population nearly tripled by 1990, when it reached 21%, and has remained at close to that level since then. The proportion of federal prisoners held for drug violations doubled during the past 10 years. In 1985, 34% of federal prisoners were

incarcerated for drug violations. By 1995, the proportion had risen to 60%. (See Figure 2.)

We note in passing that these three interrelated trends—the extraordinary increase in the numbers of persons in prison, the disproportionate incarceration of minorities, and the high percentage of persons incarcerated for drug offenses—reflect a consistent disregard of context and situation in the criminal justice policies of the past 25 years. The unprecedented use of imprisonment per se manifests a policy choice to incarcerate individual lawbreakers instead of targeting the criminogenic social conditions and risk factors that have contributed to their criminality. Sentencing models that ignore situation and context inevitably lead to higher rates of incarceration among groups of citizens who confront race-based poverty and deprivation and other social ills that are related to discrimination. The failure to address the differential opportunity structure that leads young minority group members into certain kinds of drug-related activities and the conscious decision to target those activities for criminal prosecution and incarceration, rather than to attempt to improve the life chances of the urban Black underclass, reflect dispositional—and discriminatory—views of crime control.

Moreover, excessive and disproportionate use of imprisonment ignores the secondary effects that harsh criminal justice policies eventually will have on the social contexts and communities from which minority citizens come. Remarkably, as the present decade began, there were more young Black men (between the ages of 20 and 29) under the control of the nation's criminal justice system (including probation and parole supervision) than the total number in college (Mauer, 1990). Thus, one scholar has predicted that "imprisonment will become the most significant factor contributing to the dissolution and breakdown of African American families during the decade of the 1990s" (King, 1993, p. 145), and another has concluded that "crime control policies are a major contributor to the disruption of the family, the prevalence of single parent families, and children raised without a father in the ghetto, and the 'inability of people to get the jobs still available'" (Chambliss, 1994, p. 183).

The Rise of the "Supermax" Prison

In addition to becoming dangerously overcrowded and populated by a disproportionate number of minority citizens and drug offenders over the past 25 years, many U.S. prisons also now lack meaningful work, training, education, treatment, and counseling programs for the prisoners who are confined in them. Plagued by increasingly intolerable living conditions where prisoners serve long sentences that they now have no hope of having reduced through "good time" credits, due to laws imposed by state legislatures, many prison officials have turned to punitive policies of within-prison segregation in the hope of maintaining institutional control (e.g., Christie, 1994; Haney, 1993a; Haney & Lynch, 1997; Perkinson, 1994). Indeed, a penal philosophy of sorts has emerged in which prison systems use long-term solitary confinement in so-called supermax prisons as a proactive policy of inmate management. Criticized as the "Marionization" of U.S. prisons, after the notorious federal penitentiary in Marion, Illinois, where the policy seems to have originated (Amnesty International, 1987; Olivero & Roberts, 1990), one commentator referred to the "accelerating movement toward housing prisoners officially categorized as violent or disruptive in separate, free-standing facilities where they are locked in their cells approximately 23 hours per day" (Immarigeon, 1992, p. 1). They are ineligible for prison jobs, vocational training programs, and, in many states, education.

Thus, in the 25 years since the SPE was conducted, the country has witnessed the emergence of a genuinely new penal form—supermax prisons that feature state-of-the-art, ultra secure, long-term segregated confinement supposedly reserved for the criminal justice system's most troublesome or incorrigible offenders. Human Rights Watch (1997) described the basic routine imposed in such units: Prisoners "are removed from general population and housed in conditions of extreme social isolation, limited environmental stimulation, reduced privileges and service, scant recreational, vocational or educational opportunities, and extraordinary control over their every movement" (p. 14). (See also Haney, 1993a, 1997d, and Haney and Lynch, 1997, for discussions of the psychological effects of these special conditions of confinement.) By 1991, these prisons imposing extreme segregation and isolation were functioning in some 36 states, with many others in the planning stages (e.g., "Editorial," 1991). A newly opened, highly restrictive, modern "control unit" apparently committed the federal penitentiary system to the use of this penal form for some time to come (Dowker & Good, 1992; Perkinson, 1994). Thus, by 1997 Human Rights Watch expressed concern over what it called "the national trend toward supermaximum security prisons" (p. 13), noting that in addition to the 57 units currently in operation, construction programs already underway "would increase the nationwide supermax capacity by nearly 25 percent" (p. 14).

A constitutional challenge to conditions in California's supermax—one that many legal observers viewed as a test case on the constitutionality of these "prisons of the future"—resulted in a strongly worded opinion in which the federal court condemned certain of its features, suggesting that the prison, in the judge's words, inflicted "stark sterility and unremitting monotony" (*Madrid V. Gomez,* 1995, p. 1229) on prisoners and exposed them to overall conditions that "may press the outer bounds of what most humans can psychologically tolerate" (p. 1267) but left the basic regimen of segregation and isolation largely intact.

Here, too, the importance of context and situation has been ignored. Widespread prison management problems and gang-related infractions are best understood in systematic terms, as at least in large part the products of worsening overall institutional conditions. Viewing them instead as caused exclusively by "problem prisoners" who require nothing more than isolated and segregated confinement ignores the role of compelling situational forces that help to account for their behavior. It also overlooks the capacity of deteriorated prison conditions to continue to generate new replacements who will assume the roles of those prisoners who have been taken to segregation. Finally, the continued use of high levels of punitive isolation, despite evidence of significant psychological trauma and psychiatric risk (e.g., Grassian, 1983; Haney, 1997d; Haney & Lynch, 1997), reflects a legal failure to fully appreciate the costs of these potentially harmful social contexts—both in terms of immediate pain and emotional damage as well as their long-term effects on post-segregation and even post-release behavior.

The Retreat of the Supreme Court

The final component in the transformation of U.S. prison policy during this 25-year period came from the U.S. Supreme Court, as the Justices significantly narrowed their role in examining and correcting unconstitutionally cruel prison conditions as well as drastically redefining the legal standards that they applied in such cases. Ironically, the early constitutional review of conditions of confinement at the start of this historical period had begun on an encouraging note. Indeed, it was one of the things that helped fuel the early optimism about "evolving standards" to which we earlier referred. For example, in 1974, just three years after the SPE, the Supreme Court announced that "there is no iron curtain drawn between the Constitution and the prisons of this country" (*Wolff v. McDonnell*, 1974, pp. 556–567). Given the Warren Court's legacy of protecting powerless persons who confronted potent situations and adverse structural conditions, and the Court's legal realist tendencies to look carefully at the specific circumstances under which abuses occurred (e.g., Haney, 1991), hopes were raised in many quarters that a majority of the Justices would carefully evaluate the nation's worst prison environments, acknowledge their harmful psychological effects, and order badly needed reform.

However, a sharp right turn away from the possibility and promise of the Warren Court's view became evident at the start of the 1980s. The first time the Court fully evaluated the totality of conditions in a particular prison, it reached a very discouraging result. Justice Powell's majority opinion proclaimed that "the Constitution does not mandate comfortable prisons, and prisons which house persons convicted of serious crimes cannot be free of discomfort" (*Rhodes v. Chapman*, 1981, p. 349). None of the Justices attempted to define the degree of acceptable discomfort that could be inflicted under the Constitution. However, Powell used several phrases that were actually taken from death penalty cases to provide a sense of just how painful imprisonment could become before beginning to qualify as "cruel and unusual": Punishment that stopped just short of involving "the *unnecessary* and *wanton* infliction of pain" (p. 345, citing *Gregg v. Georgia*, 1976, p. 173) would not be prohibited, pains of imprisonment that were not "*grossly* disproportionate to the severity of the crime" (p. 345, citing *Coker v. Georgia*, 1977, p. 592) would be allowed, and harm that was not "*totally* without penological justification" (p. 345, citing *Gregg v. Georgia*, p. 183) also would be acceptable (italics added).

The Supreme Court thus set a largely unsympathetic tone for Eighth Amendment prison cases and established a noninterventionist stance from which it has rarely ever wavered. Often turning a blind eye to the realities of prison life and the potentially debilitating psychological effects on persons housed in badly overcrowded, poorly run, and increasingly dangerous prisons, the Court developed several constitutional doctrines that both limited the liability of prison officials and further undermined the legal relevance of a careful situational analysis of imprisonment. For example, in one pivotal case, the Court decided that the notion that "overall prison conditions" somehow could produce a cruel and unusual living environment—a view that not only was psychologically straightforward but also had guided numerous lower court decisions in which overall conditions of confinement in particular prisons were found unconstitutional—was simply "too amorphous" to abide any longer (*Wilson v. Seiter*, 1991, p. 304).

In the same case, the Court decisively shifted its Eighth Amendment inquiry from the conditions themselves to the thought processes of the officials responsible for creating and maintaining them. Justice Scalia wrote for the majority that Eighth Amendment claims concerning conduct that did not purport to be punishment required an inquiry into prison officials' state of mind—in this case, their "deliberate indifference" (*Wilson v. Seiter*, 1991). Justice Scalia also had rejected a distinction between short-term deprivations and "continuing" or "systemic" problems of the sort that might have made state of mind less relevant. The argument here had been that evidence of systemic problems would obviate the need to demonstrate state of mind on the part of officials who had presumably known about and tolerated them as part of the correctional status quo. Scalia said instead that although the long duration of a cruel condition might make it easier to establish knowledge and, hence, intent, it would not eliminate the intent requirement.

Prison litigators and legal commentators criticized the decision as having established a constitutional hurdle for conditions of confinement claims that was "virtually insurmountable" and speculated that the impossibly high threshold "reflects recent changes in public attitudes towards crime and allocation of scarce public resources" (Hall, 1993, p. 208). Finally, in 1994, the Court seemed to raise the hurdle to a literally insurmountable level by explicitly embracing the criminal law concept of "subjective recklessness" as the Eighth Amendment test for deliberate indifference (*Fanner v. Brennan*, 1994). In so doing, the Court shunned the federal government's concern that the new standard meant that triers of fact would first have to find that "prison officials acted like criminals" before finding them liable (*Farmer v. Brennan*, 1994, p. 1980).

This series of most recent cases has prompted commentators to speculate that the Supreme Court is "headed toward a new hands-off doctrine in correctional law" (Robbins, 1993, p. 169) that would require lower courts "to defer to the internal actions and decisions of prison officials" (Hall, 1993, p. 223). Yet, the narrow logic of these opinions suggests that the Justices intend to keep not only their hands off the faltering prison system but their eyes averted from the realities of prison life as well. It is difficult to avoid the conclusion that the Court's refusal to examine the intricacies of day-to-day existence in those maximum security prisons whose deteriorated and potentially harmful conditions are placed at issue is designed to limit the liability of those who create and run them.

Unfortunately, the U.S. Supreme Court was not the only federal governmental agency contributing to this retreat from the meaningful analysis of conditions of confinement inside the nation's prisons and jails. In April 1996, the U.S. Congress passed legislation titled the Prison Litigation Reform Act (PLRA) that significantly limited the ability of the federal courts to monitor and remedy constitutional violations in detention facilities throughout the country. Among other things, it placed substantive and procedural limits on injunctions and consent decrees (where both parties reach binding agreements to fix existing problems in advance of trial) to improve prison conditions. The PLRA also impeded the appointment of "special masters" to oversee prison systems' compliance with court orders and appeared to forbid the filing of legal actions by prisoners for mental or emotional injury without a prior showing of physical injury. Although the full impact of this remarkable legislation cannot yet be measured, it seems to have been designed to prevent many of the problems that have befallen U.S. prisons from ever being effectively addressed. Combined with the Supreme Court's stance concerning prison conditions, the PLRA will likely contribute to the growing tendency to avoid any meaningful contextual analysis of the conditions under which many prisoners are now confined and also to a growing ignorance among the public about the questionable utility of prison as a solution to the nation's crime problem.

Responding to the Current Crisis: Some Lessons From the Stanford Prison Experiment

Where has this series of transformations left the U.S. criminal justice system? With startling speed, national prison policy has become remarkably punitive, and correspondingly, conditions of confinement have dramatically deteriorated in many parts of the country. These transformations have been costly in economic, social, and human terms. At the beginning of the present decade, a stark fact about governmental priorities was reported: "For the first time in history, state and municipal governments are spending more money on criminal justice than education" (Chambliss, 1994, p. 183). In California, the corrections budget alone has now surpassed the state's fiscal outlays for higher education (e.g., Butterfield, 1995; Jordan, 1995). Despite this historic shift in expenditures and the unprecedented prison construction that took place during the past 25 years, many commentators still lament what has been referred to as the "national scandal of living conditions in American prisons" (Gutterman, 1995, p. 373). As we have noted and one reviewer recently observed, "For over a decade, virtually every contemporary commentary on corrections in the United States has reminded us that the system [is] in crisis" (Cullen, 1995, p. 338).

The dimensions of this crisis continue to expand and do not yet reflect what promises to be an even more sig-

nificant boost in prison numbers—the effects of recently passed, so-called three-strikes legislation that not only mandates a life sentence on a third criminal conviction but, in some states, also doubles the prison sentence for a second criminal conviction and reduces existing good-time provisions for every term (so that all prisoners actually are incarcerated for a longer period of time). This three-strikes legislation was written and rapidly passed into law to capitalize on the public's fear of violent crime (Haney, 1994, 1997b). Despite the fact that the crime rate in the United States has been declining for some time in small but steady increments, many of these bills were written in such a way as to cast the widest possible net—beyond violent career criminals (whom most members of the public had in mind)—to include nonviolent crimes like felony drug convictions and minor property offenses. As a consequence, a disproportionate number of young Black and Hispanic men are likely to be imprisoned for life under scenarios in which they are guilty of little more than a history of untreated addiction and several prior drug-related offenses. The mandate to create lifetime incarceration for so many inmates under circumstances where overcrowding precludes their participation in meaningful programs, treatment, and other activities is likely to raise the overall level of prisoners' frustration, despair, and violence. States will absorb the staggering cost of not only constructing additional prisons to accommodate increasing numbers of prisoners who will never be released but also warehousing them into old age (Zimbardo, 1994).

Remarkably, the radical transformations we have described in the nation's penal policy occurred with almost no input from the discipline of psychology. Correctional administrators, politicians, policymakers, and judicial decision makers not only ignored most of the lessons that emerged from the SPE but also disregarded the insights of a number of psychologists who preceded us and the scores of others who wrote about, extended, and elaborated on the same lessons in empirical studies and theoretical pieces published over the past several decades. Indeed, there is now a vast social science literature that underscores, in various ways, the critical importance of situation and context in influencing social behavior, especially in psychologically powerful situations like prisons. These lessons, insights, and literature deserve to be taken into account as the nation's prison system moves into the next century.

Here then is a series of propositions derived or closely extrapolated from the SPE and the large body of related research that underscores the power of situations and social context to shape and transform human behavior. Each proposition argues for the creation of a new corrections agenda that would take us in a fundamentally different direction from the one in which we have been moving over the past quarter century.

First, the SPE underscored the degree to which prison environments are themselves powerful, potentially damaging situations whose negative psychological effects must be taken seriously, carefully evaluated, and purposefully regulated and controlled. When appropriate, these environments must be changed or (in extreme cases) eliminated. Of course, the SPE demonstrated the power of situations to overwhelm psychologically normal, healthy people and to elicit from them unexpectedly cruel, yet "situationally appropriate" behavior. In many instances during our study, the participants' behavior (and our own) directly contravened personal value systems and deviated dramatically from past records of conduct. This behavior was elicited by the social context and roles we created, and it had painful, even traumatic consequences for the prisoners against whom it was directed.

The policy implications of these observations seem clear. For one, because of their harmful potential, prisons should be deployed very sparingly in the war on crime. Recognition of the tendency of prison environments to become psychologically damaging also provides a strong argument for increased and more realistic legal and governmental oversight of penal institutions in ways that are sensitive to and designed to limit their potentially destructive impact. In addition, it argues in favor of significantly revising the allocation of criminal justice resources to more seriously explore, create, and evaluate humane alternatives to traditional correctional environments.

Second, the SPE also revealed how easily even a minimalist prison could become painful and powerful. By almost any comparative standard, ours was an extraordinarily benign prison. None of the guards at the "Stanford Prison" were armed, and there were obvious limits to the ways in which they could or would react to prisoners' disobedience, rebellion, or even escape. Yet, even in this minimalist prison setting, all of our "guards" participated in one way or another in the pattern of mistreatment that quickly developed. Indeed, some escalated their definition of "role-appropriate" behavior to become highly feared, sadistic tormentors. Although the prisoners' terms of incarceration were extremely abbreviated (corresponding, really, to very short-term pretrial detention in a county jail), half of our prisoner-participants left before the study was terminated because they could not tolerate the pains of this merely simulated imprisonment. The pains were as much psychological— feelings of powerlessness, degradation, frustration, and emotional distress—as physical— sleep deprivation, poor diet, and unhealthy living conditions. Unlike our participants, of course, many experienced prisoners have learned to suppress such outward signs of psychological vulnerability lest they be interpreted as weakness, inviting exploitation by others.

Thus, the SPE and other related studies demonstrating the power of social contexts teach a lesson about the way in which certain situational conditions can interact and work in combination to produce a dehumanizing whole that is more damaging than the sum of its individual institutional parts. Legal doctrines that fail to explicitly take into account and formally consider the totality of these situational conditions miss this psychological point. The effects of situations and social contexts must be assessed from the perspective of those within them. The experiential perspective of prison inmates—the meaning of the prison experience and its effects on them—is the most useful starting point for determining whether a particular set of prison conditions is cruel and unusual. But a macroexperiential perspective does not allow for the parsing of individual factors or aspects of a situation whose psychological consequences can then be separately assessed. Thus, legal regulators and the psychological experts who assist them also must be sensitive to the ways in which different aspects of a particular situation interact and aggregate in the lives of the persons who inhabit total institutions like prisons as well as their capacity to produce significant effects on the basis of seemingly subtle changes and modifications that build up over time. In contexts such as these, there is much more to the "basic necessities of life" than "single, identifiable human need[s] such as food, warmth or exercise" (*Wilson v. Seiter*, 1991, p. 304). Even if this view is "too amorphous" for members of the current Supreme Court to appreciate or apply, it is the only psychologically defensible approach to assessing the effects of a particular prison and gauging its overall impact on those who live within its walls.

In a related vein, recent research has shown how school children can develop maladjusted, aggressive behavior patterns based on initially marginal deviations from other children that get amplified in classroom interactions and aggregated over time until they become manifested as "problem children" (Caprara & Zimbardo, 1996). Evidence of the same processes at work can be found in the life histories of persons accused and convicted of capital crime (Haney, 1995). In similar ways, initially small behavioral problems and dysfunctional social adaptations by individual prisoners may become amplified and aggravated over time in prison settings that require daily interaction with other prisoners and guards.

Recall also that the SPE was purposely populated with young men who were selected on the basis of their initial mental and physical health and normality, both of which, less than a week later, had badly deteriorated. Real prisons use no such selection procedures. Indeed, one of the casualties of severe overcrowding in many prison systems has been that even rudimentary classification decisions based on the psychological makeup of entering cohorts of prisoners are forgone (see Clements, 1979, 1985). Pathology that is inherent in the structure of the prison situation is likely given a boost by the pathology that some prisoners and guards bring with them into the institutions themselves. Thus, although ours was clearly a study of the power of situational characteristics, we certainly acknowledge the value of interactional models of social and institutional behavior. Prison systems should not ignore individual vulnerabilities in attempting to optimize institutional adjustment, minimize behavioral and psychological problems, understand differences in institutional adaptations and capacities to survive, and intelligently allocate treatment and other resources (e.g., Haney & Specter, in press).

Third, if situations matter and people can be transformed by them when they go into prisons, they matter equally, if not more, when they come out of prison. This suggests very clearly that programs of prisoner change cannot ignore situations and social conditions that prevail after release if they are to have any hope of sustaining whatever positive gains are achieved during periods of imprisonment and lowering distressingly high recidivism rates. Several implications can be drawn from this observation. The first is that prisons must more routinely use transitional or "decompression" programs that gradually reverse the effects of the extreme environments in which convicts have been confined. These programs must be aimed at preparing prisoners for the radically different situations that they will enter in the free world. Otherwise, prisoners who were ill-prepared for job and social situations before they entered prison become more so over time, and the longer they have been imprisoned, the more likely it is that rapid technological and social change will have dramatically transformed the world to which they return.

The SPE and related studies also imply that exclusively individual-centered approaches to crime control (like imprisonment) are self-limiting and doomed to failure in the absence of other approaches that simultaneously and systematically address criminogenic situational and contextual factors. Because traditional models of rehabilitation are person-centered and dispositional in nature (focusing entirely on individual-level change), they typically have ignored the postrelease situational factors that help to account for discouraging rates of recidivism. Yet, the recognition that people can be significantly changed and transformed by immediate situational conditions also implies that certain kinds of situations in the free world can override and negate positive prison change. Thus, correctional and parole resources must be shifted to the transformation of certain criminogenic situations in the larger society if ex-convicts are to meaningfully and effectively adapt. Successful post-release adjustment may depend as much on the criminal justice system's ability to change certain components of an ex-convict's situation *after* imprisonment—helping to get housing, employment, and drug or alcohol counseling for starters—as it does on any of the positive rehabilitative changes made by individual prisoners during confinement itself.

This perspective also underscores the way in which long-term legacies of exposure to powerful and destructive situations, contexts, and structures means that prisons themselves can act as criminogenic agents—in both their primary effects on prisoners and secondary effects on the lives of persons connected to them—thereby serving to increase rather than decrease the amount of crime that occurs within a society. Department of corrections data show that about a fourth of those initially impris-

oned for nonviolent crimes are sentenced a second time for committing a violent offense. Whatever else it reflects; this pattern highlights the possibility that prison serves to transmit violent habits and values rather than to reduce them. Moreover, like many of these lessons, this one counsels policymakers to take the full range of the social and economic costs of imprisonment into account in calculations that guide long-term crime control strategies. It also argues in favor of incorporating the deleterious effects of prior terms of incarceration into at least certain models of legal responsibility (e.g., Haney, 1995).

Fourth, despite using several valid personality tests in the SPE, we found that we were unable to predict (or even postdict) who would behave in what ways and why (Haney et al., 1973). This kind of failure underscores the possibility that behavioral prediction and explanation in extreme situations like prisons will be successful only if they are approached with more situationally sensitive models than are typically used. For example, most current personality trait measures ask respondents to report on characteristic ways of responding in familiar situations or scenarios. They do not and cannot tap into reactions that might occur in novel, extreme, or especially potent situations—like the SPE or Milgram's (1974) obedience paradigm—and thus have little predictive value when extrapolated to such extreme cases. More situationally sensitive models would attend less to characteristic ways of behaving in typical situations and more to the characteristics of the particular situations in which behavior occurs. In prison, explanations of disciplinary infractions and violence would focus more on the context in which they transpired and less on the prisoners who engaged in them (e.g., Wenk & Emrich, 1972; Wright, 1991). Similarly, the ability to predict the likelihood of reoffending and the probability of repeated violent behavior should be enhanced by conceptualizing persons as embedded in a social context and rich interpersonal environment, rather than as abstract bundles of traits and proclivities (e.g., Monahan & Klassen, 1982).

This perspective has implications for policies of crime control as well as psychological prediction. Virtually all sophisticated, contemporary accounts of social behavior now acknowledge the empirical and theoretical significance of situation, context, and structure (e.g., Bandura, 1978, 1991; Duke, 1987; Ekehammar, 1974; Georgoudi & Rosnow, 1985; Mischel, 1979; Veroff, 1983). In academic circles at least, the problems of crime and violence—formerly viewed in almost exclusively individualistic terms—are now understood through multilevel analyses that grant equal if not primary significance to situational, community, and structural variables (e.g., Hepburn, 1973; McEwan & Knowles, 1984; Sampson & Lauritsen, 1994; Toch, 1985). Yet, little of this knowledge has made its way into prevailing criminal justice policies. Lessons about the power of extreme situations to shape and transform behavior—independent or in spite of pre-existing dispositions—can be applied to contemporary strategies of crime control that invest more substantial resources in transforming destructive familial and social contexts rather than concentrating exclusively on reactive policies that target only individual lawbreakers (cf. Masten & Garmezy 1985; Patterson, DeBaryshe, & Ramsey, 1989).

Fifth, genuine and meaningful prison and criminal justice reform is unlikely to be advanced by persons who are themselves "captives" of powerful correctional environments. We learned this lesson in a modest but direct way when in the span of six short days in the SPE, our own perspectives were radically altered, our sense of ethics, propriety, and humanity temporarily suspended. Our experience with the SPE underscored the degree to which institutional settings can develop a life of their own, independent of the wishes, intentions, and purposes of those who run them (Haney & Zimbardo, 1977). Like all powerful situations, real prisons transform the worldviews of those who inhabit them, on both sides of the bars. Thus, the SPE also contained the seeds of a basic but important message about prison reform—that good people with good intentions are not enough to create good prisons. Institutional structures themselves must be changed to meaningfully improve the quality of prison life (Haney & Pettigrew, 1986).

Indeed, the SPE was an "irrational" prison whose staff had no legal mandate to punish prisoners who, in turn, had done nothing to deserve their mistreatment. Yet, the "psychologic" of the environment was more powerful than the benign intentions or predispositions of the participants. Routines develop; rules are made and applied, altered and followed without question; policies enacted for short-term convenience become part of the institutional status quo and difficult to alter; and unexpected events and emergencies challenge existing resources and compromise treatment in ways that persist long after the crisis has passed. Prisons are especially vulnerable to these common institutional dynamics because they are so resistant to external pressures for change and even rebuff outside attempts at scrutinizing their daily operating procedures.

These observations certainly imply that the legal mechanisms supposedly designed to control prison excesses should not focus exclusively on the intentions of the staff and administrators who run the institution but would do well to look instead at the effects of the situation or context itself in shaping their behavior (cf. *Farmer v. Brennan*, 1994). Harmful structures do not require ill-intentioned persons to inflict psychological damage on those in their charge and can induce good people with the best of intentions to engage in evil deeds (Haney & Zimbardo, 1977; Zimbardo, 1979a). "Mechanisms of moral disengagement" distance people from the ethical ambiguity of their actions and the painful consequences of their deeds, and they may operate with destructive force in many legal and institutional contexts, facilitating cruel and unusual treatment by otherwise caring and law-abiding persons (e.g., Bandura, 1989; Browning, 1993; Gibson, 1991; Haney, 1997c).

In addition, the SPE and the perspective it advanced also suggest that prison change will come about only when those who are outside of this powerful situation are empowered to act on it. A society may be forced to presume the categorical expertise of prison officials to run the institutions with which they have been entrusted, but this presumption is a rebuttable one. Moreover, to depend exclusively on those whose perspectives have been created and maintained by these powerful situations to, in turn, transform or control them is shortsighted and psychologically naive. This task must fall to those with a different logic and point of view, independent of and free from the forces of the situation itself. To be sure, the current legal retreat to hands-off policies in which the courts defer to the presumably greater expertise of correctional officials ignores the potency of prison settings to alter the judgments of those charged with the responsibility of running them. The SPE and much other research on these powerful environments teach that this retreat is terribly ill-advised.

Finally, the SPE implicitly argued for a more activist scholarship in which psychologists engage with the important social and policy questions of the day. The implications we have drawn from the SPE argue in favor of more critically and more realistically evaluating the nature and effect of imprisonment and developing psychologically informed limits to the amount of prison pain one is willing to inflict in the name of social control (Haney, 1997b, 1998). Yet, this would require the participation of social scientists willing to examine these issues, confront the outmoded models and concepts that guide criminal justice practices, and develop meaningful and effective alternatives. Historically, psychologists once contributed significantly to the intellectual framework on which modern corrections was built (Haney, 1982). In the course of the past 25 years, they have relinquished voice and authority in the debates that surround prison policy. Their absence has created an ethical and intellectual void that has undermined both the quality and the legitimacy of correctional practices. It has helped compromise the amount of social justice our society now dispenses.

Conclusion

When we conducted the SPE 25 years ago, we were, in a sense, on the cutting edge of new and developing situational and contextual models of behavior. Mischel's (1968) pathbreaking review of the inadequacy of conventional measures of personality traits to predict behavior was only a few years old, Ross and Nisbett (1991) were assistant professors who had not yet written about situational control as perhaps the most important leg in the tripod of social psychology, and no one had yet systematically applied the methods and theories of modern psychology to the task of understanding social contextual origins of crime and the psychological pains of imprisonment. Intellectually, much has changed since then. However, without the renewed participation of psychologists in debates over how best to apply the lessons and insights of their discipline to the problems of crime and punishment, the benefits from these important intellectual advances will be self-limiting. It is hard to imagine a more pressing and important task for which psychologists have so much expertise but from which they have been so distanced and uninvolved than the creation of more effective and humane criminal justice policies. Indeed, politicians and policymakers now seem to worship the very kind of institutional power whose adverse effects were so critically evaluated over the past 25 years. They have premised a vast and enormously expensive national policy of crime control on models of human nature that are significantly outmoded. In so doing, they have faced little intellectual challenge, debate, or input from those who should know better.

So, perhaps it is this one last thing that the SPE stood for that will serve the discipline best over the next 25 years. That is, the interrelated notions that psychology can be made relevant to the broad and pressing national problems of crime and justice, that the discipline can assist in stimulating badly needed social and legal change, and that scholars and practitioners can improve these policies with sound data and creative ideas. These notions are as germane now, and needed more, than they were in the days of the SPE. If they can be renewed, in the spirit of those more optimistic times, despite having lost many battles over the past 25 years, the profession still may help win the more important war. There has never been a more critical time at which to begin the intellectual struggle with those who would demean human nature by using prisons exclusively as agencies of social control that punish without attempting to rehabilitate, that isolate and oppress instead of educating and elevating, and that tear down minority communities rather than protecting and strengthening them.

REFERENCES

American Friends Service Committee. (1971). *Struggle for justice: A report on crime and punishment*. New York: Hill & Wang.

Amnesty International. (1987). *Allegations of mistreatment in Marion Prison, Illinois, USA*. New York; Author.

Bandura, A. (1978). The self system in reciprocal determinism. *American Psychologist, 33*, 344–358.

Bandura, A. (1989). Mechanisms of moral disengagement. In W. Reich (Ed.), *Origins of terrorism: Psychologies, ideologies, theologies, states of mind* (pp. 161–191). New York: Cambridge University Press.

Bandura, A. (1991). Social cognitive theory of moral thought and action. In W. Kurtines & J. Gewirtz (Eds.), *Handbook of moral behavior and development: Vol. 1. Theory* (pp. 45–102). Hillsdale, NJ: Erlbaum.

Blumstein, A. (1993). Making rationality relevant—The American Society of Criminology 1992 Presidential Address. *Criminology, 31*, 1–16.

Brodt, S., & Zimbardo, P. (1981). Modifying shyness-related social behavior through symptom misattribution. *Journal of Personality and Social Psychology, 41*, 437–449.

Browning, C. (1993). *Ordinary men: Reserve Police Battalion 101 and the final solution in Poland*. New York: Harper Perennial.

Bureau of Justice Statistics. (1991). *Sourcebook of criminal justice statistics*. Washington, DC: U.S. Department of Justice.

Bureau of Justice Statistics. (1996). *Sourcebook of criminal justice statistics, 1996*. Washington, DC: U.S. Department of Justice.

Bureau of Justice Statistics. (1997a, May). *Correctional populations in the United States, 1995* (NCJ 163916). Rockville, MD: Author.

Bureau of Justice Statistics. (1997b, November). *Criminal victimization 1996: Changes 1995–96 with trends 1993–96* (Bureau of Justice Statistics Bulletin NCJ 165812). Rockville, MD: Author.

Bureau of Justice Statistics. (1998, January 18). *Nation's prisons and jails hold more than 1.7 million: Up almost 100,000 in a year* [Press release]. Washington, DC: U.S. Department of Justice.

Burks v. Walsh, 461 F. Supp. 934 (W.D. Missouri 1978).

Butterfield, F. (1995, April 12). New prisons cast shadow over higher education. *The New York Times*, p. A21.

Cahalan, M. W. (1986, December). *Historical corrections statistics in the United States, 1850–1984* (Bureau of Justice Statistics Bulletin NCJ 102529). Rockville, MD: Bureau of Justice Statistics.

Capps v. Atiyeh, 495 F. Supp. 802 (D. Ore. 1980).

Caprara, G., & Zimbardo, P. (1996). Aggregation and amplification of marginal deviations in the social construction of personality and maladjustment. *European Journal of Personality, 10*, 79–110.

Carr, S. (1995). Demystifying the Stanford Prison Study. *The British Psychological Society Social Psychology Section Newsletter, 33*, 31–34.

Chambliss, W. (1994). Policing the ghetto underclass: The politics of law and law enforcement. *Social Problems, 41*, 177–194.

Christie, N. (1994). *Crime control as industry: Towards gulags, Western style?* (2nd ed.). London: Routledge.

Clements, C. (1979). Crowded prisons: A review of psychological and environmental effects. *Law and Human Behavior, 3*, 217–225.

Clements, C. (1985). Towards an objective approach to offender classification. *Law & Psychology Review, 9*, 45–55.

Coker v. Georgia, 433 U.S. 584, 592 (1977).

Cullen, F. (1995). Assessing the penal harm movement. *Journal of Research in Crime and Delinquency, 32*, 338–358.

Dowker, F., & Good, G. (1992). From Alcatraz to Marion to Florence: Control unit prisons in the United States. In W. Churchill & J. J. Vander Wall (Eds.), *Cages of steel: The politics of imprisonment in the United States* (pp. 131–151). Washington, DC: Maisonneuve Press.

Duke, M. (1987). The situational stream hypothesis: A unifying view of behavior with special emphasis on adaptive and maladaptive personality patterns. *Journal of Research in Personality, 21*, 239–263.

Dunbaugh, F. (1979). Racially disproportionate rates of incarceration in the United States. *Prison Law Monitor, 1*, 205–225.

Editorial: Inside the super-maximum prisons. (1991, November 24). *The Washington Post*, p. C6.

Ekehammar, B. (1974). Interactionism in personality from a historical perspective. *Psychological Bulletin, 81*, 1026–1048.

Farmer v. Brennan, 114 S. Ct. 1970 (1994).

Forer, L. (1994). *A rage to punish: The unintended consequences of mandatory sentencing.* New York: Norton.

Fowler, R. (1976). Sweeping reforms ordered in Alabama prisons. *APA Monitor, 7,* pp. 1, 15.

Freed, D. (1992). Federal sentencing in the wake of guidelines: Unacceptable limits on the discretion of sentences. *Yale Law Journal, 101,* 1681–1754.

Georgoudi, M., & Rosnow, R. (1985). Notes toward a contextualist understanding of social psychology. *Personality and Social Psychology Bulletin, 11,* 5–22.

Gibson, J. (1991). Training good people to inflict pain: State terror and social learning. *Journal of Humanistic Psychology, 31,* 72–87.

Grassian, S. (1983). Psychopathological effects of solitary confinement. *American Journal of Psychiatry, 140,* 1450–1454.

Gregg v. Georgia, 428 U.S. 153, 173 (1976) (joint opinion).

Gutterman, M. (1995). The contours of Eighth Amendment prison jurisprudence: Conditions of confinement. *Southern Methodist University Law Review, 48,* 373–407.

Hall, D. (1993). The Eighth Amendment, prison conditions, and social context. *Missouri Law Review, 58,* 207–236.

Haney, C. (1976). The play's the thing: Methodological notes on social simulations. In P. Golden (Ed.), *The research experience* (pp. 177–190). Itasca, IL: Peacock.

Haney, C. (1982). Psychological theory and criminal justice policy: Law and psychology in the "Formative Era." *Law and Human Behavior, 6,* 191–235.

Haney, C. (1983). The good, the bad, and the lawful: An essay on psychological injustice. In W. Laufer & J. Day (Eds.), *Personality theory, moral development, and criminal behavior* (pp. 107–117). Lexington, MA: Lexington Books.

Haney, C. (1991). The Fourteenth Amendment and symbolic legality: Let them eat due process. *Law and Human Behavior, 15,* 183–204.

Haney, C. (1993a). Infamous punishment: The psychological effects of isolation. *National Prison Project Journal, 8,* 3–21.

Haney, C. (1993b). Psychology and legal change: The impact of a decade. *Law and Human Behavior, 17,* 371–398.

Haney, C. (1994, March 3). Three strikes for Ronnie's kids, now Bill's. *Los Angeles Times,* p. B7.

Haney, C. (1995). The social context of capital murder: Social histories and the logic of mitigation. *Santa Clara Law Review, 35,* 547–609.

Haney, C. (1997a). Psychological secrecy and the death penalty: Observations on "the mere extinguishment of life." *Studies in Law, Politics, and Society, 16,* 3–68.

Haney, C. (1997b). Psychology and the limits to prison pain: Confronting the coming crisis in Eighth Amendment law. *Psychology, Public Policy and Law, 3,* 499–588.

Haney, C. (1997c). Violence and the capital jury: Mechanisms of moral disengagement and the impulse to condemn to death. *Stanford Law Review, 46,* 1447–1486.

Haney, C. (1997d). *The worst of the worst: Psychological trauma and psychiatric symptoms in punitive segregation.* Unpublished manuscript, University of California, Santa Cruz.

Haney, C. (1998). *Limits to prison pain: Modern psychological theory and rational crime control policy.* Washington, DC: American Psychological Association.

Haney, C., Banks, W., & Zimbardo, P. (1973). Interpersonal dynamics in a simulated prison. *International Journal of Criminology and Penology, 1,* 69–97.

Haney, C., & Lynch, M. (1997). Regulating prisons of the future: A psychological analysis of supermax and solitary confinement. *New York Review of Law and Social Change, 23,* 101–195.

Haney, C., & Pettigrew, T. (1986). Civil rights and institutional law: The role of social psychology in judicial implementation. *Journal of Community Psychology, 14,* 267–277.

Haney, C., & Specter, D. (in press). Legal considerations in treating adult and juvenile offenders with special needs. In J. Ashford, B. Sales, & W. Reid (Eds.), *Treating adult and juvenile offenders with special needs.* Washington, DC: American Psychological Association.

Haney, C., & Zimbardo, P. (1977).The socialization into criminality: On becoming a prisoner and a guard. In J. Tapp & F. Levine (Eds.), *Law, justice, and the individual in society: Psychological and legal issues* (pp. 198–223). New York: Holt, Rinehart & Winston.

Hepburn, J. (1973). Violent behavior in interpersonal relationships. *Sociological Quarterly, 14,* 419–429.

Hilliard, T. (1976). The Black psychologist in action: A psychological evaluation of the Adjustment Center environment at San Quentin Prison. *Journal of Black Psychology, 2,* 75–82.

Human Rights Watch. (1997). *Cold storage: Super-maximum security confinement in Indiana.* New York: Author.

Immarigeon, R. (1992). The Marionization of American prisons. *National Prison Project Journal, 7(4),* 1–5.

Jackson, G. (1970). *Soledad brother: The prison letters of George Jackson.* New York: Coward-McCann.

Jordan, H. (1995, July 8). '96 budget favors prison over college; "3 strikes" to eat into education funds. *San Jose Mercury News,* p. 1A.

King, A. (1993). The impact of incarceration on African American families: Implications for practice. *Families in Society: The Journal of Contemporary Human Services, 74,* 145–153.

Madrid v. Gomez, 889 F Supp. 1146 (N.D. Cal. 1995).

Maguire, K., & Pastore, A. (Eds.). (1997). *Sourcebook of criminal justice statistics 1996* (NCJ 165361). Washington, DC: U.S. Government Printing Office.

Masten, A., & Garmezy, N. (1985). Risk, vulnerability and protective factors in developmental psychopathology. In F. Lahey & A. Kazdin (Eds.), *Advances in clinical child psychology* (pp. 1–52). New York: Plenum.

Mauer, M. (1990). *More young Black males under correctional control in US than in college.* Washington, DC: The Sentencing Project.

Mauer, M. (1992). Americans behind bars: A comparison of international rates of incarceration. In W. Churchill & J. J. Vander Wall (Eds.), *Cages of steel: The politics of imprisonment in the United States* (pp. 22–37). Washington, DC: Maisonneuve Press.

Mauer, M. (1995). The international use of incarceration. *Prison Journal, 75,* 113–123.

Mauer, M. (1997, June). *Americans behind bars: U.S. and international use of incarceration, 1995.* Washington, DC: The Sentencing Project.

McConville, S. (1989). Prisons held captive. *Contemporary Psychology, 34,* 928–929.

McEwan, A., & Knowles, C. (1984). Delinquent personality types and the situational contexts of their crimes. *Personality & Individual Differences, 5,* 339–344.

Milgram, S. (1974). *Obedience to authority: An experimental view.* New York: Harper & Row.

Miller, G. (1980). Giving psychology away in the '80s. *Psychology Today, 13,* 38ff.

Mischel, W. (1968). *Personality and assessment.* New York: Wiley.

Mischel, W. (1979). On the interface of cognition and personality: Beyond the person-situation debate. *American Psychologist, 34,* 740–754.

Mitford, J. (1973). *Kind and usual punishment: The prison business.* New York: Knopf.

Monahan, J., & Kiassen, D. (1982). Situational approaches to understanding and predicting individual violent behavior. In M. Wolfgang & G. Weiner (Eds.), *Criminal violence* (pp. 292–319). Beverly Hills, CA: Sage.

Mumola, C. J., & Beck, A. J. (1997, June). *Prisoners in 1996* (Bureau of Justice Statistics Bulletin NCJ 164619). Rockville, MD: Bureau of Justice Statistics.

National Advisory Commission on Criminal Justice Standards and Goals. (1973). *Task force report on corrections.* Washington, DC: U.S. Government Printing Office.

Newman, G. (1988). Punishment and social practice: On Hughes's *The Fatal Shore. Law and Social Inquiry, 13,* 337–357.

Olivero, M., & Roberts, J. (1990). The United States Federal Penitentiary at Marion, Illinois: Alcatraz revisited. *New England Journal of Criminal and Civil Confinement, 16,* 21–51.

Patterson, G., DeBaryshe, B., & Ramsey, E. (1989). A developmental perspective on antisocial behavior. *American Psychologist, 44,* 329–335.

Perkinson, R. (1994). Shackled justice: Florence Federal Penitentiary and the new politics of punishment. *Social Justice, 21,* 117–132.

Pugh v. Locke, 406 F. Supp. 318 (1976).

Rhodes v. Chapman, 452 U.S. 337 (1981).

Robbins, I. (1993). The prisoners' mail box and the evolution of federal inmate rights. *Federal Rules Decisions, 114,* 127–169.

Ross, L., & Nisbett, R. (1991). *The person and the situation: Perspectives of social psychology.* New York: McGraw-Hill.

Sampson, R., & Lauritsen, 1. (1994). Violent victimization and offending: Individual-, situational-, and community-level risk factors. In A. Reiss, Jr. & J. Roth (Eds.), *Understanding and preventing violence: Vol. 3. Social influences* (pp. 1–114). Washington, DC: National Research Council, National Academy Press.

Sandin v. Conner, 115 S. Ct. 2293 (1995).

Scull, A. (1977). *Decarceration: Community treatment and the deviant: A radical view.* Englewood Cliffs, NJ: Prentice Hall.

Smith, C. (1993). Black Muslims and the development of prisoners' rights. *Journal of Black Studies, 24,* 131–143.

Spain v. Procunier, 408 F. Supp. 534 (1976), aff'd in part, rev'd in part, 600 F.2d 189 (9th Cir. 1979).

Toch, H. (1985). The catalytic situation in the violence equation. *Journal of Applied Social Psychology, 15,* 105–123.

Tonry, M. (1995). *Malign neglect: Race, crime, and punishment in America.* New York: Oxford University Press.

Trop v. Dulles, 356 U.S. 86 (1958).

Veroff, J. (1983). Contextual determinants of personality. *Personality and Social Psychology Bulletin, 9,* 331–343.

von Hirsch, A. (1976). *Doing justice: The choice of punishment.* New York: Hill & Wang.

Wenk, E., & Emrich, R. (1972). Assaultive youth: An exploratory study of the assaultive experience and assaultive potential of California Youth Authority wards. *Journal of Research in Crime & Delinquency, 9,* 171–196.

Wicker, T. (1975). *A time to die.* New York: New York Times Books.

Wilson v. Seiser. 501 U.S. 294 (1991).

Wolff v. McDonnell, 418 U.S. 554, 556–7 (1974).

Wright, K. (1991). The violent and victimized in the male prison. *Journal of Offender Rehabilitation, 16,* 1–25.

Yackle, L. (1989). *Reform and regret: The story of federal judicial involvement in the Alabama prison system.* New York: Oxford University Press.

Yee, M. (1973). *The melancholy history of Soledad Prison.* New York: Harper's Magazine Press.

Zimbardo, P. (1973). On the ethics of intervention in human psychological research: With special reference to the Stanford Prison. Experiment. *Cognition, 2,* 243–256.

Zimbardo, P. (1975). On transforming experimental research into advocacy for social change. In M. Deutsch & H. Hornstein (Eds.), *Applying social psychology: Implications for research, practice, and training* (pp. 33–66). Hillsdale, NJ: Erlbaum.

Zimbardo, P. G. (1977). *Shyness: What it is and what to do about it.* Reading, MA: Addison-Wesley.

Zimbardo, P. G. (1979a). The psychology of evil: On the perversion of human potential. In T. R. Sarbin (Ed.), *Challenges to the criminal justice system: The perspective of community psychology* (pp. 142– 161). New York: Human Sciences Press.

Zimbardo, P. G. (1979b). Testimony of Dr. Philip Zimbardo to U.S. House of Representatives Committee on the Judiciary. In J. J. Bonsignore et al. (Eds.), *Before the law: An introduction to the legal process* (2nd ed., pp. 396–399). Boston: Houghton Mifflin.

Zimbardo, P. G. (1994). *Transforming California's prisons into expensive old age homes for felons: Enormous hidden costs and consequences for California's taxpayers.* San Francisco: Center on Juvenile and Criminal Justice.

Zimbardo, P. G., & Andersen, S. (1993). Understanding mind control: Exotic and mundane mental manipulations. In M. Langone (Ed.), *Recover from cults: Help for victims of psychological and spiritual abuse* (pp. 104–125). New York: Norton.

Zimbardo, P. G., Haney, C., Banks, C., & Jaffe, D. (1974). The psychology of imprisonment: Privation, power, and pathology. In Z. Rubin (Ed.), *Doing unto others: Explorations in social behavior* (pp. 61–73). Englewood Cliffs, NJ: Prentice Hall.

Zimbardo, P. G., Pilkonis, P. A., & Norwood, R. M. (1975, May). The social disease called shyness. *Psychology Today,* pp. 69–70, 72.

Editor's note. Melissa G. Warren served as action editor for this article.

Author's note. Craig Haney, Department of Psychology, University of California, Santa Cruz; Philip Zimbardo, Department of Psychology, Stanford University.

We would like to acknowledge our colleague and coinvestigator in the original Stanford Prison Experiment, W. Curtis Banks, who died last year. We also acknowledge the assistance of Marc Mauer and The Sentencing Project, who granted permission to reprint Figure Al and helped us locate other sources of information, and Sandy Pisano, librarian at the Arthur W. Melton Library, who helped compile some of the data that appear in the tables and figures.

Correspondence concerning this article should be addressed to Craig Haney, Department of Psychology, University of California, Santa Cruz, CA 95064. Electronic mail maybe sent to psylaw@cats.ucsc.edu. Readers interested in the corrections system may contact the American Psychology–Law Society or Psychologists in Public Service, Divisions 41 and 18, respectively, of the American Psychological Association.

APPENDIX

Table A1
Number and Rate (Per 100,000 Resident Population in Each Group) of Sentenced Prisoners in State and Federal Institutions on December 31 (Not Including Local Jails)

Year	Total	Rate	Year	Total	Rate
1925	91,669	79	1960	212,953	117
1926	97,991	83	1961	220,149	119
1927	109,983	91	1962	218,830	117
1928	116,390	96	1963	217,283	114
1929	120,496	98	1964	214,336	111
			1965	210,895	108
1930	129,453	104	1966	199,654	102
1931	137,082	110	1967	194,896	98
1932	137,997	110	1968	187,914	94
1933	136,810	109	1969	196,007	97
1934	138,316	109			
1935	144,180	113	1970	196,429	96
1936	145,038	113	1971	198,061	95
1937	152,741	118	1972	196,092	93
1938	160,285	123	1973	204,211	96
1939	179,818	137	1974	218,466	102
			1975	240,593	111
1940	173,706	131	1976	262,833	120
1941	165,439	124	1977[a]	278,141	126
1942	150,384	112	1977[b]	285,456	129
1943	137,220	103	1978	294,396	132
1944	132,456	100	1979	301,470	133
1945	133,649	98			
1946	140,079	99	1980	315,974	139
1947	151,304	105	1981	353,167	154
1948	155,977	106	1982	394,374	171
1949	163,749	109	1983	419,820	179
			1984	443,398	188
1950	166,123	109	1985	480,568	202
1951	165,680	107	1986	522,084	217
1952	168,233	107	1987	560,812	231
1953	173,579	108	1988	603,732	247
1954	182,901	112	1989	680,907	276
1955	185,780	112			
1956	189,565	112	1990	739,980	297
1957	195,414	113	1991	789,610	313
1958	205,643	117	1992	846,277	332
1959	208,105	117	1993	932,074	359
			1994	1,016,691	389
			1995	1,085,363	411

Note. These data represent prisoners sentenced to more than one year. Both custody and jurisdiction figures are shown for 1977 to facilitate year-to-year comparison. Adapted from *Sourcebook of Criminal Justice Statistics 1996* (NCJ 165361,p. 518), by K. Maguire and A. Pastore (Eds.), 1997, Washington,DC: U.S. Government Printing Office. In the public domain.

[a]Custody counts.

[b]Jurisdiction counts.

Table A2
Number and Rate (Per 100,000 Residents) of Adults in Custody of State and Federal Prisons and Local Jails

Year	Total custody	Federal prisons	State prisons	Local jails	Total rate[a]
1985	744,208	35,781	451,812	256,615	313
1990	1,148,702	58,838	684,544	405,320	461
1991	1,219,014	63,930	728,605	426,479	483
1992	1,295,150	72,071	778,495	444,584	508
1993	1,369,185	80,815	828,566	459,804	531
1994	1,476,621	85,500	904,647	486,474	567
June 30, 1995	1,561,836	89,334	965,458	507,044	594
December 31, 1995		89,538	989,007		
June 30, 1996	1,630,940	93,167	1,019,281	518,492	615

Note. Jail counts are for June 30; counts for 1994–1996 exclude persons who were supervised outside of a jail facility. State and federal prisoner counts for 1985 and 1990–1994 are for December 31. Adapted from *Sourcebook of Criminal Justice Statistics 1996* (NCJ 165361, p. 510), by K. Maguire and A. Pastore (Eds.), 1997, Washington, DC: U.S. Government Printing Office. In the public domain.

[a]Total number of adults held in the custody of state, federal, or local jurisdictions per 100,000 U.S. residents on July 1 of each reference year.

Figure A1
Percent of U.S. Adult Population in State or Federal Prisons or in Local Jails, by Race and Sex, 1984–1995

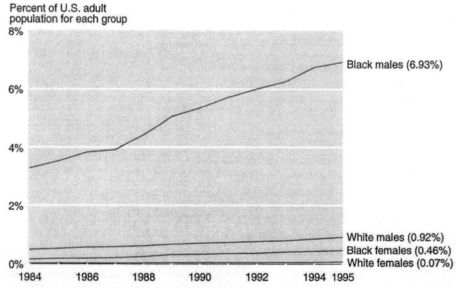

Note. Reprinted from *Correctional Populations in the United States, 1995* (NCJ 163916), by the Bureau of Justice Statistics, 1997, Rockville, MD: Author. In the public domain.

Table A3
Number of Adults Held in State or Federal Prisons or Local Jails, by Sex and Race, 1985–1995

Year	White		Black	
	Males	**Females**	**Males**	**Females**
1985	382,800	21,400	309,800	19,100
1986	417,600	23,000	342,400	19,900
1987	439,000	27,700	356,300	23,200
1988	469,200	32,600	407,400	28,000
1989	516,000	38,500	472,800	35,500
1990	545,900	39,300	508,800	38,000
1991	566,800	42,200	551,000	40,600
1992	598,000	44,100	590,300	42,400
1993	627,100	46,500	624,100	47,500
1994	674,400	51,800	676,000	52,300
1995	726,500	57,800	711,600	55,300

Note. Populations are estimated and rounded to the nearest 100. Adapted from *Correctional Populations in the United States, 1995* (NCJ 163916), by the Bureau of Justice Statistics, 1997, Rockville, MD: Author. In the public domain.

Table A4
Number of Adults Held in State or Federal Prisons or Local Jails Per 100,000 Adult Residents in Each Group, by Sex and Race, 1985–1995

Year	White		Black	
	Males	**Females**	**Males**	**Females**
1985	528	27	3,544	183
1986	570	29	3,850	189
1987	594	35	3,943	216
1988	629	41	4,441	257
1989	685	47	5,066	321
1990	718	48	5,365	338
1991	740	51	5,717	356
1992	774	53	6,015	365
1993	805	56	6,259	403
1994	851	61	6,682	435
1995	919	68	6,926	456

Note. Data are based on resident population for each group on July 1 of each year. Reprinted from *Correctional Populations in the United States, 1995* (NCJ 163916), by the Bureau of Justice Statistics, 1997, Rockville, MD: Author. In the public domain.

Bringing College Back to Bedford Hills

With Help From Glenn Close and Paul Newman, Volunteers Revive a Prison Program After Government Funds Are Cut Off

By ROBERT WORTH

BEDFORD HILLS

LAST month, nine women wearing black caps and gowns walked onto a podium here and received their college diplomas as their friends and family members wept and cheered.

It was an unusual ceremony, because all the graduates were convicted felons, and it took place in a gym ringed by locked metal gates and razor wire at the Bedford Hills Correctional Facility, a maximum security women's prison.

At most prisons, higher education was swept away when the federal and state governments withdrew all tuition grants to inmates in the mid-1990's. But at Bedford, volunteers have helped create a college program so successful that one in five of the 850 inmates is pursuing a college or postgraduate degree. Hardened criminals arriving at the prison discover that the inmate leaders are not gang members but women who stay up late reading Romantic poetry and studying for sociology exams.

"Girls are like, 'Can you just read my paper?' " said Rhonda Covington, a tall woman with a gentle smile who came to Bedford almost 17 years ago after she was convicted of assisting in a homicide, and who is working on a master's degree in English literature. "They seek you out, they find you. And you're happy to help because there was always someone helping you when you got started."

Although many Americans remain uneasy about giving convicts a free college education, volunteers at Bedford point to studies showing that education reduces recidivism and makes prisons easier to manage. The program, which is privately financed and involves 13 area colleges, has been held up as a model and is being imitated elsewhere.

"It's the largest, most robust, most linked to the community of any program in the country," said William Ayers, a professor of education at the University of Illinois at Chicago.

In some ways Bedford's example is hard to follow. Surrounded by moneyed enclaves of Bedford Hills and Katonah, Bedford's college program has become a pet cause for the actress Glenn Close, who lives in Bedford, and the playwright Eve Ensler, the author of "The Vagina Monologues," both of whom have visited the prison or taught there. Other volunteers and contributors include Ruby Dee and Ossie Davis, Paul Newman and Joanne Woodward, and Camille Cosby, Bill Cosby's wife.

The prison has its own gallery of celebrities. There is Pamela Smart, whose story inspired the movie "To Die For"; Kathy Boudin and Judith Clark, the 1960's radicals who were convicted of robbing an armored car in 1981; and Caroline Warmus, convicted of murdering her lover's wife in 1991. Former inmates include Amy Fisher, who was convicted of shooting her lover's wife, and Jean S. Harris, who served 12 years for killing Herman Tarnower, the "Scarsdale Diet" doctor.

Some of the prison's famous inmates—"trackers" in inmates' lingo—are among the most prominent students. Ms. Boudin and Ms. Clark, who were well educated before arriving in prison, helped found the college program in 1996 and have been mentors to many other women.

Yet despite its blend of Hollywood and tabloid glamour, much of what happens at Bedford could be replicated anywhere. On a recent Thursday evening, a dozen students sat at their desks in a classroom decorated with maps and blackboards, listening intently as a guest speaker described her book, a study of communities that practice voodoo.

"Do you think American attitudes toward voodoo are more about what happened with colonialism in Africa, or is it just the fact that the people who practice voodoo are dark-skinned, and there's racism in this country?" asked one inmate with a pair of purple sunglasses pushed onto her forehead.

To an outsider, it could have been an ordinary college seminar, except that all the students wore the same state-issued green pants.

Getting a college degree in prison is not easy. The students spend their days on work details and take classes at night. Many of them have earned their G.E.D.'s in prison too; two-thirds of those entering the state's prisons lack a high school diploma. The state requires inmates without basic English to take classes, and it pays for G.E.D. classes. But after that, students are on their own. And they often require months of arduous course work before they are even ready to begin college-level classes.

But Bedford's example has already inspired similar efforts. Volunteers at Sing Sing Correctional Facility in Ossining set up the Hudson Link for Higher Education in Prison last year, citing Bedford as a model; 44 students are now taking classes there through Mercy College.

"I get phone calls, e-mails and letters from people at other prisons and universities all the time," said Michelle Fine, a sociology professor at the City University of New York who has taught at Bedford and supervised a research project documenting the program's positive effects.

The Bedford program emerged from what most inmates see as a terrible injustice: the collapse of government support for prison education.

Until 1995, inmates at Bedford, like those around the country, relied on state and federal grants, with classes at Bedford provided by Mercy College. Although the nation's prisoners had accounted for only one half of one percent of all federal Pell grants, Congress dropped them in the face of public pressure to cut back on any perceived amenities in prisons. The next year New York and most other states eliminated their own tuition assistance for higher education. The nation's 300 prison college programs soon dwindled to a handful.

"Not being able to continue with new students was a devastating trauma," said Precious Bedell, who earned her B.A. at the prison in 1990 and was released in 1999. When the last group graduated in May 1995, many of the inmates and some administrators wept openly, believing the ceremony would never be repeated.

In the following year a group of seven inmates met with Superintendent Elaine Lord and asked if they could work with Theodora Jackson, a frequent visitor and volunteer at the prison, to try to bring back the college program. She agreed at once.

"We thought it would take about three years, and we'd have maybe a course," said Ms. Lord, who has been struggling for years to finish a Ph.D. in criminal justice at the State University of New York at Albany. "They did the whole thing in about 18 months."

Ms. Jackson arranged a meeting with a group of local people including her friend Dr. Regina Peruggi, who was then president of Marymount Manhattan College.

"A very exciting thing happened," Ms. Jackson recalled. "During the second meeting, we broke into three task groups. One was mostly academics, another was people who had some experience in fund-raising, and the third was interested in educating the public as to why college in prison would be beneficial to the entire society."

Before long 12 other college presidents had agreed to join a consortium, donating faculty, books, computers and other materials for the program. It was agreed that Marymount Manhattan would grant the degrees and supervise the program, and because of logistical difficulties in scheduling, there would be only one undergraduate concentration, sociology. And because many of the women who have a high school diploma or G.E.D. lack an adequate background for college, there are precollege courses as well. Mercy College offers a separate master's program in English literature.

A year later the group's fund-raising jumped into high gear with a performance called "Net of Souls" featuring readings of inmate writings by Ms. Close, Ms. Ensler and other celebrities at the Mount Kisco Presbyterian Church. (Both Ms. Close and Ms. Ensler, who declined to comment on their efforts at Bedford, had been active at the prison for years.) The event was repeated twice, and in 1989 it took place at Lincoln Center and brought in about $163,000 for the nonprofit group, the Center for Redirection through Education, that Ms. Jackson and her fellow volunteers had founded.

The annual budget is now $480,000, with foundation grants and a donor base of several thousand people, mostly Westchester residents, said Jim Payne, the group's executive director.

Many inmates and volunteers said the program would not exist if not for Ms. Lord. As the superintendent, she could easily have refused to allow a program that is vulnerable to criticism and that involves an arduous transfer of 60 volunteers in and out of the prison every week. "Her job would be easier without it," said Jane Maher, the coordinator of the prison's precollege and master's degree programs.

To Ms. Lord, "in order for people to understand why have college at prison, you need to focus on children." About 75 percent of the prison's inmates have children, and there is strong evidence that the level of education in children corresponds to their mother's, she said.

"One big way to keep kids out of prison is to keep their mothers in school," she added. "The woman is here—she's committed a crime—but her children are not."

Several inmates agreed that their children had been a powerful motivating factor in getting an education.

"Children want to be like their mom," Ms. Covington said. "For once, Mommy is doing something positive and productive." Last year Ms. Covington's son Calvin, a freshman in college, gave a speech at the graduation ceremony at Bedford in which he said he would never have believed he could make it to college if he hadn't seen his mother do so behind bars.

But children are not the only beneficiaries. Several inmates and faculty members will soon publish a study that documents the programs' effects on recidivism and prison management. Although the study grew out of a class on social science research methods taught by Ms. Fine of CUNY, prison administrators helped conduct interviews, and state officials compiled the statistics on recidivism.

The results are striking: only 7.7 percent of the inmates who attended college while at Bedford ended up in prison again, compared with 29.9 percent of those who did not. There was no significant difference in race, ethnicity, or crime committed between the two groups, according to the report.

A number of other studies in prisons have found roughly parallel results. "Nationally, getting a G.E.D. drops recidivism rates from 70 percent to 45 percent, and once you get through a four-year B.A. degree it gets down to 10 to 12 percent," said Richard Tewksbury, a professor of justice administration at the University of Louisville who has studied prison education programs.

Some criminologists point out that such studies are not pure measures of the power of education, because inmates who choose to get a high school or college degree might also be those who would have gone straight anyway. But most academics say that the career opportunities education provides do appear to make an enormous difference for many prisoners after they leave.

The report also documents the program's calming effect on the prison.

"It makes you think about your actions—you don't want to blow school," said Viniece Walker, who got her B.A. at Bedford in 1994 and is now working on a master's in English literature. "Little slights you might have responded to, you don't."

Inmates and volunteers said the college fever had spread to women who would never have chosen school independently. "It's become the hip thing to do," said Benay Rubenstein, who ran the college program from its inception in 1997 until last year. "And these are women who might otherwise be involved in problematic behavior."

'They're like sponges, they're really ready to learn something.'

Ms. Johnson, for instance, said, "I don't like school." Working on a master's in English has been difficult, she said, because "I have a tendency to destroy the English language," and writing papers about Beowulf and Edmund Spenser has been excruciating. But she has continued because she needed a goal, she said, and because of the example set by other women.

Between classes women often tutor one another informally. Even the guards get involved, reminding the women about their homework and asking them how they did on tests, several inmates said.

For volunteers, working with inmates is often a life-changing experience.

"It's an incredible high for a teacher," said Louise Feroe, the provost of Mercy College, who directed the program before public financing was cut off in 1995. "They're like sponges, they're really ready to learn something."

Hetty Jones, a poet who has taught creative writing at Bedford and other prisons for many years, said teaching there has been "one of the most rewarding experiences of my life."

Ms. Jones is the chairwoman of the prison writing committee of P.E.N., an international association of writers, which holds a prison writing contest every year. Two Bedford inmates, Ms. Boudin and Ms. Clark, have won in recent years. (The State Department of Correctional Services would not allow Ms. Boudin, Ms. Clark or Ms. Smart to be interviewed for this article, saying that they were not direct participants in the college program and that they get too much media attention already. The department also rejected a request to attend this year's graduation ceremony.

The inmates also bring a different perspective to class. "It's our life experience," Ms. Johnson said. "We never had a silver spoon in our mouths like some of their other students." As an example, she described a paper she wrote about Charlotte Perkins Gilmans' story "The Yellow Wallpaper," in which a depressed woman is confined to her bed against her will. "I wrote about how it's like being in a cell, and the professor said no one else saw that," she said.

A number of Bedford inmates have continued their studies after being released. Ms. Rubenstein, the former director of the prison's college program, now runs a nonprofit based at the CUNY graduate center called the College and Community Fellowship program. About 20 former inmates are getting help from the center to finish their degrees, and another 20 will start this fall, she said.

Many have found work in social service professions, according to the report. "If I hadn't gone to college I would never have been able to do the job I have," said Ms. Bedell, who is the prison family coordinator for the Osborne Association, a nonprofit group in Manhattan.

As a national model, Bedford clearly has its limitations. First, other prisons are not generally surrounded by wealthy liberal neighbors who place a tremendous value on education.

And male prisoners generally have a harder time drawing community support than women do.

"Charitable organizations and civic groups are a lot more likely to see women as salvageable and worthy of their efforts and resources," said Mr. Tewksbury, the professor who has studied prison education programs. Some advocates say that is why the government should start financing prison education programs again.

"Bedford is clearly a model, it is where the state ought to be," said Jeffrion L. Aubry, a state assemblyman from Queens who said he hoped to bring back state tuition assistance programs for prisoners.

But it will not be easy. Even the privately financed Bedford program remains politically vulnerable. Administrators are careful not to allow visitors to photograph the few computers inmates use, out of fear that outsiders would complain that the inmates were being coddled.

"I think maintaining the program is really difficult because people don't want prisons to be anything but punishment," said Geraldine Downey, a psychology professor at Columbia University who has taught at Bedford on and off for years.

From the state's perspective, paying for college programs does not make sense in light of the relatively small number of inmates who benefit, said James B. Flateau, a spokesman for the state Department of Corrections. There are now between 23,000 and 25,000 inmates taking G.E.D. and adult basic English classes, but only a few thousand took college classes when the state financed them. And the cost to the state of a G.E.D. is about $500 a year, compared with about $2,500 for a year of state-financed college classes, Mr. Flateau said.

The forthcoming study of Bedford's program offers an answer to that; $2,500 is not so much when you consider that it could prevent many released inmates from returning to crime and ending up in prison again at a cost to taxpayers of at least $25,000 a year.

The arguments are likely to go on. In the meantime, one thing is clear: the Bedford program keeps many inmates from losing hope, even if they know they will never be released.

"You can't undo what brought you here," Rosalie Cutting, a middle-aged woman with gray hair and calm blue eyes, said as they sat at a table reading an abstract of Sigmund Freud's works in the prison's Learning Center. But she has earned her bachelor's and master's degrees since arriving here in 1989, something she never thought she could do before coming to prison.

"There is an irony: I bloomed in a very dark place," she said.

From the *New York Times*, June 24, 2001, pp. 1, 8. © 2001 by The New York Times Company. Reprinted by permission.

Crime and Punishment

Think that stuffing prisons with lawbreakers makes sense? You clearly haven't run the numbers. Here are some better ways to buy safety.

BY CAIT MURPHY

america is an exceptional country. Compared with citizens of other nations, Americans tend to be more religious and more entrepreneurial. We send more people to university, have more millionaires, and enjoy more living space. We are the world leaders in obesity and Nobel Prizes.

And we send people to prison at a rate that is almost unheard of. Right now, almost two million Americans are either in prison (after conviction) or jail (waiting for trial). Of every 100,000 Americans, 481 are in prison. By comparison, the incarceration rate for Britain is 125 per 100,000, for Canada 129, and for Japan 40. Only Russia, at 685, is quicker to lock 'em up.

America was not always so exceptional in this regard. For the 50 years prior to 1975, the U.S. incarceration rate averaged about 110, right around rich-world norms. But then, in the 1970s, the great prison buildup began. This was a bipartisan movement. Democrats like Jerry Brown of California and Ann Richards of Texas, for example, presided over prison population booms, as did Republican governors like John Ashcroft of Missouri and Michael Castle of Delaware. Bill Clinton worried in public about rising prison populations but signed legislation, much of it Republican sponsored, that kept the figures rising. No surprise, then, that spending on incarceration has ballooned from less than $7 billion in 1980 to about $45 billion today.

Just because the U.S. is different doesn't mean it is wrong. But prison is a serious matter in a way that, say, Amer-

ica's inexplicable affection for tractor pulls is not. Accordingly, a number of people—social scientists, prison professionals, even a few politicians—have begun to examine how and why the U.S. sends people to prison. What they are finding, in broad terms, is that there is a substantial minority of prisoners for whom incarceration is inappropriate—and much too expensive.

The amount spent on incarceration has ballooned to about $45 billion a year.

Who deserves to be imprisoned is, of course, partly a question of moral values. Prison keeps criminals off the streets; it punishes transgressors and deters people from committing crimes. But it is also a question of economic values. Everyone agrees that caging, say, John Wayne Gacy is worth whatever it costs, but that locking up a granny caught shoplifting makes no sense. The question to consider, then, is not "Does prison work?" but *"When* does prison work?" Economics can help draw the line.

ON ONE LEVEL, IT MAKES SENSE that America imprisons more people than its peers. The U.S. has historically been more

violent than Europe, Japan, or Canada—in particular, our homicide rate is well above world norms—and the public wants violent people punished while freeing society from their presence. "We are a culture that believes change is possible, that human beings can be saved," says Francis Cullen of the University of Cincinnati, who specializes in public attitudes toward crime and rehabilitation. "The dividing line is violence. That's where people start becoming unwilling to take risks."

Fundamentally, America's prison population grew because people got sick of feeling scared and elected politicians who promised to deliver freedom from that fear. Moreover, it could be argued that America had some catching up to do: From the early 1960s to the early 1970s, the violent-crime rate rose sharply while the incarceration rate actually fell. Those trends probably helped spawn the "tough on crime" mentality that has reigned since. In the 1980s lawmakers delivered mandatory minimums—statutory requirements for harsh sentences for certain offenses, mostly gun- and drug-related. In the 1990s came "three-strikes" laws, designed to target repeat felons; truth-in-sentencing legislation; and the abolition of parole in many states.

All those policies filled prisons, but not necessarily with the hardened thugs people thought they were putting away. Though there are now 400,000 more violent offenders behind bars than there were in 1980, the proportion of violent offenders in the prison population has actually fallen.

The land of the free?

Incarceration rate per 100,000 residents

Russia	685
USA	481
Singapore	465
Canada	129
Britain	125
China	115
Spain	110
Australia	95
Germany	90
France	90
Italy	85
Japan	40

Sources: U.S. Department of Justice, World Prison Population List, Statistics Canada

U.S. prison population*

Drug-only offenders 7%▶ 1980

◀24% 1998

*In state and federal prisons. Does not include the 76,000 people in private prisons, or those in jail awaiting trial.

FORTUNE CHARTS

According to the Bureau of Justice Statistics, the percentage of violent offenders in state prisons has dropped from almost 60% in 1980 to 48% at the end of 1999; 21% were in prison in 1999 for property crimes, 21% for drug crimes, and the rest for public-order offenses, such as immigration, vice, or weapons violations. In the federal system, home to about 145,000 offenders, 58% are in for drug offenses (compared with 25% in 1980) and only 12% for violent crimes—down from 17% in 1990. Of the six crimes that account for the great majority of prisoners (murder, robbery, aggravated assault, burglary, drugs, and sexual assault), drug offenders made up 45% of the growth from 1980 to 1996, figures Allan Beck of the BJS. Every year from 1990 through 1997, more people were sentenced to prison for drug offenses than for violent crimes.

Because imprisonment went up in the 1990s and crime went down, you might conclude that locking up so many criminals bought us less crime. Up to a point that's true. Steven Levitt, a professor of economics at the University of Chicago, has cleverly provided an empirical foundation to prove the link between incarceration and crime reduction. In 1996 he

studied what happened after the courts ordered 12 states to reduce overcrowding in their prison systems. By looking at how the states responded, either by releasing convicts or by building new prisons, he estimated that the effect of imprisoning one additional lawbreaker for a year was to prevent two fewer violent crimes and about a dozen fewer property crimes. The social costs of these crimes Levitt estimated at $53,900 (a figure derived from published estimates commonly used by social scientists). That's well above the $25,000 or so it costs to keep a prisoner behind bars for a year.

But that doesn't prove that every prison cell built in America's 25-year construction spree was worth it. There could be ways to deliver just as much public safety for less money. Take Canada. Like the U.S., Canada saw a sharp decline in violent crime in the 1990s—but while America's prison population almost doubled, Canada's rose only slightly. Or take next-door neighbors New Hampshire and Maine. In the first half of the 1990s, both saw similar declines in crime, but New Hampshire sharply increased the number of people it imprisoned, while Maine did not. Ditto for Kansas and Missouri; the latter built lots

more new prisons, but the crime rates in the two states remained similar. In short, building prisons is not the only way to fight crime—and often not a cost-effective way to do so. In economic terms, this is because not every prison cell delivers equal returns, in terms of havoc unwreaked. As more and more people are imprisoned, the nastiness of the inmate population diminishes, so the crime control delivered per convict drops. Consider the research of John DiIulio, the new director of President Bush's office of faith-based programs; Bert Useem, director of the Institute for Social Research at the University of New Mexico; and Anne Morrison Piehl, a professor of public policy at Harvard's Kennedy School of Government. In 1999 the trio surveyed male inmates in Arizona, New Mexico, and New York about their criminal pasts. Then they multiplied each crime by its social cost, using National Institute of Justice numbers. (The cost of a rape, for example, is estimated at $98,327; of a burglary, $1,271.)

They found that the social cost of the crimes committed by the median inmate in New York—that is, one whose crimes rank 50 on a scale of 100 in terms of seriousness—was $31,866; in New Mexico,

$26,486; and in Arizona, $25,472. That's slightly more than the $25,000 cost of incarceration. For the 40th percentile, though, that figure dropped to less than $14,000 in all three states, and for the 20th, less than $7,000. At the 80th percentile, the monetary value of crime caused was almost $240,000 for New York and $163,311 for New Mexico—marking the perpetrator as the type of person for whom prison is clearly an appropriate solution.

The major dividing line between cost-effective and non-cost-effective incarceration? That turns out to be fairly easy to figure. As a general rule, those who were imprisoned for property or violent crimes caused damage to society that cost more than their incarceration; those convicted solely of drug offenses did not.

Drug dealing is not harmless, of course. Having an open-air crack market on the corner kills commerce and devastates neighborhoods. But the authors became convinced that the incarceration of so many drug-only offenders—28% in New York and 18% in Arizona—made no economic sense, because one drug seller sent to prison just created a job opening for another seller. Consider the example of a Milwaukee street corner. In 1996 a Wisconsin task force noted that although the police had made 94 drug-related arrests in three months at the corner of 9th and Concordia, most of them leading to prison sentences, the drug market continued and public safety did not improve. And the price was substantial: It costs about $23 million to jail 94 people for a year.

In short, the authors found that for drug offenders, "the crime averted by incarceration is low," says Piehl. "We need to come up with sanctions that are graduated so that our only options are not nothing, or prison, or probation." What made that conclusion particularly noteworthy was that Piehl and DiIulio had argued for years in favor of more prisons. But by last year DiIulio, who is no one's idea of a bleeding-heart liberal, was writing an article for the editorial page of the *Wall Street Journal* titled "Two Million Prisoners Is Enough."

ARE THERE BETTER, LESS COSTLY alternatives to prison for drug offenders? Lisa Roberson offers one answer to that question. She is a resident at the Phoenix Career Academy in Brooklyn, N.Y., which offers residents—many of them repeat offenders who would otherwise be in prison—intensive drug treatment, vocational training, and after-care assistance. Roberson, 31, who started selling drugs at

17 and using them at 21, spent four years at Clinton State in New Jersey for selling drugs to an undercover cop. "All I did there is learn how to jail," she says. When she was arrested again in 2000, the court gave her a choice: prison or two years at Phoenix.

This is no country club. Residents sleep ten to a room. Just about every minute of their day, starting with a 6 A.M. wake-up call, is plotted for them. If Roberson makes it through the program—and about 60% do—she will be drug-free and will have completed training as a drug counselor. Phoenix will help her find a job, an apartment, and child care for her 4-year-old son. Yes, Roberson may regress—of those who complete the course, about a third eventually go back to drugs—but clearly she has a much better shot at establishing a real life than if she had spent several more years "learning how to jail." The cost of her treatment, funded mostly by state and local governments: $17,000 to $18,000 a year.

Many successful drug-treatment programs are run out of prisons too—such as Amity Rightturn, a program in a medium-security facility in San Diego that provides more than a year of assessment and counseling, plus further treatment after the inmates have left prison. A 1999 study found that three years after release, 27% of inmates who completed all three parts of the program had returned to prison; among those who got no treatment, 75% did.

On the subject of drug treatment, cost-benefit analysis has something to say: It works. Numerous studies have concluded that well-run drug-treatment programs, particularly long-term residential ones with follow-up care, can pay for themselves just by reducing crime. Add in the value of incarceration avoided and taxes paid by the freed, and it adds up.

The incarceration of so many drug-only offenders makes no economic sense.

Given this context, it's little short of tragic that drug-treatment programs in prison are not keeping pace with the need for them. In 1991 about a third of the inmates who reported drug use in the month prior to their arrest were getting treatment; by 1999 that was down to less than 15%, according to the Department of Justice,

and much of that was of the nonintensive variety that has little long-term effect. Treatment is no panacea: Lots of people will drop out or go back to their bad habits. The point is simply that treatment works often enough for the benefits to outweigh the costs—the exact opposite of the economics of prison for drug offenders.

What about other prison programs? Social scientists have applied cost-benefit analysis to those too. They have found that busy inmates—those given the chance to learn to read, to finish high school, to learn basic job skills—are significantly less likely than idle ones to return to prison. In Maryland, for example, a follow-up analysis published last October of 1,000 former inmates found a 19% lower recidivism rate for those who had taken education programs in prison than for those who hadn't. Extrapolating that 19% figure for the state as a whole suggests that Maryland could save $23.2 million a year in reduced incarceration—double what it spends on prison education programs.

More evidence that educational programs save money: In 1999 analysts from the state of Washington surveyed studies dating back to the mid-1970s on what works and what fails in reducing crime. The researchers concluded that for every dollar spent on basic adult education in prison, there was $1.71 in reduced crime; for every dollar on vocational education, $3.23.

If you think such data have prompted more educational programs in prisons, think again. Congress passed "get tough" legislation in the 1990s that eliminated Pell grants to prisoners for college courses; it also reduced the requirements for basic and vocational education for prisoners. Many states have therefore taken the opportunity to cut back. Prisoners have a limited constituency, after all, and nixing programs for them is a politically painless way to cut budgets.

Ironically, surveys show that the public strongly supports prisoner-rehabilitation programs. So do many who run the prisons. Tommy Douberley, warden of Florida's Moore Haven Correctional Facility, is convinced that no-frills prisons are a mistake. "These people are going to be returned to society," he says. "We need to make some provision for them that when they get out they are better than when they went in." Politicians, however, seem to have interpreted the public's clear desire for greater safety as a mandate for more and harsher prisons. And they are not the same thing at all.

THERE ARE SIGNS THAT AMERICA IS beginning to recognize the limits of prison. Drug offenders are less likely to be sentenced to prison today than they were in 1992 (though still more than three times as likely as in 1980), in part because of the emergence of drug courts in many states, which force defendants into treatment on pain of prison. But past policies continue to exert expansionary pressure. From June 1999 to June 2000, the last 12-month period for which figures are available, the incarcerated population rose 3%. Though the smallest rise in decades, that still meant that 31,000 more Americans were behind bars. To house them means building a prison every ten days or so—an expensive hobby, considering that a medium-security facility for 1,000 inmates can cost $50 million.

Make no mistake: A large proportion of inmates thoroughly deserve to be exactly where they are. Incarceration is an effective way to isolate really awful people. But too many prisons stuffed with nonviolent, idle inmates is simply wasteful, of both people and money. We would do better to learn from several states that have lowered the crime rate without substantially raising prison populations—as New York did at least in part by aggressively funneling drug offenders into treatment, for example. Instead of being exceptional for its willingness to jail its citizens, the goal for America should be to become exceptional in the application of wisdom to its criminal population. At the moment, it is not even close.

Ex-cons on the street

The crime crackdown produces a record flow of ex-offenders with nowhere to go

By Jeff Glasser

L AS VEGAS—Twenty-one days out of prison, convicted drug dealer Wodabá Ahkeem Jones has job prospects as bleak as the dusty urban landscape of this old, west-side, working-class neighborhood. Five employers have rejected the three-time ex-felon. At $9 an hour, the part-time maintenance work he managed to find does not begin to pay the bills, which include $550 in monthly child support for his four kids. The stocky, 41-year-old former salesman wants to go straight, but he says the lack of opportunity has him contemplating a return to crime. "I ain't going to eat out of no can in a park," he says. "I'm going to do what I got to do to survive. I ain't going to rape no one, but I will do what's necessary to feed my family."

Jones's struggles are bitterly familiar to the legions of ex-felons returning to Sin City. Some 2,300 of 4,000 Nevada inmates released last year—part of a growing wave of prisoners being freed nationwide— were "dumped" onto city streets, Mayor Oscar Goodman says, with little more than $21 from the state and a free van ride. Michael "Muhammad" Staley, 36, lasted 90 days on the outside. The habitual criminal returned to the Strip last year after more than 11 years in prison. It was a disaster from the get-go: He had no

job skills and no place to stay. His new girlfriend ended up pregnant. "I was frustrated so much that I laid on my bed and thought, 'Well, I wish I was back in prison,'" he says. His wish was granted when a parole officer nabbed him after he was in a fight. "It's like a cub being taken out of the wilderness and then you throw him back in the wilderness when he's grown," he says from the familiar confines of Southern Desert Correctional Center shortly before being paroled again. "He doesn't know how to survive."

Five minutes away. The discharge of Staley and a record 585,000 other inmates this year raises serious public safety concerns. Communities will have to reabsorb a group larger than the entire 320,000 U.S. prison population in 1980. Two thirds of them will be rearrested for committing a crime within three years, at current national recidivism rates. More than 40 percent will end up back in prison. "Anybody who lives in a metropolitan area in the United States is going to be living within five minutes of tens of thousands of prisoners released from prison," says Leonard Sipes, a Maryland Department of Public Safety official.

The numbers are a consequence of the nation's get-tough-on-crime laws. The prison population grew by more

than 60 percent in the 1990s, to nearly 1.9 million people. Crooks are serving longer sentences now, an average of 27 months, but 95 percent of them will eventually re-enter society. When they arrive home, most will report to parole officers responsible for dozens, if not hundreds, of parolees; 19 percent of the offenders, about 110,000 this year, will "max out," meaning they have completed their sentences and face no state supervision. Often, these are the worst criminals, who have acted up in the penitentiary or failed to make parole because of the severity of their crimes. "It cries out for reform," says Stephen Rickman, who supervises federal "Weed and Seed" projects in 240 struggling urban neighborhoods. Otherwise, he warns, "you could see an explosive increase in crime."

Sobered by the statistics, criminal justice professionals are wrestling with ways to manage the felon influx. The Clinton administration has proposed a $145 million package to provide drug treatment, court supervision, and job training to returning offenders. Attorney General Janet Reno calls inmates' aftercare a "public safety" issue. "They're going to victimize [the community] again" in the absence of new programs, she tells *U.S. News.* "Why don't we stop it with

One city tries rebuilding lives

BALTIMORE—The seven ex-convicts hammering away in a dilapidated row house share a lifetime of splintered dreams. Ranging in age from 18 to 47, they are all former addicts or dealers with little education and few skills, the detritus of the drug-ravaged Druid Heights section. "If I wasn't working, I'd probably be out there selling drugs, whatever I need to get some money," says André Smothers, 18, who started stealing cars and dealing when he was 14.

Smothers and the others have jobs today because of a rare community development project. Recognizing that construction companies were not hiring unskilled workers with criminal pasts, community leaders decided to build their own construction crew. The workers rehabilitate abandoned or rundown houses that are then rented to low-income families. They earn $9-an-hour paychecks from the nonprofit Druid Heights Community Development Corp. More importantly, they learn how to frame houses, put up

drywall, and do sheetwork. "We're creating a trained pool of men," says the organization's Kelly Little.

Many temptations. The three-year-old program addresses in a small way one of Druid Heights' biggest problems: how to handle returning offenders who know more about life behind bars than simple, everyday living. In 1998 alone, almost 900 ex-convicts were released into the neighborhood of less than 5,000 residents. The great majority—about three fourths if Druid Heights mimics national figures—have drug or alcohol problems. "For the majority of guys, when they're out a couple of weeks, the street gets them," says André Fisher, a former addict and at 47, the "grandfather" of the crew. Guys fall back to what they know." Fisher says people re-entering society have to be reprogrammed. "You need to help with being on time, being taught the basics," he says. "A lot of them still don't have a clue about the boundaries."

Some ex-cons returning to Druid Heights may soon have an opportunity

to get that kind of preparation. The area will be one of 17 in a public-private pilot program to reduce recidivism. In the Druid Heights version, 20 offenders will be trained in construction, food preparation, or computers. Money management, substance-abuse prevention, and life-skills classes will accompany the job instruction. If the program works, community leaders will ask for funds to expand it.

The experience of the construction crew suggests the task will not be easy. Four of the original six members fell back into drugs, Little says. But for those who stuck it out, there's been a payoff. When foreman Eric Lee, 41, returned from prison a recovering drug addict more than three years ago, he lived with his mother. Now he owns a home with his fiancée and just bought a black Chevy Blazer. "I'm really grateful somebody saw something in me when I always thought I was nothing," he says. "I found a new way to live."

—J.G.

a carrot-and-stick approach?" Skeptical police groups say the money would be better spent hiring more people to keep an eye on the lawbreakers. "What they need to do is put 50,000 to 60,000 additional parole and probation officers on the streets so we can monitor these people," says James Fotis, director of the Law Enforcement Alliance of America.

Across the country, 17 communities are devising pilot projects to reduce the recidivism rate. Nine of the test sites will set up "re-entry courts," where convicts will have to appear regularly before judges to earn their way back into society or be sent back to prison. In western Iowa, the court will target the 22 percent of violent offenders, including sex felons, who have finished their sentences and refused treatment. Successful inmates will "graduate" into the community. Justice Department officials point to the nation's 300 drug courts as a successful model for such court supervision.

Critics caution that this system could turn judges into super-parole officers and that mass re-entry courts could lead to greater prison populations if inmates fail to meet the courts' terms.

A more effective tactic, some community activists say, would be to establish programs in prisons, where they have a captive audience. Along with seven other jurisdictions, Nevada plans to test that idea at its Southern Desert correctional facility, a desultory fortress of buildings some 40 miles north of Las Vegas. Low-risk offenders will be required to draw up re-entry plans outlining where they will live, work, and get needed treatment. Mayor Goodman applauds the concept: "There should be alternative means to work with human beings other than to just throw them away like pieces of meat and then wait until the meat ages and let it come back into the community."

Surveillance is the alternative of choice in Lowell, Mass. Police have

identified the 77 prisoners due back this year. "If each commits four or five crimes, that's a significant impact," says Ed Davis, Lowell's police chief. He says the department arrested the first two who came home "almost immediately" for larceny and drug offenses. They'll warn the others in coming months. "It seems to me 200 people in this city are committing all the crime," says Davis. "It's just a matter of getting them."

State response. Apart from the pilots, a number of states have designed programs to reduce recidivism. On July 1 Washington will become the first state to require that the corrections budget be divvied up based on the risk that ex-offenders represent to the community. In Maryland, 19,500 habitual drug offenders must submit to regular urinalysis in one of the nation's most ambitious drug-testing programs. The "Break the Cycle" initiative reduced drug use among participants by 53 percent and cut the recidivism rate by 23 percent. Florida has electronically monitored 778 released violent and sex offenders and has revoked just two for new felonies. Richard Nimer, a Florida corrections official, was among those who initially had privacy concerns about the big-brother technology. He's since decided it's well worth the $9.26 daily price tag per inmate: "The way you have to look at it is that these are people who have given up the rights they had with their crimes."

Some victims' rights advocates say even electronic monitoring isn't enough. "I don't think they should be let out," says Christine Long, 47. "I don't think rapists can change." She's speaking from a horrific perspective. In 1988, parolee Robert Blankenship broke into her Columbus home and raped her. The Ohio parole board had released him after he served 7½ years of a 15-to-75-year sentence on earlier rape convictions. Out on the streets, Blankenship was allowed to skip counseling because "the class was full," she later learned.

It's this kind of story that turns the public away from any programs for ex-offenders and makes it difficult for parole boards to predict how an inmate will react to freedom. Consider the case of convicted murderer Jimmy Keys, who will make parole in June. Southern Desert's warden, Sherman Hatcher, initially says Keys has as good a chance as any well-behaved inmate of successfully re-entering the Las Vegas community. "He's going to try much harder," he says. "He's learned a work ethic." Then he reconsiders. Keys hasn't crossed a street or driven a car in 15 years. He sports a curly perm and an early 1980s mesh cap. At the age of 42, he is a relic of another era. How will he react if he cannot follow his dream and become a stockbroker because of his criminal record? What will prevent him or any other released inmate with unreasonable expectations from snapping? "That's where the frustration sets in, when they set these lofty goals," Hatcher says. "They're setting themselves up for failure."

For many ex-convicts, a new start depends on trading the fast life for menial wages. One of the relatively few to make the trade is Noel Johnson, 33, who lived a thug's life for most of his adolescent and adult years. A former Crip from Compton with a "Gangster Man" tattoo, Johnson used to clear thousands of dollars a day selling drugs. Today, seven months fresh from a California prison, he feels lucky to make $8 an hour as a porter at a Las Vegas car dealership. "I had to put down my pride," says Johnson. "But I don't have to look over my back. When the police pull me over, I don't have to be nervous."

THE DEATH PENALTY ON TRIAL

Special Report: DNA and other evidence freed 87 people from death row; now Ricky McGinn is roiling Campaign 2000. Why America's rethinking capital punishment.

BY JONATHAN ALTER

H E STOOD AT THE THRESHOLD OF THE execution chamber in Huntsville, Texas, 18 minutes from death by lethal injection, when official word finally came that the needle wouldn't be needed that day. The rumors of a 30-day reprieve were true. Ricky McGinn, a 43-year-old mechanic found guilty of raping and killing his 12-year-old stepdaughter, will get his chance to prove his innocence with advanced DNA testing that hadn't been available at the time of his 1994 conviction. The double cheeseburger, french fries and Dr Pepper he requested for dinner last Thursday night won't be his last meal after all.

Another galvanized moment in the long-running debate over capital punishment: last week Gov. George W. Bush granted his first stay of execution in five years in office not because of deep doubts about McGinn's guilt; it was hard to find anyone outside McGinn's family willing to bet he was truly innocent. The doubts that concerned Bush were the ones spreading across the country about the fairness of a system with life-and-death stakes. "These death-penalty cases stir emotions," Bush told NEWSWEEK in an exclusive interview about the decision. Imagine the emotions that would have been stirred had

McGinn been executed, then proved innocent after death by DNA. So, Bush figured, why take the gamble?

"Whether McGinn is guilty or innocent, this case has helped establish that all inmates eligible for DNA testing should get it," says Barry Scheck, the noted DNA legal expert and coauthor of "Actual Innocence." "It's just common sense and decency."

Even as Bush made the decent decision, the McGinn case illustrated why capital punishment in Texas is in the cross hairs this political season. For starters, McGinn's lawyer, like lawyers in too many capital cases, was no Clarence Darrow. Twice reprimanded by the state bar in unrelated cases (and handling five other capital appeals simultaneously), he didn't even begin focusing on the DNA tests that could save his client until this spring. Because Texas provides only $2,500 for investigators and expert witnesses in death-penalty appeals (enough for one day's work, if that), it took an unpaid investigator from out of state, Tina Church, to get the ball rolling.

After NEWSWEEK shone a light on the then obscure case ("A Life or Death Gamble," May 29), Scheck and the A-team of

the Texas defense bar joined the appeal with a well-crafted brief to the trial court. When the local judge surprised observers by recommending that the testing be done, it caught Bush's attention. The hard-line higher state court and board of pardons both said no to the DNA tests—with no public explanation. This time, though, the eyes of the nation were on Texas, and Bush stepped in.

But what about the hundreds of other capital cases that unfold far from the glare of a presidential campaign? As science sprints ahead of the law, assembly-line executions are making even supporters of the death penalty increasingly uneasy. McGinn's execution would have been the fifth in two weeks in Texas, the 132d on Bush's watch. Is that pace too fast? We now know that prosecutorial mistakes are not as rare as once assumed; competent counsel not as common. Since the Supreme Court allowed reinstatement of the death penalty in 1976, 87 death-row inmates have been freed from prison. With little money available to dig up new evidence and appeals courts usually unwilling to review claims of innocence (they are more likely to entertain possible procedural trial-court errors), it's impossible to

THEY'RE ON DEATH ROW. BUT SHOULD THEY BE?

Five cases where there may be big questions

Groups like the Death Penalty Information Center monitor cases of prisoners on death row whose guilt, the advocates believe, may not be beyond a reasonable doubt. A few top candidates, from the DPIC and others:

Gary Graham

Graham has been on death row in Texas for nearly 20 years for killing a man during a 1981 supermarket robbery. A 17-year-old at the time, he was convicted on the testimony of a single eyewitness who claimed she saw Graham from 30 to 40 feet away in a dark parking lot. Three other eyewitnesses could not make a positive identification of Graham at the crime scene. A store employee who said he saw the shooter fleeing told police Graham was not the killer—but he was never called to testify. And none of Graham's fingerprints or DNA was found at the scene. Last week the U.S. Supreme Court declined to hear his case; he is scheduled for execution June 22.

Joe Amrine

Amrine was sentenced to death for stabbing a man with an ice pick in a Missouri prison in 1985. The conviction was based on the testimony of two fellow prisoners who said they witnessed the murder. But the two told different stories, and both later said they had lied under pressure from a prison investigator.

Larry Osborne

Osborne—at 20 Kentucky's youngest death-row inmate—was convicted of killing an elderly couple by setting their house on fire when he was 17. His conviction was based primarily on statements from a 15-year-old friend, who Osborne's lawyer says was pressured to snitch by investigators. The friend then drowned before he could be cross-examined at the trial. There was no compelling physical evidence. An appeal is pending.

John Francis Wille

A drifter from Florida, Wille was convicted along with his girlfriend in the 1985 kidnapping and murder of an 8-year-old girl in Louisiana. Their convictions were based entirely on confessions they made at the time. (His girlfriend is currently serving a life sentence.) But Wille's lawyer claims they both have histories of false confessions. And he says the forensic evidence contradicts their stories.

John Spirko

Spirko was convicted in 1984 of killing the Elgin, Ohio, postmaster. But the chief witness against Spirko said he was only 70 percent sure of his identification. And records indicate that Spirko's codefendant was actually 600 miles away at the time of the crime. Evidence implicates others in the murder. Spirko remains on death row, but in 1995 a judge granted him an indefinite stay.

know just how many other prisoners are living the ultimate nightmare.

So for the first time in a generation, the death penalty is in the dock—on the defensive at home and especially abroad for being too arbitrary and too prone to error. The recent news had prompted even many conservative hard-liners to rethink their position. "There seems to be growing awareness that the death penalty is just another government program that doesn't work very well," says Stephen Bright of the Southern Center for Human Rights.

When Gov. George Ryan of Illinois, a pro-death-penalty Republican, imposed a moratorium on capital punishment in January after 13 wrongly convicted men were released from Illinois's death row, it looked like a one-day event. Instead, the decision has resonated as one of the most important national stories of the year. The big question it raises, still unanswered: how can the 37 other states that allow the death penalty be so sure that their systems don't resemble the one in Illinois?

In that sense, the latest debate on the death penalty seems to be turning less on

moral questions than on practical ones. While Roman Catholicism and other faiths have become increasingly outspoken in their opposition to capital punishment (even Pat Robertson is now against it), the new wave of doubts seems more hardheaded than softhearted; more about justice than faith.

The death penalty in America is far from dead. All is takes to know that is a glimpse of a grieving family, yearning for closure and worried about maximum sentences that aren't so long. According to the NEWSWEEK Poll, 73 percent still support capital punishment in at least some cases, down only slightly in five years. Heinous crimes still provoke calls for the strongest penalties. It's understandable, for instance, how the families victimized by the recent shooting at a New York Wendy's that left five dead would want the death penalty. And the realists are right; the vast majority of those on death row are guilty as hell.

But is a "vast majority" good enough when the issue is life or death? After years when politicians bragged about streamlining the process to speed up executions, the

momentum is now moving the opposite way. The homicide rate is down 30 percent nationally in five years, draining some of the intensity from the pro-death-penalty argument. And fairness is increasingly important to the public. Although only two states—Illinois and New York—currently give inmates the right to have their DNA tested, 95 percent of Americans want that right guaranteed, according to the NEWSWEEK Poll. Close to 90 percent even support the idea of federal guarantees of DNA testing (contained in the bipartisan Leahy-Smith Innocence Protection bill), though Bush and Gore, newly conscious of the issue, both prefer state remedies.

The explanation for the public mood may be that cases of injustice keep coming, and not just on recent episodes of "The Practice" that (with Scheck as a script adviser) uncannily anticipated the McGinn case. In the last week alone Bush pardoned A. B. Butler after he served 17 years in prison for a sexual assault he didn't commit, and Virginia Gov. James Gilmore ordered new testing that will likely free Earl Washington, also after 17 years behind

TO LIVE AND TO DIE

After a spate of well-publicized cases in which innocent men were sentenced to die, the nation's death-penalty debate seems to be taking on new urgency. Crime, after all, is down. But the annual total of executions in the United States is still rising, principally because appeals create long delays between a prisoner's sentencing and execution. A graphic history of the American way of death:

Inmates Executed Each Year in the United States

1930 155 EXECUTED
1930s Executions rise to an average 167 a year, the highest for any decade in U.S. history
1933 Giuseppe Zangara gets the death penalty for killing Chicago Mayor Anton Cermak during an assassination attempt on FDR. The execution takes place exactly 33 days after the shooting.

1935 199 EXECUTED
1942 147 EXECUTED
1953 62 EXECUTED
1953 Julius and Ethel Rosenberg, convicted of giving U.S. atomic-bomb secrets to the Soviet Union, become the first U.S. civilians to be executed for espionage

1957 65 EXECUTED
1966 Crime is down, the economy is up and public support for the death penalty falls to 42 percent in the Gallup poll

1968–76 0 EXECUTED
1972 In a landmark case, *Furman v. Georgia*, the U.S. Supreme Court effectively voids death-penalty laws
1976 The court rules that mandatory death-penalty laws are unconstitutional—but refuses to ban the death penalty altogether
1977 After a series of high-court rulings clarifying legal standards, executions resume after a 10-year pause. In Utah, convicted murderer Gary Gilmore is the first to die—by firing squad.
1982 Convicted in Texas of killing a man while trying to steal a car, Charles Brooks becomes the first person to be executed by lethal injection

1984 21 EXECUTED

1992 31 EXECUTED
1994 Timothy W. Spence, a Virginia rapist and murderer, becomes the first person to be executed in a case in which DNA evidence is pivotal
1995 New York reinstates the death penalty after Republican George Pataki is elected governor. Nationwide, the number of executions rises to 56, the highest total since 1957.

1997 74 EXECUTED
1998 Despite protests from supporters who claimed her religious beliefs had earned her clemency, Karla Faye Tucker becomes the first woman to be executed in Texas since the Civil War. Her crime: killing two people with a pickaxe.

1999 98 EXECUTED
1999 In St. Louis, Pope John Paul II calls for an end to the death penalty, and the U.N. Human Rights Commission passes a resolution urging a worldwide moratorium

They Shall Be Released

Since the 1970s, 87 inmates have been freed from death row because of problems or errors in the legal process. Common reasons for reversal include:
- Key witnesses lied or recanted their testimony
- Police overlooked or withheld important evidence
- DNA testing showed someone else committed the crime
- The defense lawyer was incompetent or negligent
- Prosecutors withheld exculpatory evidence from the defense

World Leaders

In 1999, China easily led all nations with 1,077 executions, followed distantly by Iran (165), Saudi Arabia (103), Democratic Republic of the Congo (100) and the United States (98)

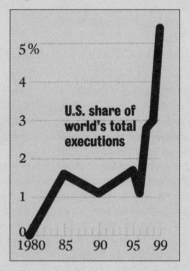

U.S. share of world's total executions

SOURCES: AMNESTY INTERNATIONAL, BUREAU OF JUSTICE STATISTICS, DEATH PENALTY INFORMATION CENTER. GRAPHIC BY STANFORD KAY AND KARL GUDE.

bars. All told, more than 70 inmates have been exonerated by DNA evidence since 1982, including eight on death row.

Death-penalty advocates often point out that no one has been proved innocent after execution. But the DNA evidence that could establish such innocence has fre-quently been lost by prosecutors with no incentive to keep it. In a recent Virginia case, a court actually prevented posthumous examination of DNA evidence. On the defense side, lawyers and investigators concentrate their scarce resources on cases where lives can be spared.

And while DNA answers some questions, it raises others: if so many inmates are exonerated in rape and rape-murder cases where DNA is obtainable, how about the vast majority of murders, where there is no DNA? Might not the rate of error be comparable?

The Executioner's Song Can Last for Years

How long death-row inmates must wait for execution varies sharply from state to state. Nebraska, where the delay averages 11.3 years, is slowest. But the interval between sentencing and execution is getting longer nationwide.

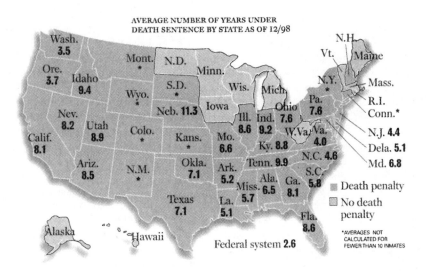

AVERAGE NUMBER OF YEARS UNDER
DEATH SENTENCE BY STATE AS OF 12/98

Wash. 3.5
Ore. 3.7
Idaho 9.4
Mont. *
N.D. *
Minn. *
Wyo. *
S.D. *
Wis. *
Mich. *
N.H.
Vt.
Maine
N.Y. *
Mass.
R.I.
Conn. *
Neb. 11.3
Iowa *
Ohio *
Pa. 7.6
Nev. 8.2
Utah 8.9
Calif. 8.1
Colo. *
Kans. *
Mo. 6.6
Ill. 8.6
Ind. 9.2
W.Va. Va. 4.0
Ky. 8.8
N.J. 4.4
Dela. 5.1
Md. 6.8
Ariz. 8.5
N.M. *
Okla. 7.1
Ark. 5.2
Tenn. 9.9
N.C. 4.6
S.C. 5.8
Texas 7.1
La. 5.1
Miss. 5.7
Ala. 6.5
Ga. 8.1
Fla. 8.6
Alaska
Hawaii
Federal system 2.6

■ Death penalty
□ No death penalty

*AVERAGES NOT CALCULATED FOR FEWER THAN 10 INMATES

Politics, for once, seems to be in the background, largely because views of the death penalty don't break down strictly along party lines. Ryan of Illinois is a Republican; Gray Davis, the hard-line governor of California, a Democrat. The Republican-controlled New Hampshire Legislature recently voted to abolish the death penalty; the Democratic governor vetoed the bill. Perhaps the best way to understand how the politics of the death penalty is shifting is to view it as a tale of two Rickys:

In January 1992, Arkansas Gov. Bill Clinton interrupted his presidential campaign to return home to preside over the execution of Ricky Ray Rector, a black man convicted of killing a police officer. Rector had lobotomized himself with a bullet to his head; he was so incapacitated that he asked that the pie served at his last meal be saved for "later." By not preventing the execution of a mentally impaired man, Clinton was sending a strong message to voters: the era of soft-on-crime Democrats was over. Even now, Al Gore doesn't dare step out front on death-penalty issues.

Ricky McGinn's case presented a different opportunity for Bush. While the decision to grant a stay was largely based on common sense and the merits of the case, it was convenient, too. In 1999, Talk magazine caught Bush making fun of Karla Faye Tucker, the first woman executed in Texas since the Civil War. Earlier this year, at a campaign debate sponsored by Ann, the cameras showed the governor chuckling over the case of Calvin Brine, whose lawyer fell asleep at his trial. In going the extra mile for Ginn over the objections of the objections of the appeals court and parole board, Bush looked prudent and blunted some of the criticism of how he vetoed a bill establishing a public defenders' office in Texas and made it harder for death-row inmates to challenge the system.

In the NEWSWEEK Poll, **73%** support the death penalty, down slightly from five years ago; **38%** say only the most brutal murderers should be executed.

Bush stayed McGinn's execution for political reasons, say **59%**, not because of evidence; **55%** say other governors also put politics first in capital cases

95% say states should permit DNA testing whenever it might prove guilt or innocence; **88%** think Washington should require states to permit such testing

72% say they are confident that those sentenced to death are guilty, but **82%** agree at least a few innocent people have been executed since the '70s

FOR THIS NEWSWEEK POLL, PRINCETON SURVEY RESEARCH ASSOCIATES INTERVIEWED 750 ADULTS BY TELEPHONE JUNE 1–2. THE MARGIN OF ERROR IS +/- 4 PERCENTAGE POINTS, THE NEWSWEEK POLL © 2000 BY NEWSWEEK, INC.

That system has scheduled 19 more Texas executions between now and Election Day. Gary Graham, slated to die June 22, was convicted on the basis of one sketchy eye-witness account when he was 17. The absence of multiple witnesses would make him ineligible for execution in the Bible ("At the mouth of one witness he shall not be put to death"—Deuteronomy 17:6); and Graham's age at the time he was convicted of the crime in 1981 would make him too young to be executed in all but four other nations in the world.

Americans might not realize how upset the rest of the world has become over the death penalty. All of our major allies except Japan (with a half-dozen executions a year) have abolished the practice. Only China, Iran, Saudi Arabia and Congo execute more than the United States. A draft version of the European Union's Bill of Rights published last week bars DU countries from extracting a suspected criminal to a country with a death penalty. (If approved, this could wreak havoc with international law enforcement). Admission to the DU is now contingent on ending capital punishment, which will force Turkey to abolish its once harsh death-penalty system.

The execution of juvenile offenders is a particular sore spot abroad. The United States has 73 men on death row for crimes committed when they were too young to drink or vote (mostly age 17); 16 have been executed, including eight in Texas. That's more than the rest of the world combined.

HOW BUSH MADE THE CALL
A huddle with aides and a sharp sense of the media play

BY HOWARD FINEMAN

When the faxes arrived on the plane, the "body guy" didn't think the governor had to see them right away. Karen Hughes, George W. Bush's right hand, knew better. She'd checked in with Austin. Ricky McGinn's appeals were failing. The DNA issue was hot. The execution was set for 6 p.m. the next day. With Bush out of state, any reprieve technically was up to the acting governor, a Democrat who hoped to grant one. If Bush wanted to deny a reprieve, he'd have to rush home.

So in a car in Albuquerque last Wednesday morning, Bush focused intently on the case. He'd tentatively signed off on it 13 days before—but only as one of four cases in a two-hour briefing during a busy day at home for "state business." Now he read the faxes from his counsel, Margaret Wilson. He spoke to her by mobile phone, hashed things out with Hughes and made his call: yes, new DNA technology might well cast doubt on McGinn's guilt. Bush would tell the press that he was "inclined" to give a reprieve. The story made headlines, and McGinn was given a stay the next day.

The episode was revealing: a real-time example of Bush's leadership style. He sets and clings to broad goals, in this case "swift and just" execution of death-row inmates. He relies heavily on trusted aides—more than ever since he is holding one job while running for another. He has a visceral feel for the media and their discontents, and jumps ahead to the next safe spot.

Reviewing death-penalty cases, Bush says, is his "most profound" duty as governor, his "worst nightmare" the death of an innocent convict. But while executions are practically an industry in Texas, Bush doesn't think he needs to scrutinize the innards of the system he oversees. In a NEWSWEEK interview last week he didn't know how much the state pays attorneys to represent defendants on appeal—a figure reform groups have loudly complained is far too low. Nor did Bush think he should assume the likelihood of error or injustice. "I trust the juries," he said. He denied that the sheer volume of executions raised the risk of a nightmare mistake. "We take lots of time on these cases, " he said. "I'm talking about my staff, the attorney general's office and me."

But in Bush's intensely personal world, decision making is less about judging the facts than reading people. He asks his aides blunt questions and scrutinizes them for signs of uncertainty. It seems there were none in the mansion meeting of May 18, though reform advocates had been agitating about the case. It was press coverage—and the resultant involvement of DNA experts—that forced Bush's hand.

Bush denies that politics drove his decision—though 59 percent of voters in the NEWSWEEK Poll thought so. He also claimed not to care that the likes of well-known DNA expert Barry Scheck had descended on Texas. "With all due respect to Mr. Scheck, he had nothing to do with my decision," Bush said. "People like to read all kinds of motives into these things, and I understand that. These death-penalty cases stir emotions. But all I ever ask are two questions: is there doubt about guilt based on the evidence, and did the defendant have full access? In this case, there was doubt." But what about the next batch, and the one after that? After last week, chances are, the briefings will run a little longer.

So far, opposition abroad has had little effect at home. What changed the climate in the United States was a series of cases in Illinois. The story traces back to the convictions of four black men, two of whom were condemned to die, for the 1978 murders of a white couple in the Chicago suburb of Ford Heights. In the early 1980s, Rob Warden and Margaret Roberts, the editors of a crusading legal publication called The Chicago Lawyer, turned up evidence that the four might be innocent. The state's case fell apart in 1996, after DNA evidence showed that none of the so-called Ford Heights Four could have raped the woman victim. It was only one case, but it had a searing effect in Illinois for this reason: three other men confessed to the crime and were convicted of it. The original four were unquestionably innocent—and two of them had nearly been executed.

By then other Illinois capital cases were falling apart. Some of the key legwork in unraveling bum convictions came from Northwestern University journalism students. Late in 1998 their school hosted a conference on wrongful convictions. The event produced a stunning photo op: 30 people who'd been freed from death rows across the country, all gathered on one Chicago stage.

But it was another Illinois case, early in 1999, that really began to tip public opinion. A new crop of Northwestern students helped prove the innocence of Anthony Porter, who at one point had been just two days shy of lethal injection for a pair of 1982 murders. Once again, the issue in Illinois wasn't the morality of death sentences, but the dangerously sloppy way in which they were handed out. Once again a confession from another man helped erase doubt that the man convicted of the crime, who has an IQ of 51, had committed it.

By last fall the list of men freed from death row in Illinois had grown to 11. That's when the Chicago Tribune published a lavishly researched series explaining why so many capital cases were suspect. The Tribune's digging found that almost half of the 285 death-penalty convictions in Illinois involved one of four shaky components: defense attorneys who were later suspended or disbarred, jailhouse snitches eager to shorten their own sentences, questionable "hair analysis" evidence or black defendants convicted by all-white juries. What's more, in the weeks after those stories appeared, two more men were freed from death row. That pushed the total to 13—one more than the number of inmates Illinois had executed since reinstating the death penalty in 1977.

The Porter case and the Tribune series were enough for Governor Ryan. On Jan. 31, he declared a moratorium on Illinois executions, and appointed a commission to see whether the legal process for handling capital cases in Illinois can be fixed. Unless he gets a guarantee that the system can be made perfect, Ryan told NEWSWEEK last week, "there probably won't be any more deaths," at least while he's governor. "I believe there are cases where the death penalty is appropriate," Ryan said. "But

THE CENTER OF THE STORM
McGinn gets a last shot to prove a lot of evidence wrong

BY MARK MILLER

Ricky McGinn is nobody's poster boy for ending capital punishment. Even before he got the death sentence for the 1993 rape and bludgeon murder of his 12-year-old stepdaughter, Stephanie Rae Flanary, McGinn, 43, had been tried and acquitted of murder in an unrelated case. He was once accused of rape—no charges were filed—and his daughter by a previous marriage has testified that McGinn molested her (again, he was not charged). He is also a key suspect in two unsolved murders of women that occurred in Brown County, Texas, in 1989 and in 1992.

Now McGinn's life may be hanging by a tiny fragment of hair—a pubic hair found in the victim's vagina during autopsy. Some time soon, this crucial piece of evidence will be subjected to mitochondrial DNA testing, a new lab technique. If the test proves the hair was McGinn's, his execution will be rescheduled and he will likely die later this year. But if the hair is someone else's, he may escape death and, possibly, get a new trial.

When McGinn was tried, the prosecution theorized that he killed the girl while raping her. Rape was the "aggravating circumstance" that persuaded the jury to impose the death penalty. Brown County District Attorney Lee Haney says McGinn was convicted of killing the girl on a compelling array of evidence that included a roofer's hammer that bore traces of Stephanie's blood and was found under a seat in McGinn's truck. Investigators also found blood in his Ford Escort, a drop of blood on his shoe and another drop on his shorts; all were type A positive, Stephanie's blood type.

But DNA testing at the time wasn't able to identify the pubic hair (prosecutors said it was "microscopically similar" to McGinn's) or to find DNA in a possible semen stain on Stephanie's shorts. The mitochondrial DNA testing will probably identify the hair, and another new DNA-analysis technique, known as STR (for short-tandem repeat) testing, may identify the semen.

McGinn still insists he was framed. He points out that the bloody hammer wasn't found during repeated searches of his truck by sheriff's deputies, implying that it was planted, and he cites a trial witness who said Stephanie's body wasn't in a culvert at a time when the authorities said it should have been there. He says testimony about the approximate time of death eliminates him as a suspect because he was already in custody. He also denies that he sexually abused his stepdaughter. "My wife kept me satisfied," he says. "I didn't need to go anywhere else, especially a 12-year-old girl." Those are hardly comforting words, but now McGinn will have a chance—and by law at least 61 days—to try to prove the rest of the evidence wrong.

we've got to make sure we have the right person. Every governor who holds this power has the same fear I do."

But few are acting on it. In the wake of the Illinois decision, only Nebraska, Maryland, Oregon and New Hampshire are reviewing their systems. The governors of the other states that allow the death penalty apparently think it works adequately. If they want to revisit the issue, they might consider the following factors:

Race: The role of race and the death penalty is often misunderstood. On one level, there's the charge of institutional racism: 98 percent of prosecutors are white, and according to the NAACP Legal Defense Fund, they are much more likely to ask for the death penalty for a black-on-white crime than when blacks are the victims. Blacks convicted of major violent offenses are more likely than white convicts to end up on death row. But once they get there, blacks are less likely than white death-row inmates to be executed because authorities are on the defensive about seeming to target African-Americans. The result is both discrimination and reverse discrimination—with deadly consequences.

The risk of errors: The more people on death row, the greater chance of mistakes. There are common elements to cases where terrible errors have been made: when police and prosecutors are pressured by the community to "solve" a notorious murder; when there's no DNA evidence or reliable eyewitnesses; when the crime is especially heinous and draws large amounts of pretrial publicity; when defense attorneys have limited resources. If authorities were particularly vigilant when these issues were at play, they might identify problematic cases earlier.

Deterrence: Often the first argument of death-penalty supporters. But studies of the subject are all over the lot, with no evidence ever established of a deterrent effect. When parole was more common, the argument carried more logic. But nowadays first-degree murderers can look forward to life without parole if caught, which should in theory deter them as much as the death penalty. It's hard to imagine a criminal's thinking; "Well, since I might get the death penalty for this crime, I won't do it. But if it was only life in prison, I'd go ahead."

Inadequate counsel: Beyond the incompetent lawyers who populate any court-appointed system, Congress and the Clinton administration have put the nation's 3,600 death-row inmates in an agonizing Catch-22. According to the American Bar Association Death Penalty Representation Project, in a state like California, about one third of death-row inmates must wait for years to be assigned lawyers to handle their state direct appeals. And at the postconviction level in some states, inmates don't have access to lawyers at all. The catch is that the 1996 Anti-Terrorism and Effective Death Penalty Act has a statute of limitations requiring that inmates file federal habeas corpus petitions (requests for federal court review) within one year after the end of their direct state appeal. In other words, because they have no lawyer after their direct appeals, inmates often helplessly watch the clock run out on their chance for federal review. This cuts down on frivolous appeals—but also on ones that could reveal gross injustice.

Fact-finding: Most states aren't as lucky as Illinois. They don't have reporters and investigators digging into the details of old cases. As the death penalty becomes routine and less newsworthy, the odds against real investigation grow even worse. And even when fresh evidence does surface, most states place high barriers against its use after a trial. This has been standard in the legal system for generations, but it makes little sense when an inmate's life is at stake.

Standards of guilt: In most jurisdictions, the judge instructs the jury to look for "guilt beyond a reasonable doubt." But is that the right standard for capital cases? Maybe a second standard like "residual doubt" would help, whereby if any juror harbors any doubt whatsoever, the conviction would stand but the death penalty would be ruled out. The same double threshold might apply to cases involving single eyewitnesses and key testimony by jailhouse snitches with incentives to lie.

Cost: Unless executions are dramatically speeded up (unlikely after so many mistakes), the death penalty will remain far more expensive than life without parole. The difference is in the upfront prosecution costs, which are at least four times greater than in cases where death is not sought. California spends an extra $90 million on its capital cases beyond the normal costs of the system. Even subtracting pro bono defense, the system is no bargain for taxpayers.

Whether you're for or against the death penalty, it's hard to argue that it doesn't need a fresh look. From America's earliest days, when Benjamin Franklin helped develop the notion of degrees of culpability for murder, this country has been willing to reassess its assumptions about justice. If we're going to keep the death penalty, the public seems to be saying, let's be damn sure we're doing it right. DNA testing will help. So will other fixes. But if, over time, we can't do it right, then we must ask ourselves if it's worth doing at all.

With JOHN MCCORMICK in Chicago, MARK MILLER in Livingston, Texas, and KEVIN PERAINO in New York

Appendix I

AE: Criminal Justice 02/03– CHARTS AND GRAPHS

Below, we have provided the page numbers and titles for the individual charts and graphs that can be found within the articles in this volume. We hope you find this resource useful.

Appendix II

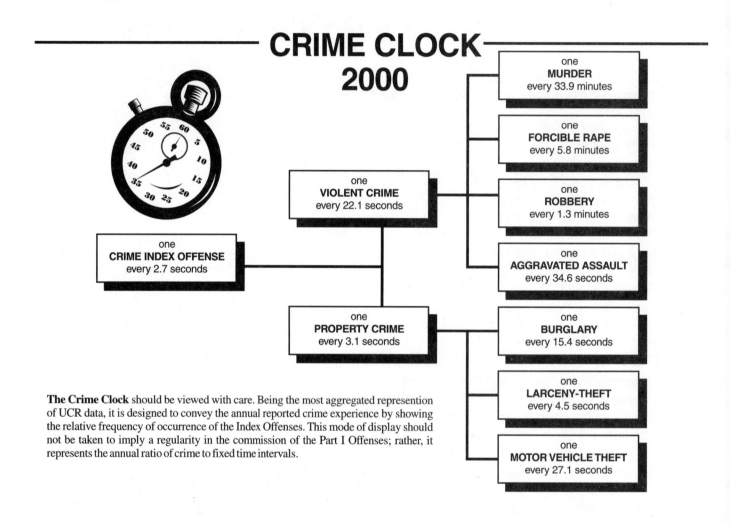

CRIME CLOCK 2000

one
CRIME INDEX OFFENSE
every 2.7 seconds

one
VIOLENT CRIME
every 22.1 seconds

one
PROPERTY CRIME
every 3.1 seconds

one
MURDER
every 33.9 minutes

one
FORCIBLE RAPE
every 5.8 minutes

one
ROBBERY
every 1.3 minutes

one
AGGRAVATED ASSAULT
every 34.6 seconds

one
BURGLARY
every 15.4 seconds

one
LARCENY-THEFT
every 4.5 seconds

one
MOTOR VEHICLE THEFT
every 27.1 seconds

The Crime Clock should be viewed with care. Being the most aggregated represention of UCR data, it is designed to convey the annual reported crime experience by showing the relative frequency of occurrence of the Index Offenses. This mode of display should not be taken to imply a regularity in the commission of the Part I Offenses; rather, it represents the annual ratio of crime to fixed time intervals.

Crime in the United States, 2000

The Crime Index total, a measure of serious crime, decreased 0.2 percent to an estimated 11.6 million offenses in 2000. This marked the lowest measure since 1978 and remained relatively unchanged from 1999 numbers. Collectively, the Nations' cities showed a 0.1-percent decline in serious crime. However, cities with populations of less than 50,000 showed increases in the Crime Index. Cities with populations of 10,000 to 24,999 had an increase of 0.8 percent, and cities with populations under 10,000 were up 0.6 percent. In cities with populations of 25,000 to 49,999, the Crime Index was up 0.4 percent. Cities with populations of 100,000 and over had an overall decrease of 0.4 percent in Crime Index offenses, and cities with populations of 50,000 to 99,999 saw serious offenses fall an average of 0.7 percent. Suburban counties

had a 1.8-percent decrease in Crime Index offenses, and rural counties had a 0.5-percent increase.

Five- and 10-year trends indicate the 2000 national total was 14.0 percent lower than in 1996 and 22.0 percent lower than in 1991.

By region, the largest volume of Crime Index offenses was reported in the most populous area, the Southern States, which accounted for 41.0 percent of the total. The Western States made up 23.0 percent of the total; the Midwestern States, 21.9 percent; and the Northeastern States, 14.2 percent. The Western States showed an increase in Crime Index offenses, up 1.0 percent from the 1999 totals. The Northeastern States had a 2.0-percent decrease, the Midwestern States noted a 0.6-percent drop, and the Southern States registered a 0.1-percent decrease.

Table 1 Index of Crime, United States, 1981-2000

Population[1]	Crime Index total	Modified Crime Index total[2]	Violent crime[3]	Property crime[3]	Murder and non-negligent man-slaughter	Forcible rape	Robbery	Aggra-vated assault	Burglary	Larceny-theft	Motor vehi-cle theft	Arson[2]
					Number of Offenses							
Population by year:												
1981-229,465,714	13,423,800		1,361,820	12,061,900	22,520	82,500	592,910	663,900	3,779,700	7,194,400	1,087,800	
1982-231,664,458	12,974,400		1,322,390	11,652,000	21,010	78,770	553,130	669,480	3,447,100	7,142,500	1,062,400	
1983-233,791,994	12,108,630		1,258,087	10,850,543	19,308	78,918	506,567	653,294	3,129,851	6,712,759	1,007,933	
1984-235,824,902	11,881,755		1,273,282	10,608,473	18,692	84,233	485,008	685,349	2,984,434	6,591,874	1,032,165	
1985-237,923,795	12,430,357		1,327,767	11,102,590	18,976	87,671	497,874	723,246	3,073,348	6,926,380	1,102,862	
1986-240,132,887	13,211,869		1,489,169	11,722,700	20,613	91,459	542,775	834,322	3,241,410	7,257,153	1,224,137	
1987-242,288,918	13,508,708		1,483,999	12,024,709	20,096	91,111	517,704	855,088	3,236,184	7,499,851	1,288,674	
1988-244,498,982	13,923,086		1,566,221	12,356,865	20,675	92,486	542,968	910,092	3,218,077	7,705,872	1,432,916	
1989-246,819,230	14,251,449		1,646,037	12,605,412	21,500	94,504	578,326	951,707	3,168,170	7,872,442	1,564,800	
1990-249,464,396	14,475,613		1,820,127	12,655,486	23,438	102,555	639,271	1,054,863	3,073,909	7,945,670	1,635,907	
1991-252,153,092	14,872,883		1,911,767	12,961,116	24,703	106,593	687,732	1,092,739	3,157,150	8,142,228	1,661,738	
1992-255,029,699	14,438,191		1,932,274	12,505,917	23,760	109,062	672,478	1,126,974	2,979,884	7,915,199	1,610,834	
1993-257,782,608	14,144,794		1,926,017	12,218,777	24,526	106,014	659,870	1,135,607	2,834,808	7,820,909	1,563,060	
1994-260,327,021	13,989,543		1,857,670	12,131,873	23,326	102,216	618,949	1,113,179	2,712,774	7,879,812	1,539,287	
1995-262,803,276	13,862,727		1,798,792	12,063,935	21,606	97,470	580,509	1,099,207	2,593,784	7,997,710	1,472,441	
1996-265,228,572	13,493,863		1,688,540	11,805,323	19,645	96,252	535,594	1,037,049	2,506,400	7,904,685	1,394,238	
1997-267,783,607	13,194,571		1,636,096	11,558,475	18,208	96,153	498,534	1,023,201	2,460,526	7,743,670	1,354,189	
1998-270,248,003	12,485,714		1,533,887	10,951,827	16,974	93,144	447,186	976,583	2,332,735	7,376,311	1,242,781	
1999-272,690,813	11,634,378		1,426,044	10,208,334	15,522	89,411	409,371	911,740	2,100,739	6,955,520	1,152,075	
2000-281,421,906	11,605,751		1,424,289	10,181,462	15,517	90,186	407,842	910,744	2,049,946	6,965,957	1,165,559	
Percent change, number of offenses:												
2000/1999	-0.2		-0.1	-0.3	[4]	+0.9	-0.4	-0.1	-2.4	+0.2	+1.2	
2000/1996	-14.0		-15.6	-13.8	-21.0	-6.3	-23.9	-12.2	-18.2	-11.9	-16.4	
2000/1991	-22.0		-25.5	-21.4	-37.2	-15.4	-40.7	-16.7	-35.1	-14.4	-29.9	
					Rate per 100,000 Inhabitants							
Year:												
1981	5,850.0		593.5	5,256.5	9.8	36.0	258.4	289.3	1,647.2	3,135.3	474.1	
1982	5,600.5		570.8	5,029.7	9.1	34.0	238.8	289.0	1,488.0	3,083.1	458.6	
1983	5,179.2		538.1	4,641.1	8.3	33.8	216.7	279.4	1,338.7	2,871.3	431.1	
1984	5,038.4		539.9	4,498.5	7.9	35.7	205.7	290.6	1,265.5	2,795.2	437.7	
1985	5,224.5		558.1	4,666.4	8.0	36.8	209.3	304.0	1,291.7	2,911.2	463.5	
1986	5,501.9		620.1	4,881.8	8.6	38.1	226.0	347.4	1,349.8	3,022.1	509.8	
1987	5,575.5		612.5	4,963.0	8.3	37.6	213.7	352.9	1,335.7	3,095.4	531.9	
1988	5,694.5		640.6	5,054.0	8.5	37.8	222.1	372.2	1,316.2	3,151.7	586.1	
1989	5,774.0		666.9	5,107.1	8.7	38.3	234.3	385.6	1,283.6	3,189.6	634.0	
1990	5,802.7		729.6	5,073.1	9.4	41.1	256.3	422.9	1,232.2	3,185.1	655.8	
1991	5,898.4		758.2	5,140.2	9.8	42.3	272.7	433.4	1,252.1	3,229.1	659.0	
1992	5,661.4		757.7	4,903.7	9.3	42.8	263.7	441.9	1,168.4	3,103.6	631.6	
1993	5,487.1		747.1	4,740.0	9.5	41.1	256.0	440.5	1,099.7	3,033.9	606.3	
1994	5,373.8		713.6	4,660.2	9.0	39.3	237.8	427.6	1,042.1	3,026.9	591.3	
1995	5,274.9		684.5	4,590.5	8.2	37.1	220.9	418.3	987.0	3,043.2	560.3	
1996	5,087.6		636.6	4,451.0	7.4	36.3	201.9	391.0	945.0	2,980.3	525.7	
1997	4,927.3		611.0	4,316.3	6.8	35.9	186.2	382.1	918.8	2,891.8	505.7	
1998	4,620.1		567.6	4,052.5	6.3	34.5	165.5	361.4	863.2	2,729.5	459.9	
1999	4,266.5		523.0	3,743.6	5.7	32.8	150.1	334.3	770.4	2,550.7	422.5	
2000	4,124.0		506.1	3,617.9	5.5	32.0	144.9	323.6	728.4	2,475.3	414.2	
Percent change, rate per 100,000 inhabitants:												
2000/1999	-3.3		-3.2	-3.4	-3.1	-2.3	-3.5	-3.2	-5.4	-3.0	-2.0	
2000/1996	-18.9		-20.5	-18.7	-25.6	-11.7	-28.2	-17.2	-22.9	-16.9	-21.2	
2000/1991	-30.1		-33.2	-29.6	-43.7	-24.2	-46.9	-25.3	-41.8	-23.3	-37.2	

[1] Populations are Bureau of the Census provisional estimates as of July 1 for each year except 1990 and 2000 which are the decennial census counts. The 1981 through 1999 population and Crime Index offense and rate counts have been adjusted.

[2] Although arson data are included in the trend and clearance tables, sufficient data are not available to estimate totals for this offense.

[3] Violent crimes are offenses of murder, forcible rape, robbery, and aggravated assault. Property crimes are offenses of burglary, larceny-theft, and motor vehicle theft.

[4] Less than one-tenth of 1 percent.

In 2000, Crime Index offenses occurred most often in July and August and least often in February.

Rate

At 4,124.0 offenses per 100,000 inhabitants in the United States, the Crime Index rate for 2000 is the lowest since 1972. By population grouping, cities outside metropolitan areas had a Crime Index rate of 4,485.0 offenses per 100,000 inhabitants, and metropolitan areas, a rate of 4,428.0 offenses per 100,000 inhabitants. Rural counties had 1,864.0 offenses per 100,000.

Overall, the 2000 Crime Index rate dropped 3.3 percent from the 1999 rate, 18.9 percent from the 1996 rate, and 30.1 percent from the 1991 rate.

Of the Nation's four regions, the South had the highest Crime Index rate with 4,743.4 offenses per 100,000 inhabitants. The West followed with a rate of 4,222.4; the Midwest with 3,945.0; and the Northeast with 3,064.3. All four regions experienced a decline in the rate per 100,000 inhabitants from 1999 to 2000.

By region, the Northeastern region experienced a decrease in the rate of serious crime of 5.2 percent, and the Southern Region recorded a 3.9-percent drop. The Midwestern Region had a 2.4-percent decrease, and the Western Region had a 2.3-percent decline.

Nature

The Crime Index is composed of the total of violent and property crimes. Violent crimes comprised 12.3 percent of Crime Index offenses, and property crimes made up 87.7 percent. Larceny-theft, a property crime, was the offense most often reported to law enforcement. Murder, a violent crime, was least often reported.

An estimated $16.4 billion in stolen property was reported for all Crime Index offenses in 2000. Thefts of motor vehicles accounted for the greatest loss, followed by jewelry and precious metals; televisions, radios, stereos, etc.; and currency, notes, etc.

The recovery rate for monetary losses from stolen property as reported to law enforcement agencies around the Nation in 2000 was 34.8 percent. With regard to percentage of monetary recovery, stolen motor vehicles had the highest followed by clothing and furs, and consumable goods.

Law Enforcement Response

Law enforcement agencies throughout the United States reported an estimated 2.2 million arrests for Index crimes and cleared 20.5 percent of serious crimes. Clearances can occur by arrest or by exceptional means when some element beyond law enforcement control precludes the placing of formal charges against the offender. The arrest of one person may clear several crimes, or several persons may be arrested in connection with the clearance of one offense.

Five- and 10-year clearance rates show a 21.7-percent clearance rate in 1996, and a 21.2-percent clearance rate in 1991.

In 2000, Crime Index arrests fell 3.7 percent from 1999 arrest numbers. With the exception of motor vehicle theft, which rose 1.2 percent, each offense in the Crime Index reflected a drop in the number of persons arrested from 1999 to 2000. Among violent crimes, arrests for murders were down 7.5 percent, and arrests for forcible rape decreased 3.6 percent. Robbery arrests declined 2.5 percent, and aggravated assault arrests went down 0.9 percent. Among the property crimes, arrests for larceny-theft dropped 5.5 percent, and arrests for burglary were down 3.4 percent. Arrests for arson declined 4.3 percent.

Adult arrests dropped 3.1 percent, and juvenile arrests declined 5.1 percent. By gender, male arrests fell 4.1 percent, and female arrests dipped 2.4 percent.

The highest volume of Crime Index arrests were for larceny-thefts with nearly 1.2 million estimated arrests.

Crime Index Offenses Reported

MURDER AND NONNEGLIGENT MANSLAUGHTER

DEFINITION
Murder and nonnegligent manslaughter, as defined in the Uniform Crime Reporting Program, is the willful (nonnegligent) killing of one human being by another.

Year	Number of offenses	Rate per 1000,000 inhabitants
1999	15,522	5.7
2000	15,517	5.5
Percent change	Less than 0.1 percent	

The estimated number of persons murdered in the United States in 2000 was 15,517, virtually no change from the 1999 estimate. The national estimate for 2000 fell 21.0 percent below the 1996 estimate and 37.2 percent below that of 1991.

Collectively, the Nation's cities registered a 0.7-percent increase in murder as compared to 1999 figures. The greatest rise, 11.7 percent, was recorded by cities with less than 10,000 inhabitants. Collectively, cities with populations of 250,000 or more had a decline of 0.3 percent. Among the Nation's counties, murder volumes declined 3.8 percent in suburban counties and 3.5 percent in rural counties.

By region, 44.0 percent of murders occurred in the South, the country's most populous region. Murders in the Midwest comprised 21.2 percent of the total; the West, 21.0 percent; and the Northeast, 13.9 percent. Two of the Nation's four regions showed increases in the number of murders when 2000 data are compared to 1999. The South and the Northeast each recorded increases of 2.4 percent, and the West and the Midwest showed decreases of 3.4 and 2.9 percent, respectively.

Considering the volume of monthly occurrence for 2000, murder was committed most frequently in July and least often in February.

Murder by Month
Percent distribution, 1996–2000

Month	1996	1997	1998	1999	2000
January	8.7	8.7	9.1	8.8	8.6
February	7.8	7.3	7.3	7.1	7.0
March	7.5	8.5	8.3	7.6	7.5
April	7.5	7.6	7.7	7.7	7.8
May	8.3	7.9	8.4	8.3	8.4
June	8.8	8.7	8.4	8.1	8.7
July	8.8	9.0	8.7	9.1	9.5
August	9.1	8.7	9.2	9.1	9.5
September	8.1	8.2	8.3	8.7	8.3
October	8.5	8.6	8.3	8.4	8.7
November	8.0	8.2	7.6	8.2	7.6
December	8.9	8.6	8.8	8.8	8.7

Rate

The national murder rate for 2000, down 3.1 percent from the 1999 rate, was the lowest since 1965, 5.5 murders per 100,000 inhabitants. Trends for 5 and 10 years show that the 2000 rate was 25.6 percent lower than in 1996 and 43.7 percent lower than in 1991.

Among the Nation's regions, the South had a rate of 6.8 victims per 100,000 inhabitants; both the West and the Midwest, 5.1 per 100,000; and the Northeast, 4.0 per 100,000. Murder rates declined in all four of the geographic areas in comparison to 1999 figures. The West registered a decrease of 6.5 percent; the Midwest, 4.7 percent; the Northeast, 1.6 percent; and the South, 1.5 percent.

Collectively, metropolitan areas throughout the country had a rate of 5.9 murders per 100,000 inhabitants for 2000. Both rural counties and cities outside metropolitan areas reported murder rates of 3.8 per 100,000 inhabitants.

Nature

In 2000, contributing agencies submitted supplemental homicide data for 12,943 of the estimated 15,517 murders. These supplemental data provide the age, sex, and race of both victims and offenders; the types of weapons used; the relationships of the victims to the offenders; and the circumstances surrounding the murders.

Murder Victims
by Race and Sex, 2000

Race of victim	Total	Sex of victim		
		Male	Female	Unknown
Total white victims	6,263	4,453	1,809	1
Total black victims	6,193	5,049	1,144	–
Total other race victims	319	230	89	–
Total unknown race	168	108	34	26
Total victims[1]	12,943	9,840	3,076	27

[1] Total number of murder victims for whom supplemental homicide data was received.

According to 2000 supplemental homicide data, males comprised 76.0 percent of the murder victim total. By age, the greatest percentage of victims, 89.7 percent, were persons aged 18 or older. Of all victims, 45.1 percent were 20 to 34 years old. Of the victims for whom race was known, 49.0 percent were white, 48.5 percent were black, and persons of others races accounted for the remaining 2.5 percent.

Regarding offender data, supplemental homicide figures were available for 14,697 murder offenders in 2000 with males accounting for 90.2 percent of those for whom gender was known. Of the murder offenders for whom age was known, 91.3 percent were persons aged 18 or older. Of all offenders, 69.1 percent were persons aged 17 through 34. Blacks accounted for 51.4 percent of those offenders for whom race was known, whites for 46.1 percent, and persons of other races for the remainder.

Based on supplemental homicide data, the racial correlation of murder victims to murder offenders is usually intraracial. Figures based on one victim/one offender incidents in 2000 indicate that 93.7 percent of black murder victims were killed by black offenders, and 86.2 percent of white murder victims were slain by white offenders.

Supplemental homicide data reveal that males were most often murdered by males in 2000. Both victim and offender were male in 88.5 percent of single-victim! single-offender incidents. In addition, the data show that 90.8 percent of female victims were murdered by males.

Available weapon data indicate that 65.6 percent of murder weapons in 2000 were firearms, making them the most frequently used weapons in the commission of murder. By firearm type, handguns accounted for 51.7 percent of the murder total; shotguns, 3.6 percent; rifles, 3.1 percent; and other or unknown types of firearms, another 7.3 percent. Knives or cutting instruments were employed in 13.5 percent of murders; personal weapons (hands, fists, feet, etc.) in 7.0 percent; blunt objects (clubs, hammers, etc.) in 4.7 percent; and other dangerous weapons (poison, explosives, etc.) in the remainder.

Supplemental homicide data for relationships between victims and offenders in 2000 indicate that 44.3 percent of all murder victims knew their offenders: 30.9 percent of victims were acquainted with their assailants and 13.4 percent were related to them. Husbands or boyfriends murdered 33.0 percent of female victims, and wives or girlfriends killed 3.2 percent of male victims. Thirteen percent of all murder victims were slain by strangers. Relationships were not known for 42.6 percent of the murders.

When examining circumstance data, arguments were the circumstance attributed to 29.4 percent of the murders in 2000. Felonious activities such as robbery, arson, etc., occurred in conjunction with 16.7 percent, and 0.5 percent of homicides were suspected to have been the result of a felonious activity.

Law Enforcement Response

Typically, murder is cleared at a higher rate than any other Crime Index offense. In 2000, law enforcement agencies nationwide recorded a 63.1 percent clearance rate for the crime. The highest clearance rate, 77.6 percent, was reported by cities with populations under 10,000. Cities with populations of 250,000 and over cleared 56.1 percent, and cities collectively cleared 61.0 percent. Law enforcement agencies in the Nation's rural counties cleared 76.8 percent of reported murders, and in suburban counties, 66.9 percent.

Regionally, the Northeastern States registered the highest murder clearance rate at 72.8 percent. The Southern States recorded a clearance rate of 65.0 percent. The Midwestern and Western States followed with clearance rates of 59.2 percent and 57.6 percent, respectively.

FORCIBLE RAPE

DEFINITION

Forcible rape, as defined in the Uniform Crime Reporting Program, is the carnal knowledge of a female forcibly and against her will. Assaults or attempts to commit rape by force or threat of force are also included; however, statutory rape (without force) and other sex offenses are excluded.

Year	Number of offenses	Rate per 1000,000 inhabitants
1999	89,411	32.8
2000	90,186	32.0
Percent change	+0.9	–2.3

The estimated 90,186 forcible rapes of females nationwide in 2000 represented the first increase in forcible rape since 1992. A comparison of 2000 figures to those of the previous year demonstrates an increase of 0.9 percent. However, the 2000 totals are 6.3 percent below the 1996 level and 15.4 percent below the 1991 level.

The greatest volume of rapes, 38.0 percent, was reported in the most populous area of the Nation, the South. Twenty-five percent of rapes were reported in the Midwest, 23.8 percent in the West, and 13.2 percent in the Northeast, respectively. Two-year trends for forcible rapes indicate that forcible rape offenses increased in three of the four regions. From 1999 to 2000, forcible rapes increased 3.5 percent in the West, 1.9 percent in the Northeast, and 1.6 percent in the Midwest. The South showed a drop of 1.5 percent.

A study of the monthly variations for this offense indicates that in 2000 the highest number of forcible rapes were recorded in July. The lowest number were reported in December.

Forcible Rape by Month
Percent distribution, 1996–2000

Month	1996	1997	1998	1999	2000
January	7.9	7.9	7.9	8.1	8.0
February	7.9	7.0	7.4	7.3	7.6
March	8.1	8.0	8.6	8.2	8.4
April	8.1	8.2	8.2	8.2	8.0
May	9.0	9.1	8.8	8.6	9.1
June	8.8	9.5	8.7	8.8	9.1
July	9.5	9.7	9.6	9.6	9.5
August	9.1	9.4	9.3	9.5	9.2
September	8.8	8.8	8.8	8.3	8.4
October	8.5	8.2	7.9	8.3	8.4
November	7.4	7.4	7.6	7.9	7.5
December	6.9	6.7	7.1	7.2	6.8

Rate

As stated in the UCR Program, the victims of rape are always female. In 2000, an estimated 62.7 of every 100,000 females in the country were victims of rape. The 2000 rate for forcible rape decreased 1.6 percent compared to the previous year's figures and declined 11.3 percent compared to the rates for 1996.

For 2000, cities outside metropolitan areas recorded the highest rate for rape in the Nation, 69.0 per 100,000 females. This figure represents a 3.0-percent increase in the rate of rape in these types of communities from the 1999 rate. Metropolitan Statistical Areas recorded a rate of 65.0 rapes per 100,000 females. This number represents a 28.6-percent decrease in the rate of rape from the 1991 rate, when there were 91 forcible rapes for every 100,000 females. Rural counties reported a rate of 43.4 rapes per 100,000 females, a rate that is 6.5 percent lower than in 1991.

Of the four regions, the rate of 68.4 rapes per 100,000 females reported by the Midwestern States was the highest. Rates of 66.9 in the Southern States, 66.5 in the Western States, and 43.5 in the Northeastern States followed. Two of the four regions experienced rate declines when compared to the 1999 figures. Rates in the South fell 4.3 percent and in the Northeast 2.3 percent. The rate of female forcible rape increased 1.5 percent in the West, and the rate in the Midwest showed no change from 1999.

Over the past decade, all four regions have experienced declines in the rate of female forcible rape. The West showed a 26.4-percent decrease when compared with 1991 figures. The Northeast experienced a decrease of 24.6 percent. A decline of 23.9 percent was recorded for the South, and a 23.6-percent decline was computed for the Midwest.

Nature

Rapes by force accounted for 89.5 percent of rapes reported in 2000. The remaining 10.5 percent were accounted for by attempts or assaults to commit forcible rape. Compared to 1999, the volume of rapes by force in 2000 increased 1.8 percent. A 5.0-percent decrease in attempts to rape was noted nationwide.

Law Enforcement Response

Overall, law enforcement cleared 46.9 percent of reported forcible rapes in 2000. The highest clearance rate for forcible rapes was reported by rural counties, 52.4 percent. Rapes occurring in suburban counties were cleared at a rate of 47.4 percent. In the Nation's cities, forcible rape had a clearance rate of 46.2 percent. Law enforcement in cities of 250,000 and over in population cleared 48.6 percent, and those with populations of less than 10,000 recorded a clearance rate of 49.1 percent.

Regionally, 2000 forcible rape clearance rates were 51.1 percent in the Northeast, 49.2 percent in the South, 43.9 percent in the West, and 43.6 percent in the Midwest.

Juveniles (persons under 18 years of age) were involved in 12.1 percent of the total clearances for forcible rape nationwide. The percentage of juvenile involvement varied by community type. In the Nation's cities collectively, juveniles were involved in 11.8 percent of clearances. Clearances in cities having populations of 25,000 to 49,999 revealed the highest level of juvenile involvement, 16.0 percent. In rural counties, 15.0 percent of clearances involved juveniles. Suburban counties reported juvenile clearance rates of 12.1 percent.

In 2000, law enforcement across the country arrested an estimated 27,469 persons for forcible rape. Of those arrested, 45.4 percent were under age 25 and 63.7 percent were white.

Compared to figures from 1999, a 3.6-percent decrease in the national arrest total for forcible rape was recorded in 2000. Arrests for forcible rape in suburban and rural counties increased 2.4 percent and 2.1 percent, respectively. A 5.5-percent decrease in arrests was recorded in the Nation's cities collectively.

ROBBERY

DEFINITION

Robbery is the taking or attempting to take anything of value from the care, custody, or control of a person or persons by force or threat of force or violence and/or by putting the victim in fear.

Year	Number of offenses	Rate per 1000,000 inhabitants
1999	409,371	150.1
2000	407,842	144.9
Percent change	–0.4	–3.5

The 2000 estimated national total of 407,842 robberies is 0.4 percent lower than the 1999 figure, and it is the lowest estimate in 27 years. Collectively, cities across the Nation also experienced a 0.4-percent decline in the numbers of robberies. The largest drop, 2.9 percent, was seen in the Nation's largest cities, those with more than 1 million inhabitants. Suburban counties registered a decline of 2.3 percent. On the other hand, the Nation's smallest cities, those with fewer than 10,000 population, saw a 3.1-percent increase in robberies. Rural counties recorded a 3.2-percent increase, and cities with populations in the range of 10,000–49,999 experienced a 2-percent increase.

In the Nation's regions, 37.4 percent of the estimated robberies occurred in the most heavily populated Southern Region. The Western, Northeastern, and Midwestern Regions recorded

22.0 percent, 20.5 percent, and 20.0 percent, respectively. In comparing the 2000 robbery figures against those for 1999, the volume fell by 5.0 percent in the Northeast; all other regions experienced slight increases. The South noted an increase of 1.2 percent; the West, 0.9 percent; and the Midwest, 0.3 percent.

A review of the 5- and 10-year trends indicate that the robbery volume fell 23.9 percent compared to 1996 totals and 40.7 percent from the 1991 level. Robbery rates for 1996–2000 steadily declined as well.

The highest number of robberies during the year 2000 occurred in October and the lowest number occurred in February.

Robbery by Month
Percent distribution, 1996–2000

Month	1996	1997	1998	1999	2000
January	9.2	9.2	9.5	8.9	8.6
February	8.0	7.6	7.5	7.3	7.1
March	8.1	7.9	8.0	7.7	7.7
April	7.5	7.6	7.6	7.6	7.6
May	7.9	8.2	7.9	8.1	8.1
June	7.9	8.0	7.7	8.1	7.9
July	8.5	8.6	8.5	8.7	8.7
August	8.6	8.8	8.7	8.8	8.9
September	8.2	8.5	8.5	8.3	8.5
October	8.6	8.8	9.0	8.8	9.1
November	8.4	8.2	8.3	8.6	8.7
December	9.1	8.6	8.8	9.2	9.0

Rate

Nationally, there were 144.9 robberies for every 100,000 persons in 2000, a rate that was 3.5 percent lower than the rate for 1999. By population groups, metropolitan areas recorded a robbery rate of 173.0 per 100,000 inhabitants; cities outside metropolitan areas, 59.9; and rural areas, 15.9. The Nation's cities collectively experienced 212.8 robberies per 100,000 inhabitants. The rate at which robberies occurred in the Nation's 8 cities with over 1 million in population, 440.2 per 100,000, was the highest robbery rate calculated. Cities with populations over 250,000 had a rate of 413.4 per 100,000 inhabitants. Robbery rates computed for suburban and rural counties were 67.6 and 15.5 per 100,000 inhabitants, respectively.

Regionally, the highest robbery rate was noted by the Northeast at 156.0 per 100,000 population. The South had a rate of 152.3, the West a rate of 142.3, and the Midwest a rate of 126.8. For 2000, the rates declined 8.2 percent in the Northeast, 2.6 percent in the South, 2.4 percent in the West, and 1.5 percent in the Midwest from 1999 figures.

Nature

During 2000, robbers stole more than $477 million from their victims. The average dollar loss, $1,170, was an increase from the $1,077 average calculated for 1999. Monetary losses ranged from an average of $544 taken during robberies of convenience stores to $4,437, the average amount stolen during bank robberies. The crime of robbery, which involves the taking of money or other valuables by the use of force or the threat of force, is classified by the Uniform Crime Reporting Program as a crime of violence. The victims of robberies often suffer personal injuries, the impact of

which may be immeasurable. Computing the dollar losses, however, does offer a means by which to measure one of the impacts of this violent crime.

Robberies of financial establishments and commercial businesses, accounting for 25.3 percent of total robberies, increased 0.3 percent over the 1999 figure. However, robberies on streets and highways, which made up 49 percent of all robberies in 1999, accounted for only 46 percent of the total offenses in 2000, a decline of 3.6 percent. Robberies of residences remained relatively unchanged from 1999 figures at 12.2 percent of all robberies.

Robbery
Percent distribution by region, 2000

Type	United States Total	North-eastern States	Mid-western States	Southern States	Western States
Total[1]	100.0	100.0	100.0	100.0	100.0
Street/highway	46.0	59.0	51.0	40.3	43.7
Commercial house	13.9	8.5	11.1	14.7	17.4
Gas or service station	2.9	2.5	3.5	2.6	2.8
Convenience store	6.4	6.3	4.4	7.7	5.9
Residence	12.2	9.7	9.7	16.2	9.2
Bank	2.1	2.1	2.0	1.8	2.8
Miscellaneous	16.5	11.9	18.4	16.7	18.3

[1] Because of rounding, the percentages may not add to total.

Offenders in 2000 relied almost equally upon firearms (40.9 percent) and strong-armed tactics (40.4 percent) to rob their victims. Other dangerous weapons were used in 10.3 percent and knives or cutting instruments in 8.4 percent of robberies. A comparison of 1999 and 2000 figures indicates that the use of other dangerous weapons in robberies increased 3.3 percent and the use of firearms increased 2.7 percent.

Law Enforcement Response

The national clearance rate for robbery was 25.7 percent in 2000. Law enforcement agencies in rural counties reported the highest clearance rate for robbery at 36.5 percent. A robbery clearance rate of 25.1 percent was registered for all cities collectively. Law enforcement agencies in suburban counties cleared 29.6 percent of robberies.

Regional robbery clearances were 29.4 percent in the Northeast, 26.1 percent in the South, 25.5 percent in the West, and 21.5 percvent in the Midwest.

Juvenile offenders (those under the age of 18) were involved in 15.5 percent of all robbery clearances in 2000. By community type, this age group accounted for 16.5 percent of the robbery clearances in suburban counties, 15.5 percent in the Nation's cities overall, and 10.2 percent in rural counties. The greatest percentage of juvenile involvement for robbery occurred iin cities with populations of 50,000 to 99,999, where juveniles totaled 18.4 percent of robbery clearances.

There were 2.5 percent fewer robbery arrests during the year 2000 than during the previous year. Arrests of juveniles fell 4.6 percent, and arrests of adults were down 1.8 percent from the 1999 figures. Declines were noted in both male and female arrests; male arrests declined 2.5 percent and female arrests dropped 2.6 percent. By community type, rural counties registered a 1.5-percent increase in the number of arrests for robbery, while suburban counties recorded a slight (0.8 percent) decrease. Collectively, cities reported a 2.8-percent decrease.

The 5-year trend in robbery arrests nationally indicates a 23.0-percent decrease when comparing 2000 to 1996 figures. The 10-year trend reveals a 31.4-percent decrease when comparing robbery arrests for the current year and those for 1991.

Of those arrested for robbery in 2000, 62.9 percent were under 25 years of age. By gender, males accounted for 89.9 percent of arrestees. By race, blacks comprised 53.9 percent of robbery arrestees, whites 44.2 percent, and all other races accounted for the remainder.

AGGRAVATED ASSAULT

DEFINITION

Aggravated assault is an unlawful attack by one person upon another for the purpose of inflicting severe or aggravated bodily injury. This type of assault is usually accompanied by the use of a weapon or by means likely to produce death or great bodily harm.

Year	Number of offenses	Rate per 1000,000 inhabitants
1999	911,740	334.3
2000	910,744	323.6
Percent change	–0.1	–3.2

Reported aggravated assault figures showed a slight decline from the preceding year's figures. The 2000 estimated total of 910,744 aggravated assaults represented a 0.1-percent decrease from 1999 data for this offense. Aggravated assault comprised 63.9 percent of all the violent crimes in 2000.

Among the Nation's regions, the Midwest had a 2.1-percent decline in reported aggravated assaults and the Northeast a 0.5-percent decrease. Aggravated assault volumes rose 0.9 percent in the West and 0.4 percent in the Southern Region. The geographic distribution among the regions in 2000 shows that the most populous Southern Region had 42.6 percent of the aggravated assault volume. The Western Region followed with 23.6 percent, the Midwestern Region with 18.4 percent, and the Northeastern Region with 15.4 percent.

The highest number of aggravated assaults, according to 2000 monthly distribution figures, took place in May, with 9.3 percent of the total reported. The fewest incidents occurred in February, November, and December, with 7.5 percent of the total distribution recorded for each of those months.

Aggravated Assault by Month
Percent distribution, 1996–2000

Month	1996	1997	1998	1999	2000
January	7.8	7.5	7.9	7.9	7.6
February	7.4	7.0	7.0	7.0	7.5
March	8.0	8.3	8.1	8.0	8.5
April	8.1	8.2	8.1	8.3	8.4
May	8.9	9.3	9.1	9.1	9.3
June	9.1	9.0	8.9	8.8	8.6
July	9.4	9.5	9.4	9.5	9.0
August	9.3	9.4	9.4	9.2	8.8
September	8.6	8.8	8.7	8.5	8.6
October	8.5	8.4	8.3	8.6	8.7
November	7.4	7.5	7.4	7.7	7.5
December	7.6	7.2	7.4	7.5	7.5

Rate

Nationwide during 2000, there were 323.6 victims of aggravated assault per 100,000 inhabitants. The rate was 3.2 percent lower than in 1999 and represented a 17.2 percent drop from the 1996 rate. The 2000 rate was down 25.3 percent from the 1991 rate.

Aggravated assaults occurred in metropolitan areas at a rate of 349.2 per 100,000 inhabitants, somewhat higher than the national average. Cities outside metropolitan areas experienced a rate of 302.5 and rural counties a rate of 167.8.

Compared to the preceding year's rate, aggravated assault rates during 2000 were down in all regions. The aggravated assault rate was 387.3 per 100,000 people in the South, 339.5 in the West, 261.2 in the Northeast, and 260.9 in the Midwest. The Northeast and Midwest each registered a 3.8-percent drop; the South decreased by 3.4 percent; and the West experienced a 2.3-percent decline.

Nature

Blunt objects or other dangerous weapons accounted for 35.9 percent of the weapons used in aggravated assaults in 2000. Personal weapons such as hands, fists, feet, etc., were used in 28.0 percent of all aggravated assaults. Firearms were used in 18.1 percent of aggravated assaults, and knives or cutting instruments were employed in 18.0 percent.

Aggravated Assault, Types of Weapons Used
Percent distribution by region, 2000

Region	Total all weapons[1]	Firearms	Knives or cutting instruments	Other weapons (clubs, blunt objects, etc.)	Personal weapons
Total	100.0	18.1	18.0	35.8	28.1
Northeastern States	100.0	13.5	17.7	32.9	35.8
Midwestern States	100.0	19.9	18.3	35.5	26.3
Southern States	100.0	19.7	19.9	39.0	21.4
Western States	100.0	16.4	14.9	32.1	36.7

[1] Because of rounding, the percentages may not add to total.

Aggravated assaults using firearms decreased 1.3 percent from 1999 to 2000 figures. Aggravated assaults with knives or cutting instruments and those with personal weapons showed virtually no change. However, those committed with blunt instruments or other dangerous weapons increased 1.7 percent.

Law Enforcement Response

Law enforcement agencies nationwide recorded a 56.9-percent aggravated assault clearance rate during 2000. Rural and suburban county law enforcement agencies cleared 64.0 and 60.6 percent, respectively, and cities collectively recorded 55.4 percent cleared. Among the city groupings, those with populations under 10,000 recorded the highest aggravated assault clearance rate at 66.1 percent.

Regional aggravated assault clearances were highest in the Northeast at 63.9 percent. The West recorded a clearance rate of 57.2 percent, followed by the South at 55.9 percent and the Midwest at 53.5 percent.

Law enforcement personnel identified juveniles, persons under age 18, to be the assailants in 11.7 percent of the aggravated assaults cleared nationally. Persons in this age group were involved in 11.8 percent of these clearances in the Nation's cities and 11.9 percent of aggravated assault clearances in suburban counties. In rural counties, law enforcement cleared 9.8 percent of aggravated assaults committed by juveniles.

Arrests for aggravated assaults represented 76.2 percent of violent crime arrests in 2000. By race, 63.5 percent of the estimated 478,417 persons arrested were white, 34.0 percent were black, and other races comprised the remainder. Persons under the age of 25 were the offenders in 39.9 percent of aggravated assault arrests. The majority of aggravated assault offenders, 79.9 percent, were male.

Arrests for aggravated assaults were down 0.9 percent in 2000 from the preceding year's totals. Arrests were also down 0.3 and 4.2 percent for adults and juveniles, respectively. The 5-year trend comparing 1996 to 2000 shows a decrease of 7.2 percent for total aggravated assault arrests. Adult arrest totals were also down 6.1 percent when compared to 1996 figures, and juvenile aggravated assault arrests decreased 13.7 percent.

BURGLARY

DEFINITION

The Uniform Crime Reporting Program defines burglary as the unlawful entry of a structure to commit a felony or theft. The use of force to gain entry is not required to classify an offense as burglary. Burglary in this Program is categorized into three subclassifications: forcible entry, unlawful entry where no force is used, and attempted forcible entry.

Year	Number of offenses	Rate per 1000,000 inhabitants
1999	2,100,739	770.4
2000	2,049,946	728.4
Percent change	−2.4	−5.4

For the ninth straight year, the estimated number of burglary offenses declined; the estimated 2,049,946 offenses nationwide represents the lowest measure since 1969. The Southern States, the Nation's most populous region, recorded the highest burglary volume, 44.2 percent. The Western States followed with 22.5 percent of the Nation's burglaries, the Midwestern States with 20.8 percent, and the Northeastern States with 12.5 percent.

Burglary by Month
Percent distribution, 1996–2000

Month	1996	1997	1998	1999	2000
January	8.3	8.4	8.9	8.3	8.2
February	7.6	7.2	7.5	7.2	7.3
March	7.8	7.9	8.2	7.9	8.0
April	7.8	7.8	8.0	7.7	7.8
May	8.3	8.3	8.3	8.2	8.6
June	8.1	8.2	8.2	8.4	8.4
July	9.1	9.1	9.0	9.0	9.2
August	8.9	9.0	9.0	9.1	9.2
September	8.6	8.7	8.4	8.7	8.5
October	8.8	8.8	8.4	8.6	8.7
November	8.0	8.2	7.9	8.4	8.2
December	8.6	8.6	8.2	8.5	8.0

Monthly figures for 2000 revealed that the greatest number of burglaries occurred in July and August, and the lowest volume was recorded during February.

Compared to the 1999 national volume, burglary declined 2.4 percent in 2000. By community type, suburban counties experienced the greatest decline, 4.6 percent. Meanwhile, rural counties showed a 0.9-percent decrease in burglary volumes between 1999 and 2000. Collectively, the Nation's cities showed a decline of 2.2 percent in burglary volume. By city group, cities with populations of 100,000 to 499,999 showed the greatest decrease, down 3.2 percent.

In 2000, decreases from the previous year's burglary volumes were recorded in all four regions of the United States. The greatest decrease, 5.1 percent, was registered in the Northeastern States. The Midwestern States reported a 3.5-percent decline, and the Southern and Western States recorded burglary volumes decreases of 2.2 and 0.2 percent, respectively.

National 5- and 10-year trends indicate burglary was down 18.2 percent from the 1996 level and has dropped 35.1 percent when compared to the 1991 volume.

Rate

National offense rates for burglary in 2000—728.4 offenses per 100,000 inhabitants—were the lowest in more than three decades. The rate was 5.4 percent lower than the 1999 rate, 22.9 percent below the 1996 rate, and had dropped 41.8 percent from the 1991 rate. In metropolitan areas, the burglary rate was reported at 754.9 offenses for every 100,000 in population; cities outside metropolitan areas recorded a rate of 759.2; and rural counties showed a rate of 532.3 per 100,000 inhabitants.

Among the Nation's four regions, the Southern States experienced the highest burglary rate, 903.0 offenses per 100,000 inhabitants. The Western States reported a rate of 730.3, and the Midwestern States registered a rate of 663.7. The lowest rate, 477.4, was recorded in the Northeastern States. All regions indicated declines in burglary rates compared to the previous year's numbers. The Northeastern Region recorded the greatest decline at 8.2 percent. The Southern and Midwestern Regions showed decreases of 5.9 percent and 5.2 percent, respectively, and the Western Region reported a decrease of 3.4 percent.

Nature

When considering distribution by type of burglary, forcible entry was involved in 63.7 percent of all burglaries in 2000, unlawful entries (without force) made up 29.5 percent of all burglaries, and the remaining 6.8 percent were forcible entry attempts. In 2000, 2 of every 3 burglaries were residential in nature. Offenses for which time of occurrence was reported showed that burglaries occurred more commonly during the daytime, 54.5 percent, than at night, 45.5 percent. Burglaries of residences occurred more frequently during the daytime, 60.7 percent, and burglaries of nonresidences occurred more frequently at night, 57.7 percent.

Victims experienced an estimated loss of nearly $3 billion in 2000. The average dollar loss per burglary was $1,462. For residential offenses, the average loss was reported at $1,381 and for nonresidential burglaries at $1,615.

Residential burglary volumes declined in 2000, down 3.9 percent from 1999 figures, and nonresidential burglary volumes increased 0.3 percent over the previous year's numbers.

Law Enforcement Response

A clearance rate of 13.4 percent was recorded for burglary offenses known to law enforcement in 2000. By region, the Northeast had a clearance rate of 16.8 percent; the South, 13.7 percent; the West, 12.3 percent; and the Midwest, 11.6 percent.

Law enforcement agencies in rural counties cleared 17.0 percent of the burglaries reported in their jurisdictions and suburban county law enforcement agencies cleared 14.0 percent. Cities as a whole cleared 12.8 percent. Cities with populations of less than 10,000 cleared the greatest percentage of burglaries among city types, 16.8. Those cities with populations over 250,000 had the lowest burglary clearance rate, 11.1.

Adult offenders were involved in the highest percentage of burglary clearances, 80.8 percent. Juvenile offenders (people under 18 years of age) were involved in the remaining 19.2 percent of clearances. The highest measure of juvenile clearances occurred in the Nation's smallest cities (under 10,000 in population) with 24.8 percent. Juveniles made up 20.8 percent of the burglary clearances in suburban counties. In both cities as a whole and rural counties, juveniles comprised 19 percent of clearances.

In the UCR Program, several persons may be arrested in connection with the clearance of one crime, or the arrest of one individual may clear numerous offenses. The latter is often true in cases of burglary, for which an estimated 289,844 arrests were made in 2000.

Total burglary arrests were down 3.4 percent from 1999. Arrests of juveniles and adults declined by 5.0 and 2.6 percent, respectively. Burglary arrests in the Nation's cities overall fell 4.6 percent for the same timeframe. In rural counties, burglary arrests declined slightly, 0.5 percent, and arrests for the same offense in suburban counties were up 0.4 percent.

Males comprised the greatest number of arrestees for burglary, at 86.7 percent of the total, in 2000. The majority of arrestees were persons under the age of 25, 63.8 percent. By race, whites accounted for 69.4 percent of all persons arrested for burglary, blacks for 28.4 percent, and other races for the remainder.

LARCENY-THEFT

DEFINITION

Larceny-theft is the unlawful taking, carrying, leading, or riding away of property from the possession or constructive possession of another. It includes crimes such as shoplifting, pocket-picking, purse-snatching, thefts from motor vehicles, thefts of motor vehicle parts and accessories, bicycle thefts, etc., in which no use of force, violence, or fraud occurs.

Year	Number of offenses	Rate per 1000,000 inhabitants
1999	6,955,520	2,500.7
2000	6,965,957	2,475.3
Percent change	+0.2	–3.0

Estimated at nearly 7 million offenses in 2000, larceny-theft made up 60 percent of the Crime Index total and 68.4 percent of the property crime total. Larceny-thefts occurred most often in August and least often in February.

Remaining relatively unchanged, larceny-thefts nationwide registered a slight increase, up 0.2 percent in 2000 compared to the 1999 figure. Cities as a whole also remained nearly unchanged

Larceny-theft by Month
Percent distribution, 1996–2000

Month	1996	1997	1998	1999	2000
January	7.8	8.0	8.4	7.8	7.7
February	7.5	7.2	7.5	7.2	7.4
March	7.9	8.0	8.2	8.0	8.3
April	8.0	8.0	8.1	8.0	7.9
May	8.6	8.4	8.4	8.4	8.7
June	8.6	8.6	8.6	8.7	8.7
July	9.3	9.2	9.0	9.1	9.1
August	9.2	9.1	9.0	9.2	9.2
September	8.4	8.5	8.4	8.5	8.4
October	8.8	8.8	8.5	8.7	8.8
November	7.8	7.9	7.8	8.1	8.0
December	8.1	8.3	8.2	8.3	7.8

with a 0.1-percent increase in larceny-theft from 1999. Among city population groups, the Nation's smallest cities, those with populations of less than 50,000, rose by 1.0 percent. Among the county groupings, rural counties experienced an increase of 1.8 percent and suburban counties as a whole fell 1.7 percent.

The South, the Nation's most populous region, accounted for 40.9 percent of the larceny-theft total in 2000. The Midwest accounted for 22.9 percent of the total, the West recorded 22.2 percent, and the Northeast 14.0 percent.

Two of the Nation's four geographic regions recorded increases in larceny-theft in 2000. The Southern States reported a 0.6-percent increase, and the Western States a 0.2-percent increase. Midwestern States reported no change from the previous year, and the Northeastern States reported a 0.9-percent decline in larceny-thefts.

Despite the similarity of the larceny-theft total when compared to the previous year's total, an examination of the long-term national trends indicated a decline in larceny-theft. The 2000 larceny-theft total shows an 11.9-percent drop when compared to 1996 figures and a 14.4-percent decrease when compared to figures from 1991.

Rate

The 2000 larceny-theft rate of 2,475.3 per 100,000 population represented a 3.0-percent drop when compared to the previous year's data. The rate fell 16.9 percent below 1996 figures and was 23.3 percent lower than the 1991 rate. Rates for community types in the Nation revealed 3,125.1 reports of larceny-theft per 100,000 inhabitants in cities outside metropolitan areas, 2,631.9 for metropolitan areas, and 999.7 in rural counties.

All four geographic regions reported declines in the 2000 larceny-theft rate per 100,000 inhabitants. The Northeast showed a 4.2-percent drop, the South and West decreased 3.2 and 3.1 percent, respectively, and the Midwest reported a 1.8-percent decline. As for larceny-theft rates in 2000, the South reported a rate of 2,842.7 larceny-thefts per 100,000 population. The Midwest registered a rate of 2,475.1, the West experienced a rate of 2,447.1, and the Northeast recorded 1,821.4 larceny-thefts per 100,000 inhabitants.

Nature

In 2000, the average value of property stolen as a result of larceny-theft was $735, down from the 1999 value of $913. The aggregate loss to victims, when applying the average value to the estimated number of larceny-thefts nationally, was over $5.1 billion for the year. This estimated dollar loss is considered conservative since many offenses in the larceny category never come to the attention of law enforcement, particularly if the value of the stolen goods is small. Losses over $200 accounted for 38.9 percent of reported larceny-thefts, and losses under $50 comprised 37.7 percent. The remaining 23.4 percent involved losses ranging from $50 to $200.

By type of larceny-theft, losses of goods and property reported stolen as a result of thefts from buildings averaged $1,176; thefts from motor vehicles had an average loss of $712; and thefts from coin-operated machines, averaged $500. Thefts of motor vehicle accessories averaged a loss of $445; pocket-picking resulted in an average loss of $408; and purse-snatching, $356. Thefts of bicycles resulted in an average loss of $276 and losses from shoplifting averaged $181.

Larceny-theft
Percent distribution by region, 2000

Type	United States Total	North-eastern States	Midwest-ern States	Southern States	Western States
Total[1]	100.0	100.0	100.0	100.0	100.0
Pocket-picking	0.5	0.9	0.4	0.4	0.5
Purse-snatching	0.5	1.1	0.5	0.4	0.5
Shoplifting	13.8	15.0	12.4	12.8	15.6
From motor vehicles (except accessories)	25.2	21.9	23.6	23.9	30.1
Motor vehicle accessories	9.7	7.7	10.3	10.0	10.1
Bicycles	4.5	5.5	5.0	3.6	4.9
From buildings	13.1	16.2	15.3	10.9	13.2
From coin-operated machines	0.7	0.6	0.6	0.7	0.7
All others	32.0	31.2	32.1	37.2	24.3

[1] Because of rounding, the percentages may not add to total.

Thefts of motor vehicle parts, accessories, and contents accounted for the largest segment of larceny-theft, 34.9 percent. Shoplifting made up 13.8 percent of larceny-thefts, and thefts from buildings, 13.1 percent. The remainder of larceny-thefts were attributed to pocket-picking, purse-snatching, bicycle thefts, thefts from coin-operated machines, and all other types of larceny-thefts.

Law Enforcement Response

The national clearance rate for larceny-theft offenses in 2000 was 18.2 percent. Cities with populations from 10,000 to 24,999 recorded the highest clearance rate, 22.9 percent. The Nation's cities collectively cleared 18.5 percent of larceny-thefts, and rural counties reported an 18.4-percent clearance rate. Suburban counties had a 16.8-percent clearance rate.

Law enforcement agencies in the Northeast cleared 21.6 percent of reported larceny-theft offenses in 2000. Agencies in the Midwest cleared 17.9 percent; the South, 17.8 percent; and the West, 17.4 percent.

Larceny-theft clearances involving juveniles (person under age 18), both nationally and in the Nation's cities were measured at 23.0 and 23.5 percent, respectively. Juveniles comprised 21.6 percent of larceny-theft clearances in suburban counties, and 16.8

percent in rural counties. Cities with populations of 50,000 to 99,999 inhabitants showed the greatest juvenile involvement in larceny-theft, 26.5 percent.

The number of persons arrested for larceny-theft in 2000 fell 5.5 percent in comparison to 1999 data. Arrests of males and females decreased 6.6 percent and 3.4 percent, respectively. Arrests of juveniles dropped 5.6 percent during this same period, and arrests of adults declined 5.4 percent.

A comparison of 1996 and 2000 data, revealed that larceny-theft arrests have declined 21.2 percent. The number of adult arrests dropped 18.3 percent in this 5-year period, and arrests of persons under the age of 18 fell 26.9 percent. Arrests of males were 23.6 percent lower in 2000 than in 1999, and arrests of females were down 16.5 percent.

Of the arrests for all Crime Index offenses reported to law enforcement in 2000, larceny-theft accounted for 52.3 percent. Larceny-theft comprised 72.4 percent of all arrests for property crimes. Of those individuals arrested for larceny-theft, 46.5 percent were persons under 21 years of age, and 31.2 percent of the arrestees were under 18. Females were arrested more often for this offense than for any other and made up 35.9 percent of larceny-theft arrestees.

Of the total number of persons arrested for larceny-theft offenses, 66.7 percent were white, 30.4 percent were black, and the remaining 2.9 percent were of all other races.

MOTOR VEHICLE THEFT

DEFINITION

Defined as the theft or attempted theft of a motor vehicle, this offense category includes the stealing of automobiles, trucks, buses, motorcycles, motorscooters, snowmobiles, etc. The definition excludes the taking of a motor vehicle for temporary use by those persons having lawful access.

Year	Number of offenses	Rate per 1000,000 inhabitants
1999	1,152,075	422.5
2000	1,165,559	414.2
Percent change	+1.2	−2.0

For the first time since 1990, the number of motor vehicle thefts reported in the United States increased from the previous year's figures as the volume of thefts in 2000 showed a 1.2-percent increase over 1999 totals. Of the nearly 1.2 million estimated thefts of motor vehicles, the Western States recorded the largest increase at 7.1 percent. Motor vehicle thefts increased in Midwestern States by 0.9 percent. The Northeastern States reported the largest decrease of motor vehicle theft with a 2.9-percent decline. In the Southern States, motor vehicle thefts were down 1.3 percent.

The 2000 figures show that the greatest number of motor vehicle thefts was recorded during the month of August and the fewest thefts occurred in February.

Collectively, the Nation's cities had a 1.4-percent increase in motor vehicle theft. Among city population groupings, those with populations of 100,000 to 249,999 experienced a 4.1-percent rise in motor vehicle theft and those with populations of 250,000 to 499,999 had a similar increase of 4.0 percent. Suburban counties experienced a 2.9-percent increase, and rural counties recorded a 1.6-percent rise in motor vehicle thefts from 1999 figures.

Looking at the 5- and 10-year trends, the volume of motor vehicle thefts in 2000 was down 16.4 percent from the 1996 figure and fell 29.9 percent from the 1991 figure.

Motor Vehicle Theft by Month
Percent distribution, 1996–2000

Month	1996	1997	1998	1999	2000
January	8.8	9.0	9.1	8.5	8.2
February	8.0	7.6	7.9	7.3	7.5
March	8.2	8.2	8.5	7.9	8.0
April	7.9	7.9	7.9	7.7	7.6
May	8.1	8.2	8.3	8.0	8.2
June	8.0	8.1	8.1	8.2	8.3
July	8.8	8.7	8.7	8.8	8.9
August	8.6	8.7	8.8	9.0	9.1
September	8.2	8.3	8.3	8.5	8.5
October	8.6	8.6	8.4	8.8	8.7
November	8.3	8.2	7.9	8.5	8.5
December	8.6	8.3	8.1	8.8	8.6

Rate

In 2000, the national rate of 414.2 motor vehicle thefts per 100,000 inhabitants recorded for the year was 2.0 percent lower than the previous year's rate. The 2000 rate is 21.2 percent lower than the 1996 rate, and 37.2 percent below the 1991 rate.

For every 100,000 inhabitants living in metropolitan areas, 479.9 motor vehicle thefts were reported in 2000. The Nation's most heavily populated municipalities, cities with populations over 250,000, experienced the highest rate of motor vehicle theft during the year—929.1 for every 100,000 inhabitants, and the Nation's smallest cities, those with fewer than 10,000 inhabitants, recorded a rate of 217.3 per 100,000. In cities outside metropolitan areas, 199.2 motor vehicle thefts were reported per 100,000 in population. In rural counties, 122.3 motor vehicle thefts were recorded per 100,000 inhabitants.

Regionally, the highest motor vehicle theft rate was recorded in the Western States at 524.1 per 100,000 people. The Southern States reported a rate of 417.1; the Midwestern States, a rate of 378.3; and the Northeastern States, a rate of 322.1 per 100,000 inhabitants. Three regions registered declines in 2000 compared to 1999 data. The Northeast reported a 6.1-percent decrease, the South a drop of 5.0 percent, and the Midwest a decline of 0.9 percent. The West's rate of motor vehicle thefts per 100,000 in population increased 3.6 percent.

Nature

The value of motor vehicles stolen in the Nation during 2000 was estimated at nearly $7.8 billion. At the time of theft, the average value per vehicle was $6,682. The recovery rate for the value of vehicles stolen was higher than for any other property type.

Of all motor vehicles reported stolen during the year, 74.5 percent were automobiles, 18.7 percent were trucks or buses, and the remainder were other types of vehicles.

Motor Vehicle Theft
Percent distribution by region, 2000

Race Region	Total[1]	Autos	Trucks and buses	Other vehicles
Total	100.0	74.5	18.7	6.8
Northeastern States	100.0	88.2	6.2	5.6
Midwestern States	100.0	80.0	13.7	6.3
Southern States	100.0	71.8	20.1	8.1
Western States	100.0	69.7	24.2	6.1

[1] Because of rounding, the percentages may not add to total.

Law Enforcement Response

Law enforcement agencies across the Nation reported a 14.1-percent motor vehicle theft clearance rate in 2000. Motor vehicle theft clearance rates in the Nation's cities overall ranged from a 27.7-percent clearance rate in cities with less than 10,000 inhabitants to 9.9 percent in cities with populations of 1 million and over. Law enforcement agencies in rural counties reported a 29.3-percent clearance rate, and those in suburban counties reported a 15.8-percent clearance rate.

Regionally, the Southern States had a motor vehicle theft clearance rate of 15.9 percent and Midwestern States recorded 15.6 percent. The Northeastern and the Western States experienced 13.7- and 11.4-percent clearance rates, respectively.

Nationally, persons in the under-18 age group were involved in 19.8 percent of the motor vehicle thefts cleared. This group also comprised 19.9 percent of those cleared in cities collectively, 19.6 percent of those cleared in suburban counties, and 19.4 percent of the motor vehicle thefts cleared in rural counties.

Persons under the age of 25 made up the largest percentage of persons arrested for motor vehicle theft, 66.5. Arrestees under the age of 18 accounted for 34.3 percent of the total in 2000, although arrests of persons under age 18 were down 2.6 percent from 1999. Juvenile female and male arrests decreased, 1.2 percent and 2.8 percent, respectively.

Adults comprised 65.7 percent of all motor vehicle theft arrestees. The number of adults arrested in 2000 increased 3.3 percent from the previous year's figures.

Males accounted for 84.2 percent of the estimated 148,225 arrestees for motor vehicle theft in 2000. By race, 55.4 percent of the arrestees were white, 41.6 percent were black, and the remainder were of other races.

In 2000, total motor vehicle theft arrests were up 1.2 percent from the 1999 numbers. The 2000 arrest totals were 18.5 percent below the 1996 level and 35.2 percent lower than the 1991 figure.

Glossary

A

Abet To encourage another to commit a crime.

Accessory One who harbors, assists, or protects another person, although he or she knows that person has committed or will commit a crime.

Accomplice One who knowingly and voluntarily aids another in committing a criminal offense.

Acquit To free a person legally from an accusation of criminal guilt.

Adjudicatory hearing The fact-finding process wherein the court determines whether or not there is sufficient evidence to sustain the allegations in a petition.

Administrative law Regulates many daily business activities, and violations of such regulations generally result in warnings or fines, depending upon their adjudged severity.

Admissible Capable of being admitted; in a trial, such evidence as the judge allows to be introduced into the proceeding.

Affirmance A pronouncement by a higher court that the case in question was rightly decided by the lower court from which the case was appealed.

Affirmation Positive declaration or assertion that the witness will tell the truth; not made under oath.

Aggravated assault The unlawful attack by one person upon another for the purpose of inflicting severe or aggravated bodily injury.

Alias Any name by which one is known other than his or her true name.

Alibi A type of defense in a criminal prosecution that proves the accused could not have committed the crime with which he or she is charged, since evidence offered shows the accused was in another place at the time the crime was committed.

Allegation An assertion of what a party to an action expects to prove.

American Bar Association (ABA) A professional association, comprising attorneys who have been admitted to the bar in any of the 50 states, and a registered lobby.

American Civil Liberties Union (ACLU) Founded in 1920 with the purpose of defending the individual's rights as guaranteed by the U.S. Constitution.

Amnesty A class or group pardon.

Annulment The act, by competent authority, of canceling, making void, or depriving of all force.

Antisocial personality disorder Refers to individuals who are basically unsocialized and whose behavior pattern brings them repeatedly into conflict with society.

Appeal A case carried to a higher court to ask that the decision of the lower court, in which the case originated, be altered or overruled completely.

Appellate court A court that has jurisdiction to hear cases on appeal; not a trial court.

Arbitrator The person chosen by parties in a controversy to settle their differences; private judges.

Arraignment The appearance before the court of a person charged with a crime. He or she is advised of the charges, bail is set, and a plea of "guilty" or "not guilty" is entered.

Arrest The legal detainment of a person to answer for criminal charges or civil demands.

Autopsy A postmortem examination of a human body to determine the cause of death.

B

Bail Property (usually money) deposited with a court in exchange for the release of a person in custody to ensure later appearance.

Bail bond An obligation signed by the accused and his or her sureties that ensures his or her presence in court.

Bailiff An officer of the court who is responsible for keeping order in the court and protecting the security of jury deliberations and court property.

Behavior theory An approach to understanding human activity that holds that behavior is determined by consequences it produces for the individual.

Bench warrant An order by the court for the apprehension and arrest of a defendant or other person who has failed to appear when so ordered.

Bill of Rights The first 10 amendments to the U.S. Constitution that state certain fundamental rights and privileges that are guaranteed to the people against infringement by the government.

Biocriminology A relatively new branch of criminology that attempts to explain criminal behavior by referring to biological factors which predispose some individuals to commit criminal acts. *See also Criminal biology.*

Blue laws Laws in some jurisdictions prohibiting sales of merchandise, athletic contests, and the sale of alcoholic beverages on Sundays.

Booking A law-enforcement or correctional process officially recording an entry-into-detention after arrest and identifying the person, place, time, reason for the arrest, and the arresting authority.

Breathalizer A commercial device to test the breath of a suspected drinker and to determine that person's blood-alcohol content.

Brief A summary of the law relating to a case, prepared by the attorneys for both parties and given to the judge.

Burden of proof Duty of establishing the existence of fact in a trial.

C

Calendar A list of cases to be heard in a trial court, on a specific day, and containing the title of the case, the lawyers involved, and the index number.

Capital crime Any crime that may be punishable by death or imprisonment for life.

Capital punishment The legal imposition of a sentence of death upon a convicted offender.

Glossary

Career criminal   A person having a past record of multiple arrests or convictions for crimes of varying degrees of seriousness. Such criminals are often described as chronic, habitual, repeat, serious, high-rate, or professional offenders.

Case   At the level of police or prosecutorial investigation, a set of circumstances under investigation involving one or more persons.

Case law   Judicial precedent generated as a by-product of the decisions that courts have made to resolve unique disputes. Case law concerns concrete facts, as distinguished from statutes and constitutions, which are written in the abstract.

Change of venue   The removal of a trial from one jurisdiction to another in order to avoid local prejudice.

Charge   In criminal law, the accusation made against a person. It also refers to the judge's instruction to the jury on legal points.

Circumstantial evidence   Indirect evidence; evidence from which a fact can be reasonably inferred, although not directly proven.

Civil law   That body of laws that regulates arrangements between individuals, such as contracts and claims to property.

Clemency   The doctrine under which executive or legislative action reduces the severity of or waives legal punishment of one or more individuals, or an individual exempted from prosecution for certain actions.

Code   A compilation, compendium, or revision of laws, arranged into chapters, having a table of contents and index, and promulgated by legislative authority. *See also Penal code.*

Coercion   The use of force to compel performance of an action; the application of sanctions or the use of force by government to compel observance of law or public policy.

Common law   Judge-made law to assist courts through decision making with traditions, customs, and usage of previous court decisions.

Commutation   A reduction of a sentence originally prescribed by a court.

Complainant   The victim of a crime who brings the facts to the attention of the authorities.

Complaint   Any accusation that a person committed a crime that has originated or been received by a law enforcement agency or court.

Confession   A statement by a person who admits violation of the law.

Confiscation   Government seizure of private property without compensation to the owner.

Conspiracy   An agreement between two or more persons to plan for the purpose of committing a crime or any unlawful act or a lawful act by unlawful or criminal means.

Contempt of court   Intentionally obstructing a court in the administration of justice, acting in a way calculated to lessen its authority or dignity, or failing to obey its lawful order.

Continuance   Postponement or adjournment of a trial granted by the judge, either to a later date or indefinitely.

Contraband   Goods, the possession of which is illegal.

Conviction   A finding by the jury (or by the trial judge in cases tried without a jury) that the accused is guilty of a crime.

Corporal punishment   Physical punishment.

Corpus delicti (Lat.)   The objective proof that a crime has been committed as distinguished from an accidental death, injury, or loss.

Corrections   Area of criminal justice dealing with convicted offenders in jails, prisons, on probation, or parole.

Corroborating evidence   Supplementary evidence that tends to strengthen or confirm other evidence given previously.

Crime   An act injurious to the public, which is prohibited and punishable by law.

Crime Index   A set of numbers indicating the volume, fluctuation, and distribution of crimes reported to local law enforcement agencies for the United States as a whole.

Crime of passion   An unpremeditated murder or assault committed under circumstances of great anger, jealousy, or other emotional stress.

Criminal biology   The scientific study of the relation of hereditary physical traits to criminal character, that is, to innate tendencies to commit crime in general or crimes of any particular type. *See also Biocriminology.*

Criminal insanity   Lack of mental capacity to do or refrain from doing a criminal act; inability to distinguish right from wrong.

Criminal intent   The intent to commit an act, the results of which are a crime or violation of the law.

Criminalistics   Crime laboratory procedures.

Criminology   The scientific study of crime, criminals, corrections, and the operation of the system of criminal justice.

Cross examination   The questioning of a witness by the party who did not produce the witness.

Culpable   At fault or responsible, but not necessarily criminal.

D

Defamation   Intentional causing, or attempting to cause, damage to the reputation of another by communicating false or distorted information about his or her actions, motives, or character.

Defendant   The person who is being prosecuted.

Deliberation   The action of a jury to determine the guilt or innocence, or the sentence, of a defendant.

Demurrer   Plea for dismissal of a suit on the grounds that, even if true, the statements of the opposition are insufficient to sustain the claim.

Deposition   Sworn testimony obtained outside, rather than in, court.

Deterrence   A theory that swift and sure punishment will discourage others from similar illegal acts.

Dilatory   Law term that describes activity for the purpose of causing a delay or to gain time or postpone a decision.

Direct evidence   Testimony or other proof that expressly or straightforwardly proves the existence of fact.

Direct examination   The first questioning of witnesses by the party who calls them.

Directed verdict   An order or verdict pronounced by a judge during the trial of a criminal case in which the evidence presented by the prosecution clearly fails to show the guilt of the accused.

District attorney   A locally elected state official who represents the state in bringing indictments and prosecuting criminal cases.

DNA fingerprinting   The use of biological residue found at the scene of a crime for genetic comparisons in aiding the identification of criminal suspects.

Docket   The formal record of court proceedings.

Double jeopardy   To be prosecuted twice for the same offense.

Due process model   A philosophy of criminal justice based on the assumption that an individual is presumed innocent until proven guilty.

Due process of law   A clause in the Fifth and Fourteenth Amendments ensuring that laws are reasonable and that they are applied in a fair and equal manner.

E

Embracery   An attempt to influence a jury, or a member thereof, in their verdict by any improper means.

Entrapment   Inducing an individual to commit a crime he or she did not contemplate, for the sole purpose of instituting a criminal prosecution against the offender.

Evidence   All the means used to prove or disprove the fact at issue. *See also Corpus delicti.*

Ex post facto (Lat.)   After the fact. An *ex post facto law is a criminal law that makes an act unlawful although it was committed prior to the passage of that law. See also Grandfather clause.*

Exception   A formal objection to the action of the court during a trial. The indication is that the excepting party will seek to reverse the court's actions at some future proceeding.

Exclusionary rule   Legal prohibitions against government prosecution using evidence illegally obtained.

Expert evidence   Testimony by one qualified to speak authoritatively on technical matters because of her or his special training or skill.

Extradition   The surrender by one state to another of an individual accused of a crime.

F

False arrest   Any unlawful physical restraint of another's freedom of movement; unlawful arrest.

Felony   A criminal offense punishable by death or imprisonment in a penitentiary.

Forensic   Relating to the court. Forensic medicine would refer to legal medicine that applies anatomy, pathology, toxicology, chemistry, and other fields of science in expert testimony in court cases or hearings.

G

Grand jury   A group of 12 to 23 citizens of a county who examine evidence against the person suspected of a crime and hand down an indictment if there is sufficient evidence. *See also Petit jury.*

Grandfather clause   A clause attempting to preserve the rights of firms in operation before enactment of a law by exempting these firms from certain provisions of that law. *See also Ex post facto.*

H

Habeas corpus (Lat.)   A legal device to challenge the detention of a person taken into custody. An individual in custody may demand an evidentiary hearing before a judge to examine the legality of the detention.

Hearsay   Evidence that a witness has learned through others.

Homicide   The killing of a human being; may be murder, negligent or nonnegligent manslaughter, or excusable or justifiable homicide.

Hung jury   A jury which, after long deliberation, is so irreconcilably divided in opinion that it is unable to reach a unanimous verdict.

I

Impanel   The process of selecting the jury that is to try a case.

Imprisonment   A sentence imposed upon the conviction of a crime; the deprivation of liberty in a penal institution; incarceration.

In camera (Lat.)   A case heard when the doors of the court are closed and only persons concerned in the case are admitted.

Indemnification   Compensation for loss or damage sustained because of improper or illegal action by a public authority.

Indictment   The document prepared by a prosecutor and approved by the grand jury that charges a certain person with a specific crime or crimes for which that person is later to be tried in court.

Injunction   An order by a court prohibiting a defendant from committing an act, or commanding an act be done.

Inquest   A legal inquiry to establish some question of fact; specifically, an inquiry by a coroner and jury into a person's death where accident, foul play, or violence is suspected as the cause.

Instanter   A subpoena issued for the appearance of a hostile witness or person who has failed to appear in answer to a previous subpoena and authorizing a law enforcement officer to bring that person to the court.

Interpol (International Criminal Police Commission)   A clearing house for international exchanges of information, consisting of a consortium of 126 countries.

J

Jeopardy   The danger of conviction and punishment that a defendant faces in a criminal trial.

Judge   An officer who presides over and administers the law in a court of justice.

Judicial notice   The rule that a court will accept certain things as common knowledge without proof.

Judicial process   The procedures taken by a court in deciding cases or resolving legal controversies.

Jurisdiction   The territory, subject matter, or persons over which lawful authority may be exercised by a court or other justice agency, as determined by statute or constitution.

Jury   A certain number of persons who are sworn to examine the evidence and determine the truth on the basis of that evidence. *See also Hung jury.*

Justice of the peace   A subordinate magistrate, usually without formal legal training, empowered to try petty civil and criminal cases and, in some states, to conduct preliminary hearings for persons accused of a crime, and to fix bail for appearance in court.

Juvenile delinquent   A boy or girl who has not reached the age of criminal liability (varies from state to state) and who commits an act that would be a misdemeanor or felony if he

Glossary

or she were an adult. Delinquents are tried in Juvenile Court and confined to separate facilities.

L

Law Enforcement Agency   A federal, state, or local criminal justice agency or identifiable subunit whose principal functions are the prevention, detection, and investigation of crime and the apprehension of alleged offenders.

Libel and slander   Printed and spoken defamation of character, respectively, of a person or an institution. In a slander action, it is usually necessary to prove specific damages caused by spoken words, but in a case of libel, the damage is assumed to have occurred by publication.

Lie detector   An instrument that measures certain physiological reactions of the human body from which a trained operator may determine whether the subject is telling the truth or lying; polygraph; psychological stress evaluator.

Litigation   A judicial controversy; a contest in a court of justice for the purpose of enforcing a right; any controversy that must be decided upon evidence.

M

Mala fides (Lat.)   Bad faith, as opposed to *bona fides, or good faith.*

Mala in se (Lat.)   Evil in itself. Acts that are made crimes because they are, by their nature, evil and morally wrong.

Mala prohibita (Lat.)   Evil because they are prohibited. Acts that are not wrong in themselves but which, to protect the general welfare, are made crimes by statute.

Malfeasance   The act of a public officer in committing a crime relating to his official duties or powers, such as accepting or demanding a bribe.

Malice   An evil intent to vex, annoy, or injure another; intentional evil.

Mandatory sentences   A statutory requirement that a certain penalty shall be set and carried out in all cases upon conviction for a specified offense or series of offenses.

Martial law   Refers to control of civilian populations by a military commander.

Mediation   Nonbinding third-party intervention in the collective bargaining process.

Mens rea (Lat.)   Criminal intent.

Miranda rights   Set of rights that a person accused or suspected of having committed a specific offense has during interrogation and of which he or she must be informed prior to questioning, as stated by the Supreme Court in deciding *Miranda v. Arizona in 1966 and related cases.*

Misdemeanor   Any crime not a felony. Usually, a crime punishable by a fine or imprisonment in the county or other local jail.

Misprison   Failing to reveal a crime.

Mistrial   A trial discontinued before reaching a verdict because of some procedural defect or impediment.

Modus operandi   A characteristic pattern of behavior repeated in a series of offenses that coincides with the pattern evidenced by a particular person or group of persons.

Motion   An oral or written request made to a court at any time before, during, or after court proceedings, asking the court to make a specified finding, decision, or order.

Motive   The reason for committing a crime.

Municipal court   A minor court authorized by municipal charter or state law to enforce local ordinances and exercise the criminal and civil jurisdiction of the peace.

N

Narc   A widely used slang term for any local or federal law enforcement officer whose duties are focused on preventing or controlling traffic in and the use of illegal drugs.

Negligent   Culpably careless; acting without the due care required by the circumstances.

Neolombrosians   Criminologists who emphasize psychopathological states as causes of crime.

No bill   A phrase used by a grand jury when it fails to indict.

Nolle prosequi (Lat.)   A prosecutor's decision not to initiate or continue prosecution.

Nolo contendre (Lat., lit.)   A pleading, usually used by a defendant in a criminal case, that literally means "I will not contest."

Notary public   A public officer authorized to authenticate and certify documents such as deeds, contracts, and affidavits with his or her signature and seal.

Null   Of no legal or binding force.

O

Obiter dictum (Lat.)   A belief or opinion included by a judge in his or her decision in a case.

Objection   The act of taking exception to some statement or procedure in a trial. Used to call the court's attention to some improper evidence or procedure.

Opinion evidence   A witness's belief or opinion about a fact in dispute, as distinguished from personal knowledge of the fact.

Ordinance   A law enacted by the city or municipal government.

Organized crime   An organized, continuing criminal conspiracy that engages in crime as a business (e.g., loan sharking, illegal gambling, prostitution, extortion, etc.).

Original jurisdiction   The authority of a court to hear and determine a lawsuit when it is initiated.

Overt act   An open or physical act done to further a plan, conspiracy, or intent, as opposed to a thought or mere intention.

P

Paralegals   Employees, also known as legal assistants, of law firms, who assist attorneys in the delivery of legal services.

Pardon   There are two kinds of pardons of offenses (1) the absolute pardon, which fully restores to the individual all rights and privileges of a citizen, setting aside a conviction and penalty, and (2) the conditional pardon, which requires a condition to be met before the pardon is officially granted.

Parole   A conditional, supervised release from prison prior to expiration of sentence.

Penal code   Criminal codes, the purpose of which is to define what acts shall be punished as crimes.

Penology   The study of punishment and corrections.

Peremptory challenge   In the selection of jurors, challenges made by either side to certain jurors without assigning any reason, and which the court must allow.

Perjury   The legal offense of deliberately testifying falsely under oath about a material fact.

Perpetrator   The chief actor in the commission of a crime, that is, the person who directly commits the criminal act.

Petit jury   The ordinary jury composed of 12 persons who hear criminal cases and determines guilt or innocence of the accused. *See also Grand jury.*

Plaintiff   A person who initiates a court action.

Plea bargaining   A negotiation between the defense attorney and the prosecutor in which the defendant receives a reduced penalty in return for a plea of "guilty."

Police power   The authority to legislate for the protection of the health, morals, safety, and welfare of the people.

Postmortem   After death. Commonly applied to an examination of a dead body. *See also Autopsy.*

Precedent   Decision by a court that may serve as an example or authority for similar cases in the future.

Preliminary hearing   The proceeding in front of a lower court to determine if there is sufficient evidence for submitting a felony case to the grand jury.

Premeditation   A design to commit a crime or commit some other act before it is done.

Presumption of fact   An inference as to the truth or falsity of any proposition or fact, made in the absence of actual certainty of its truth or falsity or until such certainty can be attained.

Presumption of innocence   The defendant is presumed to be innocent and the burden is on the state to prove his or her guilt beyond a reasonable doubt.

Presumption of law   A rule of law that courts and judges must draw a particular inference from a particular fact or evidence, unless the inference can be disproved.

Probable cause   A set of facts and circumstances that would induce a reasonably intelligent and prudent person to believe that a particular person had committed a specific crime; reasonable grounds to make or believe an accusation.

Probation   A penalty placing a convicted person under the supervision of a probation officer for a stated time, instead of being confined.

Prosecutor   One who initiates a criminal prosecution against an accused; one who acts as a trial attorney for the government as the representative of the people.

Public defender   An attorney appointed by a court to represent individuals in criminal proceedings who do not have the resources to hire their own defense council.

R

Rap sheet   Popularized acronym for record of arrest and prosecution.

Reasonable doubt   That state of mind of jurors when they do not feel a moral certainty about the truth of the charge and when the evidence does not exclude every other reasonable hypothesis except that the defendant is guilty as charged.

Rebutting evidence   When the defense has produced new evidence that the prosecution has not dealt with, the court, at its discretion, may allow the prosecution to give evidence in reply to rebut or contradict it.

Recidivism   The repetition of criminal behavior.

Repeal   The abrogation of a law by the enacting body, either by express declaration or implication by the passage of a later act whose provisions contradict those of the earlier law.

Reprieve   The temporary postponement of the execution of a sentence.

Restitution   A court requirement that an alleged or convicted offender must pay money or provide services to the victim of the crime or provide services to the community.

Restraining order   An order, issued by a court of competent jurisdiction, forbidding a named person, or a class of persons, from doing specified acts.

Retribution   A concept that implies that payment of a debt to society and thus the expiation of one's offense. It was codified in the biblical injunction, "an eye for an eye, a tooth for a tooth."

S

Sanction   A legal penalty assessed for the violation of law. The term also includes social methods of obtaining compliance, such as peer pressure and public opinion.

Search warrant   A written order, issued by judicial authority in the name of the state, directing a law enforcement officer to search for personal property and, if found, to bring it before the court.

Selective enforcement   The deploying of police personnel in ways to cope most effectively with existing or anticipated problems.

Self-incrimination   In constitutional terms, the process of becoming involved in or charged with a crime by one's own testimony.

Sentence   The penalty imposed by a court on a person convicted of a crime, the court judgment specifying the penalty, and any disposition of a defendant resulting from a conviction, including the court decision to suspend execution of a sentence.

Small claims court   A special court that provides expeditious, informal, and inexpensive adjudication of small contractual claims. In most jurisdictions, attorneys are not permitted for cases, and claims are limited to a specific amount.

Stare decisis (Lat.)   To abide by decided cases. The doctrine that once a court has laid down a principle of laws as applicable to certain facts, it will apply it to all future cases when the facts are substantially the same.

State's attorney   An officer, usually locally elected within a county, who represents the state in securing indictments and in prosecuting criminal cases.

State's evidence   Testimony by a participant in the commission of a crime that incriminates others involved, given under the promise of immunity.

Status offense   An act that is declared by statute to be an offense, but only when committed or engaged in by a juvenile, and that can be adjudicated only by a juvenile court.

Statute   A law enacted by, or with the authority of, a legislature.

Statute of limitations   A term applied to numerous statutes that set limits on the length of time after which rights cannot be enforced in a legal action or offenses cannot be punished.

Stay   A halting of a judicial proceeding by a court order.

Sting operation   The typical sting involves using various undercover methods to control crime.

Subpoena   A court order requiring a witness to attend and testify as a witness in a court proceeding.

Subpoena *duces tecum*   A court order requiring a witness to bring all books, documents, and papers that might affect the outcome of the proceedings.

Glossary

Summons   A written order issued by a judicial officer requiring a person accused of a criminal offense to appear in a designated court at a specified time to answer the charge(s).

Superior court   A court of record or general trial court, superior to a justice of the peace or magistrate's court. In some states, an intermediate court between the general trial court and the highest appellate court.

Supreme court, state   Usually the highest court in the state judicial system.

Supreme Court, U.S.   Heads the judicial branch of the American government and is the nation's highest law court.

Suspect   An adult or juvenile considered by a criminal agency to be one who may have committed a specific criminal offense but who has not yet been arrested or charged.

T

Testimony   Evidence given by a competent witness, under oath, as distinguished from evidence from writings and other sources.

Tort   A breach of a duty to an individual that results in damage to him or her, for which one may be sued in civil court for damages. Crime, in contrast, may be called a breach of duty to the public. Some actions may constitute both torts and crimes.

U

Uniform Crime Reports (U.C.R.)   Annual statistical tabulation of "crimes known to the police" and "crimes cleared by arrest," published by the Federal Bureau of Investigation.

United States Claims Court   Established in 1982, it serves as the court of original and exclusive jurisdiction over claims brought against the federal government, except for tort claims, which are heard by district courts.

United States district courts   Trial courts with original jurisdiction over diversity-of-citizenship cases and cases arising under U.S. criminal, bankruptcy, admiralty, patent, copyright, and postal laws.

V

Venue   The locality in which a suit may be tried.

Verdict   The decision of a court.

Vice squad   A special detail of police agents, charged with raiding and closing houses of prostitution and gambling resorts.

Victim and Witness Protection Act of 1984   The federal VWP Act and state laws protect crime victims and witnesses against physical and verbal intimidation where such intimidation is designed to discourage reporting of crimes and participation in criminal trials.

Victimology   The study of the psychological and dynamic interrelationships between victims and offenders, with a view toward crime prevention.

Vigilante   An individual or member of a group who undertakes to enforce the law and/or maintain morals without legal authority.

Voir dire (Fr.)   The examination or questioning of prospective jurors in order to determine his or her qualifications to serve as a juror.

W

Warrant   A court order directing a police officer to arrest a named person or search a specific premise.

White-collar crime   Nonviolent crime for financial gain committed by means of deception by persons who use their special occupational skills and opportunities.

Witness   Anyone called to testify by either side in a trial. More broadly, a witness is anyone who has observed an event.

Work release (furlough programs)   Change in prisoners' status to minimum custody with permission to work outside prison.

World Court   Formally known as the International Court of Justice, it deals with disputes involving international law.

SOURCES
The Dictionary of Criminal Justice, Fourth Edition, © 1994 by George E. Rush. Published by McGraw-Hill/Duchkin, Guilford, CT 06437.

Index

Index

Test Your Knowledge Form

We encourage you to photocopy and use this page as a tool to assess how the articles in *Annual Editions* expand on the information in your textbook. By reflecting on the articles you will gain enhanced text information. You can also access this useful form on a product's book support Web site at *http://www.dushkin.com/online/*.

NAME: DATE:

_____

TITLE AND NUMBER OF ARTICLE:

_____

BRIEFLY STATE THE MAIN IDEA OF THIS ARTICLE:

_____

LIST THREE IMPORTANT FACTS THAT THE AUTHOR USES TO SUPPORT THE MAIN IDEA:

_____

WHAT INFORMATION OR IDEAS DISCUSSED IN THIS ARTICLE ARE ALSO DISCUSSED IN YOUR TEXTBOOK OR OTHER READINGS THAT YOU HAVE DONE? LIST THE TEXTBOOK CHAPTERS AND PAGE NUMBERS:

_____

LIST ANY EXAMPLES OF BIAS OR FAULTY REASONING THAT YOU FOUND IN THE ARTICLE:

_____

LIST ANY NEW TERMS/CONCEPTS THAT WERE DISCUSSED IN THE ARTICLE, AND WRITE A SHORT DEFINITION:

We Want Your Advice

ANNUAL EDITIONS revisions depend on two major opinion sources: one is our Advisory Board, listed in the front of this volume, which works with us in scanning the thousands of articles published in the public press each year; the other is you—the person a ctually using the book. Please help us and the users of the next edition by completing the prepaid article rating form on this page and returning it to us. Thank you for your help!

ANNUAL EDITIONS: Criminal Justice 02/03

ARTICLE RATING FORM

Here is an opportunity for you to have direct input into the next revision of this volume.
We would like you to rate each of the articles listed below, using the following scale:

1. **Excellent: should definitely be retained**
2. **Above average: should probably be retained**
3. **Below average: should probably be deleted**
4. **Poor: should definitely be deleted**

Your ratings will play a vital part in the next revision.
Please mail this prepaid form to us as soon as possible.
Thanks for your help!

RATING	ARTICLE	RATING	ARTICLE
	1. What Is the Sequence of Events in the Criminal Justice System?		30. Bringing College Back to Bedford Hills
	2. The Road to September 11		31. Crime and Punishment
	3. America Is Getting Even Safer		32. Ex-Cons on the Street
	4. Toward the Ideal of Community Justice		33. The Death Penalty on Trial
	5. Making Computer Crime Count		
	6. When It's No Longer a Game: Pathological Gambling in the United States		
	7. Land of the Stupid: When You Need a Used Russian Submarine, Call Tarzan		
	8. The Well-Marked Roads to Homicidal Rage		
	9. Coping in Tragedy's Aftermath		
	10. In the Campus Shadows, Women Are Stalkers as Well as the Stalked		
	11. Telling the Truth About Damned Lies and Statistics		
	12. Sexual Violence: Current Challenges and Possible Responses		
	13. A LEN Interview With Susan Herman, Director of the National Center for Victims of Crime		
	14. Ethics and Criminal Justice: Some Observations on Police Misconduct		
	15. On-the-Job Stress in Policing—Reducing It, Preventing It		
	16. Crime Story: The Digital Age		
	17. Policing the Police		
	18. Police Officer Candidate Assessment and Selection		
	19. Improving the Recruitment of Women in Policing		
	20. How to Improve the Jury System		
	21. Q: Should Juries Nullify Laws They Consider Unjust or Excessively Punitive?		
	22. Looking Askance at Eyewitness Testimony		
	23. The Creeping Expansion of DNA Data Banking		
	24. Community Prosecution		
	25. Why the Young Kill		
	26. Juvenile Justice: A Century of Experience		
	27. Juvenile Probation on the Eve of the Next Millennium		
	28. Judging Juveniles		
	29. The Past and Future of U.S. Prison Policy: Twenty-Five Years After the Stanford Prison Experiment		

(Continued on next page)

BUSINESS REPLY MAIL
FIRST-CLASS MAIL PERMIT NO. 84 GUILFORD CT

POSTAGE WILL BE PAID BY ADDRESSEE

**McGraw-Hill/Dushkin
530 Old Whitfield Street
Guilford, Ct 06437-9989**

- -

ABOUT YOU

Name   Date

Are you a teacher? ☐   A student? ☐
Your school's name

Department

Address   City   State   Zip

School telephone #

YOUR COMMENTS ARE IMPORTANT TO US!

Please fill in the following information:
For which course did you use this book?

Did you use a text with this ANNUAL EDITION?   ☐ yes ☐ no
What was the title of the text?

What are your general reactions to the *Annual Editions* concept?

Have you read any pertinent articles recently that you think should be included in the next edition? Explain.

Are there any articles that you feel should be replaced in the next edition? Why?

Are there any World Wide Web sites that you feel should be included in the next edition? Please annotate.

May we contact you for editorial input?   ☐ yes ☐ no
May we quote your comments?   ☐ yes ☐ no